NEOLIBERAL CHICAGO

D1559134

NEOLIBERAL CHICAGO

Edited by
LARRY BENNETT, ROBERTA GARNER,
AND EUAN HAGUE

UNIVERSITY OF ILLINOIS PRESS
Urbana, Chicago, and Springfield

Published with support from DePaul University's
College of Liberal Arts and Social Sciences.

© 2017 by the Board of Trustees
of the University of Illinois
All rights reserved
Manufactured in the United States of America
1 2 3 4 5 C P 5 4 3 2 1
∞ This book is printed on acid-free paper.

Library of Congress Control Number: 2016952446
ISBN 978-0-252-04059-7 (hardcover)
ISBN 978-0-252-08209-2 (paperback)
ISBN 978-0-252-09903-8 (e-book)

JKM.
1100 East 55th Street
Chicago, IL 60615

CONTENTS

PREFACE

On November 19, 2015, a Cook County judge ordered the release of a video recording documenting the death of Chicago teenager Laquan McDonald. McDonald had been fatally shot by police officer Jason Van Dyke in late October 2014. Van Dyke and fellow officers present at the October 2014 encounter on the city's Southwest Side claimed that McDonald had approached them threateningly, with knife in hand. The video recording of the event, retrieved from a camera positioned on a police patrol car, was shockingly inconsistent with the officers' account. In the video, one observes McDonald walking away from the police, and though he is holding a knife, he is in no way using it to provoke them. Van Dyke fired sixteen shots at McDonald. After an initial burst of gunfire, McDonald slumped to the ground. The majority of Van Dyke's shots were directed at the clearly disabled McDonald.

In the months following McDonald's death, attorneys representing the young man's family insisted that contrary to Van Dyke's claims, Laquan McDonald had posed no threat to the police officers. The existence of the police dash-cam video was known both to McDonald family attorneys and lawyers representing the City of Chicago. In negotiations between the two parties, city attorneys sought to have the video suppressed as part of a legal settlement. Just after Chicago's mayoral election in early spring 2015, Chicago's city council—without discussion—approved a $5 million dollar settlement between the city and the McDonald family. This settlement did, however, permit release of the dash-cam video pending a criminal investigation of Officer Van Dyke.

In the wake of the release of the McDonald/Van Dyke video, Chicago was thrown into a maelstrom of recrimination, political confusion, and self-doubt. Very shortly after the release of the dash-cam video, Officer Van Dyke was indicted on a first-degree murder charge. Local Black Lives Matter activists, perceiving a direct connection between the McDonald shooting and recent notorious incidents such as the deaths of Michael Brown, Freddie Gray, Eric Garner, and Tamir Rice (each in the presence of or while in the custody of police officers) in Ferguson, Missouri; Baltimore; New York City; and Cleveland, mounted a series of demonstrations across Chicago. Other organizations, such as We Charge Genocide, connected McDonald's death to a long list of other African Americans who have died in encounters with the Chicago Police Department. Mayor Rahm Emanuel initially called for a local task force to investigate Laquan McDonald's death and other violent incidents involving Chicago police and young African American men. However, bowing to political pressure from a variety of sources, Emanuel acquiesced in December 2015 to an investigation by the U.S. Department of Justice.

At this writing, street demonstrations in Chicago have subsided and the federal examination of local police practices has just begun. It does appear that the political fortunes of Mayor Emanuel, who was reelected in a runoff election in April 2015, have been seriously damaged. In addition to the uproar caused by the McDonald shooting, Emanuel has struggled to put the city government's finances in order and has badly mismanaged efforts to reshape the Chicago Public Schools. By early 2016, public opinion polling found that the majority of Chicagoans—in particular African Americans—had lost faith in the mayor.

These details all point to a city in crisis, but the editors and contributors to this volume view Chicago's current crisis as the outgrowth of a deeper core condition. Neoliberal Chicago is, in fact, two cities that can be distinguished in terms of economic condition, neighborhood quality of life, and demographics. One of those cities, which geographically includes the downtown Loop and adjoining areas, runs north along the shore of Lake Michigan and encompasses patches of gentrification south, west, and northwest of the Loop. This city has generally prospered over the last quarter-century. The other Chicago spans the band of neighborhoods running west from the Loop and south and southwest of downtown Chicago. It was in the latter area, a short distance from Interstate 55, that Jason Van Dyke shot Laquan McDonald. The residents of this other Chicago are mainly African Americans and Latinos, and their neighborhoods suffer from the array of disadvantages all too familiar to social scientists and journalists: fiscal disinvestment and the resulting "hollowing out" of the local economy and abandonment of residential areas, poor public services (not least ineffective policing that is compounded by dysfunctional police/community relations), and disastrous levels of crime and personal disorder.

The circumstances that we have just described are not new conditions, and are well known to attentive observers of American cities. However, the civic outcry that followed the Laquan McDonald killing reveals a social divide that is greater than most politicians, journalists, and even social scientists have acknowledged. Why, one might ask, has this gap grown rather than shrunk in recent decades? In the chapters that follow, we and our contributors examine the impact of neoliberal politics and policy in Chicago over the past twenty-five years. As a philosophy and an approach to governance, neoliberalism privileges economic growth and understands the primary role of citizens to be consumers while reducing the role of government in addressing social ills, rolling back the state in favor of the private sector. It is an approach that has exacerbated class and racial inequality, deepening the divide between the two Chicagos.

Neoliberal Chicago is the product of many hands. At the University of Illinois Press we wish to acknowledge the early support of Bill Regier and the contributions of Danny Nasset, Marika Christofides, Jennifer Comeau, and Kate Babbitt. University Research Council grants at DePaul University enabled us to produce just the volume we envisioned several years back. Other important contributors to this volume do not appear in our table of contents. Nemoy Lewis, David Schalliol, and Deena Weinstein, respectively, contributed the text boxes on antiforeclosure activism, Norfolk Southern/Englewood, and the daily press. We also salute David's photo that graces the cover of *Neoliberal Chicago*. The insights of two colleagues/friends, Pat Callahan and Daniel Tucker, contributed much to our initial articulation of *Neoliberal Chicago*. Finally, Nandhini Gulasingam of DePaul's Social Science Research Center made an important contribution to our preliminary discussions of this book by preparing a series of maps that were instrumental in our specifying the geography of neoliberal Chicago.

EH: For Esther and Isla
RG: For my family
LB: For Julia

NEOLIBERAL CHICAGO

Introduction

Chicago: Neoliberal City

EUAN HAGUE, MICHAEL J. LORR,
AND CAROLINA STERNBERG

On the evening of April 7, 2015, following a runoff election in which he received 56 percent of the votes cast, Rahm Emanuel won a second term as mayor of Chicago. The contest was much closer than many had expected, particularly as Emanuel's predecessor, Richard M. Daley, routinely received around 70 percent support (on the first ballot) when achieving reelection. Yet because Emanuel had failed to get more than 50 percent of the vote in the first-round mayoral ballot on February 24, he was forced into the runoff against his second-place challenger, Cook County commissioner Jesus "Chuy" Garcia.

As the runoff contest developed, it became less about the specifics of policies and budgets offered by the two candidates and more about the visions of Chicago's future that each was perceived to represent. Although both Emanuel and Garcia belong to the Democratic Party, Garcia was understood to be significantly to Emanuel's political left, speaking for Chicago's outlying neighborhoods, the working class, the immigrant made good, the city's ethnic minorities, and older counterculturalists who had arrived in Chicago in the 1960s and stayed. Additionally, Garcia promised to support public education irrespective of Chicago's budget deficit. Emanuel, in turn, was aligned with local corporations and elites, those working in financial services, real estate, technology, and the like. In Garcia's words, Emanuel's constituency was the "rich and powerful . . . [the] millionaires and billionaires" (Martin and Bosman, 2015). The runoff election gained national and international attention, and for many observers it became a referendum on neoliberal urban policies. Though Emanuel was ultimately victorious, Garcia's grassroots campaign had the legs to seriously press the extremely well-funded incumbent, a turn of events that suggested that many Chicagoans were (and are) discontented with Emanuel's policies and their impacts on the life and landscapes of the city. As pursued by Emanuel and his predecessor Richard M. Daley over the past twenty-five years, these policies have exemplified what we call neoliberal Chicago.

Neoliberal Chicago

Neoliberalism, as we explain below, is a political economic theory that in public administrative practice and legislation marketizes public services and privatizes public sector functions (see Harvey 2005; Klein 2007). As government at all scales reduces its direct involvement in the day-to-day provision of services, neoliberal city halls pursue public-private partnerships or privatization to fill the gaps and generate short-term revenue through leasing or selling public assets. In Chicago, neoliberalism is the new reality: the city leases its parking meters and sections of its highways, sells advertising space for billboards, and uses tax money to lure corporate headquarters, fund stadium development, and build charter schools. It has tried, but has so far failed, to lease Midway Airport. Chicago in the twenty-first century is, as the *Chicago Reader*'s Mick Dumke (2012, 23, 28) has opined, a "City for Sale" in which there is "a price tag on everything from parking meters to CTA [Chicago Transit Authority] stops, billboards to city departments" and corporations are "invited . . . to come forward with ideas for how they'd like to make money off city properties."

Since taking office in May 2011, Rahm Emanuel has pursued neoliberal governance with the zeal of a true believer, accelerating the policies and fiscal practices of his predecessor, Richard M. Daley, Chicago's longest-serving mayor (1989–2011). Over the past quarter-century, the City of Chicago has sought to entrepreneurialize government actions, create more responsible citizens and citizens who are more business-oriented, build a strong local business climate, encourage upmarket real estate development, and fashion a globally competitive, consumption-oriented city. This has been accompanied by a radical overhaul of the troubled Chicago Public Schools (CPS), which has led to the closure of numerous neighborhood schools and the opening of charter schools across the city with such rapidity that in some areas parents do not know where their children will go to school from one year to the next (Lipman 2011). It has established over 160 Tax Increment Financing districts (TIFs) to route property tax revenue toward economic development in "blighted" neighborhoods (Weber and O'Neill-Kohl 2013; see Box I-1). In some cases this has been successful; in others it has generated some very curious definitions of blight, for example, a definition that made it possible to spend $21 million to bring Boeing's head office to the city's downtown Loop (Washburn and Ciokajlo 2001). In neoliberal Chicago, the Chicago Housing Authority's (CHA) Plan for Transformation means that the agency provides "opportunities" for residents to use vouchers to

Box I.1: Tax Increment Financing

Tax increment financing (TIF) was introduced to the United States in the 1950s and was codified by the Illinois General Assembly in 1977. TIF was brought to Chicago by Mayor Harold Washington's administration in 1984, when the Central Loop TIF district was created. A geographical approach to land use planning and development, TIF districting is designed to target neighborhoods deemed "blighted" and unable to attract private investment "*but for*" TIF-funded direct public investments and development incentives. TIF dollars are drawn upon to fund infrastructure improvements, beautification projects, site cleanup and remediation, economic development, job training and job creation, and a host of other related activities. TIF districts generate resources from property taxes collected within the district boundaries, which are used to fund projects within the same bounded area. Property taxes collected within a TIF district are divided among the city's general budget and the budgets of several other local jurisdictions, notably the Chicago Public Schools (the baseline levy that preceded TIF designation) and the TIF district. The money accrued by the TIF district is called the "increment." The city's general budget (and the other taxing jurisdictions) receives a fixed dollar amount from the property taxes raised within that TIF district throughout the duration of the TIF. As property tax revenues within a TIF district rise, the increase in revenue goes directly into the increment for reinvestment within district boundaries. Chicago also permits TIF money to be "ported," or moved from the district within which it has been raised to a physically adjacent district. The Illinois TIF statute mandates that TIF districts have a lifespan of twenty-three years (though in the case of some districts, the city extends the TIF designation beyond the 23-year termination point). The presumption is that at the end of twenty-three years, property values within the TIF district will have increased substantially and the sum of property tax revenues will be routed to the city's general fund and the other local jurisdictions that collect property taxes. By 2015, more than 160 TIF districts dotted Chicago, making it the one of the world's most notable implementers of this development tool.

live in "mixed-income" communities rather than providing actual homes made of bricks and mortar.

There is another side to neoliberal urbanism: surveillance, security, and social exclusion. Across Chicago, thousands of CCTV cameras have been installed to monitor streets and sidewalks, their blue lights flashing nightly as they send data to a high-technology "fusion center" at the Chicago Police Department called the Crime Prevention and Information Center (CPIC). Segway-riding security staff patrol the city's popular Millennium Park, a TIF-funded public-private partnership. In 2004–2005, taxpayer money bought and then demolished an 85-year old homeless shelter in the increasingly expensive South Loop neighborhood to provide a prime site for the expansion of a selective-enrollment public high school focused on college preparatory courses. To soften the blow, a "starchitect" was commissioned to design a replacement homeless shelter, located alongside rail yards just over a mile farther away from the city center. As public housing has been demolished and gentrification has resulted in the construction of thousands of new luxury condominiums that cater to white-collar urban professionals, long-term renters have been forced to leave their homes and neighborhoods to find somewhere cheaper to live. Rising rents and real estate prices have made a three- to five-mile radius around the Loop unaffordable to most of the city's residents. Arguably, the last piece in Chicago's real-estate-upgrade jigsaw puzzle would have been the 2016 Olympics, which was planned for the city's South Side (see Chapter 10 of this volume). Supported by a partnership of public agencies and private sponsors, the games would have transformed the low-income, African American Douglas, Oakland, and Grand Boulevard community areas that are sandwiched between the new condominium towers of the South Loop and the wealthy Hyde Park enclave around the University of Chicago. The International Olympic Committee, however, had not read the city's script and decided to host the 2016 Games in Rio de Janeiro.

Neoliberal Urban Policies

Policies such as those that have been pursued in Chicago constitute the conventional wisdom in many cities, and not just in the United States. Cutting spending on social services, using tax monies to attract business and leverage corporate investment, encouraging real estate markets, and removing fiscal protections in favor of laissez-faire market-driven capitalism, neoliberalism has arguably become the globe's characteristic framework for conceiving and executing urban public policy. Chicago, as we explain in this collection, is a paradigmatic neoliberal city. Its embrace of neoliberal urban policies has paralleled, and in some cases influenced, similar trends in metropolises as far afield as Toronto, London, Paris, Buenos Aires, and Sydney. Although neoliberalism is "variegated"

(Brenner, Peck, and Theodore 2010), meaning that urban governance operates differently in each city and each city exhibits its own distinct set of policies responding to its specific circumstances, a number of common processes and policies are shared by cities that pursue neoliberal urban governance:

- Privatize public assets and reduce the role of government in service provision
- Encourage city authorities to guide and/or aid private investment and development through practices such as public-private development partnerships and use of tax monies to leverage private investment
- Structure zoning and other land use policies to stimulate real estate markets, for example encouraging gentrification, and understand property solely in terms of monetary value (as opposed to social or residential worth)
- Promote the city as an urban entertainment complex, a place of and for consumption (e.g., tourism, trade shows and conventions, festivals, dining)
- Pursue practices that exclude or displace nonconsumers and low-income populations (e.g., the homeless) and "unproductive" or less lucrative land uses, particularly in central areas
- Increase policing and surveillance

David Harvey (2005, 35, 26) argues that the cumulative effects of such policies has been a "radical reconfiguration of class relations" in which the post–World War II welfare state and regulatory apparatus are replaced by neoliberal polices that, when taken together, generate a "momentous shift towards greater social inequality and the restoration of economic power to the upper class." In cities such as Chicago that were once strongholds of union labor and working-class jobs, these disappear, and with them the communities they once supported, as major corporations, formerly producers of materials and consumer goods, "become more and more financial in their orientation." For example, U.S. Steel has renamed itself USX and now focuses on real estate and insurance rather than iron ore and steel (Harvey 2005, 32). The result is a bifurcation of urban populations divided between white-collar jobs in finance, insurance, real estate, and other high-paying tertiary sector occupations and precarious, low-wage service sector positions that are primarily filled by employees who are recent immigrants and/or members of ethnic minority groups. Yet the ghosts of the industrial past linger: in warehouses converted to luxury condominiums with exposed brick interior walls, in restaurants and nightclubs that tout their authentic urban grittiness, and in political and commercial appeals to "blue-collar" values and attributes of hard work and honest toil.

In its essence, neoliberalism is a theory and practice of political economy that demands a reduction in government provision of services and advocates for the primacy of private markets, producing a hypercommodification in which almost everything becomes something to sell or a selling point. At its core, neo-liberalism, which draws upon the thinking of Friedrich Hayek (1899–1992; e.g., 1944, 1960a, [1948] 1960b) and Milton Friedman (1912–2006; e.g., 1962, 1984)—both of whom had taught economics at the University of Chicago—is a quest to dismantle policies that are presumed to impede the operations of markets (Harvey 2005). To generate an ideal free market, according to neoliberal beliefs, governments should pursue privatization, deregulation, and the withdrawal of the state from areas of social provision (e.g., welfare, education, and housing). The animating logic of these principles is that government interventions and regulations disrupt "natural" relationships of supply and demand, introducing inefficiency to markets and unduly bureaucratizing society. By stripping away government regulations and interventions, the capitalist free market will operate as a system in which individual self-seeking also maximizes the social good. Within this logic, individuals acting on their own self-interest will optimize their particular material standing. This, in turn, will create maximum benefits for all. Thus, the greatest good will be encouraged by using government not to provide social services or oversee regulatory measures but instead to minimally intervene in very specific circumstances, as a protector and arbitrator of free ex-change (Hackworth 2007). Advocates of neoliberalism insist that it is necessary to end welfare and social service programs and instead stimulate job creation through tax cuts and relaxed governmental regulation of industry; these are often referred to as "supply-side" economic policies. Through these processes, people will no longer need state assistance because they will benefit from the new jobs that have been thus created. These workers, in turn, will generate wealth for employers, which will lead to more investment, jobs, economic growth, and rising incomes and living standards for all (Leitner, Peck, and Sheppard 2007).

As geographers Don Mitchell and Clayton Rosati (2006, 145) explain, this approach to public policy came to the fore following General Augusto Pinochet's takeover of the Chilean government in 1973:

> Chile became perhaps the earliest test case for implementing what we now recognize as the neoliberal model of capitalist development . . . a model that depends on the almost total eradication of alternative means of livelihood, civic life and culture, and its replacement with a highly commodified, market-driven way of living in the world and relating to culture. The "social market economy" implemented in Chile (under the advice of consulting economists from the University of Chicago)[1] demanded the rapid withdrawal of the state from the economy, except, as Marc Cooper (2001, 62) succinctly puts it, "for limiting wages, smashing unions, and jailing their leaders." The very fabric of social welfare quickly unraveled in Chile, even as essential services like gar-bage collection, water and sewage, healthcare and pensions were privatized.

Conservatives on both sides of the Atlantic, in turn, began to revise their economic policy prescriptions. By the 1980s, neoliberalism was politically ascendant, in large part through the influence of the Thatcher and Reagan administrations in the United Kingdom and United States, respectively (Harvey 2005). Both of these heads of state initiated policies that dramatically cut social programs and urban funding, attacked labor unions, and removed financial regulations. Global financial institutions like the International Monetary Fund and World Bank also moved to adopt and mandate neoliberal approaches. By the 1990s, neoliberalism was virtually hegemonic, naturalized as the proper mode of governance in a variety of countries and institutional contexts, and followed by the state at all scales: national, regional, urban, and local. Across the globe neoliberal administrations "rolled back" financial regulations and social welfare safety nets and "rolled out" market-oriented policies that subsidized businesses and expanded the operations of security organizations, be these the military, police, or private contractors (Peck and Tickell 2002). Neoliberal polices became a way both to generate profits and reorder spatial relations. As central cities gentrified, public-private partnerships hosted downtown festivals and built stadiums and convention centers, city administrations began to think of spending in terms of investment and profitability rather than as providing essential services to all local residents (including the neediest). With economic growth considerations driving urban governance, typically to the detriment of other prospective policy priorities such as poverty alleviation, neoliberalism has physically reshaped urban areas. As urban planner and geographer Jason Hackworth (2007, 78) explains, the spatial order of the early twenty-first-century neoliberal city

> is increasingly characterized by a curious combination of inner city and ex-urban private investment, disinvestment in the inner suburbs, the relaxation of land use controls, and the reduction of public investment that is not likely to lead to an immediate profit. If public housing and middle-class suburban housing were icons of the Keynesian managerialist city, then gentrified neighborhoods and downtown commercial mega-projects are the icons of the neoliberal city.

The rise and subsequent acceptance of the belief that municipal governments should be entrepreneurial actors means that urban administrations increasingly perform like businesses: competing with other locations for investment, headquarters, and "mega-events"; construing urban spaces in terms of their monetary potential and profitability, rather than as particular locales embodying what sociologists John Logan and Harvey Molotch (1987) call "use value."

This neoliberal vision of the city also presumes that there is an ideal urban resident, a member of what planner and urban futurist Richard Florida (2002, 2005) has called the "creative class": perhaps a software engineer who bikes to work from a newly built condominium in a once majority-Hispanic neighborhood, or a pair of doctors who have moved into a row house loaded with new appliances and send their children to an exclusive selective enrollment charter school? There is less room in this neoliberal city, and when real estate trends are factored in, literally less space, for those who have not completed a high school diploma, for those who rely on public housing or other assistance, for those who, in the past, would have worked in Chicago's famed stockyards and steel mills.

Neoliberalism in One City

In 1999, the Commercial Club of Chicago (CCC)[2], a civic group with numerous ties to the city's leading corporations, released *Chicago Metropolis 2020*, its vision for the first decades of the twenty-first century. Articulating a program that found a receptive audience among city officials, developers, corporations, and civic organizations, the CCC proclaimed that its objective was to "mold Chicago into one of the great cities of the world." The ultimate aim was to

> bring the resources and participation of the business community together with other outstanding regional civic organizations and governmental leaders that have both the expertise and commitment to help promote and implement the goals of the plan. It will convene these organizations and their leaders and seek to unite them in a common mission to enhance the region's position as one of the world's foremost economic centers and as a place known worldwide for the quality of life and equity of opportunity that its residents enjoy. (Johnson 1999)

A major component of the *Chicago Metropolis 2020* vision, and of municipal policy for many decades, has been the physical and aesthetic upgrading of the downtown Loop and its immediately adjoining neighborhoods, through the beautification of parks, streets, and plazas; the promotion of gentrification; and the construction of a global downtown. From the standpoint of *Chicago Metropolis 2020*, a healthy metropolitan region is unthinkable unless the geographic core of that region is also healthy. Yet far from producing a regionally encompassing "equity of opportunity," as espoused by *Chicago Metropolis 2020*, the main track of city- and business-driven development activity in the subsequent years ignored large parts of Chicago or, worse, targeted neighborhoods for redevelopment while paying little heed to local needs. Already marginalized African American and Latino communities were especially impacted. On the South Side and the West Side, economic restructuring, deindustrialization, and the shifting geography of employment had already undermined working-class neighborhoods. These long-term trends were then amplified by the foreclosure crisis that accompanied the Great Recession of 2008. School closures and the aggressive scaling down of the city's public housing stock have further disrupted these neighborhoods, particularly since 1999 through the Chicago Housing Authority's (CHA) Plan for Transformation (Hyra 2008).

Built from the late 1930s to 1969, Chicago's public housing projects were racially segregated. Many were constructed in or became African American "ghettos" (Hirsch 1998) and were located in areas that were viewed by developers and city officials as lacking investment potential. By the 1990s, however, as gentrification encroached from adjacent neighborhoods, several of the sites occupied by public housing appeared to offer new opportunities for high-end residential development. The CHA's Plan for Transformation mandated that high-rise public housing be demolished and replaced by mixed-income development. This displaced thousands of Chicago families, a situation that was exacerbated by the fact that the mixed-income communities built on former CHA sites typically reserved less than one-third of the new units for low-income renters (Bennett, Smith, and Wright 2006). In Bronzeville, which had been the site of the South Side's largest concentration of public housing, the demolition of the Robert Taylor Homes, Stateway Gardens, Dearborn Homes, Harold Ickes Homes, and the Madden Park–Wells–Darrow Homes from 2002 to 2006 cleared 300 acres of land, half of which was targeted for private-sector redevelopment (Wilson and Sternberg 2012). Elsewhere in the city, residential property conversions transformed 100,000 units of housing from rentals to condominiums from 1989 to 2004, thus further tightening the housing market for those unable to afford for-purchase housing (Briggs 2007).

The transformation of Chicago's housing stock and real estate market as a result of the pursuit of neoliberal urban policies has been reflected in a similar polarization of employment opportunities. Like many global metropolises, neoliberal Chicago's economy is split between high-wage white-collar jobs and low-wage unskilled jobs. In the early 2000s, by one estimate, Chicago had amassed the largest concentration of high-tech workers of any U.S. city, but it also had the second-largest number of low-wage unskilled workers (Koval et al. 2006). Propelled by the ascendant service economy and the low wages earned by most of its work force, increased poverty has been the certain result. The share of Chicago's workers earning less than $7.00 per hour doubled from 1983 to 2004, from 2.7 to 5.4 percent, and growing unemployment and homelessness are omnipresent in the city's poorest neighborhoods (Wilson and Sternberg 2012).

Although ascendant, urban neoliberalism in Chicago has faced resistance and contestation since its onset (see Sternberg and Anderson 2014). For example, for many years the Chicago Coalition to Protect Public Housing waged a campaign to stop public housing demolitions, and in 2012, the Chicago Teachers Union led the first strike by public school teachers in a generation (see Box C-1). Many Chicagoans are questioning particular privatization initiatives such as the leasing of parking meters (Farmer 2014; see Box 3.2), parents have angrily protested as the CPS has closed neighborhood schools, community groups mobilized to resist the 2016 Olympic bid (see Chapter 10), and local environmentalists are attempting to ensure that the greening of their city prioritizes social justice, not just tax breaks for developers who "go green" (Lorr 2012).

Neoliberalism in Chicago and Beyond

Post–World War II Chicago has experienced three phases of urban governance and fiscal policy: the Richard J. Daley Democratic Party machine that dominated from the 1950s to the 1970s, the brief urban populist regime that was still in the making when Mayor Harold Washington died in 1987, and, most recently, the neoliberal era of mayors Richard M. Daley and Rahm Emanuel. Contemporary Chicago, or "the Third City," as Larry Bennett (2010) has characterized it, is a metropolis of themed neighborhoods, multiple entertainment facilities and districts, highly publicized corporate patronage, and new condominiums in "up-and-coming" neighborhoods. In neoliberal Chicago, few Greeks live in Greektown but numerous Greek restaurants sit side by side on streets featuring faux classical columns; a once-notorious high-rise public housing complex (Cabrini-Green) has been demolished and a Target store rises on its footprint, new brew pubs regularly open in some of the hippest (and hottest) real estate markets in the nation, and tourists delight in the mirrored surface of "The Bean" in the Loop's glittering Millennium Park, the epitome of a public-private partnership.

At the same time, schoolchildren are beaten and killed as they walk across gang turf boundaries to reach their new schools, shootings in African American neighborhoods are a daily occurrence, long-term renting Chicagoans flee to less expensive inner-ring suburbs, and some of the most toxic sites in the United States just happen to be located in the city's poorest neighborhoods. In his first term as mayor, Rahm Emanuel supported the closure of fifty public schools and advocated for the expansion of charter schools, continued to promote redevelopment through TIF districting despite his initial promises of reform, cut city spending on libraries, and shuttered public mental health facilities (Lydersen 2013).

The central issue we address in this collection, therefore, is how neoliberalism works on the ground in Chicago at the start of the twenty-first century. How have neoliberal processes and policies in this particular city impacted race relations, schooling, housing, the use of public spaces, the urban landscape, and the environment? What kind of city is neoliberal Chicago likely to become? We hope this collection can contribute to meaningful discussions about the future of Chicago and offer insights to examine similar or emergent urban scenarios in both the United States and beyond.

The Book to Come

Our book is organized via four sections.[3] In Part I, Context, the editors and several collaborators describe contemporary Chicago from three perspectives: race relations, with an emphasis on the continuing gap that divides African Americans from other Chicagoans; contemporary Chicago's multilayered geography of inequality; and the political and public policy landscape of early twenty-first-century Chicago, with special attention to *how* Chicago became a neoliberal city. The two chapters of Part II, the first by Michael Lorr and the second by Sean Dinces and Christopher Lamberti, address aspects of what may be considered the "neoliberal vision": how local environmental policy, on the one hand, and the promotion of enthusiasm for professional sports figures, on the other, reflect the broader neoliberal construction of society. The chapters of Part III examine three locally iconic spaces and explore how their meaning has been transformed as neoliberalism remakes and rebrands them, turning them into spaces of consumption. Alex Papadopoulos details the emergence of contemporary Chicago's North Side "gay neighborhood," locally known as Boystown. Carrie Breitbach contrasts the new—the Lakeside mixed-use development proposal—and old—the South Works steel mill complex—in far South Side Chicago. Yue Zhang's profile of the downtown block formed by the Medinah Temple and Tree Studios explores how neoliberal assumptions shape what is construed as worthy of historic preservation. In Part IV, the focus is on how neoliberalism "works." Martha Martinez documents the uneven effect of the foreclosure crisis on neighborhoods across Chicago. Larry Bennett, Michael Bennett, and Stephen Alexander analyze the neoliberal ends and means that were revealed by the city's campaign from 2007 to 2009 to host the 2016 Olympics. Rajiv Shah and Brendan McQuade, in turn, track the spread of surveillance technology—and the logic of enhanced surveillance—in contemporary Chicago. In the book's concluding chapter, the editors seek to place contemporary Chicago within a broader context, first by assessing just what sort of neoliberal city Chicago is and second by discussing how this city might chart an alternative path toward socially just urbanism.

Notes

1. This training was the result of the Chile Project, organized in the 1950s by the U.S. State Department and funded by the Ford Foundation, which sought to influence Chilean economic thinking. The project was unsuccessful until the early 1970s. Later, the training was extended to other Latin American countries such as Argentina and Uruguay. Naomi Klein (2007) persuasively argues that the economic policies the Pinochet regime pursued in Chile constitute the basic tenets of neoliberalism's "shock doctrine" of "disaster capitalism."

2. The CCC was founded in 1877 in order to "advance the public welfare and the commercial interests of metropolitan Chicago by co-operative effort, social intercourse, and a free interchange of views. . . . [The membership] is limited to residents of the Chicago metropolitan area who shall be deemed qualified by reason of their personality, general reputation, position in their business or profession, and service in the public welfare" (Johnson 1999, 3). Today, the city's most prominent business and corporate leaders are represented in this organization, including the Chicago Urban League, the Chicago Community Trust, the John D. and Catherine T. MacArthur Foundation, the McCormick Tribune Foundation, the Sara Lee Corporation, the Elizabeth Morse Genius Charitable Trust, McDonalds, Motorola, Price Waterhouse Coopers, and Sears. Among the many other organizations that are devoted to various aspects of the region's economic, environmental, and social well-being are Business and Professional People for the Public Interest, the Center for Neighborhood Technology, Chicago United, Inc., the Civic Federation, the Leadership Council for Metropolitan Open Communities, the Local Initiatives Support Corporation, and the Environmental Law and Policy Center. In addition, the CCC has benefited from consultation with many universities in the region, including DePaul University, Northwestern University, Roosevelt University, the University of Chicago, and the University of Illinois at Chicago (Johnson 1999).

3. Several of the chapters include boxes, short essays that amplify themes of the particular chapters or of the book generally.

Bibliography

Bennett, Larry. 2010. *The Third City: Chicago and American Urbanism*. Chicago: University of Chicago Press.

Bennett, Larry, Janet Smith, and Patricia Wright, eds. 2006. *Where Are Poor People to Live?: Transforming Public Housing Communities*. Armonk, N.Y.: M.E. Sharpe.

Brenner, Neil, Jamie Peck, and Nik Theodore. 2010. "Variegated Neoliberalization: Geographies, Modalities, Pathways." *Global Networks* 10, no. 2: 182–222.

Briggs, Johnathon E. 2007. "Condo Boom Thunderous." *Chicago Tribune*, April 30.

Cooper, Marc. 2001. *Pinochet and Me: A Chilean Anti-Memoir*. London: Verso.

Dumke, Mick. 2012. "City for Sale." *Chicago Reader*, December 12.

Farmer, Stephanie. 2014. "Cities as Risk Managers: The Impact of Chicago's Parking Meter P3 on Municipal Governance and Transportation Planning." *Environment and Planning A* 46, no. 9: 2160–2174.

Florida, Richard. 2002. *The Rise of the Creative Class: And How It's Transforming Work, Leisure, Community and Everyday Life*. New York: Basic.

———. 2005. *Cities and the Creative Class*. New York: Routledge.

Friedman, Milton. 1962. *Capitalism and Freedom*. Chicago: University of Chicago Press.

———. 1984. *Market or Plan? An Exposition of the Case for the Market*. London: Centre for Research into the Communist Economies.

Hackworth, Jason. 2007. *The Neoliberal City: Governance, Ideology, and Development in American Urbanism*. Ithaca, N.Y.: Cornell University Press.

Harvey, David. 2005. *A Brief History of Neoliberalism*. New York: Oxford University Press.

Hayek, Friedrich. 1944. *The Road to Serfdom*. Chicago: University of Chicago Press.

———. 1960a. *The Constitution of Liberty*. Chicago: University of Chicago Press.

———. (1948) 1960b. *Individualism and Economic Order*. Chicago: University of Chicago Press.

Hirsch, Arnold. 1998. *Making the Second Ghetto: Race and Housing in Chicago, 1940–1960*. Chicago: University of Chicago Press.

Hyra, Derek. 2008. *The New Urban Renewal: The Economic Transformation of Harlem and Bronzeville*. Chicago: University of Chicago Press.

Johnson, Elmer W. 1999. *Chicago Metropolis 2020: Preparing Metropolitan Chicago for the 21st Century*. Chicago: Chicago Metropolis 2020.

Klein, Naomi. 2007. *The Shock Doctrine: The Rise of Disaster Capitalism*. New York: Picador.

Koval, John P., Larry Bennett, Michael I. J. Bennett, Fassil Demissie, Roberta Garner, and Kiljoong Kim, eds. 2006. *The New Chicago: A Social and Cultural Analysis*. Philadelphia: Temple University Press.

Leitner, Helga, Jamie Peck, and Eric S. Sheppard, eds. 2007. *Contesting Neoliberalism: Urban Frontiers*. New York: Guilford.

Lipman, Pauline. 2011. *The New Political Economy of Urban Education: Neoliberalism, Race, and the Right to the City*. New York: Routledge.

Logan, John, and Harvey Molotch. 1987. *Urban Fortunes: The Political Economy of Place*. Berkeley: University of California Press.

Lorr, Michael J. 2012. "Defining Urban Sustainability in the Context of North American Cities." *Nature and Culture* 7, no. 1: 16–30.

Lydersen, Kari. 2013. *Mayor 1%: Rahm Emanuel and the Rise of Chicago's 99%*. Chicago: Haymarket Books.

Martin, Jonathon, and Julie Bosman. 2015. "Chicago Mayor's Race Is Cast as a Test of Liberalism." *New York Times*, March 21.

Mitchell, Don, and Clayton Rosati. 2006. "The Globalization of Culture: Geography and the Industrial Production of Culture." In *Globalization's Contradictions: Geographies of Discipline, Destruction and Transformation*, ed. Dennis Conway and Nik Heynen, 144–160. New York, Routledge.

Peck, Jamie, and Adam Tickell. 2002. "Neoliberalizing Space." *Antipode* 34, no. 3: 380–404.

Sternberg, Carolina, and Matthew Anderson. 2014. "Contestation and the Local Trajectories of Neoliberal Urban Governance in Chicago's Bronzeville and Pilsen." *Urban Studies* 51, no. 15: 3198–3214.

Washburn, Gary, and Mickey Ciokajlo. 2001. "Chicago Snags Boeing—Price Was High, But Was It Worth It?" *Chicago Tribune*, May 11.

Weber, Rachel, and Sara O'Neill-Kohl. 2013. "The Historical Roots of Tax Increment Financing, or How Real Estate Consultants Kept Urban Renewal Alive." *Economic Development Quarterly* 27, no. 4: 193–207.

Wilson, David, and Carolina Sternberg. 2012. "Changing Realities: The New Racialized Redevelopment Rhetoric in Chicago." *Urban Geography* 33, no. 7: 979–999.

PART I

CONTEXT

Neoliberal Chicago was not built in a day. As African Americans flooded north to the city in the first decades of the twentieth century, the great majority of the new arrivals were forced by white hostility and real estate practices to settle in the narrow band of neighborhoods running south from downtown, the area that came to be known as the Black Belt. The job prospects Chicago's diverse array of commercial establishments and manufacturers offered far exceeded the opportunities the agrarian economies of Arkansas, Louisiana, or Mississippi presented. Nonetheless, many employers routed African Americans into the least desirable jobs or did not hire them at all. In recent decades, Chicago Latinos have encountered other obstacles to accessing good jobs in an economy that is now less driven by overt racism but is increasingly structured in terms of specialized skills and educational credentials. Compared to African Americans, Latinos have been able to settle across a broader range of city neighborhoods and suburban communities. Meanwhile, a new tier of private sector technical, clerical, and salaried professional workers emerged in the city's post-industrial economy. Its boundary with the more affluent "creative class" is blurry and this group is substantially white. In essence, neoliberal politics, policy, and culture have amplified the effects of long-standing inequalities in economic opportunity, quality of housing and neighborhood life, and access to high-quality public services.

CHAPTER 1

Class and Race-Ethnicity in a Changing City

A Historical Perspective on Inequalities

ROBERTA GARNER, BLACK HAWK HANCOCK,
AND KENNETH FIDEL

This chapter traces the dynamics of race-ethnicity and class in the Chicago metropolitan area, with an emphasis on both change in recent decades and persistent disparities. The strong link between racial disparities and class inequality is our focal point, and we discuss why African Americans remained relatively disadvantaged during the economic, social, and political transition to a new class structure as Chicago changed from a declining industrial city to the revitalized "third city."

In his book *The Third City: Chicago and American Urbanism* (2010), Larry Bennett developed a model that is useful for organizing our discussion. Bennett proposes that Chicago moved through three stages in the twentieth century, passing from an ethnically divided industrial city in the early twentieth century into a difficult period as a racially divided Rust Belt city facing demise from the mid-twentieth century to the 1990s and finally emerging as a postindustrial global city. Bennett (2010, 8) describes what he terms the Third City as featuring "a revitalized urban core, which at present coexists uncomfortably with a belt of very poor to working-neighborhoods reaching west and south," and as "home to a shifting population mix, including a very large segment drawn from Mexico; a smaller but significant immigrant stream from south and east Asia; a substantial population of middle-class professionals working in corporations, universities, and other 'creative class' economic niches." The transition from the declining Second City to the flourishing Third City was accomplished during the neoliberal era of the last decades of the twentieth century, powered by institutional structures, policies, and practices of neoliberalism as we have defined it. This transition paralleled similar transitions in many other cities (see, for example, Boudreau, Keil, and Young 2009 for an analysis of the process in Toronto). In this chapter we examine these emerging structures, policies, and practices and attempt to understand how many people in Chicago—especially African Americans—remained poor and in the marginalized parts of the working class.

The transition to the Third City was marked by globalization and the incorporation of immigrants into the new structure of occupations in a form that made the intertwining of class and ethnicity more complicated than in the industrial era. The occupations of the middle class changed during this transition, as did their household structure, as fewer lived in nuclear families. We conclude the chapter by looking at some of the many political and ideological features of neoliberalism that impact the dynamics of class and race-ethnicity, specifically the ebbing political engagement of disadvantaged communities, new cognitive maps of class and race-ethnicity that emphasize individual attainment, and a general thinning out of opportunities for public discussion of inequalities.

Racial Isolation and Persistent Disparities: New Structure, Old Inequality

Chicago is a city of persistent disparities. How is it possible that fifty years after the March on Washington, so many African Americans in Chicago remain racially isolated and economically disadvantaged? The data suggest that African Americans are disproportionately located in disadvantaged sections of the new working class, and consequently, disproportionately exposed to unemployment and low-wage work. Although the occupational and class structures have changed with the transition to the Third City, the situation of African Americans, on average, has not improved in the ways that were hoped for in the civil rights era.

Segregation and Racial Isolation

Chicago has long been known as one of the most racially segregated cities in the United States (although at times the index of dissimilarity—a measure of segregation—has been even higher for New York and Detroit).[1] The decline in segregation since the 1960s has been minimal. In 1960, 69 percent of African Americans in Chicago lived in neighborhoods in which at least 95 percent of the residents were African Americans; in 2011, 63 percent of African Americans lived in neighborhoods in which at least 94 percent of the residents were African Americans. Almost two-thirds of African Americans live in twenty-two of Chicago's seventy-seven community areas, and of the total population of these areas, 95 percent is African American. In short, about two-thirds of Chicago's African American residents live in racially isolated areas (Bogira 2013).

Economic Disadvantage

These overwhelmingly African American areas are not just racially segregated; they are also profoundly unequal in economic terms. In 1963, the March on Washington called for jobs and equality in employment (Jones 2013), as did the 1968 Report of the National Advisory Commission on Civil Disorders (the Kerner Report). Fifty years after the March on Washington, this promise remains unfulfilled both nationally and locally. In Chicago in 1968, the unemployment rate for African Americans was 7.8; for whites it was 2.3 percent. By 2012, the situation was considerably worse for both racial categories, and though the racial gap had decreased proportionally, the percentage gap had increased. The unemployment rate for whites was 8.1 percent, and it was 19.5 percent for African Americans. (The national percentages were 6.6 and 12.6, respectively). Poverty rates for both categories also increased in Chicago from 1960 to 2011, and over one-third of African Americans now live in poverty. For whites, the poverty rate increased from 7.4 percent to 10.9 percent; for African Americans, it increased from 29.7 percent to 34.1 percent (Bogira and Dumke 2013).

Median income figures tell the same story of little or no change in racial economic disparities. In Chicago in 1960, the median family income of African Americans was $4,800; for white families it was $7,700. In 2010, the median household income was $29,371 for African American households and $58,752 for white households (and $64,692 for non-Hispanic whites), reflecting an exacerbation rather than amelioration of the racial income gap (Bogira and Dumke 2013; U.S. Census Bureau 2011).

Income dispersion is also part of the story, and the national income distribution for African American households is more unequal than that of other major ethnoracial categories, although income inequality has increased in all of them (Macewan 2013; U.S. Census Bureau 2013). The data from the 2000 Census for Chicago (Bruch 2014) suggested that both in Chicago and nationally there is considerably greater income inequality among black households than among white households (the Gini ratios for income, a commonly used measure of inequality, are, respectively, .45 and .38). The growing disparities among African Americans are beginning to have a complicated impact on politics, opportunities, and lifestyles in Chicago, as sociologist Mary Pattillo (2007) charts in *Black on the Block,* her study of class relationships within a predominantly African American community poised on the verge of gentrification.

Crime and "Hyper-Incarceration"

There is a concentration of violent crime in predominantly African American neighborhoods in Chicago. The community areas of Washington Park, Englewood, West Garfield Park, North Lawndale, and several other South and West Side areas persistently appear at the top of the violent crime rankings. Homicide "hot spots" are similarly concentrated. Although murder rates actually declined in Chicago from the early 1990s to the late 2000s, Daniel Hertz (2013) of the University of Chicago's Harris School of Public Policy has found that they declined on the South and West Sides less than they did on the North Side. Murder rates actually increased in seven South and West Side police districts, a trend that widened the racial/geographic gap in the incidence of homicides.

Some of these disparities were already visible in the 1960s, but at present many predominantly African American neighborhoods are experiencing a spiraling of consequences due to intense policing, mass incarceration, and the challenges of "reintegrating" the formerly incarcerated. Using the phrases "incarceration regime" and "hyper-incarceration," sociologist Robert Sampson points to an astonishing gap between the incarceration rates for white and black communities. For example, the highest incarceration rate in a predominantly black community area (West Garfield Park, where the rate is 4,226/100,000) is 42 times greater than the highest incarceration rate in any white community (103/100,000)! The new burden of incarceration and the problems of "reentry" that former inmates face exacerbate the older legacies of inequality in many African American neighborhoods.

Education

Individuals of color vastly predominate among the students of Chicago Public Schools (CPS). Currently, only 9 percent of the students are white. CPS students, by and large, are also very poor. Eighty-five percent of CPS students receive free or reduced-price lunches, which means that their families report less than 185 percent of poverty-level income. In contrast, a slight majority (52 percent) of Chicago families with children under 18 are low-income, as defined by the criteria for free or reduced-price lunches. Both white and middle-income parents continue to live in Chicago, but many send their children to parochial or other private schools. Those who cannot afford to do so often move to suburban school districts. Yet CPS policies of closing schools, firing teachers, and opening charter schools have resulted in whiter (and younger) teaching staffs.

Young African American men in 2007 had only a 39 percent chance of completing a diploma in the Chicago Public Schools. For Hispanic males the comparable figure was 51 percent. Drop-out rates were also high for African

American women and Latinas (Allensworth and Easton 2007). More recently the graduation rate has risen to 70 percent for African American men (and to higher levels for others), in part due to a program called Freshmen on Track that has been described as "a central-office mandate that teachers and principals do whatever it takes to make sure that no ninth-grader receives a failing grade in any subject" (Joravsky 2014, 9; see also Knowles 2014; and University of Chicago Consortium on Chicago School Research 2014). The logic of this initiative turns on the high correlation between failure in the ninth grade and subsequent dropping out of school. Charges are also circulating that drop-outs are being recorded as "transfers out of the district" to mitigate the drop-out statistics.

Mayor Rahm Emanuel's administration has determined that closing "underperforming" and "underutilized" schools will solve the problem of unacceptable educational outcomes. Before the start of the 2013–2014 school year, CPS closed forty-seven elementary schools and one high school and slated two more elementary schools for closure within two years. Almost all of these schools were in predominantly African American neighborhoods. The CPS closed these schools and cut teaching jobs instead of viewing low enrollments as an opportunity to develop innovative programs with smaller class sizes and specialized services. In part this is a union-busting move, and some portion of the shuttered schools will reopen as charter schools with nonunion teachers.

The school closings of 2013 were met by community protests, and the issues that surfaced during these protests and debates revealed (once again) the siege-like conditions of the neighborhoods that were affected. In many instances parents and children are afraid to walk to nearby schools in hostile gang territory. The fears are real enough, and media accounts make visible living conditions that are unimaginable to viewers and readers living as nearby as Chicago's North Side.

Health Indicators

Juliet Yonek and Romana Hasnain-Wynia's noteworthy study for the Feinberg School of Medicine at Northwestern University in collaboration with the Chicago Department of Public Health (2011) provides a comprehensive profile of health disparities and the geographical and racial-ethnic distribution of health issues and health resources in Chicago. Their findings reveal major disparities in the proportions of overweight African American and Latino high school students compared to whites, a very disproportionate rate of HIV diagnosis among blacks (who constituted 60 percent of individuals diagnosed in 2008), a motor vehicle accident death rate that was twice as high among blacks as among whites, and a breast cancer mortality rate that is three-fifths greater for black women than for white women. The last of these comparisons reflects a disturbing divergence since the early 1980s, when the rates were essentially similar. Yonek and Hasnain-Wynia discuss the very marked differences in the distribution of health-related resources across the city, including bike paths, access to mammograms, HIV clinics, and food stores with healthy options. Recent media reports have likewise focused on the shortage of trauma centers on the South Side.

Foreclosures

The current home foreclosure rate is about three times as high in predominantly African American and Latino communities as it is in predominantly white areas. In terms of socioeconomic status, the rate is twice as high for families with incomes under $80,000 as for more affluent families. (These disparities are discussed in more detail in Chapter 9; see also Immergluck and Smith [2005] and Rugh and Massey [2010] for more about the role of racial segregation in foreclosures and the effects of sub-prime lending on neighborhoods.)

Concentrated Disadvantage

The information we have reviewed in the preceding pages underlines the cumulative disparities that divide white and African American Chicagoans and suggests that even middle-income African Americans have a more fragile hold on day-to-day well-being than whites do. In addition to this series of disparities, sociologist Robert Sampson (2012) draws attention to "concentrated disadvantage" in his analysis of community areas marked by unemployment, poverty, welfare dependency, family disruption, high infant mortality rates, low birth weight, homicide, and others forms of violence (and by the effects of mass incarceration). These indicators are strongly correlated with one another and are spatially clustered in a fraction of African American neighborhoods in which about 20 percent of the city's population lives. Already in the 1960s, many of these areas had high rates of poverty, but mass incarceration and the challenges posed by reintegration of the formerly incarcerated represent new obstacles to efforts to improve the quality of neighborhood life.

A Historical Perspective on Racial Segregation and Inequality

To understand the disparities we see in the present we need to trace the historical process in which the marked segregation and inequality of the industrial First City were exacerbated during the deindustrialization of the Second City and then were not relieved by the neoliberal restructuring that yielded the Third City. In effect, the economic and social aspirations of the civil rights movement in the 1960s were curtailed by the linked processes of deindustrialization, economic restructuring, and globalization as they impacted racially isolated African American communities in Chicago.

The neoliberal era has meant privatization, deregulation, and the shrinkage of the welfare state. These forces further unleashed a process of globalization characterized by financial flows across borders, the offshoring of jobs, and accelerated changes in production that were commonly referred to as deindustrialization, though this term (as it is widely understood) is a misnomer for workplace shifts to flexible production and the spread of industrial processes into formerly white-collar work. Because neoliberal restructuring is based on faith in the market and decreased government intervention, these shifts occurred without recourse to buffering policies such as retraining, new educational initiatives, or regional development. The foregoing has been visible in both the United Kingdom and the United States and can be traced regionally and locally in much of the former U.S. industrial heartland running from the Northeast across to the Great Lakes states, the so-called Rust Belt. Some cities, including Chicago, have enjoyed rebirth into employment and prosperity as "Third Cities" while others (Detroit and cities in the north of England, for example) have not. The impact has also been uneven within cities. Who enjoyed rebirth into employment and prosperity in the Third City? Who was left behind or stranded in the transition?

The native-born working class took the brunt of the impact in most countries experiencing deindustrialization, and in the United States, the industrial working class had become increasingly African American by the 1970s. How are we to understand the process that stranded African Americans in Chicago (and elsewhere) in conditions of high unemployment and the accompanying deterioration in social capital and living conditions while other residents of the city and the metropolitan area successfully entered the new Third City? A generation ago, the initial, overly simple answer to this question was the mismatch hypothesis that posited a spatial disconnect between the concentration of African Americans in inner cities and the development of new jobs in the suburbs (when such employment opportunities did not leave the region or the country altogether), but this hypothesis has only limited explanatory power (see the discussion among sociologists and urban policy makers in articles by Kasarda 1985; Kain 1992; and Ihlanfeldt and Sjoquist 1998).

A better answer with more explanatory depth is offered by examining the institutional racism that preceded the high levels of unemployment accompanying the emergence of the Second City. The mismatch hypothesis, which is essentially descriptive, overlooks the racialized sources of the spatial gap that seemed to produce job opportunities for whites and unemployment for blacks. African Americans were locked into inner-city, racially isolated areas by decades of institutionally sanctioned racism, as exemplified by redlining (the refusal of banks to issue mortgage loans in African American or racially mixed areas), "racial steering" by real estate agents, and informal use of violence when African Americans tried to settle in white neighborhoods. Sociologist William Julius Wilson has been a meticulous observer of the ways that institutional racism and segregation preceded joblessness, creating the conditions under which many African Americans were unable to make the transition into the new economy. In the pages that follow we first summarize Wilson's main arguments and several important amendments to his work that other researchers have offered. We then sketch out a causal narrative that places the African American socioeconomic lag within the context of Chicago's transition from the Second to the Third City.

The Wilson School and Chicago's Persistent Racial Disparities

The most coherent and expansive explanation of how Chicago's Third City failed to reduce the racial disparities so emblematic of the Second City is Wilson's *When Work Disappears* (1997), which details the transformation of African American communities from "institutional ghettos" (i.e., places of involuntary racial isolation) to ghettos of joblessness. Wilson shows the devastating effect of deindustrialization and unemployment in areas of the city that were already subject to extreme segregation and racial isolation. Wilson further documents how employers' perceptions, the poorly developed state of mass transit on Chicago's South and West Sides, and the contingencies of everyday life created accelerating problems of unemployment and precarious employment that were not remedied by government intervention. Wilson (1987) had earlier suggested that the poverty of inner-city African Americans may be in part a result of more prosperous households moving to the suburbs, but these were predominantly African American suburbs (such as Harvey, Markham, and Dolton in the Chicago area) that are also poorer than diverse or predominantly white suburbs. Such contemporary suburbs, in fact, replicate long-observed inner-city racial disparities.

In a volume that might be viewed as a successor to *When Works Disappears*, Robert Sampson in *Great American City* (2012) reports on the effects of this transition—segregation followed by deindustrialization—on Chicago neighborhoods. Sampson's analysis focuses on differences among community areas that are associated with concentrated disadvantages in health, safety, and economic conditions. Looking at data from a number of predominantly African American community areas, he reaches the pessimistic assessment that little has changed for the better since the 1960s, and indeed, he argues that the effects of mass incarceration have worsened conditions. The percentage of families living in poverty in an area in 1960 was a strong predictor of the proportion in poverty in 2000, even though many individuals and families have moved in or out of these areas. All the areas Sampson identified as subject to concentrated disadvantage are predominantly African American and are home to about 20 percent of the city's residents. However, one should also bear in mind that not all African American communities experience concentrated disadvantage. Yet compared to middle-income whites, middle-income African Americans are more likely to live near areas with high levels of poverty (Mendell and Little 2003).

One very significant factor differentiates life in communities of concentrated disadvantage in the 2000s, compared to the 1960s and 1970s. This is the unnatural disaster of mass incarceration, which Sampson seems to naturalize as an outgrowth of altered behavior. In *Great American City* Sampson does not delve very deeply into the forces that have propelled mass incarceration, which include not only actual behaviors but also criminal code provisions, policing practices, pretrial processes, and sentencing policies that have racial effects despite "color-blind" statutes (such as the variation in sentencing for possession of crack in contrast to other forms of cocaine). Journalists such as Steve Bogira (2006; observing a Chicago criminal courtroom) and Mick Dumke (2013; looking at bond-court and pretrial decision making) have shed particular light on the racial disparities in the criminal-legal system in Chicago.

In *Black Picket Fences* (1999), Mary Pattillo used historical and ethnographic data to trace the declining economic fortunes of a South Side Chicago neighborhood as it slid from a lower middle- and solidly working-class community into one in which young people faced much diminished economic prospects. In particular, she highlights the negative cultural consequences of the broader economic context, such as the increasing impact of drug-trafficking gangs from adjacent areas, intense consumerism (the "reign of Nike"), and ultimately, the "ghetto trance" (styles of resistance that celebrate the rejection of "white" or mainstream culture).

These Chicago-focused studies are complemented by the national perspective offered in Patrick Sharkey's *Stuck in Place* (2012). Sharkey analyzes data from a number of U.S. cities and demonstrates that a sizable portion of African Americans have had their economic mobility blocked relative to white counterparts who grew up in families whose initial economic status was essentially similar. His fundamental argument, echoing one of Sampson's principal contentions, is that "neighborhood effects" substantially limit the life chances of young people living in poor, racially isolated areas.

Why the Third City Failed to Rectify the Racial Disparities of the Second City

The work of William Julius Wilson and his followers is a powerful explanation for persistent racial disparities, but it has also generated counterarguments and substantial amendments. One especially notable amendment is the finding by William Sites and Virginia Parks (2011) that even before the rush of deindustrialization, African Americans throughout the United States were excluded from more secure and better paid sectors of the working class. They were not only excluded from the mainstream in terms of residence and education; they were also marginalized in terms of occupation, and their economic status was generally not "essentially similar" to that of whites. In comparison to immigrants and native-born whites, social networks linking blacks to employers were more tenuous, and this situation exacerbated the effects of racial preferences in hiring. Political scientist Ira Katznelson (2006) further argues that New Deal policies, due in large part to the intransigence of southern congressional leadership, did not give African Americans access to many of the state-sponsored social benefits that helped build the post–World War II middle class.

The high rates of unemployment and poverty of African Americans after 1980 were not new phenomena resulting from a new economy. Instead, they were long-standing conditions of disadvantage and occupational marginalization. In the late 1960s and early 1970s, the African American unemployment rate was double that of whites (a condition that persisted into the 1980s), and African American workers were disproportionately concentrated in low-wage work (Davis 1986). In the 1970s, Andrew Levison of the Martin Luther King Jr. Center for Social Change wrote:

> The majority of black Americans are working people. . . . An increase in the minimum wage and serious enforcement of minimum wage laws would do more to end black poverty than anything an army of social workers will ever be able to accomplish. The problem is not values or culture. For the majority it is the typically working-class issue—the size of the paycheck. (1974, 48)

In the terminology of the period, researchers concluded that African Americans were disproportionately in the peripheral labor force rather than in the high-wage core. French social scientist Loïc Wacquant now uses the term precariat ("precarious" plus "proletariat") to refer to a stratum of workers that faces low wages, job insecurity, and frequent periods of unemployment and underemployment. Whatever the label, this tier of the working class is still disproportionately composed of African Americans and other people of color.

Employer preferences were and continue to be a key element in persistent high levels of unemployment among African Americans. Employer preferences tilted away from hiring African Americans, reflecting a cluster of causes that include not only racist attitudes but also the lower educational attainment of African Americans, inadequate preparation in the public school system, and a greater propensity to unionize or express job dissatisfaction. In the transition to the new economy, employers preferred to hire immigrants both at the high end of the new occupational structure (where a high-quality education was decisive) and in the lower tier, where docility and accommodation to unfavorable working conditions constituted desirable traits. This indirect discrimination further impinged on African Americans' efforts to enter the new economy.

Discrimination against African Americans as militant workers requires a word of explanation because it not as well understood as the more obvious factors of inadequate educational preparation, employer racism, and social networks disconnected from job networks. By the 1960s, African Americans had become more likely to unionize, perhaps in part because they had been confined to particularly dangerous and low-paying jobs within industrial sectors. Because of their greater propensity to unionize, employers saw them as a less attractive labor force for jobs in the lower tier of the new economy. After decades of exclusion from many unions and from good jobs in core sectors of the economy, African Americans had begun to unionize and to demand better pay and working conditions. Political scientist Michael Goldfield (1982, 1987) has documented African Americans' greater propensity to vote for union representation. Dan Georgakas and Marvin Surkin (1975) describe African American workers' militancy in the Detroit-area automobile industry by the 1970s. Sociologist Kathleen Schwartzman's (2008) brilliant analysis of ethnic succession in the poultry industry shows that the process was often driven by employers' preferences for immigrant workers over the native born. In the particular case she examined, this was expressed by replacing increasingly militant and unionizing African American workers with immigrants.

When deindustrialization struck communities that had formed in racial isolation during decades of de facto segregation, the upcoming generation experienced great difficulty entering the increasingly globalized, hypermarketized economy. In some form, industrial working classes across the globe encountered these difficulties, but in the Rust Belt of the United States—including the South and West Sides of Chicago—the existing pattern of racial segregation created an exceptional level of disadvantage for African Americans. The impact was primarily intergenerational. Working-class and lower-middle-class African American families faced daunting challenges to their ability to pass on their socioeconomic position to their children. The neighborhood Pattillo profiled in *Black Picket Fences* is a representative case of how these barriers to preserving middle-class employment for young people played out at the local level. The emerging job categories in the new economy—at the top and at the bottom—were more often filled by children of the affluent white middle class in the top tier and by immigrants in both the top and bottom tiers than by young African Americans.

Immigrants have brought a host of skills to the new economy, and many were educated prior to their arrival in the United States. Their skills are a good match for the new economy, not only as manual workers and care providers but also as nurses, physicians, technical workers, software engineers, and entrepreneurs. The investments in human capital that have prepared them for the full range of positions were made wholly or at least in part in their countries of origin. Contrary to stereotypes, immigrants do not just fill the lower tier of the new economy; they also find work in its middle and even upper tiers, although this varies considerably by country of origin (see Koval 2006 for a detailed analysis of the occupational distribution of immigrants in the Chicago area by country of origin).

A brief comparative look at this economic transition suggests both broad overall similarities and national differences and complex regional variation. For example, in Britain the process has had a regional dynamic; the South has become the site of the new economy while the North has experienced high unemployment and limited investment. In Torino, Italy, children of postwar migrants from southern Italy made a reasonably good adjustment as the city reinvented itself as a financial center and tourist destination of baroque palaces, outstanding restaurants, nightlife, and nearby ski slopes. Marginal working-class positions in Torino and other Italian cities are increasingly filled by immigrants from outside the European Union, while the Italian South remains relatively poorer and beset by higher unemployment. In the United States (and certainly in Chicago), the foundation of profound racism and residential segregation created conditions of exclusion for the African American working class that largely prohibited entry into the new economy (Sharkey 2012). The term Rust Belt can be viewed as spatial metaphor that veils a racial dynamic.

The fiscal crisis of governments at the state, municipal, and federal levels and the subsequent waves of public-sector downsizing have also contributed to the racialized impact of the transition to the Third City economy. During the early post–World War II period and particularly in the civil rights era, public sector employment became more open to African Americans. Many of these jobs conferred middle-class status and income. However, across the United States, the shrinkage of the public sector in the last decades of the twentieth century hit African Americans especially hard.

Theorists disagree about how to conceptualize the disadvantaged tier of the class structure. Marxists such as Deepankar Basu (2013) conceptualize a proletariat that includes a reserve army of labor (the unemployed and underemployed). Saskia Sassen (2011) describes global cities as having an hourglass class structure in which a lower tier of low-wage jobs is often filled by immigrants. Wacquant's term precariat captures the insecurity of this tier. Whatever terms and concepts are used, it is difficult to escape the conclusion that in Chicago, African Americans are disproportionately located in the lower paid, less secure, and less skilled portions of the class structure, its most disadvantaged and chronically unemployed portion. Although a substantial number of African

Americans have experienced upward mobility in recent decades, the occupational equality and full employment that were central aspirations of the civil rights movement have not been realized. On the contrary, many children of the African American urban industrial working class have sunk into increasingly precarious employment and unemployment.

The spatial and occupational segregations of the pre–civil rights First and Second Cities thus laid the foundation for the devastating impact of deindustrialization as the Second City wound down. The Third, neoliberal city has not undone these conditions. If anything, it has extended their reach across Chicago's South and West Sides. Although Chicago may well have made the turn from what Bennett calls the Second City to the Third City, many African Americans—and many other persons of color and recent immigrants—are locked in circumstances, neighborhoods, and institutions that amplify the inequalities that were so characteristic of the First and Second Cities.

The Emerging Class-Ethnic Structure

The shift to the Third City has produced a new structure of occupations and a new configuration of social classes that is markedly different from the industrial city's heavily blue-collar manufacturing work force. Jobs involving manual labor are increasingly to be found in the service sector, light industry, and construction. White-collar jobs encompass both a well-paid segment of attractive "creative class" occupations and a larger and much less remunerative sphere of retail and clerical positions. These two segments are often blurred together with the term "middle class."

Immigrants in the Emerging Class Structure

The presence of immigrants is closely linked to these occupational changes, and they have added new elements to the persistent baseline of racial inequality. Even though people cross national boundaries far less easily than capital does, a rapid rise in immigration has taken place in the neoliberal era, in sharp contrast to the early to mid-twentieth century's restrictive immigration regime. Currently, about one-fifth of the population of the Chicago metropolitan region is foreign born. In 2011, more than half a million immigrants lived in Chicago, and Hispanics constituted about half of that population. Individuals of Mexican origin (many of whom are American born) constituted 80 percent of the Hispanic population. Across the six-county metropolitan area, the immigrant population numbered 1,700,000 and Hispanic immigrants constituted 44.3 percent of the total. Other major countries of origin for the foreign born are Poland (8 percent), China (5 percent), the Philippines (4 percent), and India (3 percent).

As Chicago's ethnoracial structure has become much more complicated than simply black and white, the imaginary of race and ethnicity is often viewed as a threefold structure of whites, blacks, and Hispanics, each constituting about a third of the city's population (with "Asians" forming a much smaller fourth group). Currently, non-Hispanic whites constitute 31.7 percent of the population, African Americans 32.9 percent, Hispanics (including all nations of origin) 28.9 percent, and Asians 5.5 percent (U.S. Census Bureau 2015b). Although these "lumped" folk categories are of very limited use in understanding culture, history, and contemporary conditions, they increasingly have come to replace the older notion of "nationality," and many Chicagoans use them to talk about racial and ethnic difference and political interests.

In this model of race, class, and ethnicity, Hispanics are seen as intermediate in socioeconomic status between whites and blacks. Their presence appears to fill in the gap between the two racial groups of the Second City and seems to promise a less polarized racial divide. This perception is neither completely accurate nor a complete misrecognition. In median household income, high school completion rates, and poverty rates, Hispanics do indeed fall into an intermediate place.

But in terms of other characteristics, Hispanics are quite different from both whites and African Americans. Hispanics tend to be younger, and the age difference may account for their higher labor force participation rate. The number of workers per household is considerably higher for Hispanic immigrants (especially Mexicans) than for immigrants from other global regions. Both whites and African Americans are more likely to depend on Social Security and retirement income (which is much higher for whites than for blacks). Among the three large ethnoracial categories, Hispanics lag behind whites and African Americans in educational achievement. Fifty-six percent of whites report having earned a bachelor's degree or higher, more than three times the rate for African Americans and four times the rate for Hispanics. This disparity is related to occupational status. Over half of white workers are employed at better-paid managerial, business, science, and arts occupations and in the FIRE (finance, insurance, and real estate) sector, compared to 29 percent of African Americans and only 16.4 percent of Hispanics. One out of five African American workers is employed by a government agency, a sector that has provided job security, a decent income, and opportunities for advancement but is now experiencing job contraction. Hispanics have a more dispersed residential distribution than African Americans, and one recent national study (Iceland and Wilkes 2006) suggests that they (and Asian Americans) are reluctant to live in majority African American neighborhoods.

In short, a more careful look at residential patterns and preferences, educational levels, and occupational distributions suggests that one cannot simply place the three large ethnoracial categories on a single fixed scale of advantage and disadvantage. It is probably more accurate to think of Hispanics as replicating immigrant upward mobility along the lines of previous generations of European immigrants, moving from low-wage labor into a wider range of occupations, often—as Cynthia Cranford (2005) and Roger Waldinger (2005) have found—through the effective use of social networks. But they are doing so in a new, bifurcated economy that contains major barriers that separate lower- from upper-tier jobs.

In addition to the popular imagery of three major ethnic groups, another new cognitive map encompasses immigration and diversity. The highly diversified socioeconomic status of immigrants (once one looks beyond the social position of Mexican immigrants) supports an image of cultural diversity and contributes to the perception that the preceding black-white division is obsolete, fragmented into a mosaic formed by many ethnicities, religions, cultures, and nationalities. In this image, race has indeed declined in significance, and we live in an increasingly color-blind society in which what matters are cultural heritage and the decisions of individuals to invest in their own human capital. We will return to this imagery in our discussion of political and discursive responses to the emerging class/ethnic structure.

Stratification: Color, Country, Class, and Capital

A closer look at immigrants and their national origins allows us to see the complex relationship between ethnicity and socioeconomic status and the marked differences in the socioeconomic situations among immigrants depending on regional and national origin. In the Chicago metropolitan area, measures of central tendency (in other words, means and medians) of indicators of immigrant socioeconomic status are heavily weighted by the large presence of Latin American immigrants, particularly Mexicans, who are relatively disadvantaged educationally and economically. However, a more detailed breakdown shows considerable across-group variation, and many immigrants (and their children) are entrepreneurs, professionals, and skilled technical workers. Within the very broad categories of Asian or Latin American there are marked differences in education and socioeconomic status. Table 1.1 displays some of the disparities and the overall diversity.

The data in Table 1.1 suggest broad conclusions about the socioeconomic status of immigrants:

- Northern and western European immigrants and those from Oceania and Northern America (i.e., Canada) are at least as prosperous as native-born whites. Eastern and southern Europeans are somewhat less so.

Table 1.1. Socioeconomic status indicators by place of origin of immigrants

Region of Birth	Population*	% with College or Graduate Degree†	% with White Collar Occupations‡	Median Household Income	% Earning Less than 100% of Poverty Level
Africa	19,994	40.2	44.2	$32,162	28.6
Northern America	4,445	74.0	90.6	$84,741	11.3
Oceania	1,161	63.3	91.8	$116,250	21.2
Northern & Western Europe	17,137	50.9	79.3	$65,691	5.4
Southern and Eastern Europe	86,329	28.7	40.0	$41,064	9.6
Eastern Asia§	40,694	44.6	62.6	$37,063	25.8
South Central Asia§	28,812	66.1	79.6	$59,164	20.1
South Eastern Asia§	34,167	52.7	63.3	$65,172	12.2
Western Asia§	13,272	40.1	69.5	$39,585	27.2
Mexico	260,967	4.8	21.2	$39,475	23.4
Central America	23,669	11.2	29.6	$39,354	16.8
Caribbean	11,947	23.7	51.8	$39,375	21.9
South America	27,050	26.5	37.1	$49,017	14.5

Source: U.S. Census 2008.

*Estimate

†Age 25+

‡Managerial, professional, sales, and office work

§Asian country classification:

Eastern Asia: China, Hong Kong, Taiwan, Japan, Korea, Macau, Mongolia

Western Asia: Armenia, Azerbaijan, Georgia, Bahrain, Cyprus, Iraq, Israel, Jordan, Kuwait, Lebanon, Oman, Qatar, Saudi Arabia, Syria, Turkey, United Arab Emirates, Yemen

South Central Asia: Afghanistan, Bangladesh, India, Iran, Kazakhstan, Kyrgyzstan, Nepal, Pakistan, Sri Lanka, Turkistan, Turkmenistan, Uzbekistan

South Eastern Asia: Myanmar, Cambodia, Laos, Malaysia, Philippines, Singapore, Thailand, Vietnam

- "Asian" is a very heterogeneous category of immigrants, and there are considerable differences among the better educated and more prosperous Southern Asians and immigrants from Eastern Asia and from Western Asia (who, at present, are often refugees from regional conflicts). Within these broad regional categories there are further differences by national origin (both in educational and economic circumstances), for example, between Pakistani and Indian immigrants, as sociologists John Koval and Ken Fidel (2006) have charted.
- Latin Americans include both immigrants from South America with a higher median level of income and education and generally less well educated and lower income immigrants from Mexico and Central America.
- African immigrants have lower median incomes and are more likely to be impoverished than both other immigrants (including Latinos) and the native-born white population.
- For virtually every region-of-origin category and socioeconomic status rubric (with the exception of education level for Mexican immigrants), immigrants fare better than African Americans and appear to have directly stepped onto a higher rung of the stratification system.

When the data are further broken down by country of origin (rather than region), the disparities and diversity become even more striking. Sociologist John Koval (2006), who has looked at the occupations of immigrants by country of origin, has uncovered remarkable differences. To cite but one of his findings, the modal occupation of women immigrants from India in 2000 was physician!

One interpretation of Table 1.1 is that it confirms the persistence of racial dominance and a pattern of white supremacy that were already apparent in the First and Second Cities. We still see whites at the top of the socioeconomic hierarchy and African Americans at the bottom, with immigrants of color generally in less favorable positions than European immigrants (as measured by indicators of socioeconomic status). This conclusion matches sociologist Eduardo Bonilla-Silva's (2013) analysis of the emerging racial hierarchy of the United States. It also corresponds to the observation offered by Canadian scholars Boudreau, Keil, and Young about Toronto's patterns of labor market segregation, unemployment, poor working conditions, substandard housing, and distressed neighborhoods: "Multiculturalism, in other words, has not prevented the racialization of poverty but has led to inequalities in the well-being of visible minority populations" (Boudreau, Keil, and Young 2009, 92).

However, to use only "race" (i.e., skin color or visible-minority status) as a predictor of the class position of immigrants is oversimplified and neglects other relevant factors, above all the economic condition of their country of origin and furthermore their own class position within that country. World Bank analyst Branko Milanovic (2005) has assembled data demonstrating that the purchasing power of individuals in the global system can largely be predicted by two variables. The most important is the position of their country of residence in the global economic system, and the second most important is their own class location within that country. The class situation of immigrants (measured by their purchasing power or income) is more complicated than that of nonmigrants because not only is it shaped by the economic position of their new country of residence but it is also influenced by the economic position of their country of origin and by their own class location within the country of origin prior to their migration. The data reporting socioeconomic status characteristics of immigrants in the Chicago area (Table 1.1) clearly reflect the position of their countries of origin in the global system, including economic level and ability to offer emigrants a strong foundation of skills and education. For example, Polish immigrants have generally benefited from a better educational system in their country of origin than immigrants from Mexico. The historic relationship between the country of origin and the United States is also related to the differences among countries that affect the circumstances of immigration and the life opportunities of immigrants. Moreover, individuals and families of immigrants experience very different class situations and opportunities for increasing their human capital in their countries of origin, and they arrive in the United States with very different levels of skill and education. This factor complicates the tendency toward a "color hierarchy," as demonstrated by the case of well-educated Asian Indian immigrants (Rangaswamy 2006).

The Realigning Significance of Class

The occupations, households, and life experiences of the new middle strata are quite distinct from those of the middle class in the industrial era. Though still majority white, they are now more diverse than in the past, and members of this group are more likely to live as singles rather than within nuclear family households (Klinenberg 2012). And of course, there are a wide array of new occupations and professions.

However, U.S. census and other data sources only take us only so far in understanding how middle-class life in the Third City diverges from its preceding iteration in the Second City. Stand at the corner of Clark Street and Diversey Parkway on Chicago's North Side on a warm Saturday afternoon or a cold weekday rush hour. Around you swirl the faces of 30-year olds and millennials. Many (but not all) of them are white and appear to be middle-class. Who are all these hip-looking people talking on their phones or stroking their tablets, typically while toting shopping bags? Are they representatives of Richard Florida's creative class, the well-educated "smart" young professionals with college educations and high-tech skills who are lifting cities out of the doldrums of deindustrialization

Box 1.1: The Emerging Class-Ethnic Structure, Occupations, and Demographics in a Large Hospital

In this brief excerpt from a sociologist's field notes in a hospital, we catch a glimpse of the emerging class-ethnic structure at the "cell level," in a single institution or organization. This middle level of analysis (between micro-level interactions and macro-level stratification systems) enables us to analyze how institutions both reflect and reproduce the larger structure as individuals with a wide range of educational qualifications and demographic backgrounds work in different types of jobs. Neither plutocrats nor the homeless are visible among hospital personnel, but we can see how the occupational rungs of new class structures in a global city tend to be filled by individuals with different characteristics than those of their predecessors.

Physicians: At the top of the professional hierarchy, the physicians are predominantly white or (especially at the more junior ranks of hospitaliers—physicians on the floor) Southern Asian (both immigrant and native-born) and evenly balanced by gender.

Registered Nurses and Professional-Technical Staff: The RNs are predominantly young white women (including a few European immigrants), while tech professionals are somewhat more diverse and include more men.

PCTs (patient-care technicians) and non-professional staff: This large component of the hospital work force that includes nurses' assistants, food service workers, transport workers, housekeeping, and clerical staff is the most diverse, with African Americans forming a relative majority, though there are also many immigrants in this segment of the workforce. Gender is evenly balanced.

The example shows a fairly typical "cell" within the emerging structure in the Chicago area. This structure is substantially white in the upper occupational tiers, though it is more ethnically diverse than in the past; it includes immigrants (and second-generation Americans) throughout the structure in a wide range of occupations and incorporates African Americans primarily in working-class positions, many of which are now in the service sector or clerical work (often within health care and educational institutions) rather than in manufacturing.

and inventing new economies based on research and development, advanced corporate services, the arts, and up-market consumption (Florida 2002)?

Or are these young people a "new proletariat," a working class condemned to a lifetime of meager earnings, life in tiny apartments in which the dining room table doubles as a work desk and an emergency storage platform, biking in the ice and snow of the Chicago winter, and postponing a family and children under the cover of an ideology of perpetual youth and carefreeness? Maybe these are not the faces of the creative class but of economist Tyler Cowen's new working class (or "lower-middle class"; as he puts it "the new below-average"), a new proletariat that seems different from the old one because of its educational attainment, cool clothes, and hipster ways, appearances that conceal its straitened earning power and diet of beans, albeit very healthy ones (Broughton 2013; Cowen 2013a). Maybe the young people are new proletarians who will never own a viable business (even though they initiate many failed startups), never attain a strong professional standing, never become rich, and perhaps never own a home or enjoy job security. This prospective proletariat can be found in a vast range of occupations associated with an advanced capitalist economy, an economy in which information and professional services are largely industrialized, or "automated," as people used to say. Many of them are in computer, software, and digital technology fields, and some are in health care (another one of Florida's creative categories). As citizens, as relatively well-educated workers, as smart consumers safely on the good side of the digital divide, they do not look as if they are in a precarious tier of the labor force, but Cowen is pretty merciless in his assessment:

> Imagine a very large bohemian class of the sort that say, lives in parts of Brooklyn. . . . It will be culturally upper or upper-middle class, but there will be the income of lower-middle class. They may have lives that are quite happy and rewarding, but they may not have a lot of savings. There will be a certain fragility to this existence. (Cowen 2013b)

This fragility is different from the pressures working-class families experienced in the past. With small households, attention can focus on food, lifestyle, DIY projects such as the ingenious fashioning of backpacks from old tweed pants and computer desks from industrial rubbish. At its lower reaches, the "creative class" gently tails off into the new "below average" without a sharp fault line, as these strata are not all that different in their ethnic composition, tastes, lifestyles, and even educational attainment. Providing city comparisons but in sharply contrasting tones, Eric Klinenberg describes opting out of family formation in his largely New York–based and cheerful *Going Solo* (2012), while Jennifer Silva offers a somber portrait of psychological fragility, political disengagement, and self-blame in *Coming Up Short* (2013), her interview-based study of white and African American working-class young adults in Lowell, Massachusetts and Richmond, Virginia.

No discussion of emerging class structure would be complete without mention of the rise of plutocracy in the uppermost tier of almost every global city. By "plutocracy" we refer not only to the increasing numbers of the very wealthy in global cities but also to their impact on real estate markets, planning and development, and political decision making. Since the nineteenth century, Chicago has been home to extremely wealthy individuals and families, so their presence and political role are not new phenomena. The Gold Coast area on the city's near North Side remains Chicago's wealthiest district.

Judging how "plutocratic" Chicago has become depends on the metric. Alan Berube (2014) of the Brookings Institution places Chicago in eighth place on an index of city inequality formed by comparing the income of households at the 95th percentile to those at the 20th percentile in the distribution of income in the city in 2012. By this measure, Chicago's ratio of 12.5 ($201,460 to $16,078) is high but considerably lower than the most unequal city, Atlanta, which has an 18.8 ratio ($280,827 to $14,850). Compared to New York, Los Angeles, or San Francisco, Chicago is home to a relatively smaller number of households whose incomes fall within the top 5 percent of the national income distribution. Not only is Chicago's plutocracy relatively smaller than the comparable cohorts in New York, Los Angeles, and San Francisco areas, Chicago does not even make the top ten list of metropolitan regions with the most sizable proportions of the affluent (Kurtzleben 2013, reporting U.S. census data). Real estate prices suggest that Chicago lags behind New York (and certainly behind London) in the extent to which the wealthy are the main beneficiaries of central city development and the driving force of real estate markets. Chicago also falls well below the top thirty in the cost-of-living rankings for global cities (Mercer 2014). Chicago's modest standing according to such measures suggests that its "home town global elite" has not yet fully detached itself from the markets in which local middle- and working-class households participate (Reich 1991). However, recently completed enclaves in the "expanded Loop" (and certainly specific projects such as Trump Tower) may be physical predictors of Chicago's convergence with global trends. In what is called the New East Side—toward the lake from Michigan Avenue and along the Chicago River—anchored by the architecturally stunning Aqua Tower and organized via a tri-level street plan, homeless people congregate in the lowest level, even as above them an expanding cohort of the very wealthy seems to monopolize the attention of those who plan the city's future physical development.

Neoliberalism, Reimagined Inequality, and Politics

Race, ethnicity, immigration trends, and social class play out in particular ways in neoliberal Chicago. On the one hand, the patterns we have described extend older conditions of social hierarchy and group separation that the Second City manifested. And in other ways—such as the very recent trends we have just discussed—globalizing forces and neoliberal policy have contributed to the shape of the emerging Chicago. Race, ethnicity, immigration, and social class also contribute to how we interpret and behave in the world or, when we reduce the scale of "the world," how we interpret and behave within our local realm, our particular city. These interpretations are not simply products of the media; they are rooted in social networks and everyday experience. As Marx said of ideology: "They do not know it, but they are doing it" (quoted in Žižek 1989, 28).

We conclude this chapter by outlining four ideological processes, broadly defined, that tend to reduce both the recognition and discussion of social inequality/disparities in neoliberal Chicago: (1) displacement of the marginalized and working class from visible public spaces; (2) the disengagement of these groups from voting and other forms of conventional political engagement; (3) the emergence of cognitive maps that encourage people to see inequality in terms of individual effort, smart choices, and cultural values; and (4) a general shrinkage of the public sphere and public discussion.

Neoliberal policies such as the redevelopment of public housing complexes and zero-tolerance policing of the Loop have literally reduced the presence of African Americans and other people of color, the poor, and the otherwise marginalized from central Chicago. According to the market logic that aligns with these public policies, valuable territory is secured where the responsible middle and upper classes can pursue entrepreneurship, management, and consumption. This reorganization of space and displacement of the marginalized is one geographic reflection of what French social scientists Pierre Bourdieu (2010) and Loïc Wacquant (2008) call the retreat by the "left hand of the state," or social functions such as public education, housing, and health care directed to those with limited economic and cultural capital, in favor of the "right hand of the state," functions such as policing and the criminal court system that seek to enforce public order and individual discipline.

"The black community is really messed up now. . . . We had leaders before. . . . We as a people have been totally forgotten," observes Morris Shadrach Davis, a relative of two recent Chicago shooting victims (quoted in Johnson and Babwin 2013). The voting participation of Chicago African Americans jumped markedly during the two elections (1983 and 1987) that brought Harold Washington—the city's first black mayor—to office. However, since the 1987 election, black voting participation has markedly declined (Lewis, Taylor, and Kleppner 1997). In all likelihood, the introduction in 1995 of nonpartisan mayoral balloting reinforced the political alienation at the heart of this decline; most observers view this change as having reduced the chances of prospective African American mayoral candidates.

This change in voting patterns and procedures has accompanied the erosion of political leadership in the African American community, marked by the weak performance of Carol Moseley Braun both as a U.S. senator and as a 2011 mayoral candidate (she received only 10 percent of the vote), the floundering of Todd Stroger as president of the Cook County Board of Commissioners, and the painful spectacle of the criminal convictions of Jesse Jackson Jr. and his wife, Alderman Sandra Jackson, on charges of illegal use of campaign funds. Although African American clergy remain engaged on many issues and at least one current African American officeholder, Cook County Board president Toni Preckwinkle, has maintained a visible and positive public profile and is widely discussed as a future candidate for Chicago mayor, the vigorous leadership of the civil rights era appears to have faded, and the names of activists such as Harold Washington, Jesse Jackson Sr., Renault Robinson, Al Raby, Ralph Metcalfe, and Richard Newhouse are rarely evoked by the media or in the conversation of Chicago's millennial generation and students.

In the view of French philosopher Michel Foucault (2008, 2009), the dynamics of late-twentieth-century capitalism, which are reflected in ever-increasing individuation, "flexibility," privatization, entrepreneurialism, and risk management operate not only on the individual level; they also operate at the level of institutions and at the level of the state. The social practices that embody individuation, privatization, entrepreneurialism, and the like, in turn, are associated with a mode of governing that promotes insecurity and instability. In this fashion, the populace becomes "entrepreneurs of themselves" navigating an "enterprise society"(Foucault 2008, 226, 147). The social world discards notions such as solidarity and common effort in favor of constant competition and performance metrics at school, in the workplace, and, not least, on the health club treadmill.

In Chicago—as across the North America, Europe, and increasing portions of Asia—market solutions have become the preferred antidote to social inequalities. The ideal citizen has become a "smart consumer" who navigates a host of complex choices in the public sector as well as private markets. Education scholar Pauline Lipman (2006) documents the welter of options offered by Chicago's "reformed" public schools, which nonetheless result in the concentration of middle-income and white students in magnet schools while youngsters in lower income communities of color typically attend neighborhood schools and military academies. In his book *Heat Wave* (2002), sociologist Eric Klinenberg discusses the disastrous consequences for elderly, ill, and poor people who were unable to identify and contact the agencies they needed for help to survive the debilitating weather conditions of July 1995. It is of course a bitter irony that more choice only seems to amplify older race- and class-derived social disparities.

Two variables—cultural heritage and human capital—are believed to account for the differences in socioeconomic outcomes. This emphasis on culture and human capital is both factual and mythical. It is not completely untrue, but it obscures the historical and economic origins of inequality between whites and African Americans and the racial dimension of socioeconomic stratification. The images of the mosaic of diversity and individual responsibility and the foregrounding of cultural difference and individual initiative dovetail well with neoliberal views of social inequality as an individual rather than a public issue. A highly differentiated ethnoracial spectrum paradoxically contributes to a deceptive color-blindness in popular discourse because the historical specificity of racial inequality is lost from view amid the emergent complexities of cultural and ethnic diversity.

Neoliberalism as an ideology of markets and individualism is associated with an ideological shift from the idea that government should and can look out for people and establish a shared common good to a belief that the role of government centers on support for entrepreneurship and control of disruptive forces. As political philosopher Michael Sandel (2012) points out, in this ideology, all political, social, and moral issues are dissolved and eliminated by the workings of the market. Racial and class inequalities are removed from an agenda of governing whose main premise is a purported equivalence between freedom and the logic of the market. What then unfolds in the management of neoliberal society is the rapidly increasing gap between upper and middle strata whose members possess the means and resources to live out their own private interests and a lower stratum whose members become the objects of displacement, surveillance, and the penal system. In Chicago, while the upper and middle strata are diverse, the lower stratum is disproportionately composed of people of color and especially African Americans.

Ultimately, an especially troubling aspect of racial and social class disparities in a neoliberal city is the difficulty of addressing these problems in public discussion and debates about policy options and an equity agenda. Commentators representing a variety of ideological positions and disciplines, including Pierre Bourdieu (1991) and American sociologist Theda Skocpol (2004), have expressed concern about the withering of public policy-oriented political discourse. In Chicago, following a general decline in the vitality, staffing, and readership of print journalism (see Box 3.2), only a small number of print journalists consistently write about racial isolation and inequality in the city. For an exception, see the work of Steve Bogira and Mick Dumke in *The Chicago Reader* (2013, 2015). Legal scholar Cass Sunstein (2009) points out that Internet forums are often marked by hyperfragmentation of interpretation and hyperpolarization of opinion.

These empirical developments seem to confirm the forebodings, expressed decades ago, by important social critics such as Jürgen Habermas (1991) and Hannah Arendt. Arendt (1977) argued that the existence of a public sphere balances and helps curb the pursuit of private interest, whereas in neoliberal ideology, it is precisely the pursuit of private interest that is supposed to produce the common good. This individualism obscures structural factors that produce inequalities by making all social and political issues appear as if they were personal matters of the work ethic, an entrepreneurial attitude, or a disposition toward self-advancement. Racial isolation exacerbates the tendencies in neoliberalism to shrink the public sphere. In a racially divided city, there are few occasions that permit, and equally few institutions that encourage, the discussion of public issues across racial and class lines.

As Chicago becomes the province of only those who can afford to live there, economic citizenship overshadows political citizenship. Although everyone is impacted by the neoliberal shrinkage of the public sphere, working-class and lower income people and persons of color are particularly hard hit, and their major resources—numbers and social capital—are diminished, even as politics as we have known it is diminished. The emergent, highly circumscribed "public" has become so privatized, so protective of private finances, and so opposed to taxation that it has become nearly impossible for the state, even if it were inclined to do so, to reassert itself and promote redistribution of income or broadly beneficial public investment. The dwindling of social programs and the privatization of all spheres of life leave people feeling disenfranchised, and this was a primary component of the political apathy characteristic of Chicago during the 1990s and the first decade of the new century.

Note

1. The index of dissimilarity is a measure used to express residential segregation or the uneven distribution of two groups in a specific territory. A high index score means that an area is very segregated and that the two groups do not live in an even distribution across the territory. The score can be read as the percentage of people in one of the groups that would have to move in order to create the same proportions in a sub-area as the proportion that pertains to the territory as a whole. (Example: While Chicago's population is about 32 percent African American, this overall proportion is found in few neighborhoods. Many neighborhood populations are either less than 10 percent African American or over 90 percent African American.)

Bibliography

Allensworth, Elaine, and John Q. Easton. 2007. *What Matters for Staying On-Track and Graduating in Chicago Public High Schools: A Close Look at Course Grades, Failures, and Attendance in the Freshman Year.* Chicago: Consortium on Chicago School Research at the University of Chicago.

———. 1977. "Public Rights and Private Interests: In Response to Charles Frankel." In *Small Comforts for Hard Times: Humanists on Public Policy,* ed. Michael J. Mooney and Florian Stuber, 103–108. New York: Columbia University Press.

Arendt, Hannah. 1998. *The Human Condition.* 2nd ed. Chicago: University of Chicago Press.

Basu, Deepankar. 2013. "The Reserve Army of Labor in the Postwar U.S. Economy." *Science and Society* 77, no. 2: 179–201.

Bennett, Larry. 2010. *The Third City: Chicago and American Urbanism.* Chicago: University of Chicago Press.

Berube, Alan. 2014. "All Cities Are Not Created Unequal." Metropolitan Opportunity Series no. 51. Washington, D.C.: The Brookings Institution. Accessed August 5, 2014. http://www.brookings.edu/research/papers/2014/02/cities-unequal-berube.

Bogira, Steve. 2006. *Courtroom 302: A Year behind the Scenes in an American Criminal Courthouse.* New York: Vintage.

———. 2012. "Concentrated Poverty and Homicide in Chicago." *Chicago Reader,* August 2.

Bogira, Steve, and Mick Dumke. 2013. "A Dream Unrealized for African Americans in Chicago." *Chicago Reader,* August 22.

———. 2015. "Still Separate, Unequal, and Ignored." *Chicago Reader,* February 5.

Bonilla-Silva, Eduardo. 2013. *Racism without Racists: Color-Blind Racism and the Persistence of Racial Inequality in America.* Lanham, Md.: Rowman & Littlefield.

Bourdieu, Pierre. 1991. *Language and Symbolic Power.* Cambridge, UK: Polity Press.

———. 2010. *Sociology Is a Martial Art.* Ed. Gisele Sapiro. New York: The New Press.

Boudreau, Julie-Anne, Roger Keil, and Douglas Young. 2009. *Changing Toronto: Governing Urban Neoliberalism.* Toronto: University of Toronto Press.

Broughton, Philip Delves. 2013. Review of *Average Is Over. Wall Street Journal,* October 2. Accessed January 3, 2015. http://online.wsj.com/news/articles/SB10001424052702303342104579097482945031804.

Bruch, Elizabeth E. 2014 "How Population Structure Shapes Neighborhood Segregation." *American Journal of Sociology,* 119, no. 5: 1221–78.

Cowen, Tyler. 2013a. *Average Is Over: Powering America Beyond the Age of the Great Stagnation.* New York: Dutton.

———. 2013b. Interview on National Public Radio, September 12. Accessed January 3, 2015. http://www.npr.org/2013/09/12/221425582/tired-of-inequality-one-economist-says-itll-only-get-worse.

Cranford, Cynthia J. 2005. "Networks of Exploitation: Immigrant Labor and the Restructuring of the Los Angeles Janitorial Industry." *Social Problems* 52, no. 3: 379–397.

Davis, Mike. 1986. *Prisoners of the American Dream.* London: Verso.

Dumke, Mick. 2013. "Our Medieval Bail System: Do We Have the Right People Locked Up?" *Chicago Reader*, October 17.

Florida, Richard. 2002. *The Rise of the Creative Class: And How It's Transforming Work, Leisure, Community and Everyday Life*. New York: Basic Books.

Foucault, Michel. 2008. *The Birth of Biopolitics: Lectures at the Collège de France, 1978–79*. New York: Palgrave-Macmillan.

———. 2009. *Security, Territory, Population: Lectures at the Collège de France, 1977–1978*. New York: Picador.

Georgakas, Dan, and Marvin Surkin. 1975. *Detroit: I Do Mind Dying*. New York: St. Martin's Press.

Goldfield, Michael. 1982. "The Decline of Organized Labor: NLRB Union Certification Election Results." *Politics and Society* 11, no. 2: 167–210.

———. 1987. *The Decline of Organized Labor in the United States*. Chicago: University of Chicago Press.

Gutstein, Eric, and Pauline Lipman. 2013. "The Rebirth of the Chicago Teachers Union and Possibilities for a Counter-Hegemonic Education Movement." *Monthly Review* 65, no. 2. Accessed July 15, 2014. http://monthlyreview.org/2013/06/01/the-rebirth-of-the-chicago-teachers-union-and-possibilities-for-a-counter-hegemonic-education-movement/.

Habermas, Jürgen. 1991. *The Structural Transformation of the Public Sphere: An Inquiry into a Category of Bourgeois Society*. Studies in Contemporary German Social Thought. Cambridge, Mass.: MIT Press.

Hertz, Daniel Kay. 2013. "We've Talked about Homicide in Chicago at Least One Million Times but I Don't Think This Has Come Up." *City Notes*, August 5. Accessed July 15, 2014. http://danielkayhertz.com/2013/08/05/weve-talked-about-homicide-in-chicago-at-least-one-million-times-but-i-dont-think-this-has-come-up/.

Iceland, John, and Rima Wilkes. 2006. "Does Socioeconomic Status Matter? Race, Class, and Residential Segregation." *Social Problems* 53, no. 2: 248–273.

Ihlanfeldt, Keith, and David Sjoquist. 1998. "The Spatial Mismatch Hypothesis: A Review of Recent Studies and Their Implications for Welfare Reform." *Housing Policy Debate* 9, no. 4: 849–857.

Immergluck, Dan, and Geoff Smith. 2005. "Measuring the Effect of Subprime Lending on Neighborhood Foreclosures: Evidence from Chicago." *Urban Affairs Review* 40: 362–389.

Johnson, Carla A. K., and Don Babwin. 2013. "Chicago Shooting Shows Gap in Stepped-Up Policing." Associated Press, September 21.

Jones, William P. 2013. *The March on Washington: Jobs, Freedom, and the Forgotten History of Civil Rights*. New York: W. W. Norton.

Joravsky, Ben. 2014. "Give the Mayor Credit: School Graduation Rates Are Up." *Chicago Reader*, November 27.

Kain, John. 1992. "The Spatial Mismatch Hypothesis: Three Decades Later." *Housing Policy Debate* 3, no. 2: 371–392.

Kasarda, John. 1985. "Urban Change and Minority Opportunities." In *The New Urban Reality*, ed. Paul Peterson, 33–68. Washington, D.C.: The Brookings Institution.

Katznelson, I. 2006. *When Affirmative Action Was White: An Untold History of Racial Inequality in Twentieth-Century America*. New York: W. W. Norton.

Klinenberg, Eric. 2002. *Heat Wave: A Social Autopsy of Disaster in Chicago*. Chicago: University of Chicago Press.

———. 2012. *Going Solo: The Extraordinary Rise and Surprising Appeal of Living Alone*. New York: Penguin Books.

Knowles, Tim. 2014. "Chicago Isn't Waiting for Superman." *U.S. News and World Report*, September 5. Accessed January 18, 2015. http://www.usnews.com/opinion /articles/2014/09/05/chicago-public-schools-show-real-graduation-rate-progress.

Koval, John P. 2006. "Immigrants at Work." In *The New Chicago: A Social and Cultural Analysis*, ed. John Koval, Larry Bennett, Michael I. J. Bennett, Fassil Demissie, Roberta Garner, and Kiljoong Kim, 197–210. Philadelphia: Temple University Press.

Koval, John P., and Kenneth Fidel. 2006. "Chicago: Immigrant Capital of the Heartland." In *The New Chicago: A Social and Cultural Analysis*, ed. John P. Koval, Larry Bennett, Michael I. J. Bennett, Fassil Demissie, Roberta Garner, and Kiljoong Kim, 97–104. Philadelphia: Temple University Press.

Koval, John P., Larry Bennett, Michael I. J. Bennett, Fassil Demissie, Roberta Garner, and Kiljoong Kim, eds. 2006. *The New Chicago: A Social and Cultural Analysis*. Philadelphia: Temple University Press.

Kurtzleben, Danielle. 2013. "Where the Richest Americans Live." *U.S. News and World Report*. Accessed December 14, 2014. http://www.usnews.com/news/articles /2013/02/12/where-the-richest-americans-live.

Levison, Andrew. 1974. *The Working-Class Majority*. New York: Penguin Books.

Lewis, James, D. Garth Taylor, and Paul Kleppner. 1997. *Metro Chicago Political Atlas '97–'98*. Springfield, Ill.: University of Illinois at Springfield, Institute for Public Affairs.

Lipman, Pauline. 2006. "Chicago School Reform: Advancing the Global City Agenda." In *The New Chicago: A Social and Cultural Analysis*, ed. John P. Koval, Larry Bennett, Michael I. J. Bennett, Fassil Demissie, Roberta Garner, and Kiljoong Kim, 248–58. Philadelphia: Temple University Press.

Macewan, Arthur. 2013. "Black-White Income Differences: What's Happened?" *Dollars and Sense*. July/August. Accessed December 4, 2015. http://dollarsandsense .org/archives/2013/0713macewan.html.

Mendell, David, and Darnell Little. 2003. "Poverty, Crime Still Stalk City's Middle-Class Blacks." *Chicago Tribune*, August 7.

Mercer. 2014. "Mercer's 2014 Cost of Living City Rankings." Accessed December 9, 2014. http://www.imercer.com/content/cost-of-living.aspx.

Milanovic, Branko. 2005. *Worlds Apart: Measuring International and Global Inequality*. Princeton, N.J.: Princeton University Press.

Pattillo, Mary. 2007. *Black on the Block: The Politics of Race and Class in the City*. Chicago: University of Chicago Press.

Pattillo-McCoy, Mary. 1999. *Black Picket Fences: Privilege and Peril among the Black Middle Class*. Chicago: University of Chicago Press.

Rangaswamy, Padma. 2006. "Asian Indians of Chicago." In *The New Chicago: A Social and Cultural Analysis*, ed. John P. Koval, Larry Bennett, Michael I. J. Bennett, Fassil Demissie, Roberta Garner, and Kiljoong Kim, 128–140. Philadelphia: Temple University Press.

Reich, Robert. 1991. *The Work of Nations*. New York: Random House.

Rugh, Jacob S., and Douglas Massey. 2010. "Racial Segregation and the American Foreclosure Crisis." *American Sociological Review* 75, no. 5: 629–651.

Sampson, Robert. 2012. *Great American City: Chicago and the Enduring Neighborhood Effect*. Chicago: University of Chicago Press.

Sandel, Michael. 2012. *What Money Can't Buy: The Moral Limits of Markets*. New York: Farrar, Strauss, and Giroux.

Sassen, Saskia. 2011. *Cities in a World Economy*. Thousand Oaks, Cal.: Sage.

Schwartzmann, Kathleen. 2008. "Lettuce, Segmented Labor Markets, and the Immigration Discourse." *Journal of Black Studies* 39, no. 1: 129–156.

Sharkey, Patrick. 2012. *Stuck in Place*. Chicago: University of Chicago Press.

Silva, Jennifer. 2013. *Coming Up Short: Working Adulthood in an Age of Uncertainty*. New York: Oxford University Press.

Sites, William, and Virginia Parks. 2011. "What Do We Really Know about Racial Inequality? Labor Markets, Politics, and the Historical Basis of Black Economic Fortunes." *Politics and Society* 39, no. 1: 40–73.

Skocpol, Theda. 2004. "The Narrowing of Civic Life." *The American Prospect*, May 17. Accessed February 14, 2015. http://prospect.org/article/narrowing-civic-life.

Sunstein, Cass. 2009. *Going to Extremes: How Like Minds Unite and Divide*. New York: Oxford University Press.

U.S. Census Bureau. 2008. American Community Survey 5-Year Estimates 2008–2012, Tables SO403-SO506, accessed August 30, 2013.

———. 2011. "American FactFinder: Median Income in the Past 12 Months, 2011 American Community Survey 1-Year Estimates." (S 1903) Accessed February 26, 2016. http://factfinder.census.gov/faces/tableservices/jsf/pages/productview.xhtml?src=bkmk.

———. 2013. "Historical Income Tables: Income Inequality." Table H-4. Gini Ratios for Households, by Race and Hispanic Origin of Householder: 1967 to 2012. Accessed December 4, 2015. http://www.census.gov/hhes/www/income/data/historical/inequality/.

———. 2015a. "Historical Income Tables: Income Inequality." Accessed February 27, 2016. http://www.census.gov/hhes/www/income/data/historical/inequality/.

———. 2015b. "State and County QuickFacts: Chicago, Illinois." Accessed May 9, 2015. http://quickfacts.census.gov/qfd/states/17/1714000.html.

University of Chicago Consortium on Chicago School Research. 2014. *Preventable Failure: Improvements in Long-Term Outcomes When High Schools Focused on the Ninth Grade Year: Research Summary*. April. Accessed December 16, 2014. http://ccsr.uchicago.edu/publications/preventable-failure-improvements-long-term-outcomes-when-high-schools-focused-ninth.

Wacquant, Loïc. 2008. *Deadly Symbiosis: Race and the Rise of the Penal State.* Cambridge, UK: Polity Press.

Waldinger, Roger. 2005. "Networks and Niches: The Continuing Significance of Ethnic Connections." In *Ethnicity, Social Mobility, and Public Policy*, ed. Glenn C. Loury, Tariq Modood, and Steven M. Teles, 324–362. Cambridge, UK: Cambridge University Press.

Western, Bruce. 2006. *Imprisonment and Inequality in America.* New York: Russell Sage Foundation.

Wilson, William J. 1987. *The Truly Disadvantaged: The Inner City, the Underclass, and Public Policy.* Chicago: University of Chicago Press.

———. 1997. *When Work Disappears.* New York: Alfred Knopf.

Yonek, Juliet C., and Romana Hasnain-Wynia. 2011. *A Profile of Health and Health Resources within Chicago's 77 Communities.* Chicago: Northwestern University Feinberg School of Medicine, Center for Healthcare Equity/Institute for Healthcare Studies.

Žižek, Slavoy. 1989. *The Sublime Object of Ideology.* London: Verso.

CHAPTER 2

Metropolitan Chicago's Geography of Inequality

COSTAS SPIROU AND LARRY BENNETT

Many years ago, English historian Asa Briggs (1980, 55–56) identified Chicago as one of the "shock cities" of the nineteenth century. In the years following the Civil War, Chicago experienced a burst of variegated growth. Major industrial complexes sprang up on the city's South and West Sides; a web of railroad lines connected the city to points east, south, and west; and each year thousands of immigrants poured into the city, initially from northern and western Europe, but as 1900 neared, increasingly from southern and eastern Europe (Cronon 1991; Miller 1996). In one sense Chicago was a shock city because of the seemingly chaotic nature of its nineteenth-century growth. In the city's downtown core—which around the turn of the century was dubbed "the Loop"—tall office buildings seemed to spring up overnight. Some of them disappeared nearly as quickly. The Montauk Block, completed in the early 1880s and designed by Daniel Burnham and John Wellborn Root, was characterized by some as Chicago's "first skyscraper." Nonetheless, it was demolished in favor of a newer, taller structure within twenty years.

Given Chicago's tumultuous growth spurt, it is not especially surprising that its civic leaders were among the nation's first local elites to promote the vision and practices of the nascent city planning profession. The famous Plan of Chicago, completed in 1909 by a team under the direction of Daniel Burnham, was the earliest effort by a major American city to shape its trajectory of growth. And though Burnham and his collaborators focused their attention on the city of Chicago, the "Plan of Chicago" looked beyond the municipal limits to sketch out the rudiments of a regional portrait (Scott 1971; Schaffer 1993; Smith 2006).

The Chicago that Burnham observed and analyzed was already a divided metropolis. Elite residential neighborhoods clung to the city's eastern margin along the shore of Lake Michigan. To the west, highly mixed-use neighborhoods of small factories, hastily constructed houses and walk-up apartment buildings, and commercial strips typified development. In the years just after the release of the Plan of Chicago, as the first great wave of African Americans settled in Chicago seeking work in its World War I–swollen local economy, the South Side Black Belt was taking form (Spear 1969; Drake and Cayton [1945] 1993). Beyond these districts, within two to three miles of the Loop, more prosperous, largely residential areas were emerging, even though on the far South Side, heavy industry—dominated by a half-dozen major steel producers—had already seized the lakefront and areas to the west.

By the middle of the twentieth century, a Chicago that was several decades past its shocking growth spurt was widely known as the most racially segregated city in the United States. But apart from intense inner-city racial segregation, mid-century metropolitan Chicago's pattern of growth reflected the suburbanization typical of American urban regions, shaped by popular culture and driven by public policy (Jackson 1985; Beauregard 2006). Enchanted by the distance-reducing automobile and lured by highway construction funded by the federal government and affordable mortgages, Chicagoans—typically white and middle-class—flocked to the suburbs. Post–World War II Chicago was a metropolis divided along the dimensions of both social class and race in which land uses, property value, and municipally controlled zoning served to spatially structure social separation.

Contemporary Chicago is, in one sense, an extension of the divided metropolis that took shape a century ago. However, in the current era of globalization—which we define as both an actual process of accelerated international linkage and an ideology of local economic development—neoliberal policy has contributed to the emergence of an updated geography of inequality. Chicago's new geography of inequality can be characterized by a group of seemingly disparate attributes: increasing racial and ethnic diversity, notably in many suburban communities; accelerated exurban development; inner-city gentrification; and advancing decline in non-gentrifying city neighborhoods and inner-ring suburbs. Broad forces such as ongoing economic restructuring and the particular impacts of the Great Recession have contributed to these trends. But also at work are specifically neoliberal, locally implemented strategies aimed at "transforming" public housing and promoting residential development in the central city.

Chicago's Highly Skewed Geography of Race and Economic Attainment

Various aspects of Chicago's evolving pattern of racial segregation since the latter part of the nineteenth and first half of the twentieth centuries have been amply documented. For all its promise, the Great Migration to the North by African Americans proved deeply ambiguous for the newcomers who sought to escape the degradations of the South, economic opportunities, and a more tolerant social climate. Most found northern social institutions to be highly unwelcoming. A host of scholars have documented these conditions in Chicago, focusing on the interactions of race with housing, political participation and representation, education, and access to social services. All of these works point to the persistent geographical clustering and isolation of African Americans within the city of Chicago (Drake and Cayton [1945] 1993; Spear 1969; Hirsch 1998; Smith 2012).

The distribution of racial/ethnic groups in Chicago changed little during the second half of the last century. An analysis of housing segregation and employment patterns conducted in the late 1960s compared Chicago and Detroit. The research findings described the residential patterns of African Americans by noting that "most Chicago Negroes live in the notorious South Side, although fingers of the ghetto extend due west and due north from the Loop. Chicago's principal ghetto houses a larger percentage of its non-white workforce than does Detroit's: 96 per cent of Chicago's nonwhite workers reside there" (Kain 1968, 179). A more recent analysis of Latinos in Chicago concluded that the combination of limited mobility opportunities and discriminatory practices caused durable residential clustering of this minority group. Specifically, "Latinos [in Chicago] bear a permanent minority condition that has translated into exclusion, economic immobility, and manipulation. This is reflected in a settlement process deeply colored by discrimination" (Betancur 1996, 1316). Another analysis of Latinos' residential patterns concluded that during the 1990s, more than half of Chicago's Latinos lived in nine of the city's seventy-seven community areas and that over three-fourths of Latino residents lived in just eighteen of those areas (Paral, Ready, Chun, and Sun 2004).

Residential segregation continues today. Most African Americans live on the city's South and West Sides, Latinos live in neighborhoods to the southwest and northwest of the Loop, and whites primarily live along the north part of the lakefront and in the far northwest neighborhoods. Chicago is also experiencing population loss. The 2010 census revealed that during the preceding decade, Chicago's population fell by 6.9 percent to 2.69 million residents (Table 2.1). That figure was lower than the 2.7 million reported by the 1920 census. Among the three largest racial/ethnic groups, the white population shrank by 52,000 to under 855,000 and the Latino population increased by 25,000 to about 780,000. But the most notable population shift can be observed among African Americans, whose numbers dropped from 1,065,009 to 887,608 (Helliker 2011). This decline of African Americans played out in the politics of drawing new ward maps as black aldermen sought to maintain their city council numbers in the face of the shrinking constituent numbers within their wards. Yet a recent examination of the 2000 and 2010 racial distribution of city council wards reveals little change in the general pattern of geographical clustering. Even as population totals rose or fell, the racial/ethnic concentrations persisted (Dardick and Mack 2011).

A 2012 report by the Manhattan Institute for Policy Research entitled *The End of the Segregated Century* examined racial segregation in American cities from 1890 to 2010. The report concluded that American cities are now more racially integrated than previously, gentrification and immigration have reduced segregation, and ghetto neighborhoods, while in decline, continue to persist. The report's findings regarding Chicago are noteworthy. Specifically, from 2000 to 2010 Chicago experienced significant declines in population variation and increases in isolation. Population variation refers to the distribution of two racial groups in a neighborhood. Isolation refers to a single racial group's dominance of a neighborhood. This combination of factors positioned Chicago as the most segregated large city in the country (Dallas and Houston were the least segregated of the group of cities examined; Glaeser and Vigdor 2012).

This degree of isolation has many social ramifications. FBI data for 2012 reveal that 500 murders were committed in Chicago, considerably more than the 431 that were recorded in far more populous New York City. The number of murders in New York actually declined from 514 in 2011 (Wilson 2013). This trend captured the interest of the national media, which raised a variety of questions about urban life, race, and public policy strategies to address crime. A *New York Times* examination of Chicago's homicides analyzed the socioeconomic composition of areas "near homicides" and those "not near homicides." Using U.S. census data, the investigation concluded that residents living near homicides had lower levels of education, lower levels of income, and were much more likely to be African Americans. Residents in neighborhoods near homicides had an average income of $38,318, were 55 percent African American, and only

Table 2.1. Population change in the Chicago metropolitan area, 1980–2010

	1980	1990	2000	2010
Chicago	3,005,072	2,783,911	2,893,666	2,695,598
Suburban Cook County	2,248,583	2,321,156	2,483,075	2,499,077
Lake, McHenry, DuPage, Kane, and Will Counties	1,849,969	2,156,109	2,741,979	3,121,975

Sources: Chicago Tribune (1991); U.S. Census Bureau (2010).

19 percent had a bachelor's degree. Conversely, the residents in communities at a distance from homicides had an average income of $61,175, were 14 percent African American, and 43 percent had a bachelor's degree. According to Chicago Police Department data, about half of the city's twenty-three police districts, mostly in the South and West Sides of the city, handled over 80 percent of the city's homicides in 2012 (Davey 2013).

The persistence of racial segregation in Chicago is also connected to the geographical distribution of income. Across Chicago's neighborhoods, the pattern of wealth inequality has been maintained over the years. As an illustration of the city's yawning income and wealth divide, consider the following contrasts. Census tract data for 2011 show that West Side and South Side residents have the city's lowest incomes and highest poverty rates. For example, census tract #3504 in the South Side community of Armour Square has a median income of just $10,152. Residents of tract #715 in Lincoln Park on the North Side have an income of $75,122. While these findings may not be surprising, the spatial proximity of income inequality in Chicago can be startling. Census tract #2519 in South Austin has a median household income of $18,818, while census tract #8125 just west in suburban Oak Park has a median income of $65,313. Similarly, tract #2809 on the city's Near West Side has a median income of $10,217, while nearby tract #8331 has a median income of $98,677 (Galland 2013).

The skewed geography of race and economic attainment in Chicago is also evident at the metropolitan level, which reveals analogous patterns of isolation and residential segregation. These trends are more recent, since in addition to the overarching and highly visible trend of population growth, a qualitative transition in suburban settlement has also emerged. The monolithic suburban communities of the early post–World War II era, which were dominated by white populations of middle- to upper middle-class status that often had a conservative political outlook, are for the most part artifacts of the past. Chicago's suburban areas have become more diverse, and in a number of suburban communities racial minorities have settled in great numbers. This emergent trend is creating new public policy challenges, especially for municipalities that are unprepared to address the unique needs of their new residents.

Clustering of Race and Social Class at the Metropolitan Scale

The Chicago metropolitan area (including northwest Indiana and southeast Wisconsin) experienced significant growth from 1950 to 2010, from about 5.5 million to nearly 9.5 million residents. This expansion spatially integrated a larger geographic area and added numerous communities to the region. The geographic expansion of metropolitan Chicago accelerated in the last two decades as many affluent Chicagoans embraced outer metropolitan areas as an attractive alternative to living and working in the city, and as a better option than the older suburban municipalities of Cook and DuPage Counties. This trend also strengthened the unique identity of the broader area as conveyed by the popular term "Chicagoland."

Two key observations can be made about the recent dynamics of population change outside Chicago's borders. The first relates to the fact that suburban communities closer to the core face either slow population growth or population loss. Conversely, communities in what once were considered to be the far outskirts of the metropolitan area have experienced significant expansion. The second observation relates to changes in composition across suburban communities. Municipalities closer to the city of Chicago tend to be socially, economically, racially, and ethnically diverse, and in many cases they are economically challenged. Housing decay, increased crime rates, and poor educational systems pose serious threats to many of these inner-ring communities.

Rapid population growth, once evident in suburban Cook County, especially during the early postwar years, has decelerated in recent decades. From 2000 to 2010, the overall Cook County population declined by 3.4 percent, though suburban Cook County beyond Chicago's municipal boundary experienced some growth. The bulk of the expansion of the metropolitan area occurred far outside Cook County and adjoining DuPage County. For example, once-exploding DuPage County grew by just 1.4 percent from 2000 to 2010. In the preceding three decades, DuPage's rate of population increase had varied from 15.6 percent (in the 1990s) to 34.1 percent (in the 1970s). The exurban communities of the Chicago metropolitan area in Will, Kane, McHenry, and Lake Counties are primarily responsible for recent metropolitan population growth (Table 2.2).

In addition to this general trend of outward growth, Chicago's suburban areas are much more ethnically diverse than they were twenty to thirty years ago, a circumstance that is the result of several contributing factors. The first of these is the rapid suburbanization of Latinos, a group that has made several suburban communities major ports of entry. In addition, other immigrant populations are both "suburbanizing"—resettling in suburban communities following a move from the city of Chicago—or making suburban towns their initial port of entry. Finally, there is a growing movement of African Americans out from Chicago and into communities to the west and south. This confluence of trends is reshaping the socioeconomic composition of many of Chicago's suburbs.

During the 1990s, Latino population growth in the suburbs outpaced that group's growth within Chicago. According to the 2000 U.S. census, 46.4 percent of Latinos lived in Chicago's suburbs, compared to 24 percent in 1970. From 1990 to 2000, more than 360,000 Latinos were added to Chicago's suburbs (124 percent growth). In comparison, the increase of suburban African Americans was

Table 2.2. County population growth in the Chicago metropolitan area, 1990, 2000, and 2010

County	1990	2000	2010	% Change 1990–2010
Cook	5,105,067	5,376,741	5,194,675	+1.75%
DuPage	781,666	904,161	916,924	+17.32%
Kane	317,471	404,119	515,269	+62.30%
Lake	516,418	644,356	703,462	+36.22%
McHenry	183,241	260,077	308,760	+68.49%
Will	357,313	502,266	677,560	+89.62%

Sources: Ebner (2005), Keating (2005), Marcus (2005), McGrath (2005), Pfannkuche (2005a, 2005b), U.S. Census Bureau (2010).

151,000 (45.5 percent growth) during the same time frame. In 2000, 12.5 percent of all suburban Chicago residents were Latinos. In 1990, the Latino share of the suburban population was 6.5 percent (Paral, Ready, Chun, and Sun 2004).

The suburbanization of Latinos intensified from 2000 to 2010. In 2010, Latinos constituted 21.6 percent of the metropolitan region's residents, a considerably higher proportion than in 2000. Indeed, the 3.6 percent population increase across the metropolitan region in the first decade of the twenty-first century is largely due to Latino population growth. While the Latino population grew in all but 15 of 284 municipalities in the region, the rate of growth was especially pronounced in a number of outlying communities (Map 2.1). In 2006, for the first time, census data revealed that more Latinos lived in the suburbs than in Chicago (Chicago Metropolitan Planning Agency 2010). The number of Latinos grew in inner-ring suburbs and in larger, more established cities such as Waukegan, Joliet, and Elgin, which at one time were satellite manufacturing hubs. For example, from 2000 to 2010, the population of Latinos in Elgin surged by 45.3 percent. The white population increased by just 7.1 percent during that time frame (Stockinger 2011).

Apart from individuals of Mexican and Polish descent, the Chicago region's largest immigrant nationalities are Asian: Indians, Chinese, and Filipinos. Many highly educated Asians initially settle in or near suburban job centers (Mihalopoulos and Yates 2001). This has produced a band of suburban municipalities with substantial Asian populations that runs, roughly speaking, across the northern margin of Cook County and into the western portions of DuPage County (Paral 2011).

Chicago's declining African American population is itself attributable to several factors. In other northern and east coast cities such as New York, the 2000s signaled the reversal of a long-standing trend as African Americans relocated to southern states and metropolitan areas, either in search of better economic opportunities or as places to retire (Bilefsky 2011). The same forces appear to

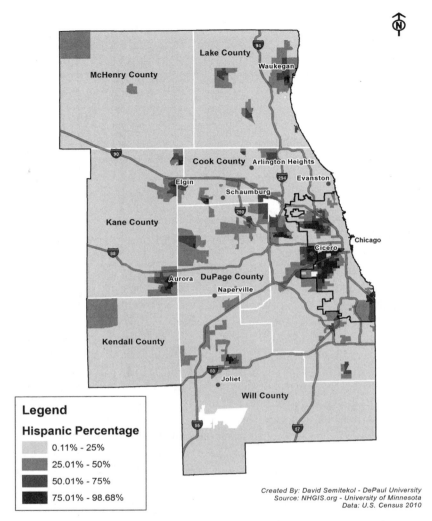

Map 2.1. Latino population concentrations across the Chicago Metropolitan Area. Source: David Semitekol.

have contributed to Chicago's loss of African American residents (Paral 2011). In addition, across the United States large numbers of African American families are moving to the suburbs. From 2000 to 2010, black residents of Atlanta, Detroit, New Orleans, Oakland, and Washington, D.C., moved outward. Each of these is a city with a long history as a center of African American commerce and culture. Atlanta lost almost 30,000 African Americans while the population of African Americans in the metropolitan suburbs shot up by 40 percent to almost 500,000 residents (Keen 2011).

In the Chicago metropolitan area a similar trend can be observed (Table 2.3). According to the Metropolitan Planning Council, Cook County communities such as Calumet City, Cicero, Lansing, Matteson, Richton Park, and Sauk Valley have received large numbers of African Americans. In addition, satellite cities of the metropolitan periphery, including Aurora, Elgin, Joliet, and Waukegan, added substantial numbers of African Americans. Another cluster of suburban communities, located in Will and southern DuPage Counties, experienced comparable growth. These included Bolingbrook, Naperville, Plainfield, and Romeoville. From 2000 to 2010, Plainfield's African American population grew by a factor of twenty, the largest rate of African American increase in the region (Trotter 2011).

Recent African American suburbanization in Chicago also has a specifically local source: building demolitions by the Chicago Housing Authority and "neighborhood flight" from adjoining areas. A recent census tract–level analysis by the *Chicago Sun-Times* shows that many of these dislocated Chicagoans have moved to the suburbs, mostly to inner-ring southern Cook County communities such as Ford Heights, Harvey, Hodgkins, Riverdale, and Robbins. The trend of resettlement from public housing in some of these communities actually accompanied total population losses in the double digits. In the face of this influx of former public housing residents, fearful longtime residents appear to have moved out. From 2000 to 2010, the white population of Hodgkins decreased by more than a quarter, while the African American population increased fivefold (Mitchell 2011).

Contemporary Chicago's more socially diverse suburban landscape, of course, overlays an older pattern of residential, commercial, and industrial development and municipal boundary-drawing that was forged in the first two decades fol-

Table 2.3. Percent change in the African American population, Chicago metropolitan area, 1990–2010

City/County	1990	2000	2010	% Change 1990–2010
Chicago	1,074,471	1,053,739	872,286	-18.81%
Cook	1,301,196	1,390,448	1,265,778	-2.72%
DuPage	15,119	26,977	41,024	+171.34%
Kane	18,353	22,477	27,819	+51.57%
Lake	33,736	43,580	46,989	+39.28%
McHenry	287	1,379	3,045	+960.97%
Will	37,752	51,980	74,419	+97.12%

Sources: Chicago Metropolis 2020 (2002), 54; USDA and Carsey School of Public Policy, University of New Hampshire n.d.

lowing World War II. That suburban Chicago was whiter and more uniformly prosperous than contemporary suburbia. Yet the spatial pattern of that preceding suburbia also could be differentiated in terms of its narrower socioeconomic gradations and by land uses. Directly north of the city of Chicago, for example, is a band of largely residential, older, and very prosperous suburban towns such as Wilmette, Highland Park, and Winnetka. Postwar suburban growth to the west of these communities—that is, north and northwest of Chicago—also tended to follow their model of development of middle- to upper middle-class and largely residential communities. To the west of Chicago, along newly constructed interstate highway segments and running toward older industrial satellites such as Elgin and Joliet, mixed commercial, light industrial, and residential development occurred. And though there are some very prosperous residential areas to Chicago's west, DuPage and Kane Counties have never approached the exclusivity of the North Shore. Finally, to the city's south and southwest, mixed-use communities, many of which have some variety of industrial heritage, have provided housing for residents of lower middle-class to middle-class status. In recent decades, nearer-in southwestern and southern suburbs have received substantial numbers of relocating African Americans (Ebner 2008).

The most advantaged suburbs have used exclusionary zoning strategies to retain their social position and control their tax bases, which has protected the quality of local public schools and other amenities (Johnson 2001; Chicago Metropolitan Agency for Planning and Chicago Fair Housing Alliance 2013). Less prosperous communities are less able to manage land uses and tax bases in this protectionist fashion. As a consequence, Chicago's increasingly diverse suburban landscape also reveals a long-standing and distinctive geographic pattern: more exclusive and *whiter* suburbs to the north; a wide array of communities, as defined by land use and degrees of social diversity, to the west; and many poorer suburban towns directly south of Chicago that function as buffers for the more characteristically prosperous suburbs at a distance from the city's South and Southwest Sides.

An examination of school spending in Chicago suburbs reveals wide variation between inner- and outer-ring communities and between northern and southern suburban municipalities. Data from the Illinois State Board of Education for the 2013–2014 academic year (Table 2.4) demonstrates how much less inner-ring and south suburban school districts spend per pupil than north suburban and outer-ring districts. Property tax differences account for the funding discrepancy. For example, in 2013–2014, Waukegan Community Unit School District 60 served 16,899 students with a budget of $220 million. Only $82 million (37 percent) came from local funding. The rest came from state (54.3 percent) and federal (8.4 percent) sources. In contrast, Naperville Community Unit School District 203 enrolled 17,271 students with a budget of $250 million. Local fund-

Table 2.4. Operating expenses per pupil, 2014, Illinois

North Suburbs (K–8)	
Rondout, SD 72 (Lake Bluff, Lake Forest, Libertyville)	$30,628.48
Kenilworth SD 38	$22,288.70
Northbrook ESD 27	$21,196.14
Winnetka SD 36	$19,774.32
South Suburbs (K–8)	
Lansing SD 158	$9,970.59
Indian Springs SD 109 (Bridgeview, Justice)	$9,759.89
Mokena SD 159	$9,551.18
Calumet Public SD 132	$9,360.92
Inner Ring Suburbs (K–8)	
Berkley SD 87	$9,632.37
Atwood Heights SD 125 (Alsip)	$9,559.48
Cicero SD 99	$9,506.07
Maywood–Melrose Park–Broadview 89	$9,144.19
Outer Ring Suburbs (K–12)	
Lisle CUSD 202	$18,319.16
CUSD 201 (Westmont, Clarendon Hills, Downers Grove)	$17,516.46
Barrington CUSD 226	$16,178.28
Geneva CUSD 304	$14,341.22
Inner Ring/South Suburbs (9–12)	
Thornton Fractional HSD 215 (Calumet City, Lansing)	$13,517.67
Lincoln Way CHSD 210 (New Lennox)	$13,224.58
Lockport Township HSD 205	$12,781.56
JS Morton HSD 201	$11,722.25

Source: Illinois State Board of Education 2014a.
Abbreviations:
SD: School District
ESD: Educational Service District
CUSD: Community Unit School District
HSD: High School District
CHSD: Community High School District

ing of $218.5 million (87.4 percent) made up the greatest share of that budget, with the remaining coming from state (9.7 percent) and federal (2.9 percent) sources (Illinois State Board of Education 2014b).

As we look at patterns of population growth during the last few decades outside the city of Chicago, it is clear that race and social class continue to loom large in shaping patterns of investment and settlement. The evolving geography of the metropolitan region is a characteristic form of uneven development. To paraphrase the aphorism, the rich tend to get richer, though the trajectory of the rest is somewhat less clear. Current trends can impact investment patterns that may eventually engender substantial economic and demographic transitions. In the following section of this chapter we focus on the convergence of a noteworthy demographic trend, exurban population growth, and a frequently employed political tactic, suburban municipal expansion through annexation.

Exurban Population Growth and Policies of Aggressive Municipal Annexation

A closer look at population growth in Chicago's suburbs offers an opportunity to identify significant trends that are reshaping the metropolitan exurbs. In addition to the general movement outward from the city, there has also been an associated movement toward the metropolitan periphery. From 2000 to 2010, the fastest growing counties in Illinois were located on the Chicago region's geographic fringe. Growth has been staggering in Kendall (110 percent), and it proceeded at a rapid pace in Will (35 percent), Grundy (33 percent), Boone (30 percent) and Kane (28 percent) Counties. These outlying counties, in fact, were already in a process of considerable growth. During the 1990s double-digit growth was observed in Will (41 percent), Kendall (38 percent), and Kane (27 percent).

Many smaller communities in these counties boomed between 1990 and 2010. These include Plainfield (652 percent population growth), Yorkville (212 percent), Hampshire (182 percent), Sugar Grove (179 percent), Manhattan (135 percent), Frankfort (129 percent), Plano (85 percent), Peotone (52 percent), and Lockport (46 percent). The larger suburban cities also experienced significant population growth. From 1990 to 2010, Aurora's population doubled, while Joliet and Elgin each grew by approximately 60 percent (Table 2.5).

Each of these three formerly industrial satellite urban centers embraced a two-pronged strategy that abetted their growth. They attempted to rehabilitate their ailing downtowns, and they pursued aggressive land annexation policies, typically on their western margins. While all three were quite successful in annexing land, the case of Elgin is notable since it also reveals the tensions such policies can produce. In 2004, western Kane County residents organized in opposition to Elgin's expansionism and formed the then-newest municipality in the Chicago metropolitan region, Campton Hills.

In unincorporated areas west of Elgin, annexation opponents contended that their bucolic lifestyle was threatened by impending traffic and the dense residential and commercial development that typically accompanies municipal annexation. Following a referendum in which 55 percent of the voters supported the creation of the new village, Elgin's persistent march westward was blocked. Campton Hills occupies more than 20 square miles in Plato and Campton Townships and has approximately 14,000 residents (Presecky 2007). The creation of the new municipality is a direct expression of the pressures caused by exurban growth, in this instance amplified by an existing municipality's efforts to profit from that growth.

Table 2.5. Population trends in Aurora, Elgin, and Joliet by race/ethnicity, 1990–2010

	Total Population	% African American	% Latino
Aurora			
1990	99,581	11.9	22.6
2000	142,990	11.1	32.6
2010	197,899	10.7	41.3
Elgin			
1990	77,010	7.3	18.4
2000	94,487	6.8	34.3
2010	108,190	7.4	43.6
Joliet			
1990	76,836	21.5	12.3
2000	106,221	18.2	18.4
2010	147,433	16.0	27.8

Sources: U.S. Census Bureau (1990, 2002, 2012a).

Neither Aurora nor Joliet faced significant opposition to their plans for geographic expansion. Land acquisition firmly positioned Aurora, with just under 200,000 residents, as the second-largest city in the state in 2010. Annexation provided much-needed revenue through an expanded property tax base. In addition, Aurora turned its attention to refurbishing its downtown. In the early 1990s, it embraced riverboat gambling, which attracted the Hollywood Casino and added 1,500 employees to the downtown work force. Tax Increment Financing (TIF) gave developers financial assistance to restore and upgrade housing in the central area by converting warehouses into lofts. Public investment in beautification programs and related infrastructure projects helped rehabilitate civic spaces. Concurrently, Downtown Alive!, a program of festivals, outdoor street performances, and seasonal entertainment venues, brought thousands of day trippers to the city's core (Spirou 2011).

In Joliet, as a direct result of its physical expansion, more than 7,600 new homes were constructed on the city's west side in the 1990s. In 2000 alone, more than 1,000 new single-family homes were built in this area. Beyond residential development, Joliet looked to annex land for other purposes. One such example is the city council decision in 2000 to annex 143 acres in unincorporated Troy Township for the construction of an "extreme sports" complex (O'Brien 2000). A few years later, in 2005, Joliet claimed a portion of a public forest preserve and annexed the land for development as an industrial park (O'Brien 2005a). Concurrently, at the request of Pasquinelli Development Group, Inc., a large housing construction company, the Joliet City Council approved the annexation of 988 acres for the development of 2,500 structures that were mainly residential but also included commercial and industrial uses (O'Brien 2005b). In

2007, Joliet annexed an additional 255 acres (Sullivan 2007). The result of this sequence of physical expansions, augmented by the creation of TIF districts to stimulate internal investment was that Joliet's population surged from 76,836 in 1990 to 147,433 in 2010. Joliet's expansion contributed greatly to the overall growth of Will County. Will County's growth, in turn, spilled over to Kendall County, whose population nearly tripled between 1990 and 2010, increasing from 39,413 to 114,736.

The Great Recession, Neoliberal Policy, and Uneven Regional Development

The broader metropolitan shifts that we have discussed can also be linked to policies and processes that played out within the city of Chicago. These include the Chicago Housing Authority's (CHA) Plan for Transformation, an ambitious program of high-rise demolition, mixed-income neighborhood redevelopment, and geographic dispersal of former public housing development residents. In addition, in the past fifteen years, neighborhoods to the west and south of the downtown Loop have experienced a marked degree of gentrification. The impacts of CHA restructuring and gentrification near the Loop were exacerbated by the devastating economic crash of 2008. Accelerated neighborhood decay in many nongentrifying Chicago neighborhoods and the "suburbanization" of poverty are two significant outgrowths of these policies and trends.

The robust growth observed in the Chicago metropolitan area during the 1990s and the first half of the next decade was derailed by the 2008 economic downturn, whose origins can be traced to a distinctly neoliberal policy turn: the federal government's easing of regulation of financial institutions in the 1990s and early 2000s (Immergluck 2009). Though the 2008 crash struck several Sunbelt metropolitan areas with particular fury, the downturn as registered by indicators such as unemployment, housing starts, housing sales and prices, and foreclosures also devastated the Chicago area. For example, in late 2007 regional unemployment hovered around 5.2 percent, but by early 2010 the proportion of unemployed workers was over 11 percent (Illinois Department of Employment Security 2013). Within the city of Chicago, unemployment numbers also spiked after 2008. In 2011, Chicago's unemployment rate exceeded 14 percent, a figure that was nearly three percentage points greater than that of New York City (Institute for Housing Studies 2013).

Swelling unemployment across the metropolitan area undercut an already weakened housing market by increasing the number of homeowners who were unable to meet their mortgage obligations. In the wake of increasing foreclosures, property abandonment increased. According to data from the American Community Survey, vacant residential units in the Chicago area grew to nearly

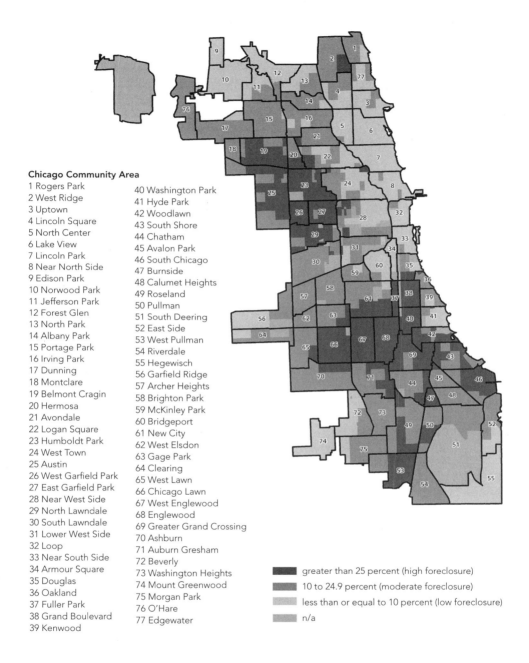

Chicago Community Area

1 Rogers Park
2 West Ridge
3 Uptown
4 Lincoln Square
5 North Center
6 Lake View
7 Lincoln Park
8 Near North Side
9 Edison Park
10 Norwood Park
11 Jefferson Park
12 Forest Glen
13 North Park
14 Albany Park
15 Portage Park
16 Irving Park
17 Dunning
18 Montclare
19 Belmont Cragin
20 Hermosa
21 Avondale
22 Logan Square
23 Humboldt Park
24 West Town
25 Austin
26 West Garfield Park
27 East Garfield Park
28 Near West Side
29 North Lawndale
30 South Lawndale
31 Lower West Side
32 Loop
33 Near South Side
34 Armour Square
35 Douglas
36 Oakland
37 Fuller Park
38 Grand Boulevard
39 Kenwood

40 Washington Park
41 Hyde Park
42 Woodlawn
43 South Shore
44 Chatham
45 Avalon Park
46 South Chicago
47 Burnside
48 Calumet Heights
49 Roseland
50 Pullman
51 South Deering
52 East Side
53 West Pullman
54 Riverdale
55 Hegewisch
56 Garfield Ridge
57 Archer Heights
58 Brighton Park
59 McKinley Park
60 Bridgeport
61 New City
62 West Elsdon
63 Gage Park
64 Clearing
65 West Lawn
66 Chicago Lawn
67 West Englewood
68 Englewood
69 Greater Grand Crossing
70 Ashburn
71 Auburn Gresham
72 Beverly
73 Washington Heights
74 Mount Greenwood
75 Morgan Park
76 O'Hare
77 Edgewater

■ greater than 25 percent (high foreclosure)
■ 10 to 24.9 percent (moderate foreclosure)
░ less than or equal to 10 percent (low foreclosure)
▨ n/a

Map 2.2. Share of parcels with at least one foreclosure filing by City of Chicago census tract, 2005 to 2011. Source: Institute for Housing Studies 2013. Map by Sara Duda

10 percent of the total housing stock by 2012. The percentage of owner-occupied residential units slumped, as did new housing construction. From 2010 to 2012, the median value of an owner-occupied home in the Chicago metro area declined by nearly $15,000 (U.S. Census Bureau n.d.).

The effects of the foreclosure crisis have been especially evident in African American and Latino communities, which had been magnets for subprime lenders in the years just before the economic crash (Bajaj and Fessenden 2007; Squires, Hyra, and Renner 2009; see also Chapter 9 of this volume). As of mid-2013, there were 33,902 vacant houses within the city of Chicago, an increase of 22 percent since 2010. During the same time frame, vacant residential units beyond the city limits in Cook County rose to 21,479, an increase of 79 percent. Communities with large racial minority populations such as Back of the Yards (Latino) and Englewood (African American) registered the highest vacancy rates in the city (Map 2.2). In the summer of 2013, just under 20 percent of the houses in Back of the Yards were vacant, while in Englewood the vacancy rate was just above 15 percent (Gallun and Maidenberg 2013). As foreclosures and property abandonment increased, the broader process of neighborhood decline, as indicated by spikes in crime and other social problems, extended its reach in many of the city's South and West Side communities.

The Geographic Consequences of Local Public Housing Policy

From 2000 to 2010, the number of African American Chicagoans declined by 17 percent. In large part this was the outcome of the outward movement of individuals and families guided by a desire for better housing, schools, and employment opportunities and safer living environments. At the same time, the city's loss of African American residents can be connected to public policy decisions. During the 1990s, Chicago responded to emergent federal policy shifts by initiating a large-scale program of high-rise building demolitions and neighborhood redevelopment featuring New Urbanist physical planning and mixed-income distributions of housing units. The impacts on several South Side and West Side neighborhoods, and on the Near North Side, have been startling. Market-driven new neighborhoods replaced the old high-rise complexes, and the numbers of public housing units were dramatically reduced (Bennett, Smith and Wright 2006; Goetz 2013; Vale 2013; Chaskin and Joseph 2015).

From the mid-1950s through the mid-1960s, the CHA built more than 10,000 public housing units. A large portion of these units was in a single development on the South Side, the huge Robert Taylor Homes complex, which had more than 4,400 apartments. On the West Side, developments such as the Henry Horner Homes were not as large as the Robert Taylor Homes, but the proximity of Horner Homes to the group of developments known as the ABLA Homes produced a concentration of public housing nearly as great as Robert Taylor and adjoining CHA projects along the State Street corridor. During this era, local city council representatives, in Chicago known as aldermen, could block the siting of public housing within their wards. Virtually without exception white aldermen exercised this option, and as a result neighborhoods that were already African American and neighborhoods in racial transition received the bulk of CHA housing. In addition, given the economic decline of West and South Side neighborhoods after the 1970s and the increasing indigence of CHA residents, West and South Side public housing neighborhoods evolved into daunting concentrations of urban poverty (Hunt 2009).

Public housing demolitions after the CHA's adoption in early 2000 of its Plan for Transformation meant that thousands of residents were forced to look for alternative housing in the private sector using Housing Choice (Section 8) Vouchers or in other public housing developments that were in the process of or were awaiting renovation. In practice, thousands of former CHA residents were "lost"; they were entitled to vouchers or relocation to other public housing, but without access to adequate relocation counseling, they were left to simply find housing where they might (Sullivan 2004; Goetz 2013).

In 1999, more than 16,500 families lived in CHA housing. By 2008, that number was less than 10,000. As the Plan of Transformation has proceeded, fewer dislocated public housing residents have exercised their court-mandated right to return than was expected. Robert Chaskin of the University of Chicago and Mark Joseph of Case-Western Reserve University, who have monitored the Plan for Transformation for more than a decade, report that as of 2011, slightly more than one-tenth of such residents had settled in one or another of the CHA's mixed-income communities (Chaskin and Joseph 2012b). And where have most of the rest resettled? According to Chaskin and Joseph, "[t]he majority of [Housing Choice] voucher holders have relocated to traditionally African American neighborhoods on the south and west sides of the city . . . leaving them in more racially segregated neighborhoods than those in traditional public housing developments" (Chaskin and Joseph 2012a, 2, 4).

Expanded Central City Gentrification

In the summer of 1988, the *Chicago Tribune* published a series of articles entitled "Chicago on Hold: The New Politics of Poverty." John McCarron, the newspaper's urban affairs writer, opened one of the essays in the series by asserting that "Chicago is being paralyzed by a self-serving political movement fueled by the fear of displacement and orchestrated by leaders determined to stop change in neighborhoods that need change the most." The primary argument that informed McCarron's perspective was that a number of politically connected community organizations, self-styled grassroots activists, and elected representatives had used the rhetoric of race and class conflict to halt desirable neighborhood change. These interests, according to McCarron, had "declared war on displacement and gentrification." In his view, members of these groups would consistently reject private investment by entrepreneurs in the form of new shopping centers or new upscale housing as the Trojan horse of a spatial conquest that would eventually tilt neighborhoods from black and Latino to white. The essential aim of these "inner-city political bosses," who embraced aggressive anti-development politics, was to present themselves as spokespersons for oppressed minority constituencies (McCarron 1988).

As a prediction of things to come, McCarron's analysis was impressively off target. Over the quarter-century following the publication of the McCarron series, Chicago neighborhoods to the west and south of the Loop underwent a significant transformation. While gentrification in the city dates to the 1950s and the era of urban renewal supported by the federal government, the socioeconomic composition of many near-Loop neighborhoods has dramatically changed in just the most recent two decades. During the 1990s and the first decade of the new century, Mayor Richard M. Daley and his administration embraced aggressive pro-growth and (in effect) pro-gentrification policies. These aided commercial and residential developers, who produced a new and rehabilitated cityscape that stretches north, northwest, west, and south of Chicago's downtown. Andersonville on the North Side, Bronzeville on the South Side, Pilsen on the Near Southwest Side, and Wicker Park and Logan Square northwest of the Loop are some of the neighborhoods that have experienced significant gentrification in the last two decades (Bennett 2010).

Large-scale residential developments directly adjoining Chicago's core (the South Loop, River West, the Near West Side, Old Town, and River East) helped fuel an outward pattern of gentrification as large numbers of young professionals settled both in newly developed residential areas and in older neighborhoods and renovated buildings. University Village, Central Station, and River East Center are just some examples of new residential communities near the Loop. Central Station, an 80-acre master-planned community directly south of downtown Grant Park, has brought thousands of condominiums and townhouses to what had previously been a largely unpopulated area. Constructed on the site of an abandoned commuter rail yard west of Lake Shore Drive and Soldier Field, the upscale development has redefined the South Loop.

Even as Chicago's overall population declined in the first decade of the new century, the near-Loop residential population expanded. The U.S. Census counted 133,426 Chicagoans living within a radius of two miles from City Hall in 2000. By 2010, the population of this area had jumped 36.2 percent to 181,714 residents, the largest absolute population increase among the nation's downtowns during that decade. The census analysis also highlighted the growth of the 25–34 age group in the Loop and near-Loop neighborhoods (U.S. Census 2012). These new residents, pulled by significant infrastructure investments in cultural attractions, beautification, and parks and a multitude of recreational facilities along the lakefront and Chicago River, were well educated, predominantly white, and high-income earners. The combination of this trend, near-Loop public housing demolitions, and weak city incentives for private affordable housing development contributed to the reorganization of Chicago's already racially and economically segregated geography.

The Suburbanization of Poverty

Over the last decade a new urban problem has drawn the interest of policy makers, academic researchers, and journalists. This is the so-called suburbanization of poverty, in large part the result of the migration of poor, racial minority residents out of the central city and into inner-ring suburban towns. Other sources of suburbanized poverty are the foreclosure crisis of the last half-decade and, over a longer span of time (at least in reference to some inner-ring suburbs), the withdrawal of major employers (Walters 2010). Increased suburban poverty rates are now placing significant fiscal pressure on many municipalities. At the same time, many of these communities are experiencing significant population turnover and a downward trend in the overall socioeconomic status of local residents. In many instances, suburban municipal leaders have been unprepared to address these changing realities.

Overall, the number of Americans whose incomes fall below the official poverty line increased from 33.9 million in 2000 to 46.2 million in 2011. Most of these individuals and families live in metropolitan areas, and the majority actually live in the suburbs. From 2000 to 2010, suburban poverty grew by 53 percent (Mertens 2013). In short, the largest and fastest-growing segment of America's impoverished population lives in suburban communities, *not* in the urban cores of metropolitan areas.

During the last few decades, these trends have played out very clearly in the Chicago metropolitan region. In 2005, DuPage County's rate of poverty growth exceeded Chicago's, in spite of the fact that DuPage County's per capita income is among the highest in the Midwest. Dealing with poverty is no longer a challenge that suburban leaders can avoid by assuming that it is an inner-city problem. While the number of poor residents in the city of Chicago increased by 13.9 percent from 2000 to 2011, the suburbs registered a near-doubling of their impoverished residents in the same time frame. However, it is worth noting that as of 2011 the suburban poverty rate continued to lag behind the city's: 11.3 percent versus 22.1 percent.

Among the Chicago suburbs with the highest rates of poverty are Ford Heights (43 percent), Harvey (34 percent), Markham (25 percent), Blue Island (21 percent), and Calumet Heights (20 percent), all located in the southern tier of the metropolitan region. In the city of Cicero, just west of Chicago, 18.7 percent of residents live in poverty, and in Waukegan in Lake County to the north, nearly the same percentage of residents, 18.8, are impoverished (U.S. Census Bureau 2012b). Within the city of Chicago, racial minorities still constitute the bulk of the impoverished population, but across the metropolitan area rates of impoverishment have increased across many demographic categories. For example, a 2013 report by the Heartland Alliance's Social IMPACT Research Center noted that between 1990 and 2011, the incidence of poverty among native-born Latinos increased by 31 percent. For native-born blacks—whose initial poverty rate was the highest among the four groups analyzed in this report—the comparable figure was 12 percent, while the rate of increase for whites was 26 percent. Among foreign-born residents of metropolitan Chicago, the incidence of poverty increased by 33 percent. Nevertheless, as of 2011, suburban poverty was especially pervasive among racial minorities. Twenty-two percent of African Americans and 13 percent of Latinos living in the suburbs were poor (Sotonoff 2013).

The Spatial and Human Distortions of Neoliberal Chicago

Since the 1980s, Chicago has experienced a remarkable transformation of its urban core (Weber 2015), ongoing and even accelerating decline in several South and West Side neighborhoods and across an arc of inner-ring suburbs running from west-central through far south Cook County, and rapid growth on the metropolitan periphery to the southwest, west, northwest, and directly north. Analogous patterns of growth and decline are evident in metropolitan regions across the United States. Metropolitan Chicago's evolving spatial organization is a function of both structure and agency. Major social and economic trends such as deindustrialization and metropolitan decentralization in combination with the particular forces that drove the Great Recession have played a major part in reshaping the Chicago region. But in addition, the actions of local policy makers have contributed to the trends we have discussed in this chapter.

From 1989 until Richard M. Daley's retirement in 2011, the neoliberal policies of his administration spatially altered the city in ways that accelerated uneven development and social inequality. The "shock therapy" of the CHA's Plan for

Transformation contributed to near-Loop neighborhood gentrification and the outward resettlement of thousands of socially and economically disadvantaged residents. Across the metropolitan area, suburban counties and municipalities—almost without exception—rejected the policy ideas of "metropolitan integrationists" such as the Chicago Metropolis 2020 organization in favor of protectionist agendas aimed at increasing local property values and avoiding redistributional measures such as the sharing of school tax bases. In the Hobbesian world of private commercial and residential investment across a landscape of competing municipalities, the rich (to the north and west) tended to win and the poor (to the south) generally lost.

Or, to focus on the people residing and working in these places, Chicago's neoliberal politics and policy have adversely impacted racial minority and already economically marginalized residents. At a time of cresting unemployment, these policies have benefited more advantaged groups within the region (investors, residential and commercial developers, construction firms, and economically secure condominium and home owners) at the expense of hourly wage earners, many service sector workers, the holders of subprime mortgages, and renters. The latter groups have been subjected to extreme economic stress, shrinking opportunities for upward social mobility, and, often, residential dislocation. Neoliberal Chicago is a very good place for some, but for many it is a far different and far less congenial place to live or work.

Bibliography

Bajaj, Vikas, and Ford Fessenden. 2007. "What's Behind the Race Gap?" *New York Times*, November 4.

Beauregard, Robert A. 2006. *When America Became Suburban*. Minneapolis: University of Minnesota Press.

Bennett, Larry. 2010. *The Third City: Chicago and American Urbanism*. Chicago: University of Chicago Press.

Bennett, Larry, Janet Smith, and Patricia Wright, eds. 2006. *Where Are Poor People to Live? Transforming Public Housing Communities*. Armonk, N.Y.: M.E. Sharpe.

Betancur, John. 1996. "The Settlement Experience of Latinos in Chicago: Segregation, Speculation, and the Ecology Model." *Social Forces* 74, no. 4: 1299–1324.

Bilefsky, Dan. 2011. "Seeking New Life, New York Blacks Heed South's Tug." *New York Times*, June 22.

Briggs, Asa. 1980. *Victorian Cities*. New York: Penguin.

Chaskin, Robert J., and Mark L. Joseph. 2012a. *Chicago's Public Housing Transformation: What Happened to the Residents?* University of Chicago School of Social Service Administration and Case Western Reserve University Mandel School of Applied Social Sciences, Mixed Income Development Study Research Brief #5.

———. 2012b. *Why Do So Few Residents Return to Mixed Income Developments? Insights into Resident Decisionmaking*. University of Chicago School of Social

Service Administration and Case Western Reserve University Mandel School of Applied Social Sciences, Mixed Income Development Study Research Brief #6.

———. 2015. *Integrating the Inner City: The Promise and Perils of Mixed-Income Public Housing Transformation.* Chicago: University of Chicago Press.

Chicago Metropolis 2020. 2002. *The Metropolis Housing Index.* Chicago: Chicago Metropolis 2020. Accessed April 5, 2016. https://www.csu.edu/cerc/documents /MetropolisHousingIndexHousingAsOpportunity_000.pdf.

Chicago Metropolitan Agency for Planning. 2010. "GOTO 2040: Comprehensive Regional Plan." Chicago: Metropolitan Agency for Planning. Accessed April 1, 2016. http://www.cmap.illinois.gov/documents/10180/17842/long_plan_FINAL_100610 _web.pdf/1e1ff482–7013–4f5f-90d5–90d395087a53.

Chicago Metropolitan Agency for Planning and Chicago Area Fair Housing Alliance. 2013. *Fair Housing and Equity Assessment: Metropolitan Chicago.* Prepared for the U.S. Department of Housing and Urban Development Office of Sustainable Housing and Communities, November.

Chicago Tribune. 1991. "Final Census Figures for Chicago Area." *Chicago Tribune,* January 24.

Cronon, William. 1991. *Nature's Metropolis: Chicago and the Great West.* New York: Norton.

Dardick, Hal, and Kristen Mack. 2011. "Chicago's Ward Remap Begins with Everyone on Alert." *Chicago Tribune,* July 14.

Davey, Monica. 2013. "In a Soaring Homicide Rate, a Divide in Chicago." *The New York Times,* January 2.

Drake, St. Clair, and Horace Cayton. (1945) 1993. *Black Metropolis: A Study of Negro Life in a Northern City.* Chicago: University of Chicago Press.

Ebner, Michael H. 2005. "Lake County." In *Encyclopedia of Chicago* (electronic version), edited by Janice L. Reiff, Ann Durkin Keating and James R. Grossman. Accessed April 6, 2016. http://www.encyclopedia.chicagohistory.org/pages/706.html.

———. 2008. "Suburbs and Cities as Dual Metropolis." In *Chicago Neighborhoods and Suburbs: A Historical Guide,* ed. Ann Durkin Keating, 29–40. Chicago: University of Chicago Press.

Galland, Zoe. 2013. "How Rich Is Your Neighborhood?" *Crain's Chicago Business,* January 8. Accessed February 27, 2016. http://www.chicagobusiness.com/article /20130108/blogs08/130109821/how-rich-is-your-neighborhood.

Gallun, Alby, and Micah Maidenberg. 2013. "Reckless Abandon." *Crain's Chicago Business,* November 11.

Glaeser, Edward, and Jacob Vigdor. 2012. *The End of the Segregated Century: Racial Separation in America's Neighborhoods, 1890–20.* Civic Report no. 66. New York: The Manhattan Institute.

Goetz, Edward G. 2013. *New Deal Ruins: Race, Economic Justice, and Public Housing Policy.* Ithaca, N.Y.: Cornell University Press.

Helliker, Kevin. 2011. "U.S. News: Chicago Population Sinks to 1920 Level." *Wall Street Journal,* February 16.

Hirsch, Arnold. 1998. *Making the Second Ghetto: Race and Housing in Chicago, 1940–1960.* Chicago: University of Chicago Press.

Hunt, D. Bradford. 2009. *Blueprint for Disaster: The Unraveling of Chicago Public Housing.* Chicago: University of Chicago Press.

Illinois Department of Employment Security. 2013. *Economic Information and Analysis.* Chicago-Joliet-Naperville, IL Metropolitan Division. Seasonally Adjusted, Revised 2008–2012 Estimates. March.

Illinois State Board of Education. 2014a. Fiscal Year 2015: Operating Expense per Pupil (OEPP), Per Capita Tuition Charge (PCTC), and 9 Month Average Daily Attendance (ADA). Accessed April 4, 2016. http://www.isbe.net/finance/verification.htm.

———. 2014b. *Illinois Report Card, 2013–2014: School Districts.* Accessed March 25, 2015. http://illinoisreportcard.com/default.aspx.

Immergluck, Dan. 2009. *Foreclosed: High-Risk Lending, Deregulation, and the Undermining of America's Mortgage Market.* Ithaca, N.Y.: Cornell University Press.

Institute for Housing Studies. 2013. "Map 10: Variation in Neighborhood Distress Level: Share of Parcels with at Least One Foreclosure Filing by City of Chicago Census Tract, 2005 to 2011." In *Overview of the Chicago Housing Market: Background Data for Chicago's 2014–2018 Housing Plan*, 18. Chicago: Institute for Housing Studies, DePaul University. Accessed May 2, 2016. https://www.housingstudies.org/media/filer_public/2013/10/01/ihs_2013_overview_of_chicago_housing_market.pdf.

Jackson, Kenneth T. 1985. *Crabgrass Frontier: The Suburbanization of the United States.* New York: Oxford University Press.

Johnson, Elmer W. 2001. *Chicago Metropolis 2020: The Chicago Plan for the Twentieth Century.* Chicago: University of Chicago Press.

Kain, John. 1968. "Housing Segregation, Negro Employment, and Metropolitan Decentralization." *Quarterly Journal of Economics* 82, no. 2: 175–197.

Keating, Ann Durkin. 2005. "Cook County." In *Encyclopedia of Chicago* (electronic version), edited by Janice L. Reiff, Ann Durkin Keating and James R. Grossman. Accessed April 6, 2016. http://www.encyclopedia.chicagohistory.org/pages/335.html.

Keen, Judy. 2011. "Blacks' Exodus Reshapes Cities." *USA Today*, May 19.

Marcus, Sasha S. 2005. "Will County." In *Encyclopedia of Chicago* (electronic version), edited by Janice L. Reiff, Ann Durkin Keating and James R. Grossman. Accessed April 6, 2016. http://www.encyclopedia.chicagohistory.org/pages/1356.html.

McCarron, John. 1988. "Chicago on Hold: Politics of Poverty: 'Reform' Takes Costly Toll." *Chicago Tribune*, August 28.

McGrath, Steph. 2005. "DuPage County." In *Encyclopedia of Chicago* (electronic version), edited by Janice L. Reiff, Ann Durkin Keating and James R. Grossman. Accessed April 6, 2016. http://www.encyclopedia.chicagohistory.org/pages/396.html.

Mertens, Richard. 2013. "Face of US Poverty: These Days, More Poor Live in Suburbs than in Cities." *Christian Science Monitor*, September 11.

Mihalopoulos, Dan, and Jon Yates. 2001. "Indian Immigrants Flock to Suburbs to Fill High-Tech Jobs." *Chicago Tribune*, May 29.

Miller, Donald L. 1996. *City of the Century: The Epic of Chicago and the Making of America*. New York: Touchstone.

Mitchell, Mary. 2011. "Not Surprised about Black Migration to Burbs." *Chicago Sun-Times*, May 22.

O'Brien, Ken. 2000. "Joliet Annexation Welcomes Extreme-Sports Complex." *Chicago Tribune*, March, 19.

———. 2005a. "Forest Preserve Annexation Opens Up Joliet Industrial Park." *Daily Journal*, February 13.

———. 2005b. "Joliet Adds 988 Acres for Growth." *Chicago Tribune*, February 3.

Paral, Rob. 2011. *What Does the 2010 Census Tell Us about Metropolitan Chicago?* Prepared by Rob Paral and Associates for the Chicago Community Trust, May. Accessed February 26, 2016. http://www.robparal.com/downloads/CCT_2010CensusFindings_0511.pdf.

Paral, Rob, Timothy Ready, Sung Chun, and Wei Sun. 2004. *Latino Demographic Growth in Metropolitan Chicago*. University of Notre Dame: Institute for Latino Studies.

Pfannkuche, Craig L. 2005a. "Kane County." In *Encyclopedia of Chicago* (electronic version), edited by Janice L. Reiff, Ann Durkin Keating and James R. Grossman. Accessed April 6, 2016. http://www.encyclopedia.chicagohistory.org/pages/685.html.

———. 2005b. "McHenry County." In *Encyclopedia of Chicago* (electronic version), edited by Janice L. Reiff, Ann Durkin Keating and James R. Grossman. Accessed April 6, 2016. http://www.encyclopedia.chicagohistory.org/pages/800.html.

Presecky, William. 2007. "Kane County's Newest Village Is Born." *Chicago Tribune*, May 15.

Schaffer, Kristen. 1993. "Fabric of City Life: The Social Agenda in Burnham's Draft of *The Plan of Chicago*." In Daniel H. Burnham and Edward H. Bennett, *Plan of Chicago*, v–xv. New York: Princeton Architectural Press.

Scott, Mel. 1971. *American City Planning since 1890*. Berkeley: University of California Press.

Smith, Carl. 2006. *The Plan of Chicago: Daniel Burnham and the Remaking of the American City*. Chicago: University of Chicago Press.

Smith, Preston H. 2012. *Racial Democracy and the Black Metropolis: Housing Policy in Postwar Chicago*. Minneapolis: University of Minnesota Press.

Sotonoff, Janie. 2013. "Report: Suburbs Have as Much Poverty as the City." *Daily Herald*, September 5.

Spear, Alan. 1969. *Black Chicago: The Making of a Negro Ghetto, 1890–1920*. Chicago: University of Chicago Press.

Spirou, Costas. 2011. "Both Center and Periphery: Chicago's Metropolitan Expansion and the New Downtowns." In *The City Revisited*, ed. Dennis Judd and Dick Simpson, 373–301. Minneapolis: University of Minnesota Press.

Squires, Gregory D., Derek S. Hyra, and Robert N. Renner. 2009. *Segregation and the Subprime Lending Crisis*. Briefing Paper no. 244. Washington, D.C.: Economic Policy Institute.

Stockinger, Josh. 2011. "Census Shows What Suburbs Grew the Most." *Daily Herald,* February 18.

Sullivan, Dennis. 2007. "Joliet Annexation Protects Creek." *Chicago Tribune,* April 18.

Sullivan, Thomas P. 2004. *Independent Monitor's Report to the Chicago Housing Authority and the Central Advisory Council Regarding Phase II-2003 of the Plan for Transformation.* Chicago: Chicago Housing Authority.

Trotter, Joanna. 2011. "2010 Census: African-Americans Leaving City for Suburbs." *The Connector,* April 12. Accessed August 10, 2013. http://www.metroplanning.org /news-events/blog-post/6140.

U.S. Census Bureau. 1990. *1990 Census of Population: General Population Characteristics: Illinois.* Washington, DC: U.S. Census Bureau. Accessed April 6, 2016. https://www2.census.gov/library/publications/decennial/1990/cp-1/cp-1-15.pdf.

———. 2002. *Illinois: 2000 Summary Population and Housing Characteristics.* Washington, DC: U.S. Census Bureau. Accessed April 6, 2016. https://www.census.gov /prod/cen2000/phc-1-15.pdf.

———. 2010. "2010 Census Population Compared to 2000: Illinois Counties." 2010 Census Redistricting Data (Public Law 94–171) Summary File, Tables P1 and H1. Accessed April 5, 2016. http://www.illinois.gov/census/Documents/2010%20 Data/2000%202010_IL%20Counties_Alpha.pdf.

———. 2012a. *Illinois: 2000 Summary Population and Housing Characteristics.* Washington, DC: U.S. Government Printing Office. Accessed April 6, 2016. http://www .census.gov/prod/cen2010/cph-1-15.pdf.

———. 2012b. *Patterns of Metropolitan and Micropolitan Population Change: 2000 to 2010.* September. Accessed May 8, 2015. http://www.census.gov/population/ metro/data/c2010sr-01patterns.html.

———.n.d. "American Fact Finder: Selected Housing Characteristics, 2006–2010, ACS 5-Year Estimates." Accessed April 1, 2016. http://factfinder.census.gov/faces/ tableservices/jsf/pages/productview.xhtml?src=bkmk.

USDA and Carsey School of Public Policy, University of New Hampshire. N.d. *Demographic Trends in U.S. Counties.* Accessed April 6, 2016. http://www.unh .edu/demographic-indicators/USFS%20DataBook.070213/Final%20Display /EntryPage.html.

Vale, Lawrence J. 2013. *Purging the Poorest: Public Housing and the Design Politics of Twice-Cleared Communities.* Chicago: University of Chicago Press.

Walters, Jonathan. 2010. "Poverty's New Population." *Governing,* October 12.

Weber, Rachel. 2015. *From Boom to Bubble: How Finance Built the New Chicago.* Chicago: University of Chicago Press.

Wilson, Reid. 2013. "FBI: Chicago Passes New York as Murder Capital of U.S." *Washington Post,* September 18.

CHAPTER 3

Contemporary Chicago Politics
Myth, Reality, and Neoliberalism

LARRY BENNETT

For many Chicagoans, one of the truisms of their city's cultural heritage is the persistence of machine politics. Given that assumption, descriptions such as the following ring true even in the absence of direct experience with such proceedings:

> The precinct captains who constitute the rank and file workers of a party machine try in every way possible to perform concrete services for the voters which will be remembered on election day. When a precinct captain is unable by himself to perform a given task, he gets in touch with some one in his party organization who can. In other words, the precinct committeeman is an agent or broker for a great variety of services which are used to cement voters to the party machine. (Gosnell [1937] 1968, 69)

Machine politics in Chicago is further linked to another of the city's widely circulated identities as the "city of neighborhoods," as the following suggests about the importance of the Democratic Party's local ward organizations:

> The most significant of all of the party's relationships with any of the constituent parts of the organization are its dealings with the ward organizations in the city. Each of Chicago's wards is an entity unto itself, a fiefdom ruled in the party's name by a committeeman who is a prince of the blood, a duke, a baron, an earl, or a mere knight. (Rakove 1975, 106)

However, these accounts, and the propositions they expressed, are decades old. The first is Harold Gosnell's mid-1930s depiction of the precinct captain's function within the Cook County Democratic organization's vote-getting efforts.

The second, from Milton Rakove's *Don't Make No Waves, Don't Back No Losers*, describes Democratic Party structural dynamics in the latter years of Richard J. Daley's mayoralty. But what is one to make of the following, an admittedly personal but nonetheless empirical observation? I have lived in the North Side's 46th Ward for twenty-five years and have been contacted by a precinct captain on one occasion. This was during the 1991 aldermanic election, and the precinct captain was not, in fact, a resident of my ward. In this 1991 city council contest, recently elected Mayor Richard M. Daley was supporting a challenger to the incumbent alderman, Helen Shiller, a former grassroots activist and at that time a critic of the mayor. The regular 46th Ward Democratic organization was so depleted that Daley's campaign operation had to recruit election workers from other wards around the city. The precinct captain who pushed my building's entrance buzzer and with whom I engaged in brief conversation had come over from the "safe" 45th Ward. By the way, Daley's man in that 1991 election did not unseat Alderman Shiller.

Yes, objections can be made to this vignette. Political machines do not triumph in every election contest. The 46th Ward has long been an outlier, populated by a shifting and diverse array of demographic groups; it is one of what were once called "lakefront liberal" wards. Over the course of six terms as alderman, Helen Shiller made peace with Richard M. Daley, though no one ever accused her of being a Daley loyalist. On the other hand, my vignette indubitably illustrates several truths about contemporary Chicago politics. At present, the resource-heavy, disciplined party organizations Gosnell, Rakove, and other observers of Chicago politics described in the middle decades of the twentieth century can be found in no more than a handful of the city's wards. Chicago remains a one-party city—in that 1991 election in the 46th Ward, Democrat Helen Shiller's chief opponent was another Democrat, Michael Quigley, who has subsequently joined the Democratic delegation in the U.S. House of Representatives—but it is a one-party city in which Democrats often capture local office having garnered no more than a few thousand votes. For example, in the city's 2011 round of aldermanic elections, five aldermen triumphed while collecting fewer than 3,000 votes (ward populations average approximately 54,000). Three other aldermanic victors won their elections with between 3,000 and 4,000 votes.[1] Chicago is a one-party city not because of an imposing Democratic machine but because of the absence of any coherent opposition to the politicians who have long been in control of local government.

From a public policy standpoint, the consequence of this situation is profound. Democratic politicians in Chicago are unburdened by ideological rectitude. Without competitors to the right, some Democrats—notably Richard J. Daley—have staked out clearly conservative positions on many issues. Conversely, given changing national political dynamics and evolving local demographics, more recent leading Democrats such as Richard M. Daley and current mayor Rahm Emanuel—proponents of what might be called lifestyle liberalism—unapologetically combine social liberalism with an unwavering faith in market economics. Without Republicans laying claim to conservative policy preferences or crying foul at ideological shape-shifting, Democrats who are well funded or personally charismatic can occupy an expansive ideological landscape bounded roughly by social democracy on the left and fascism on the right.

Nevertheless, for many observers of Chicago politics, terms such as "machine," "political boss," and "patronage army" provide a reflexive lexicon for apprehending local events. Again, to recall a personal conversation, following the 2011 mayoral election, I pointed out to a colleague that the supposedly formidable 14th Ward Democratic organization—headed by Alderman Ed Burke, who had endorsed Gerry Chico in the mayor's race—had managed to bring fewer than 4,000 voters to the polls in support of the alderman's preferred candidate. The reply to this observation typifies how the myth of the Chicago machine is sustained: "It must mean that Burke knew Chico was doomed and wanted to curry favor with [Rahm] Emanuel." Many years ago, historian Robert Wiebe ([1967] 1998, 164) wryly noted that in their efforts to blunt political machines, urban reformers at the turn of the twentieth century were prone to "attributing omnipotence to abstractions." My colleague rationalized that given that there must a Democratic machine in Chicago, the failure of the machine to perform what surely is its most basic function—getting out the vote—was wily gamesmanship. What cannot be countenanced is the possibility that the dominant Cook County Democratic Party organization is a thing of the past, that the notion of a local political machine at this time is more metaphor than descriptor.

What Happened to the Machine?

The winding down of the Cook County Democratic machine can be traced to the second half of Richard J. Daley's mayoralty. Having weathered an aggressive challenge by Democrat-turned-Republican Ben Adamowski in the 1963 mayoral election and encountering stepped-up agitation by civil rights activists over school and residential segregation, Chicago's first Mayor Daley increasingly catered to the city's "white ethnic" voting bloc, and in so doing, alienated Chicago's still-growing African American population (Biles 1995). As political scientist William Grimshaw demonstrated in his illuminating study *Bitter Fruit: Black Politics and the Chicago Machine* (1992), this alienation was initially signaled by declining voter turnout. But in the long run, the result was the atrophying of Democratic ward organizations in many parts of Chicago's South and West Sides. By around 1970, the Cook County Democratic Party was no longer, as historian John M. Allswang (1982) once put it, "a house for all peoples."

Apart from this fracturing due to the racial politics of 1960s Chicago, in the early 1970s a serious structural impediment to the Democratic machine emerged. A local attorney by the name of Michael Shakman, whose 1970 bid to win election as a state constitutional convention delegate had been thwarted due to competition by machine-backed candidates, filed a federal lawsuit claiming that his free speech rights had been violated by the Cook County Democrats' stranglehold on local elections, a domination that was made possible by the use of public employees as partisan campaign workers. In 1972, the federal district court hearing the Shakman petition ruled in the plaintiff's favor, and over the subsequent decades a series of follow-up court rulings and settlements accepted by various local jurisdictions led to a marked reduction in political patronage in the form of the hiring of party-affiliated campaign workers as public employees (Fross 2004; Freedman 1988). Are there still politically connected city, county government, and Chicago Park District employees? There most certainly are, but the numbers of such patronage workers are a small fraction of the number in the early 1970s, which is estimated to have been 25,000 to 30,000 (Rakove 1975; O'Connor 1984). Though the impact of the Shakman litigation has been gradual, over the last two generations the fifty Democratic ward organizations across Chicago have lost their most effective tool for recruiting precinct captains, a decently compensated government job (which was often accompanied by much "free time" to do political work).

The remaining stakes in the coffin of the Democratic machine have been broader shifts in demographic and neighborhood settlement patterns (Koval et al. 2006; Bennett 2010). Richard J. Daley's core constituency after the mid-1960s—second- and third-generation "ethnics" who were typically Roman Catholic and working- to lower middle-class—has aged and precipitously declined as a proportion of the Chicago electorate. This demographic group had supplied the bulk of the Daley machine's campaign workers and as constituents had accepted the myriad "favors"—garbage can lids, letters of recommendation, street-side tree-trimming, public displays of sympathy or celebration—that earned the party their votes. Chicago has become an increasingly Latino (and in particular, Mexican American) city, and many of Chicago's Latinos have service/favor needs that are comparable to those of their Euro-American predecessors. However, voter participation remains low among Chicago's Mexican Americans, yielding ward-level situations such as Alderman Burke's in the 14th Ward, secure in his incumbency but also unable to get out the vote. Postindustrial Chicago is also a city of gentrifying neighborhoods. These are located along the lakefront north from the Loop to Evanston, on the south lakefront from the Loop to Hyde Park, and in the Near West Side area and across the band of neighborhoods running northwest from the Loop along Milwaukee Avenue (West Town, Wicker Park, Logan Square). The swelling middle class in these neighborhoods has little affinity for the give-and-take mode of machine politics of the Richard J. Daley era.

The death throes of the Chicago machine occurred in the 1980s as Mayor Harold Washington's administration sought to redirect city government policy away from its fetish with downtown boosting and toward a balanced, neighborhood-oriented economic development policy (Rivlin 2013; Clavel 2010). The Washington administration signed on to the Shakman provision that limited political hiring in city government (previously, political *firing* had been banned), even as a bloc in the city council sought to stall the mayor's innovative program of city government modernization and equity-oriented economic development. In effect, the oppositionist Vrdolyak-Burke bloc on the city council desperately tried to freeze the hands of time and preserve a style of ward-based, favor-distributing politics whose fundamental preconditions had been irreparably dashed. Because of Harold Washington's death by heart attack in November 1987, the city government's "move to the left" was short lived. More than a year of political turmoil ensued, and in early 1989 many observers construed Richard M. Daley's election as mayor as a restoration of the old order. But in fact, Mayor Richard M. Daley made no effort to rebuild the Cook County Democratic Party organization, and the global, postindustrial Chicago his policies promoted bore very little resemblance to the city of heavy industry and ethnic enclaves that had given rise to the machine (Bennett 2010).

What is left of the old Democratic machine is a cluster of mutually tolerant family dynasties. Richard M. Daley has stepped down from the mayoralty, but his younger brother John remains an influential member of the Cook County Board of Commissioners. Another brother, Bill, has held important posts in the Clinton and Obama administrations and has made fitful efforts to enter Illinois electoral politics. Then there are the Burkes: long-term city council member Ed; Ed's brother Dan, who serves in the state legislature; and Ed's wife, Ann, a member of the judiciary. Twenty-third ward Democratic committeeman Mike Madigan is speaker of the Illinois House of Representatives, and his daughter Lisa is the state's attorney general. On Chicago's Northwest Side, recently retired alderman Dick Mell managed to pass on his city council seat to one of his daughters. But by far the most famous scion of the Mell dynasty was the meteoric (and now disgraced) Rod Blagojevich, former congressman and impeached governor of Illinois, currently a resident of the minimum security federal prison in Littleton, Colorado (Coen and Chase 2012). Each of these dynasties rests on the foundation of unchallenged if not necessarily robust ward organizations. But from a practical political standpoint, the influence exercised by figures such as Ed Burke or Mike Madigan is a function of the offices they hold and the political resources they can thereby muster. Burke, for example, raises far more in campaign contributions than is necessary for his reelection efforts and recycles a portion of these contributions to other aldermanic candidates, many of whom might be hard pressed otherwise to build effective electoral operations.[2] In turn, Burke's weight in the city council far exceeds his nominal status as one member among fifty.

Winning elections in Chicago—just like everywhere else in the United States—is largely a function of fund-raising and the capacity of particular candidates to intrigue, win over, or alienate the media. In both his 2011 and 2015 election campaigns, Mayor Rahm Emanuel triumphed in large part due to his name recognition, which far surpassed that of any of his competitors, a starting advantage that was reinforced by his equally dominant campaign fund-raising. To the degree that "patronage armies" still exist, during Richard M. Daley's mayoralty, constituency-focused groups such as the Hispanic Democratic Organization (HDO) and the Committee for Better Government targeted parts of the city for Daley and candidates allied to Daley (Cohen, Mota, and Martin 2002). However, each of these groups numbered, at most several hundred campaigners, many of whom were not classic local government patronage workers. As the Daley administration had expanded vendor contracting as a mode of service delivery, some of the companies doing work for the city obliged by directing employees to participate in political efforts. But crucially, operations such as the HDO bypassed the Democratic Party's ward organizations, to the chagrin of many ward-level operatives, and their "targeting"—in the case of the HDO focusing on sections of the city with significant Latino populations—was the practical consequence of an unyielding reality. There are not enough campaign workers these days to blanket the whole of Chicago, so precious resources are directed toward contested elections. Finally, election law and election practice in Illinois remain highly favorable to incumbency. Office holders in Chicago have honed a particular technique for blunting opposition: find fault in the lists of voters whose signatures are required to qualify for election candidacy and prompt the Board of Elections to strike opponents' names from the ballot. Or more prosaically, recruit faux opponents in elections whose names happen to correspond to those of real (and possibly formidable) competitors, thereby drawing off votes from the real challenger.[3]

Chicago's Brief Era of Contested Politics

Many years ago political scientist Raymond Wolfinger (1972) drew the distinction between political machines—resource-rich, disciplined political party organizations—and machine politics, an ethos that aligns political activity with the pursuit of self-interest, political mobilization through the promise or delivery of particularistic favors, and ethnic identification. As has been so clearly demonstrated by the recent, extravagantly self-interested political maneuvering of some notable Chicago political figures—former Governor Blagojevich immediately comes to mind—Wolfinger's notion of machine politics remains relevant to understanding contemporary Chicago. But in order to understand how Chicago became a notably neoliberal city, we must examine in greater detail the contested politics of the 1980s and that period's aftermath.

In the six years following the death of Richard J. Daley, the policy and political bankruptcy of the Cook County Democrats was unmistakable. Daley's first successor, former alderman Michael Bilandic, responded to emerging fiscal crisis and service breakdowns in public schools, transit, and housing with a firm commitment to the status quo. As a result, in the winter of 1979 the Cook County Democrats failed even to carry the mayoral primary for the incumbent mayor. The victor in the 1979 mayoral race, Jane Byrne, initially promoted herself as a reformer, but in four years as mayor she performed as ineptly, though far more entertainingly, as had Bilandic (Bennett 2013).

As the 1983 mayoral campaign unfolded—and over the course of the next half-decade—Chicago politics began to conform in a very rough way to a two-party system. On the one side was the party of the status quo—Mayor Byrne and other leading Democrats such as Ed Vrdolyak and Ed Burke—which pretended nothing had changed within and nothing external was threatening Chicago; therefore, nothing other than the ongoing modus operandi was in order. The opposition was a loose and frequently fractious coalition of disgruntled African American politicos (and voters), "progressive" neighborhood activists, and long-standing "good government" foes of the Daley machine. What bound together this diverse coalition was the power of Harold Washington's image and personality (Rivlin 2013).

The Washington administration was forced to expend much energy fighting off the rearguard action of the Vrdolyak-Burke city council faction, but nevertheless, it managed to shift local policy in a number of new directions. Notably, its economic development program prioritized job creation over real estate development, promoted neighborhood economic development (away from the Loop) as key to the overall well-being of the city, and introduced new industrial retention tools (Clavel 2010; Rast 1999). Shortly following Harold Washington's death, a coalition of school reform groups that he had supported won state legislation authorizing a substantial decentralization of Chicago public school governance (Mirel 1993). In areas such as neighborhood economic development and affordable housing construction, the Washington administration frequently used "delegate agencies," community-based nonprofit organizations, to oversee its initiatives (Clavel 2010, 125–126). In so doing, the administration was responding to many activists' complaint that city bureaucracies were incapable of competent (much less innovative) performance. In the long run, of course, this practice could be adapted to radically different purposes.

The Washington administration's neighborhood-oriented "local producer strategy" (Rast 1999) of economic development was spearheaded by Commis-

sioner of Economic Development Rob Mier, a leading figure in the urban populist movement that crested in many U.S. cities during the late 1970s and 1980s
(Clavel 1986; Swanstrom 1988).[4] This component of the Washington program
was of great importance to the grassroots activists who had participated in
Harold Washington's 1983 mayoral campaign, but for other Washington supporters—some portion of the long-standing group of anti–Richard J. Daley
reformers and many of the African American politicos who had been swept
into the Washington camp by the tide of popular support for the crusading
mayor—a constituent- and job-focused recasting of local government was not
a priority. Soon after Harold Washington's death, the Washington coalition
collapsed in the absence of leadership that could hold together the coalition's
various factions. In particular, the progressive economic development thinking
that animated much Washington administration action dropped out of local
political discourse. This dissipation of energy and policy direction provided an
opening for Cook County state's attorney Richard M. Daley, who triumphed in
the 1989 special election to fill out the four-year term Washington had won in
1987. This 1989 special election handed Chicago a new mayor whose fundamental
policy preferences were largely unknown, possibly even to himself. But over the
next several years Richard M. Daley found a congenial policy track and put to
an end the city's brief flirtation with "two faction" politics.

Remaking Chicago (1999), political scientist Joel Rast's study of Chicago's
evolving economic development policy, offers key insights into how Richard
M. Daley's administration developed its agenda and how neoliberal principles
have become the city government's default approach to an array public policy
challenges. Given the vituperative politics of the Washington era—and in turn,
the civic leadership's extreme discomfort with media portrayals of Chicago as
"Beirut by the Lake"—in the 1989 mayoral race, Richard M. Daley first and foremost presented himself as a stabilizing figure. In particular reference to using
city government as an engine for private investment, Daley's position could be
construed as "anything but Washington." Loop-focused public investment would
regain its place as the core city policy; reaching out to neighborhood constituencies with populist measures would come to an end. However, in the aftermath
of his failure to deliver on several big projects—a downtown casino, a streetcar
network intended to connect important downtown transit hubs and tourist
venues, an airport on the far South Side of the city—Daley's administration
embraced various components of the Washington administration's industrial
retention program as relatively inexpensive and "doable" initiatives. This drift
back to innovation was further enabled by some Washington administrations
holdovers in key planning and economic development positions and by the
continued advocacy of several nonprofit neighborhood economic development
organizations.

Box 3.1: Mayor Daley's Pet Project

In 1998, when Mayor Richard M. Daley announced that a new park within a park—Millennium Park, located on the northwest edge of downtown Grant Park—was to be constructed to celebrate the arrival of January 1, 2000, no observer could have anticipated how close this project would come to being Mayor Daley's Waterloo or the degree of praise the completed project would achieve. Initially estimated to cost $150 million, by the time Millennium Park opened in July 2004, the project's price tag had risen to approximately $500 million. The sources of the cost overrun were numerous: more complicated engineering challenges than initially anticipated, various add-on features, and a distended construction timeline. As the park's cost increased and one construction snafu followed another, criticism of Mayor Daley and his project managers mounted. Nevertheless, with the completion of the park—dubbed a "phenomenal undertaking" in one laudatory commentary—the mayor seemed to triumph. Millennium Park immediately became one of Chicago's leading tourist attractions, and for residents of the city its various allures as performance venue, picnicking site, and pastoral oasis were irresistible.

Two and half years following Daley's departure as mayor, a *Chicago Tribune* story disclosed that the fiscal footing of Millennium Park was just as shaky as the overall financial management that characterized the latter years of the Daley mayoralty. Beginning in the early 2000s the Daley administration initiated a variety of questionable financial maneuvers that included deferring contributions to employee pension plans, financing typically line-item budget items via debt, holding down short-term debt charges through "interest-rate swaps," and drawing down "rainy day" funds that had been generated through the leasing of city assets such as parking meters and municipally owned parking garages. Through these and other techniques, Mayor Daley accomplished the political miracle of funding his city's physical makeover without imposing property tax increases on his fellow Chicagoans. In the case of Millennium Park, the Daley administration borrowed $30 million to finance the day-to-day operations of its new showpiece. In late 2013, the Emanuel administration announced that it would pay down a portion of the principal on debt issued to fund Millennium Park operations but that as late as 2015 it would still need to commit $2 million dollars for interest payments on top of ongoing park expenses.

The circuitous story of Millennium Park's construction, public acclaim, and shaky financing encapsulates a key paradox of Richard M. Daley's mayoralty. He was at once a visionary municipal leader determined to renew physical Chicago *and* a flawed public manager whose fiscal practices will constrict city government for years to come.

Over the course of his two-decade mayoralty, Richard M. Daley would time and again borrow the agendas of both local and national policy advocates (Bennett 2010). Indeed, Daley's political success can be largely attributed to his skill at making other people's ideas his own and then communicating to key local constituencies the idea that his was an innovative, forward-thinking administration. But crucially, after the mid-1990s the Daley program in Chicago, broadly defined, increasingly coincided with the emergent neoliberal approach to big city governance in a globalized urban world.

The Politics of Chicago Neoliberalism

The history of neoliberalism's ascendance as a cluster of widely implemented policy prescriptions is an oft-told tale (Harvey 2005; Peck 2010). The crucial insight in Chicago's embrace of neoliberalism is that by approximately the 1990s, within the United States, neoliberalism ceased to be an inherently conservative approach to local governance.[5] Conventional urban liberalism (a city government inclined to provide a long menu of services, with particular emphasis on assisting less privileged groups)—whether fairly or not—was discredited by the series of traumas big cities experienced in the 1960s and 1970s, notably the wave of civil disturbances in the late 1960s and the catastrophic New York City fiscal crisis of the mid-1970s. Thereafter, among local government elites across the United States, the managerialist and consumer-oriented ideas of government "reinventers" David Osborne and Ted Gaebler (1993) gained wide currency. In the national political arena, New Democrat Bill Clinton and his colleagues in the Democratic Leadership Council broke with the "statist" assumptions of the fraying New Deal Coalition and proposed that Democrats could attend to society's less fortunate while also promoting business-friendly policies that would foster economic growth. The latter, of course, was expected to be the proverbial tide lifting all boats and, as such, the ultimate solution to problems of widespread poverty, high levels of urban unemployment, and the broadly corrosive effects of deindustrialization.

While it would be excessively harsh to characterize the newly elected Richard M. Daley as the empty vessel into which these new and to some degree counterintuitive ideas flowed, Daley, like many members of a new generation of mayors elected in the late 1980s and early 1990s—Rudolph Giuliani in New York City, Ed Rendell in Philadelphia, Richard Riordan in Los Angeles—adopted a very pragmatic and business-friendly approach to promoting his city (Bennett 2010). Many cities across the United States adopted the kinds of neoliberal prescriptions Richard M. Daley pushed: simplifying planning and zoning approval processes; when possible, privatizing service delivery; limiting policymaking friction attributable to excessive public input; and rebranding Chicago as a good place to do business. Moreover, presidential administrations both Republican (George W. Bush) and Democratic (Bill Clinton and Barack Obama) endorsed and helped fund major Daley initiatives such as his restructurings of public housing and the local school system.

Indeed, Chicago under Richard M. Daley and current Mayor Rahm Emanuel has become something of a showpiece for Democratic neoliberalism, as can be illustrated by considering how the Chicago Housing Authority (CHA) and the Chicago Public Schools (CPS) have been reshaped since the 1990s. In the spring of 1989, as Richard M. Daley took office, the crisis of Chicago public housing was a widely acknowledged blot on the city's reputation. Over the course of the preceding three decades the CHA's residential developments had become racially segregated, were typically in physical disrepair, and in many cases were beset by gang violence (Hunt 2009; Vale 2013). In the early 1990s, as the federal Department of Housing and Urban Development (HUD) rolled out the new HOPE VI initiative, CHA director Vince Lane applied for funds to support a modest upgrading of the North Side Cabrini-Green development. Three of Cabrini-Green's high-rise buildings would be demolished; replacement housing, in low-rise structures, would be built mainly on the grounds of the existing development (Bennett 1998; Vale 2013).

However, as the national HOPE VI agenda broadened into an aggressive program of building demolition that brought in private developers to collaborate with public housing agencies on site redevelopment, so too did Chicago's approach to public housing redevelopment. In 1995, Vince Lane was removed as head of the CHA, whose operations were taken over by HUD. During the four years that HUD oversaw the CHA, a survey of CHA developments determined that the vast majority of its high-rise structures could not be economically rehabilitated. This finding effectively set the agenda for the CHA once local control was restored in late 1999. At that point, the CHA adopted its Plan for Transformation, which proposed to reduce the CHA housing stock from 40,000 to 25,000 units, demolish all of the CHA's "family" high-rise structures, turn over property management to private firms, and redevelop the major CHA complexes—Cabrini-Green on the North Side, Robert Taylor Homes and Stateway Gardens on the South Side, and the ABLA Homes on the West Side—as

Once one of America's fabled "newspaper towns," in the second decade of the twenty-first century Chicago has long been reduced to two dailies, both of which have problematic financial futures. Caught in a process of unremitting decline, the *Chicago Tribune* and the *Chicago Sun-Times* have progressively reduced the space devoted to reporting local, national, and world events; diminished the quality of that reporting; and scaled down their staffs.

The story is not unique to Chicago. The decline in newspaper readership and revenue, in part due to competition from the Internet, is well documented. Another significant factor in the decline of newspapers that has been graphically illustrated in Chicago is the corrosive aspects of capitalism. On the surface, the *Tribune* and the *Sun-Times* are very different papers. The *Tribune* is a broadsheet that appeals to a wealthier audience and carries more national and international news than its rival. The *Sun-Times* is a tabloid with a less prosperous audience and a focus on local news. Nonetheless, although they are sharply differentiated by class constituencies, the two papers share the same conservative business ideology.

Nowhere in the American newspaper world has contemporary predatory capitalism been more on display than in Chicago. Both the *Tribune* and the *Sun-Times* were financially wrecked by a series of unscrupulous owners who, absorbed completely in their own financial gain, evinced no concern for the public function of the newspaper (accurate and comprehensive information, representation of the community, and engagement of diverse viewpoints).

The *Sun-Times* fell first under the criminally corrupt practices of its owner, the Canadian press baron Conrad Black, who used his corporate position to enrich himself personally, specifically by making bogus noncompete deals (he has since been sentenced to federal prison for pillaging his papers through "self-dealing"). After Black had gutted his empire, the *Sun-Times* went bankrupt and was taken over in severely reduced circumstances by a syndicate of local businessmen without journalistic backgrounds. Whereas Black's destructive practices were notoriously crude, the financial manipulations of Sam Zell, a Chicago real estate mogul, were byzantine. Despite these differences, Zell's policies produced the same result. Zell, who took over the *Tribune* when the Chandler family (*Los Angeles Times*) sold its stake in the Tribune Company, assumed control through a complicated deal in which he leveraged the company with so much debt that it fell into bankruptcy of its own weight and until 2011 remained there, under interim management, as conflicting groups of creditors fought over how much of what was left each would have. When the case was resolved in 2014, the *Tribune*'s former creditors and new owners engineered a spinoff of the company's newspapers into a separate corporation from its more lucrative TV stations, weakening its financial situation even further through payouts. The new *Tribune* management has attempted to resurrect the paper through printing more and higher-quality news and has achieved a measure of financial stability. Whether or not the return to more traditional journalism will last or will be economically viable remains to be seen.

mixed-income, New Urbanist residential communities. Richard M. Daley was a vocal proponent of the CHA's Plan for Transformation, which is among the most ambitious public housing redevelopment efforts across the United States, though much of the policy logic that shaped action in Chicago is attributable to the shifting aims of the national HOPE VI program (Hunt 2009; Bennett, Smith, and Wright 2006; Goetz 2013).

The story of public school restructuring in Chicago is a matter of different paths reaching the same terminus (Allensworth et al. 2011). Shortly after the death of Harold Washington, school reform groups in Chicago pressed the Illinois General Assembly to approve a decentralization law that would deliver a significant degree of oversight power to Local School Councils, elected bodies that would oversee each of Chicago's public schools (Mirel 1993). The decentralization phase of Chicago school restructuring ran until 1995, when the Richard M. Daley administration sought new state legislation that gave Chicago's mayor greater oversight of the CPS. Mayor Daley appointed a new school board and, more consequentially, selected his administration's budget director, Paul Vallas, as CEO of the CPS. From Daley's standpoint, Vallas's virtues included the fact that he had no background in teaching or education management. During his tenure as CEO, Vallas recentralized CPS decision making, emphasized student progress assessment via standardized test performance, and used school closings and teacher reassignments to spur system improvement (Shipps 2006).

Vallas's initiatives, of course, did not occur in vacuum. Across the United States, advocates of standardized testing, the sanctioning of presumably poor teachers, and charter schools were retracking education policy (Ravitch 2010). Still, Richard M. Daley made a decisive choice, based on his view of the local political/institutional landscape, in bringing in a non-educator to direct Chicago's schools. As such, Chicago public school restructuring was ahead of the curve defining the trajectory of national policy. Unlike Vallas, his successor as CPS CEO, Arne Duncan, brought to the job a background in education of a very particular sort; he had been a charter school advocate (Pattillo 2007). Following the presidential election of 2008, Duncan would go on to have a key role in defining Obama administration educational policy

Neoliberalism in Chicago has thus reflected an interplay of local circumstances and the wider circulation of new-style policy thinking in reference to public education, affordable housing, public finance, infrastructure, and even planning. Institutional factors have further shaped Chicago's embrace of neoliberalism. For instance, Richard M. Daley's political longevity was largely attributable to the civic consensus he forged in the 1990s, when he won the allegiance of a wide array of figures and organizations not otherwise directly connected to local politics that endorsed or in more practical ways supported the mayor's agenda. For example, the richly endowed MacArthur Foundation poured millions of dollars into Daley administration programs intended to support public housing resident relocation and job-training efforts (Goetz 2013). Also during the 1990s, a long-standing Chicago business group, the Commercial Club, spun off a regional planning advocacy group, Chicago Metropolis 2020. When this new organization released its eponymous regional plan, *Chicago Metropolis 2020*, it advocated a series of market-friendly education reforms that converged with the evolving agenda of CPS CEO Paul Vallas (Johnson 2001). In short, neoliberal ideas were an adhesive that permitted Richard M. Daley to build an unusually expansive local political coalition and, on some occasions, actually tap nongovernmental resources to assist in the execution of his local neoliberal agenda.

Over the first decade of his mayoralty, Richard M. Daley was a cautious privatizer of services; he contracted out only a few internal city functions, such as hauling and truck maintenance. Then, in the period 2004–2008, the Daley administration negotiated a series of long-term lease agreements with private firms to take over the management of a South Side toll highway (the Chicago Skyway), city-owned parking garages, the city's parking meters, and the city-owned Midway Airport. Daley repeatedly trumpeted these initiatives as innovative municipal management (his argument was that they improved services and allowed the city to set aside substantial cash reserves), though in fact, a large share of the up-front cash inflows these agreements produced was expended to offset a growing municipal gap in revenues versus expenditures (Hendrik, Luby, and Terzakis 2010).

One of these infrastructure leasing deals, the privatization of parking meters, generated a firestorm of public criticism (Blake 2009; Mihalopoulos and Dardick 2009), but surely the most interesting aspect of this series of "innovations" is their political and public policy lineage. Attorney John Schmidt of Mayer Brown LLC represented the City of Chicago in the Skyway, parking garage, and Midway Airport negotiations. Mayor Richard M. Daley had selected him as his first chief of staff in 1989. In 2010, reporter Mick Dumke of the free weekly *Chicago Reader* interviewed Schmidt, focusing the discussion on his role in negotiating the city's infrastructure leasing agreements. Schmidt observed that he had never had a "particular ideological point of view on it, that per se privatization is a good thing or bad thing." He then recalled that privatization ideas had circulated, years before, in the Clinton administration. At the time Schmidt was an assistant attorney general and he was in contact with "the Gore people" and their "reinventing government" initiative, which, among other things, floated the idea of privatizing federal prisons. Schmidt was dubious about such proposals, but, as he indicated to Dumke, his thinking subsequently evolved:

> There's no question that airports could be better run by experienced private operators than they're run by any public entity in the world. You know, you go to Vancouver [a privately run airport] . . . and you feel you're at a high-quality regional shopping mall compared with a typical airport. They have three spas, they have a four-star restaurant—the whole feel is different. (Dumke 2010, 14)

Here we observe neoliberal ideology—there is no other way to characterize Schmidt's certainty that privately run airports will be superior airports—trickling down from a Democratic national administration through an influential attorney (and former federal and local official) to a willfully non-ideological municipal leadership cadre, Richard M. Daley and his circle of advisors.

Under Mayor Rahm Emanuel, Chicago neoliberalism has shifted into high gear. Again, personal history and institutional networks bear mentioning as one attempts to characterize the program of Chicago's current chief executive (Lyderson 2013). Rahm Emanuel is a lifelong Democrat, but—to recall the late Minnesota Senator Paul Wellstone's typology—not a member of the democratic wing of the Democratic Party. He built his reputation as a fund-raiser for New Democrat notables including Richard M. Daley and Bill Clinton, then withdrew from politics for a few years and earned millions at the investment firm Wasserman Perella. Emanuel's politics are pragmatic to a fault, as was most visibly demonstrated in 2006, when he served as chair of the Democratic Congressional Campaign Committee and recruited a cohort of conservative "Blue Dog" Democrats to contest House of Representatives elections in the South and in border states (Tomasky 2009).

Mayor Emanuel has promoted an "on all fronts" neoliberal agenda. Richard M. Daley did not become an outspoken proponent of charter schools until the last half-decade of his mayoralty, but Mayor Emanuel has aggressively supported charters, just as aggressively closed "poor performing" public schools, and has made a point of antagonizing the Chicago Teachers Union (Ahmed-Ullah and Byrne 2013; Ahmed-Ullah 2013; Coen and Ahmed-Ullah 2012). Among Emanuel's earliest initiatives was to reorganize city trash collection and authorize private vendors to compete with the city Department of Streets and Sanitation (Mack and Chase 2011). Emanuel's aims in each of these initiatives may derive as much from political as economic calculation. He is a Democratic Party politician determined not to be pegged as captive to labor unions.

At this writing, what may be Emanuel's most telling neoliberal inclinations involve public finance and city planning matters. For many years the municipal government's chief neighborhood development tool has been tax increment financing (TIF), the specification of redevelopment areas in which anticipated future increases in property tax revenue are used to fund upfront public investments to stimulate private investment (see Box I.1). These are typically infrastructure improvements, though TIF spending in Chicago can also be devoted to activities such as job training. By the end of Richard M. Daley's mayoralty, the city had designated over 160 TIF districts that collectively covered about 30 percent of Chicago's land area. Critics of Chicago's TIF practices have identified a litany of problems. First, property tax increases within TIF districts represent public revenues that are diverted not just from the city government's general revenue but also from the coffers of other (frequently revenue-starved) local jurisdictions such as the CPS. Second, TIF districts have been declared in many areas that have not suffered from the lack of private investment and do not appear to be threatened by the prospect of disinvestment. The Central Loop TIF district is a frequently cited instance. Third, as a consequence, TIF expenditures often indirectly subsidize highly profitable corporate and real estate endeavors. Fourth, and conversely, TIF districts in many actually blighted sections of the city fail to induce any substantial private investment. Finally, the TIF process has been, effectively, a behind-closed-doors mechanism for allocating public funds to support private investment.

Public discontent with the TIF system was sufficient to induce newly elected mayor Emanuel to appoint a TIF reform panel to examine TIF practices and recommend changes. In August 2011, the panel released a report proposing modest adjustments to the TIF system (TIF Reform Panel 2011). The Emanuel administration's follow-through on the TIF reform panel's recommendations, limited though they were, has been minimal. For instance, Chicago residents and others, if they wish, can now visit an online site that provides financial data for individual TIF districts. More substantively, when what is known as the "progressive caucus" on the city council, in late 2013, proposed returning "surplus" TIF tax revenue to nonmunicipal jurisdictions such as the CPS, the majority on the council aligned with Mayor Emanuel rejected the proposal. Local journalist Ben Joravsky (2013, 10) has characterized Chicago's TIF politics in the following way: "The TIF program has one essential quality that makes it too powerful to resist. It gives Mayor Emanuel hundreds of millions of dollars that he's free to spend pretty much as he likes." Joravsky exaggerates the mayor's autonomy, not so much from the city council or other local political actors but from real estate interests, corporations proposing to expand their downtown operations, and firms scouting Chicago as a prospective relocation site. Chicago's TIF system is characteristically neoliberal: it is driven by private investment and executed in a manner that shields it from public scrutiny. As D. Bradford Hunt and Jon B. DeVries (2013, 8) have recently observed of city planning in Chicago more generally: "Rather than a systematic understanding of current problems, forecasting of human needs, and crafting of policies to address both, planning has too often been demoted and replaced by one-off projects." One-off projects epitomize the TIF process.

As to city planning more generally, the Emanuel administration has ceded that function to World Business Chicago (WBC), a nongovernmental organization that for a number of years has received public funds. In the past, it has tapped the resources of Chicago's corporations in an effort to promote Chicago as a global business node and to attract international investment. In June 2011, WBC expanded its board by adding thirty-five members. These individuals were characterized as a "who's who of Chicago business." Not one had a direct connection with any of the city's network of neighborhood economic development organizations (Harris 2011). Emanuel assumed the chairmanship of WBC, which in February 2012 issued a "blueprint for the city's future" titled *A Plan for Economic Growth and Jobs*.

A Plan for Economic Growth and Jobs is a typical corporate-produced document. It is very long on forceful rhetoric—"the Plan was designed to be *fact-based, data-driven and market disciplined*" (World Business Chicago 2012, 10, italics in original)—and equally forceful in advancing conventional wisdom as if it were innovative thinking. The plan's Strategy 2 (of ten that are proposed) is "Increase the Region's Attractiveness as Center for Business Services and Headquarters"; Strategy 4 is "Make Chicago a Premier Destination for Tourism and Entertainment." In reference to the latter, *A Plan for Economic Growth and Jobs* laments that "Chicago . . . sees below-average visitor spending" (World Business Chicago 2012, 23). Presumably, WBC's analysts anticipate that by making Chicago a more expensive destination it will become more attractive for visitors. *A Plan for Economic Growth and Jobs* is not entirely lacking in good ideas.

Its Strategy 1, "Become a Leading Hub of Advanced Manufacturing," builds on Chicago's existing and still very diverse manufacturing economy and on local initiatives to develop training centers focused on the production of physical goods. It is also a strategy that can give priority to job creation. However, when one scans the list of WBC's fifty-five board members, the representatives of manufacturers number less than a half-dozen. Apart from Mayor Emanuel there are no public officials, and possibly least surprising of all, there are no individuals affiliated with labor unions. Nor are there any grassroots-connected advocates of training initiatives in advanced manufacturing.

In addition, no public process—for instance, public hearings—contributed to the drafting of *A Plan for Economic Development and Jobs*. The document dutifully acknowledges neighborhood economic development via its Strategy 9—"Develop and Deploy Neighborhood Assets to Align with Regional Economic Growth"—but the only neighborhood project it discusses is the "South Works" plan, a mixed-use development of the old U.S. Steel complex (see Chapter 6). In the minds of WBC board members and staff, it would appear that real estate speculation constitutes the cutting edge of neighborhood development practice.

Mayor Emanuel's other noteworthy planning/public finance initiative has been the formation of the Chicago Infrastructure Trust, an independent agency mandated to contract with private investors who will fund capital projects such as mass transit improvements, highway projects, and public building renovations. In the weeks before the city council passed the Infrastructure Trust ordinance, debate over the merits of the initiative turned, first, on its sheer novelty. Few cities in the United States have attempted to fund public projects in this fashion. In addition—and in direct response to the multitude of complaints after the city contracted out the parking meter system—much concern was expressed in reference to public oversight (Mack and Bergen 2012). Critics contended that unless the Infrastructure Trust's staff and appointed board were subject to clearly defined accountability provisions, they could make fiscal commitments that might be devastating for the city government's finances (Dardick and Mack 2012).

Mayor Emanuel responded to these objections by amending the enabling ordinance to specify that all city government infrastructure initiatives would require city council approval. One of the Infrastructure Trust's initial board members, David Hoffman, had previously served as a city inspector general and in that role had confronted former Mayor Richard M. Daley on a number of public accountability matters. Hoffman's appointment to the Infrastructure Trust board signaled that the new unit's governance team would include at least one individual who did not have close ties to the current or preceding mayoral administrations. In fact, the Infrastructure Trust has gotten off to a very slow start. Its first capital project was a modest $13 million investment in efficiency

Box 3.3: The Chicago Parking-Meter Lease Agreement

Toward the end of his twenty-two years as Chicago's longest-serving mayor, Richard M. Daley pushed a measure through the city council to lease the 36,000 parking meters operated by the City of Chicago for seventy-five years, generating $1.156 billion in immediate revenue. The lessee was Chicago Parking Meters, LLC, a consortium backed by Morgan Stanley. The enabling ordinance moved from introduction to final vote in the city council in just three days in late 2008, as the city moved to immediately fill its budget hole with the proceeds of the deal. Five aldermen (of fifty) voted against the measure. On the campaign trail in 2011, mayoral candidate Rahm Emanuel questioned using the revenue from the leasing of a public asset to plug short-term budget shortfalls. The *Chicago Tribune* described the parking-meter lease as "a genuine fiasco." Previously, in a 2009 report, the city's inspector general had criticized the parking-meter agreement as a "dubious financial deal."

Driven in part by unrelenting public discontent, upon his election as mayor, Emanuel negotiated a revision to the original contract, maintaining the overall structure of the deal but allowing free parking outside the city center on Sundays in return for extended pay-to-park hours in central areas. The city also negotiated a reduction in penalty fees when it reduced access to metered spaces due to street maintenance or neighborhood festival street closures. Despite these alterations, various observers maintained that even the revised agreement substantially favored investors over the city and its residents and had the secondary effect of reducing the likelihood of legal challenges to the deal. In Chicago's downtown Loop business district, meters now operate twenty-four hours a day. Thus, a long-standing public utility and a source of consistent public-sector revenue became a private business run for corporate profit.

upgrades for city buildings (Ruthhart 2014). It is possible that Mayor Emanuel's enthusiasm for this initiative has waned. In a January 2015 campaign address reviewing his administration's progress on rebuilding Chicago's roads, transit system, and parks, the mayor failed to mention the new agency that three years previously was touted as a key part of such efforts (Spielman 2015).

A Natural Experiment Properly Understood

Politically speaking, the emergence of neoliberal Chicago, a city government that is committed to privatized policy aims and means that are aligned with an array of specific business interests (and endorsed by various civic and philanthropic organizations), is attributable to the confluence of several sources. In the most general sense, one can construe neoliberalism as a collection of broad notions and particular policy devices that reflect an economistic view of world with a very particular slant:

> a theory of political economic practices that proposes that human well-being can best be advanced by liberating individual entrepreneurial freedoms and skills within an institutional framework characterized by strong private property rights, free markets, and free trade. The role of the state is to create and preserve an institutional framework appropriate to such practices. (Harvey 2005, 7)

Given this broad precondition, the more particular sources of Chicago neoliberalism can be condensed to the drift toward neoliberal policy preferences that is associated with the New Democratic politics of national figures such as former President Bill Clinton and the particular structural situation of American municipalities (Frug 1999). Blessed with a substantial degree of policymaking leeway but cursed with limited support from fiscally straitened state and federal levels of government, U.S. cities have become increasingly entrepreneurial in the sense that they center local policy and fiscal initiatives on a single, fundamental aim: the attraction of private investment (Katz and Bradley 2013). Chicago's Democratic neoliberal mayors, Richard M. Daley and Rahm Emanuel, have operated within a universe of ideas, policy techniques, and interest configurations that are directly comparable to the environment that shaped the actions of, for example, New York City's Republican neoliberal mayor, Michael Bloomberg.[6]

Contemporary Chicago can further be understood as a natural experiment in neoliberal public policy. Will city planning and fiscal subsidy methods that give priority to recruiting footloose corporations, stimulating "new economy" business activity, and luring the creative class accelerate local growth? Will "shock therapy" techniques such as the Chicago Housing Authority's Plan for Transformation or the Chicago Public Schools' current rush to close underperforming schools, open charter schools, and even "incentivize" good parenting produce a generation of more responsible, economically self-sustaining residents? Will these and other measures "bring back" long-neglected sections of Chicago's South and West Sides? Will such neighborhood comebacks play out in a way that allows some substantial portion of their current underprivileged populations to actually benefit from new jobs, better housing, and improved local environments?

A great irony that helps explain why so few observers of Chicago politics have alerted academic or broader audiences to the emergence of local neoliberalism is the fact that weakness in the public accountability of government institutions, obscured decision-making processes, and policies tilted in favor of property or corporate interests are attributes of neoliberal governance that bear a distinct resemblance to the defects of the declining Democratic Party machine of the late 1960s and 1970s. One can hark back to a time when Chicago's ward organizations sustained some degree of grassroots connectedness, and in a general sense, an early Richard J. Daley regime that was bound to a broad agenda of municipal public service that derived from the persisting ideals of Franklin Roosevelt's New Deal, but this reaching back to another form of Chicago governance transports one across many decades.

The great challenge in the coming years for local journalists and the social scientists who will be monitoring Chicago is to assess how effectively the neoliberal experiment plays out. The term neoliberal is not part of the lexicon Chicago or national political figures use. But political figures and allied policy advocates routinely articulate the prospective neoliberal policy gains outlined in this and other chapters of this volume. It is easy enough to specify what will constitute the failure to achieve these aims if the neoliberal program does not yield what it promises. However, a continued reliance on tired but tried and true interpretive frames, notably Chicago's unceasing condition as a "machine city," will not contribute to clarity of interpretation and assessment. Over the last two generations, Chicago's political landscape has fundamentally changed. It is time for observers of the city to come to terms with the real Chicago of the early twenty-first century.

Notes

1. The aldermen in that election who won office having pulled fewer than 3,000 votes were Cardenas, Foulkes, Thompson, Cochrane, and Munoz in the 12th, 15th, 16th, 20th, and 22th Wards, respectively. The three who carried between 3,000 and 4,000 votes were Thomas, Chandler, and Solis in the 17th, 24th, and 25th Wards. Voting in a number of wards increased modestly in 2015, in large part because of the mayoral runoff campaign that pitted Jesus "Chuy" Garcia against incumbent Mayor Rahm Emanuel. However, that mayoral runoff was a rarity, the first that has occurred in the city since the two-stage nonpartisan mayoral election format was adopted in the 1990s.

2. From 2010 to 2012 (municipal elections occurred in 2011), Burke and his law firm contributed over $100,000 to local and state-level Democratic candidates, including four candidates for alderman and four Democratic ward organizations. Burke also made contributions to John Daley and Mike Madigan. This information is available at the website of the Illinois Campaign for Political Reform at http://illinois sunshine.org/sunshine/contributorSearch.php?lastName=Burke&firstName=Ed& yearFrom=2010&yearTo=2012&recipient=&doSearch=Search.

3. For a concise description of two such ballot manipulation techniques, see Joravsky (2007).

4. Urban populism, which sought to use local policies to achieve economic redistribution and emphasized broadened public participation in municipal decision making, was an important force in European as well as American cities. See, for example, Gyford (1985).

5. I wish to acknowledge Timothy P. R. Weaver's elaboration of this point in his 2012 dissertation, "Neoliberalism in the Trenches: Urban Policy and Politics in the United States and the United Kingdom."

6. Michael Bloomberg's legacy is summarized in a series of articles and graphics accompanying the heading "The Impossible Man of the Possible," which appeared on pp. 22–25 of the first section of the Sunday *New York Times*, August 18, 2013. Also see Larson (2013).

Bibliography

Ahmed-Ullah, Noreen S. 2013. "CPS Seeks New Charters to Ease Overcrowding." *Chicago Tribune*, October 1.

Ahmed-Ullah, Noreen S., and John Byrne. 2013. "At CPS, Building and Shutting." *Chicago Tribune*, September 18.

Allensworth, Elaine M., Paul Moore, Marisa de la Torre, and James Murphy with Sanja Jagesic. 2011. *Trends in Chicago's Schools across Three Eras of Reform: Summary of Key Findings.* Chicago: Consortium on Chicago School Research at the University of Chicago Urban Education Institute, September.

Allswang, John M. 1982. *A House for All Peoples: Ethnic Politics in Chicago 1890–1936.* Lexington: University Press of Kentucky.

Bennett, Larry. 1998. "Do We Really Wish to Live in a Communitarian City? Communitarian Thinking and the Redevelopment of Chicago's Cabrini-Green Public Housing Complex." *Journal of Urban Affairs* 20, no. 2: 99–116.

———. 2010. *The Third City: Chicago and American Urbanism.* Chicago: University of Chicago Press.

———. 2013. "Introduction to the Revised Edition." In Gary Rivlin, *Fire on the Prairie*, xiii–xxix. Temple University Press.

Bennett, Larry, Janet L. Smith, and Patricia A. Wright, eds. 2006. *Where Are Poor People to Live? Transforming Public Housing Communities.* Armonk, N.Y.: M.E. Sharpe.

Biles, Roger. 1995. *Richard J. Daley: Politics, Race, and the Governing of Chicago.* DeKalb: Northern Illinois University Press.

Blake, Dan P. 2009. "Daley Takes Blame for Meters." *Chicago Tribune*, May 20.

Clavel, Pierre. 1986. *The Progressive City: Planning and Participation, 1969–1984.* New Brunswick, N.J.: Rutgers University Press.

———. 2010. *Activists in City Hall: The Progressive Response to the Reagan Era in Boston and Chicago.* Ithaca, N.Y.: Cornell University Press.

Coen, Jeff, and Noreen S. Ahmed-Ullah. 2012. "Emanuel Allies Press Attack on CTU." *Chicago Tribune*, June 22.

Coen, Jeff, and John Chase. 2012. *Golden: How Rod Blagojevich Talked Himself out of the Governor's Office and into Prison.* Chicago: Chicago Review Press.

Cohen, Laurie, Jorge Luis Mota, and Andrew Martin. 2002. "Political Army Wields Clout, Jobs." *Chicago Tribune*, October 31.

Dardick, Hal, and Kristen Mack. 2012. "Emanuel's Trust Plan Lax on Oversight, Critics Say." *Chicago Tribune*, April 16.

Dumke, Mick. 2010. "The Case for Selling Off the City." *Chicago Reader*, January 14.

Freedman, Ann. 1988. "Doing Battle with the Patronage Army: Politics, Courts, and Personnel Administration in Chicago." *Public Administration Review* 48, no. 5: 847–859.

Fross, Roger R. 2004. "Shakman Decrees." In *The Encyclopedia of Chicago*, ed. James R. Grossman, Ann Durkin Keating, and Janice L. Reiff, 749. Chicago: University of Chicago Press.

Frug, Gerald E. 1999. *City Making: Building Communities without Building Walls.* Princeton, N.J.: Princeton University Press.

Goetz, Edward G. 2013. *New Deal Ruins: Race, Economic Justice, and Public Housing Policy.* Ithaca, N.Y.: Cornell University Press.

Gosnell, Harold F. (1937) 1968. *Machine Politics Chicago Model.* Chicago: University of Chicago Press.

Grimshaw, William J. 1992. *Bitter Fruit: Black Politics and the Chicago Machine, 1931–1991.* Chicago: University of Chicago Press.

Gyford, John. 1985. *The Politics of Local Socialism.* London: Allen & Unwin.

Harris, Melissa. 2011. "Mayor Emanuel Shakes Up World Business Chicago with New Appointments." *Chicago Tribune*, July 13.

Harvey, David. 2005. *A Brief History of Neoliberalism.* New York: Oxford University Press.

Hendrik, Rebecca, Martin Luby, and Jill Mason Terzakis. 2010. "The Great Recession's Impact on the City of Chicago." Great Cities Institute Working Paper GCP-10-7. Chicago: University of Illinois at Chicago.

Hunt, D. Bradford. 2009. *Blueprint for Disaster: The Unraveling of Chicago Public Housing.* Chicago: University of Chicago Press.

Hunt, D. Bradford, and Jon B. DeVries. 2013. *Planning Chicago.* Chicago: Planners Press.

Johnson, Elmer W. 2001. *Chicago Metropolis 2020: The Chicago Plan for the Twenty-First Century.* Chicago: University of Chicago Press.

Joravsky, Ben. 2007. "Forty-Eighth Ward Follies." *Chicago Reader*, November 15.

———. 2013. "Our Aldermen (at Least a Few of Them) Finally Challenge the Mayor on TIFs!" *Chicago Reader*, November 19.

Katz, Bruce, and Jennifer Bradley. 2103. *The Metropolitan Revolution: How Cities and Metros Are Fixing Our Broken Politics and Fragile Economy.* Washington, D.C.: Brookings Institution Press.

Koval, John P., Larry Bennett, Michael I. J. Bennett, Fassil Demissie, Roberta Garner, and Kiljoong Kim, eds. 2006. *The New Chicago: A Social and Cultural Analysis.* Philadelphia: Temple University Press.

Larson, Scott. 2013. *Building Like Moses with Jacobs in Mind: Contemporary Planning in New York City*. Philadelphia: Temple University Press.

Lyderson, Kari. 2013. *Mayor 1%: Rahm Emanuel and the Rise of Chicago's 99%*. Chicago: Haymarket Books.

Mack, Kristen, and Kathy Bergen. 2012. "Public-Private Is Risky Business." *Chicago Tribune*, April 13.

Mack, Kristen, and John Chase. 2011. "Mayor Hires Private Recycling Firms." *Chicago Tribune*, July 19.

Mihalopoulos, Dan, and Hal Dardick. 2009. "Outrage against the Machines." *Chicago Tribune*, May 28.

Mirel, Jeffrey. 1993. "School Reform, Chicago Style: Educational Innovation in a Changing Urban Context, 1976–1991." *Urban Education* 28, no. 2 (July): 116–149.

O'Connor, Len. 1984. *Clout: Mayor Daley and His City*. Chicago: Contemporary Books.

Osborne, David, and Ted Gaebler. 1993. *Reinventing Government*. New York: Penguin.

Pattillo, Mary. 2007. *Black on the Block: The Politics of Race and Class in the City*. Chicago: University of Chicago Press.

Peck, Jamie. *Constructions of Neoliberal Reason*. Oxford; New York: Oxford University Press, 2010.

Rakove, Milton. 1975. *Don't Make No Waves, Don't Back No Losers: An Insider's Guide to the Daley Machine*. Bloomington: Indiana University Press.

Rast, Joel. 1999. *Remaking Chicago: The Political Origins of Urban Industrial Change*. DeKalb: Northern Illinois University Press.

Ravitch, Diane. 2010. *The Death and Life of the Great American School System: How Testing and Choice Are Undermining Education*. New York: Basic Books.

Rivlin, Gary. 2013. *Fire on the Prairie: Harold Washington, Chicago Politics, and the Roots of the Obama Presidency*. Philadelphia: Temple University Press.

Ruthhart, Bill. 2014. "Council OKs First Infrastructure Trust Project." *Chicago Tribune*, January 16.

Shipps, Dorothy. 2006. *School Reform, Corporate Style: Chicago, 1880–2000*. Lawrence: University Press of Kansas.

Spielman, Fran. 2015. "Emanuel Unveils Infrastructure Agenda without Mentioning Infrastructure Trust." *Chicago Sun-Times*, January 29.

Swanstrom, Todd. 1988. "Urban Populism, Uneven Development, and the Space for Reform." In *Business Elites and Urban Development: Case Studies and Critical Perspectives*, ed. Scott Cummings, 123–152. Albany: State University of New York Press.

TIF Reform Panel. 2011. *Tax Increment Financing Task Force Final Report: Findings and Recommendations for Reforming the Use of Tax Increment Financing in Chicago: Creating Greater Efficiency, Transparency and Accountability*. Chicago: Mayor's Office.

Tomasky, Michael. 2009. "Who Are the Blue Dogs?" *New York Review of Books*, December 3.

Vale, Lawrence J. 2013. *Purging the Poorest: Public Housing and the Design Politics of Twice-Cleared Communities.* Chicago: University of Chicago Press.

Weaver, Timothy P. R. 2012. "Neoliberalism in the Trenches: Urban Policy and Politics in the United States and the United Kingdom." PhD diss., Political Science Department, University of Pennsylvania.

Wiebe, Robert H. (1967) 1998. *The Search for Order, 1877–1920.* New York: Hill and Wang.

Wolfinger, Raymond. 1972. "Why Political Machines Have Not Withered Away and Other Revisionist Thoughts" *Journal of Politics* 34, no. 2: 365–398.

World Business Chicago. 2012. *A Plan for Economic Growth and Jobs.* Chicago: World Business Chicago. http://www.cityofchicago.org/content/dam/city/depts /dcd/general/Plan-for-Economic-Growth-and-Jobs.pdf.

PART II

NEOLIBERAL VISIONS

Neoliberal Chicago is in part a social construction, a metropolis whose collective identity and characteristic approaches to public problems and their solutions are built on widely circulated presuppositions about human nature and behavior. Michael Lorr's aggressive critique of the approaches of the Richard M. Daley and Rahm Emanuel administrations to local environmental policy focuses on the consumerist presuppositions of the municipal agenda. The Chicago envisioned by the city's two most recent mayoral administrations is a uniformly prosperous place whose inhabitants, if they make informed consumer choices, will produce a greener, healthier city. Yet in fact much of Chicago is not such a prosperous place, and the residents of this other Chicago encounter a variety of environmental threats that will not be alleviated by recourse to smart shopping.

Sean Dinces and Christopher Lamberti's subject is not public policy per se, but it certainly is the neoliberal social construction of Chicago. In their analysis of how promotion of "blue-collar" athletes serves the bottom line of the city's major league sports franchises, Dinces and Lamberti explore one iteration of the most fundamental of neoliberal mystifications: how recognition of increasing economic inequality—in this instance, the exorbitant profitability of professional sports and bountiful compensation of sports personnel versus the public's decreasing earning power and reduced access to prime professional sports viewing—is deflected through the manipulation of a famous though now largely passé Chicago self-image.

CHAPTER 4

Urban Sustainability and the "Greening" of Neoliberal Chicago

MICHAEL J. LORR

During his long tenure as mayor, Richard M. Daley asserted that Chicago should become the "greenest city in America" (quoted in Saulny 2010). His successor, Rahm Emanuel, has aggressively pursued this agenda, implementing multiple environmental initiatives and ensuring that his greening programs receive wide press coverage. Yet for many of Chicago's residents, access to this "greener" city is out of reach. Since the early 1990s, the city's environmental policies have been market driven and have primarily relied on consumer preferences, public-private partnerships, and voluntary participation. Instead of directly addressing the legacies of decades of environmental injustice and inequality that have disproportionately impacted the city's lower income neighborhoods and their primarily ethnic minority and nonwhite residents via measures that toughen regulations and levy compensatory fines, Chicago has tackled its environmental concerns through a public policy approach that sees "greening" as a business- and consumer-friendly route to a cleaner environment that, proponents argue, will produce higher value real estate. The results have been policies and practices that are most responsive to the demands of residents in higher income areas of the city that subsequently get prioritized in infrastructure investment and implementation of new initiatives, while poorer, more polluted areas with greater needs get considerably less attention. In the latter neighborhoods, such as Little Village on the West Side and Altgeld Gardens on the far South Side, residents have become community activists leading a fight for environmental justice and a more sustainable city for all.

The City of Chicago and especially its Departments of Buildings (which issues permits for "green" construction projects), Planning and Development (where the city's sustainable development staff work), and Public Health (which oversees environmental health and permit standards) are among the major governmental actors attempting to make "green" Chicago a meaningful and sustainable reality. Initiatives pursued under the Daley and Emanuel administrations include the construction of 645 miles of protected bike lanes by 2020, a highly publicized green roofs program, a green alleyways program, a push for citywide recycling, interest in urban agriculture (especially through farmers markets), and the Chicago Green Homes Program. At the same time, organizations such as the U.S. Green Building Council and other interested developers, planners, and architects are creating their own versions of a greener Chicago by building LEED-certified buildings (LEED is the acronym for Leadership in Energy and Environmental Design, a certification program the U.S. Green Building Council developed). However, while Chicago's business and government elites make big green plans, it is not clear how close the "sustainable" (governmental) and/or "green" (corporate) and/or "environmentally just" (activist) visions of Chicago come to addressing environmental degradation, economic inequality, and social injustice that sustainable urban development, in theory, should deliver. These competing visions of Chicago have intensified in the decade since sociologist David Pellow (2004) argued that the city had failed to develop basic strategies for bettering the environment and, in particular, had neither recognized nor addressed the entrenched environmental injustices inherent in the city's patchwork attempts at recycling and trash management. Dorceta Taylor (2014) demonstrates how Chicago and other U.S. cities created what she calls "toxic communities" through policies of racialized residential segregation. There are still Chicago neighborhoods and communities without recycling programs, bike lanes, or other commonly initiated features of sustainable urban development because of the legacies of racial discrimination, class discrimination, residential segregation, and institutional failure. Today, Chicago's sustainability policies, programs, and developments work together to reinforce the unbalanced, neoliberal ideology of a city that addresses environmental degradation by strengthening business and government partnerships while eroding the power that citizens have to make decisions collectively about the environment in which they live.

Sustainable Chicago: What Has Been Accomplished?

Richard M. Daley, who was mayor from 1989 to 2011, spearheaded many of Chicago's initial sustainability efforts and was sometimes referred to, by groups such as the Trust for Public Land and the City Parks Alliance as the "Green

Mayor" (Crotty 2010). From calling for the city to plant more trees along boulevards, within road medians, and on roofs, to pushing businesses to create a "green economy," Daley asked Chicago's residents to become more environmentally responsible consumers. In an *NBC Nightly News* interview in June 2007, Daley responded to Brian Williams's query: "Tell me how green is profitable for the city of Chicago."

> It's very profitable.... You can save jobs; you can bring new industry in. At the same time you can adapt old industry with new technology to keep the jobs here, retaining and building new jobs.... All the mayors are concerned ... about their environment.... Nature can coexist in an urban environment. It doesn't have to be all concrete and steel ... you can soften it with trees, flowers, bushes, all type[s] of new landscaping. (NBC 2007)

Daley defined his idea of environmental policy as making improvements to urban aesthetics and creating jobs and avoided any mention of environmental justice. In a 2010 interview I conducted, First Ward alderman Manny Flores (in office 2003–2010), who said he would like to be known as the "Green Alderman," expressed how neoliberalism and the greening of Chicago mutually constitute one another: "Sustainability should be about clarifying the too often opaque interface between government, business, and the public." Emphasizing that redevelopment proposals for the Lathrop Homes public housing complex would produce a sustainable mixed-income community, Flores was attempting to infuse social justice ideas into his vision of a greener Chicago (Lorr 2012a).

The desire for a more sustainable Chicago was not entirely inspired by the benevolence of enlightened officials. Some of the impetus behind the city's environmental planning was rooted in its inept handling of the city's 1995 heat wave, which caused more than 700 deaths (Klinenberg 2002). Power failures during the heat wave led the city to restructure its relationship with Commonwealth Edison, the local power company, and in March 1999 the utility agreed to give $25 million to Chicago to improve energy efficiency (Washburn with Gaines 1999). These funds paid for the green roof on City Hall (Washburn 1999) and financed Chicago's first *Environmental Action Agenda*, which was released in 2005. Reiterating the key proposals of the 2005 document in its 2006 *Environmental Action Agenda*, the city stated that it was committed to "improving the quality of life in Chicago neighborhoods, conserving and protecting the City's natural resources, and, through the City's leadership and example, encouraging more Chicagoans to make healthy, smart and environmentally conscious decisions in their homes and businesses" (City of Chicago 2006, 2).

The combination of Chicago's *Environmental Action Agenda* and pressure from political leaders and the public created a policy window that the sustainable development division of the Chicago Department of Planning and Development used to craft the beginnings of a local sustainability policy. However, this policy was devised within the context of neoliberalism, and it focused on greening incentives rather than on environmental justice. This can be seen in the latest iteration of Chicago's environmental policies, Mayor Emanuel's *Sustainable Chicago 2015 Action Agenda* (City of Chicago 2014d). That document sets twenty-four goals for the city within the following broad areas: economic development and job creation; energy efficiency and clean energy; transportation options; water and wastewater; parks; open space and healthy food; waste and recycling; and climate change. Emanuel claims that these goals affirm that "the City of Chicago is a world-leader in fostering sustainability and has proven without question that environmentally friendly practices and good business practices go hand in hand" (Office of the Mayor 2013). Some of Chicago's *2015 Action Agenda* goals include specific benchmarks such as improving energy efficiency by 5 percent, reducing municipal fuel consumption by 10 percent, and decreasing water use by 2 percent annually (i.e., by 14 million gallons per day). Other goals are more vague, such as to "establish Chicago as a hub for the growing sustainable economy," "make Chicago the most bike and pedestrian friendly city in the country," "increase options for accessing local or healthy food in every neighborhood," and "protect the city and its residents by preparing for changes in the climate" (City of Chicago 2014d, 7, 36). Many of these goals expand upon Daley-era attempts to green the city. For example, Mayor Daley promoted cycling in the city and established the Mayor's Bicycle Advisory Council in 1991, which published its *Bike 2000* plan in 1992. Daley subsequently promised to increase marked bicycle lanes from just 35 miles in 2001 to 350 miles (Madhani 2001). This target has not been realized. According to the 2012 *Environmental Action Agenda*, the city had just 183 miles of marked on-street bicycle lanes; by 2014, Chicago claimed 225 miles of protected on-street bike lanes (City of Chicago 2014e). Mayor Emanuel's *2015 Action Agenda* called for further expansion of protected bike lanes, and the city's *Streets for Cycling Plan 2020* proposes 645 miles by 2020 (Chicago Department of Transportation 2012).

In support of the goal of diversifying the city's transportation options and creating "complete streets," a popular concept in urban planning that attempts to make the cityscape safe for individuals, communities, and multiple modes of transportation (see LaPlante and McCann 2008; Zavestoski and Agyeman 2015), the city government has entered into public-private partnerships that support alternative transportation needs. Divvy (see Box 4.1), a city-initiated bike-sharing program that began in 2013, and the Enterprise (formerly i-Go) and Zipcar car-sharing programs partner with the Chicago Transit Authority (CTA) to complement Chicago's traditional public transportation.

Chicago's Green Roofs program works to incentivize the building of green roofs on all types of local buildings: governmental, commercial, and residential.

Instead of conventional roofing, a green roof typically has a layer of sod and/ or climate-appropriate plants growing on it. The city government advanced the program as part of its larger storm water management effort. Roofs, streets, and drainage could have less impact on the municipal storm water and sewage system than they currently do. Planted roofs divert rainwater from the municipal storm water and sewage system, as do rain barrels and more porously paved streets and alleyways. However, when Dr. Milind Khire of Michigan State University was interviewed by Anthony Martinez (2012) on Chicago's WBEZ public radio station, he said: "Right now the green roof implementation is, at the best, ad hoc. We need larger scale implementation of green roofs to actually show that there are benefits. It's the catch-22; until we can demonstrate that, it's expensive to build them and realize the benefits." According to the City of Chicago (2014b), in 2010, there were 359 green roofs totaling 5,469,463 square feet of coverage within the city limits. Both the City Hall building and the Center for Green Technology showcase examples of green roof techniques that reduce heating costs and provide growing space for urban agriculture. The honey produced in the honeybee colony on the green roof on City Hall, for example, is sold at city farmers markets. Chicago's Green Roofs program supports the use of better building techniques that mitigate some environmental harms of the urban landscape. In addition, green roofs cut energy costs and taxes for the building owner. In a 2008 interview I conducted, a staff member in Chicago's Department of Planning and Development explained that "benefits for the homeowner and business owner are first and foremost a big utility saving" and praised the city's "green roof permitting program which speeds up the permit process for construction" (Lorr 2012a). The Green Roofs program is a highly visible initiative in the sense that the city's planners envision a time when observers of Chicago from the air will see green instead of gray and black roofs. The environmental and water management aims of the Green Roofs program are similar in function to Chicago's less-publicized Green Alleys program, which began in 2004; the first five prototype alleys were constructed in 2006 (Attarian 2010). This program supports the refurbishing of alleyways, often through tax increment financing (TIF; see Box I.1), for projects that use permeable paving techniques to divert water back into the aquifer, reduce standing water, and keep water out of storm drains. In 2010, the city reported it had constructed more than 100 green alleys (City of Chicago 2014c). However, the Chicago Department of Transportation does not report how many miles this equates to, and a cynic would likely suggest that this is because it is a small fraction of the nearly 2,000 miles of alleyway in Chicago.

Chicago's Green Homes program largely duplicates the standards for evaluating sustainable housing devised by the U.S. Green Building Council's LEED program. According to the council, whose stated goal is to provide all people access to green buildings within a generation, LEED is "the nationally accepted benchmark for the design, construction, and operation of high-performance green buildings and neighborhoods" (Coyle 2014). However, not all architects and sustainable building experts are so enamored of LEED (Cater 2010). Writing with two colleagues, Guy Newsham of the World Green Building Council observes that although typical LEED-certified buildings use from one-fifth to one-third less energy than conventionally built structures, "28–35% of LEED buildings used more energy than their counterparts" (Newsham, Mancini, and Birt 2009, 897). As of 2008, there were at least 250 LEED developments in Chicago, but of these developments only sixteen were individual homes. Ten were identified as "other"; fifty-two were federal, state, or local government buildings; forty-seven were nonprofit organizations; and the remaining 125 were for-profit organizations (Lorr 2012a). Two years later the Chicago Green Homes program identified approximately 250 Chicago Green Homes (U.S. Department of Energy 2014). In Chicago, a structure could be certified as a one-, two-, or three-star green home based on the criteria of site sustainability, energy efficiency, materials, health and safety, resource conservation, homeowner education, and innovation. Surprisingly—especially given the initiative's promotion in recent years—the Green Homes program has been suspended and is notably absent from the *2015 Action Agenda*, despite the agenda's goal of "doubl[ing] the number of LEED-certified buildings" in Chicago (City of Chicago 2014d, 13).

The City of Chicago has also attempted to encourage interest in urban agriculture, especially through farmers markets, the most popular of which is Lincoln Park's Green City Market. There are fifty-two smaller neighborhood markets throughout the city (City of Chicago 2014a). Many of these farmers markets accept the Supplemental Nutrition Assistance Program's (SNAP) Illinois Link card, and the city is trying to strengthen the links among regional businesses and farmers in order to deliver healthy food to more Chicago neighborhoods. According to urban landscape researchers John Taylor and Sarah Lovell (2012), Chicago had sixty-five acres of land in food production in 2010. The *2015 Action Agenda* proposes a doubling of the area of Chicago's urban farms and plans to "increas[e] residents' ability to participate in urban agriculture" (City of Chicago 2014d, 27).

These green initiatives since the mid-1990s have set the tone for what the city government considers to be the future greening of Chicago and have defined the ways this vision can be attained. They offer a trajectory that future sustainable urban development might take. However, it also appears that a narrow focus on money-saving techniques made possible through technology and efficiency savings is central to Chicago's greening agenda. These appeal to a middle- and upper-class demographic with income to spend on these amenities, creating a process that has been called "environmental gentrification" (Checker 2011).

Box 4.1: Chicago's Divvy Bike-Sharing Program

In March 2012, the Chicago Department of Transportation (CDOT) announced that the Oregon-based company Alta Bike Share (renamed Motivate in 2015) was its partner in a project to install and operate a bike-sharing program in the city. Although shared bicycle rentals first appeared on Chicago's streets in 2010 as an initiative to provide cheap transit for tourists in the city center, the new program was modeled on successful precedents in Montreal and London and aimed to serve the city's commuters. Initially projected to cost $21 million, with the city spending $3 million and receiving the additional $18 million from federal subsidies, CDOT planned to roll out a total of 5,000 bicycles and install 500 pay stations by 2014. The program, which is known locally as Divvy, features instantly recognizable sky-blue bicycles costing around $1,200 each and solar-powered bicycle docking stations provided by PBSC Urban Solutions. The bike-sharing program epitomizes the neoliberal pursuit of environmental gains through individual consumption. By mid-2015, Divvy was operating nearly 500 stations and 4,760 bicycles and was receiving major sponsorship from Blue Cross Blue Shield of Illinois, the health insurance provider.

The Divvy bike-sharing program was slated to begin in summer 2012, but delays and late delivery of equipment and vehicles meant that the first forty Divvy stations did not open for public use in the Loop and the Near North Side until June 28, 2013. During the planning stage, potential users had been invited to attend meetings and go online to vote for the locations of bike-sharing stations. By October 2012, the most popular location was the intersection of Milwaukee, Ashland, and Division in the center of a rapidly gentrifying corridor northwest of the downtown Loop. When the service opened, it was immediately apparent that the availability of Divvy mirrored existing income inequalities in Chicago. Concentrated in the Loop, the prosperous North Side, and neighborhoods such as Hyde Park, no Divvy bike rental stations were placed south of 63rd Street, north of Devon Avenue, or west of California Avenue. This meant that they were absent from most poor to working-class neighborhoods on the city's South and West Sides. Divvy's Website responded that the location of the program's rollout in the city's most densely populated areas would guarantee high use, making possible greater accumulation of user fees to fund further expansion. Within weeks of Divvy's launch, the city had other obstacles to overcome, among them, the need to move Divvy stations that blocked fire lanes or raised security and safety concerns.

In addition to the geographic inequalities of the system, it was also noted that the intended users were wealthier residents within the city and in suburbs. Divvy riders had to have a credit card and pay an annual $75 membership fee and a daily rental charge of $7 for unlimited rides under thirty minutes. Additional charges were made to users' credit cards for longer rentals and late return fees. Divvy users receive a key to access bicycles and are advised that these are "not transferable": financial penalties may be incurred and credit cards may be billed if keys are shared or used in an "inappropriate" manner. In April 2015, Divvy reported that over three million trips had been made and seven million miles traveled in its twenty-one months of operation, and it expanded its network of stations farther north to Rogers Avenue, west to Pulaski Avenue, and south to 75th Street (although again behind schedule and funded through a combination of city and federal dollars). Although this increased the area of the city within the Divvy network, much of the city's South and Southwest Sides remained without service.

In the summer of 2015, the Emanuel administration announced its Divvy for Everyone program, which offers low-cost ($5 per year) introductory Divvy memberships to individuals with annual incomes below $35,000. However, the accessibility of Divvy stations on the city's South and West Sides remains a problem. As a South Side cycling advocacy organization, Major Taylor Cycling Club (named in honor of a successful late-nineteenth-century African American bicycle racer), lamented, although Divvy rentals were for 30-minute periods, it would take many of their members at least that time to travel to and from their nearest Divvy station.

Drawing on this idea, geographers Winifred Curran and Trina Hamilton (2012, 1027) note that "while sustainability and green urbanism have become buzzwords in urban policy circles, too little analysis has focused on who gets to decide what green looks like. Many visions of the green city seem to have room only for park space, waterfront cafes, and luxury LEED-certified buildings, prompting concern that there is no place in the 'sustainable' city for industrial uses and the working class." The public policies intended to create a green Chicago embody Curran and Hamilton's concerns. The various proposals and action agendas fail to adequately address broader environmental injustices. In many respects, the direction City Hall has taken means that the greener Chicago gets, the more environmentally unequal and unjust Chicago will become. This is observable in *Building a Sustainable Region* (Green Ribbon Committee 2014), in which Mayor Emanuel sets out his vision: "A sustainable Chicago is a city that spends less on energy use with each passing year, creates good-paying jobs in up-and-coming industries, responsibly maintains and upgrades its infrastructure, and ensures every Chicagoan has the opportunity to live a healthy and active lifestyle." Yet as one looks at the corporate partnerships listed in this report, namely McDonalds, United Airlines, Boeing, Northern Trust, and MillerCoors, among others, it becomes much clearer whose interest Chicago's green amenities are serving in this brave new sustainable region.

Defining Urban Sustainability

Many urban scholars argue that sustainable urban development holds the key to creating livable cities in the twenty-first century (Wheeler and Beatley 2009; Zeemering 2009; Whitehead 2007; Agyeman, Bullard, and Evans 2003). Sustainable urban development respects the triple bottom line: bettering the environment, improving the economy, and alleviating social injustice. Academic analysts often contrast the extremely broad and generic term "green" with a slightly more defined and robust concept of sustainability. The often-cited 1987 United Nations World Commission on Environment and Development report *Our Common Future* (often referred to as the Brundtland report), defines sustainable development as the ability to "create development that meets the needs of the present without compromising the ability of future generations to meet their own needs," or the ability to sustain life at the current quality for the generations that come after ours (Brundtland and United Nations World Commission on Environment and Development 1987, 43). Although many of the ideas expressed in *Our Common Future* were not new, the Brundtland definition was one of the first acknowledgments from a global governance entity that human development intricately relates to and causes environmental degradation. The UN (United Nations 1992, 2000) revisited the idea of sustainable development at the Rio de Janeiro conference on Environment and Development in 1992, which resulted in *Agenda 21*, and in 2000, when it issued a series of Millennium Development Goals, a component of its Millennium Declaration. Goal 7 aims to ensure environmental sustainability by outlining three targets: sustainability as a governmental policy and program driver to reduce the loss of environmental resources; reducing by half the proportion of people without access to safe drinking water and basic sanitation; measurable improvement in the lives of at least 100 million slum dwellers. The UN now refers to these as sustainable development goals and at the 21st meeting of the Conference of Parties in Paris (convened in November 2015 and commonly known as COP21) attempted to make them even more specific as they relate to climate change.

In their explorations of the meanings of sustainable development, scholars such as ecological economist Herman E. Daly (1991) have suggested pursuing "steady state economics" rather than constant economic growth, and others argue that we should reassess how the environment, economy, and equity interconnect using the "ecological footprint" model (Rees and Wackernagel 1996). For some, however, any definition is problematic because the combination of the terms "sustainable" and "development" will always create an oxymoron (e.g., Mitlin 1992; Wheeler 1998; Agyeman, Bullard, and Evans 2003; Lorr 2012b). Sociologists Daniel Faber and Deborah McCarthy (2003) argue that contemporary neoliberalism forces sustainability and environmental justice to opposite ends of an environmental continuum and that expanding this narrow economic definition of sustainability to emphasize social justice would require the inclusion of a broader constituency than political and business elites. Ross Mitchell (2006b, 459; see also 2006a), among others, calls for "ecological democracy . . . an alternative democratic model that . . . strives to incorporate interested citizens into environmental decision-making, and . . . lacks structural features that systematically concentrate environmental amenities into the hands of particular social groups, while imposing environmental and ecological degradation on others." Environmental policy and planning researchers Julian Agyeman, Robert Bullard, and Bob Evans (2003, 2) succinctly state that sustainability requires "a better quality of life for all, now and into the future, in a just and equitable manner, whilst living within the means of supporting ecosystems."

Until definitions of sustainability expand to include and emphasize social and environmental justice, neoliberalism and sustainability will remain mutually reinforcing rhetorics that create green policies that typically provide environmental amenities for the middle and upper classes. These policies are facilitated by neoliberal urban development ideologies that add environmental value to select places, communities, and properties and seek to attract wealthy green-oriented consumers. In reference to local policy in Chicago, two key questions must be asked. How substantive is Chicago's greening? How capable is Chicago of enforcing policies that will deliver on its green promises?

Green Chicago Falls Short

Chicago's Green Homes program, its Green Roofs program, its recycling program, and its Divvy bike-sharing program have been structured and delivered in ways that valorize the sphere of business, cater to well-off consumers, and actively shrink the roles of government and an engaged public. In the case of the Green Homes program, the city copied an industry-defined set of green standards instead of creating its own standards. The Green Roofs program may create some level of environmental and economic efficiency, and many businesses have taken advantage of the tax incentive to create green roofs, yet researchers and news anecdotes have also documented many examples of poorly executed green roofs (Lorr 2012a). Over the long run, it is unclear how effective they will be. Chicago's most notorious "green failure" to date has been its recycling program. Since the passage in 1993 of the High Density Residential and Commercial Source Reduction and Recycling Ordinance, office blocks and multi-unit residential buildings (which in Chicago refers to properties containing at least five dwelling units and includes small condominiums, large apartment buildings, and residential towers) have been mandated to coordinate their own recycling (Schwebel 2012). This requirement was accompanied from 1995 to 2008 by the "blue bag" recycling program for smaller residential properties, which required residents to put recyclables in blue plastic bags to be placed in the same dumpsters as other trash. Abandoning the blue bag program in 2008, the city began to roll out a new "blue cart" recycling program with a projection that residential recycling would be citywide by 2011.

These programs have been beset by problems and inequalities. Large residential and office buildings across the city were mandated to be fully compliant with the recycling ordinance by 1996 (Cromidas 2014). In residential buildings, this meant drafting a written recycling plan, distributing it to residents, and contracting with a private recycling company. In addition, the city required building owners, property managers, and condominium associations to "implement an educational program that informs new residents, and at least annually all residents how to participate in the building's recycling program, including what can be recycled, how to prepare it and where to take it" (City of Chicago 2015). Commercial buildings were similarly mandated to provide written instructions and educational programs to encourage recycling. Despite the fact that this regulation has been in place for almost two decades, Rachel Cromidas (2014) reported in the Chicago Tribune that many properties fail to provide this (or any) level of recycling service, to the frustration of residents who shame building owners on the popular website "My Building Doesn't Recycle!" (Micklin, Wilhelm, and Kahn 2015), which maps complaints. Yet despite this social media campaign, building owners that do not comply with the ordinance typically go unpunished. "We're not fining high-density residential buildings," city spokeswoman Molly Poppe told Cromidas. "The city's goal is really to encourage recycling participation through conversations with residents, building managers and owners of buildings, so we're not looking to do penalties or punishments" (Cromidas 2014, 6). One community organization, the Chicago Recycling Coalition (2011), points out that because fines range from $25 to $100 per violation, "many owners of these buildings and businesses would rather risk occasionally paying the low fine, rather than pay for more costly recycling services." The result is that large volumes of recyclable material enter the waste stream and landfills.

With the aim of achieving a 25 percent rate of recycling by 1996, the blue bag system for smaller residential properties required waste management workers to separate blue bags containing recyclables from other trash at the point of collection (Pellow 2004). The city contracted with the nation's largest waste removal company, Waste Management Inc., to operate the blue bag program. David Pellow (2004) explains that in addition to reaching a recycling rate of only 6 percent, the operation also contributed to a multitude of environmental injustices, including the creation of unsafe working conditions for mainly minority, non-unionized sanitation workers whose supervisors were typically white. Pellow concludes that Waste Management's blue bag program was "possibly the most high-tech, hazardous, anti-ecological, and fiscally irresponsible waste management program ever devised" (Pellow 2004, 159–160).

In order to fix this embarrassment, the city government initiated the blue cart residential recycling program in 2008. At the time of writing in 2015, however, the blue cart program has done little to increase recycling rates in the city. Failing to learn lessons from previous missteps, the blue cart program revisited many of the same problems of the blue bag program, namely inequality of access and service. The blue cart program began in wealthy neighborhoods and spread slowly into poorer areas, reinforcing past environmental injustices (Mack and Chase 2011). In addition, blue carts were provided only to single-family homes, "two-flats," and some "three-flats," leaving larger residential condominium towers and commercial properties to make their own private arrangements.

Exacerbating these inequalities, Mayor Emanuel's reorganization of trash collection routes away from one organized by aldermanic wards to a grid system similarly overserved wealthier areas and underserved poorer areas of the city (Byrne 2013). In addition, Chicago's waste collection services offer only one household chemicals and computer recycling facility where residents can drop off hazardous waste. It is located on Goose Island, an industrial district about two miles northwest of City Hall. Major producers of hazardous waste, such as construction companies, are required to find a private recycler. Although the city reduced municipal waste by 900,000 tons between 2005 and 2010 and encouraged the marketization of recycling through the Greater Chicago Waste to Profit Network, which "diverted 182,000 tons of waste from landfills and saved companies $17 million in the Chicago region" (City of Chicago 2014d, 30), Chicago has yet to adequately address the social and environmental injustices related to these market-led greening approaches. Instead of requiring recycling, for example, the city approach largely leaves this up to the private market and individual residents to implement. Similarly, the Divvy bike-sharing program and CTA/Enterprise car-sharing program, which are intended to reduce traffic congestion, rely on consumers paying up-front fees, often with a credit card required for membership.

Alternative Forms of Sustainable Development: Resistance and Activism

In the face of the official promotion of Chicago as a cutting-edge example of greening and urban sustainability, many Chicago residents and activists are aware of the city's deficiencies in precisely these areas. As reported in my previous research (Lorr 2012a), many Chicago residents describe their consumer purchases and lifestyle choices as pieces of a potentially larger set of environmental actions. They tie their personal choices and actions involving recycling, biking or taking public transit, purchasing organic food, and seeking out sustainable housing options to the sustainability programs of the city and to addressing global climate change and environmental problems (see also Lorr forthcoming). These personal decisions are complemented by numerous activist organizations that attempt to hold the city to its promises and advance an environmentally equitable agenda. These include organizations such as the Chicago Center for Green Technology and the Center for Neighborhood Technology, individuals who work at neighborhood farmers markets, and collaborations such as Accelerate 77 (2014), a group sponsored by the nonprofit Institute of Cultural Affairs, which offers a crowd-sourced map and database of environmental groups in Chicago. Growing Home (see Growing Home 2014), Growing Power (see Growing Power 2014), the Southeast Environmental Task Force, the Pilsen Environmental Rights and Reform Organization (PERRO), Blacks in Green, A Just Harvest, and the Altgeld Gardens group People for Community Recovery (see People for Community Recovery 2014) are among the community organizations advancing alternate forms of sustainable development. Although often these groups are very localized, they emphasize environmental justice, ecological democracy, and, in many cases, a more holistic vision of an environmentally, economically, and sustainably just city. Two such organizations, the Little Village Environmental Justice Organization and the Active Transportation Alliance (formerly the Chicagoland Bicycle Federation) have been at the forefront of environmental justice advocacy in the city.

The Little Village Environmental Justice Organization

For many years, Chicago's two coal-burning power plants, Fisk, located in Pilsen, and Crawford, in Little Village, have been the most blatant examples of how the neoliberal greening of Chicago touched only certain communities.

The Fisk power plant opened in 1903, the Crawford plant in 1924. Both were once state-of-the-art facilities, but in the years before they were shut down in 2012 they had become the source of "90 percent of all annual carbon emissions from industrial sources in the City . . . releas[ing] soot and other pollutants into the air while emitting five million tons of carbon dioxide annually" (City of Chicago 2014d, 35). Journalist Peter Gorrie (2007) described the impact of these pollution sources:

> Chicago has serious environmental blind spots. One is a neighborhood called Little Village, population 95,000, mainly Mexican-American. Across 33rd [Street] and the railway tracks, white smoke belches from the stacks of the coal-fueled Crawford electricity generating station, one of two that operate in the city. Some years ago the owner, Midwest Generation—a major U.S. power producer—covered the heaps with grass, and planted trees. But there are still no scrubbers to capture sulphur dioxide and other smog chemicals, and one-third of the kids in Little Village have asthma. A study from the Harvard School of Public Health states air pollution from Chicago's two coal-fuelled plants is directly linked to more than 40 premature deaths a year.

In the face of this environmental harm, Kimberly Wasserman, a local community resident, organized the Little Village Environmental Justice Organization (LVEJO),which works to create a participatory and environmentally just city (see Little Village Environmental Justice Organization 2014). This organization, in coalition with others such as the Pilsen Alliance and PERRO, helped focus grass-roots community pressure on how the coal plants disproportionately affected poor and nonwhite communities. As they did this environmental justice work, Wasserman, LVEJO, and other organizations revealed multiple environmental injustices that usually remained hidden from the headlines and from areas well served by Chicago's neoliberal greening policies. Wasserman (2011) states,

> I'm not saying that Fisk and Crawford caused my sons' asthma. After all, there's industry everywhere in our community—it's a regular toxic soup. But Fisk and Crawford depend on outdated technology, and they're impacting my environment more than anyone else. I don't necessarily blame them for caus-ing my kids' asthma, but I do blame them for making it worse. My husband Stan and I are also trying to do our best by our kids. We try to make sure they eat healthy food and get lots of physical activity to strengthen their lungs. But we can only do so much. After that it falls on our city, state and federal government to provide Peter and Anthony and all the other little kids with a clean environment.

It took decades of organizing to close Fisk and Crawford, and low-income communities still face threats from energy companies. The Southeast Environmental Task Force, for example, is active in a campaign to remove petroleum coke storage piles on the Southeast Side of Chicago. Petroleum coke, or petcoke, is a solid carbon material that resembles coal and is a byproduct of hydraulic fracturing ("fracking") natural resource extraction techniques (Henderson 2013). The continuing uneven exposure of Chicago's residents to environmental harms and the precariousness of local environmental victories are sharp rebukes to Chicago's official claims that it seeks citywide greening.

The Active Transportation Alliance

Despite the city government's efforts, Chicago remains a dangerous place for cyclists, pedestrians, and users of public transit. The Active Transportation Alliance (2014) works to make bicycling, walking, and public transit safe and travel in Chicago environmentally cleaner and individually healthier. Advocating for transportation that encourages and promotes safety, physical activity, recreation, social interaction, equity, environmental stewardship, and resource conservation, the Active Transportation Alliance demands that the city work to reduce vehicular crashes and promote alternatives to car transportation. Rob Sadowsky, the former head of the Active Transportation Alliance (when it was still called the Chicagoland Bicycle Federation), explained in an interview (Maus 2010):

> I am not afraid of big and bold ideas. It's important to push our leaders to set some big goals and make it clear where we want to go. The vision has to be doable, and possible, but it has to be big. We're going to try to build a movement, not just around pedal-power, but also around how we relate to the streets. Incremental change may be the first step, but if all you're seeing is incremental changes and you don't know where you're headed, that can be frustrating.

While the Chicago region offers a multitude of transportation options, many of these options are not safe or feasible for substantial portions of the population. Sadowsky acknowledges that the localized particularities of the "bike lobby" constitute part of the problem, because the lobby is led for the most part by young, able-bodied white males who are oblivious to the needs of the majority of Chicagoans. Among the latter are the elderly, disabled people, parents with young children, people who have to commute long distances to work, and business owners who continue to depend on cars and find "bike-oriented planning" (such as wrong-way bike lanes on congested streets) to be a hardship. The "omni-bikers," therefore, are more representative of the much-vaunted creative class and "environmental gentrifiers" than they are of most Chicagoans. The Active Transportation Alliance, like LVEJO, practices an engaged criticism. Reflecting on Chicago's self-congratulatory promotion of its bike-friendliness, Sadowsky observed in 2010: "A strike against the greening of Chicago is also its bike lanes to nowhere. However, I ride to work every day and biking in this city is at least 10 times better and safer than it was ten years ago" (Lorr 2012a). In order to create change in Chicago, activists recognize the need to work with multiple constituencies and with public officials, even if at the same time the activists need to critique the multiple players involved. The result is piecemeal, incremental change rather than holistic sustainable urban redevelopment.

Green Neoliberalism

Both Richard M. Daley and Rahm Emanuel have constructed a political narrative of a greening Chicago that emphasizes individual consumer solutions rather than a comprehensive sustainability policy. This neoliberal greening of Chicago is a vehicle for environmental gentrification; it creates a more sustainable city for some but largely excludes poor and nonwhite people. The green upscaling of a neighborhood reduces the ability of poorer residents to remain in that area, generating displacement that reinforces the exclusion of "toxic communities" from environmental amenities. In addition, these processes make it more difficult for all of Chicago's citizens to engage in the democratic participation needed to determine how their communities will sustainably develop. Because neoliberal sustainability policies overlook the needs and demands of some of Chicago's poorest communities and presume that all residents will become environmentally conscious green consumers, they erode the power that citizens should have to create community-based and citywide solutions to environmental, economic, and social problems. To the degree that Chicago's green policies, in their current form, become a model for other cities, they will further embed in America's urban politics the belief that environmental problems can be tackled through deceptively simple, market-led solutions. While the market model for environmental change might be a first step toward a greener society—or constitute some part of a broader sustainability agenda—this approach alone is insufficient to address the varied and often daunting environmental challenges cities such as Chicago face in the twenty-first century.

Bibliography

Accelerate 77. 2014. "Resource Database." Accessed September 6, 2014. http://www.accelerate77.net/map.

Active Transportation Alliance. 2014. Active Trans. Accessed September 6, 2014. http://www.activetrans.org/.

Agyeman, Julian, Robert D. Bullard, and Bob Evans, eds. 2003. *Just Sustainabilities: Development in an Unequal World*. Cambridge, Mass.: MIT Press.

Attarian, Janet L. 2010. "Greener Alleys." *Public Roads*, May/June. Accessed May 30, 2015. http://www.fhwa.dot.gov/publications/publicroads/10mayjun/05.cfm.

Brundtland, Gro Harlem, and United Nations World Commission on Environment and Development. 1987. *Our Common Future*. Oxford: Oxford University Press.

Byrne, John. 2013. "Emanuel Garbage Pickup Changes Save Less than Touted." *Chicago Tribune*, April 11.

Cater, Franklyn. 2010. "Critics Say LEED Program Doesn't Fulfill Promises." NPR, September 8. Accessed September 6, 2014. http://www.npr.org/templates/story/story.php?storyId=129727547.

Checker, Melissa. 2011. "Wiped Out by the 'Greenwave': Environmental Gentrification and the Paradoxical Politics of Urban Sustainability." *City and Society* 23, no. 2: 210–229.

Chicago Department of Transportation. 2012. *Streets for Cycling Plan 2020*. Accessed February 24, 2015. http://www.scribd.com/doc/122665261/Streets-for-Cycling-Plan-2020.

Chicago Recycling Coalition. 2011. "Recycling: High-Density Residential and Commercial Properties Preliminary Resource Paper." Accessed February 10, 2015. http://www.chicagorecycling.org/High-Density_Res_&_Commercial_Recycling_WEB_04032011.pdf.

City of Chicago. 2006. *Environmental Action Agenda 2006: Building a Sustainable City*. Accessed September 6, 2014. http://naturalsystems.uchicago.edu/urbanecosystems/calumet/cdrom/plans/Action_Agenda_Exec_Summary_06.pdf.

———. 2014a. "Chicago Farmers Markets." Accessed September 6, 2014. http://www.cityofchicago.org/city/en/depts/dca/supp_info/farmers_market.html.

———. 2014b. "Chicago Green Roofs." Accessed September 8, 2014. http://www.cityofchicago.org/city/en/depts/dcd/supp_info/chicago_green_roofs.html.

———. 2014c. "Service: Green Alleys." Accessed September 6, 2014. http://www.cityofchicago.org/city/en/depts/cdot/provdrs/street/svcs/green_alleys.html.

———. 2014d. *Sustainable Chicago 2015: Action Agenda*. Accessed August 4, 2014. http://www.cityofchicago.org/content/dam/city/progs/env/SustainableChicago2015.pdf.

———. 2014e. "What We Do: Bicycling." Accessed September 8, 2014. http://www.cityofchicago.org/city/en/depts/cdot/provdrs/bike.html.

———. 2015. "Recycling for Multi-Unit Residential Buildings." Accessed February 10, 2015. http://www.cityofchicago.org/city/en/depts/streets/supp_info/recycling1/recycling_multi-unitresidentialbuildings.html.

Coyle, Tiffany. 2014. "Green Building 101: What Is LEED?" Accessed September 6, 2014. http://www.usgbc.org/articles/green-building-101-what-leed.

Cromidas, Rachel. 2014. "Highs and Lows: When It Comes to Multi-Unit Buildings, Chicago's Recycling Program Falls Flat." *Chicago Tribune*, September 23.

Crotty, John. 2010. "Chicago's Green Mayor: The Legacy of Richard Daley." City Parks Blog. Accessed September 6, 2014. http://cityparksblog.org/2010/10/27/chicagos-green-mayor-the-legacy-of-richard-daley/.

Curran, Winifred, and Trina Hamilton. 2012. "Just Green Enough: Contesting Environmental Gentrification in Greenpoint, Brooklyn." *Local Environment: The International Journal of Justice and Sustainability* 17, no. 9: 1027–1042.

Daly, Herman. 1991. *Steady-State Economics.* 2nd ed. Washington, D.C.: Island Press.

Faber, Daniel, and Deborah McCarthy. 2003. "Neoliberalism, Globalization and the Struggle for Ecological Democracy: Linking Sustainability and Environmental Justice." In *Just Sustainabilities: Development in an Unequal World*, ed. Julian Agyeman, Robert D. Bullard, and Bob Evans, 38–63. Cambridge, Mass.: MIT Press.

Gorrie, Peter. 2007. "Going Green But Not in All Corners." *Toronto Star*, April 28.

Green Ribbon Committee. 2014. *Building a Sustainable Region: Innovative Practices from Metro Chicago's Global Corporations.* Accessed August 4, 2014. http://www .cityofchicago.org/content/dam/city/progs/env/SustainableChicagoRegionReport .pdf.

Growing Home. 2104. "About Us." Growing Home. Accessed September 3, 2014. http://growinghomeinc.org/.

Growing Power. 2014. "Chicago Farms and Projects." Growing Power Inc. Accessed September 3, 2014. http://www.growingpower.org/chicago_projects.htm.

Henderson, Henry. 2013. "Petcoke Piles: We Should All Stand Up for Chicago's Southeast Side." *Huffington Post*, October 23. Accessed February 25, 2015. hhttp://www.huffingtonpost.com/henry-henderson/petcoke-piles-we-should -a_b_4150512.html.

Klinenberg, Eric. 2002. *Heat Wave: A Social Autopsy of Disaster in Chicago.* Chicago: University of Chicago Press.

LaPlante, John, and Barbara McCann. 2008. "Complete Streets: We Can Get There From Here." *Institute of Transportation Engineers Journal* 78, no. 5: 24–28.

Little Village Environmental Justice Organization. 2014. "About Us." Accessed September 3, 2014. http://lvejo.org/.

Lorr, Michael. 2012a. "The Popularization of Sustainable Urban Development: Chicago, Vancouver, and Marketing Environmental and Spatial Justice in an Era of Neoliberalism." PhD diss., University of Wisconsin-Milwaukee.

Lorr, Michael. 2012b. "Defining Urban Sustainability in the Context of North American Cities." *Nature and Culture* 7, no. 1: 16–30.

———. Forthcoming. "Greening Lifestyles, Homes, and Urban Infrastructure in Chicago, IL, and Jacksonville, FL." In *The Greening of Everyday Life*, ed. Jens Kersten and John Meyer. New York: Oxford University Press.

Mack, Kristen, and John Chase. 2011. "Emanuel Hires Private Firms for City Recycling." *Chicago Tribune*, July 19.

Madhani, Aamer. 2001. "City Paves Way for More Bikers." *Chicago Tribune*, May 19.

Martinez, Anthony. 2012. "A Green Roofs Check-In." Accessed September 8, 2014. http://www.wbez.org/series/curious-city/green-roofs-check-101677.

Maus, Jonathan. 2010. "Interview with BTA Board Chair and New Hire Rob Sadowsky." Accessed September 6, 2014. http://bikeportland.org/2010/03/17/interview -with-bta-board-chair-and-new-hire-rob-sadowsky-30870.

Micklin, Claire, Ben Wilhelm, and Alex Kahn. 2015. "My Building Doesn't Recycle!" Accessed November 16, 2015. http://mybuildingdoesntrecycle.com/.

Mitchell, Ross. 2006a. "Building an Empirical Case for Ecological Democracy." *Nature and Culture* 1, no. 2: 149–156.

———. 2006b. "Green Politics or Environmental Blues? Analyzing Ecological Democracy." *Public Understanding of Science* 15, no. 4: 459–480.

Mitlin, Dianna. 1992. "Sustainable Development: A Guide to the Literature." *Environment and Urbanization* 4, no. 1: 111–124.

NBC. 2007. "NBC Interviews Mayor Richard Daley on City's 'Green' Plan." *NBC Nightly News*, June 1. YouTube video. Accessed September 8, 2014. http://www.youtube.com/watch?v=B1zCcR65Kyk.

Newsham, Guy, Sandra Mancini, and Benjamin Birt. 2009. "Do LEED-Certified Buildings Save Energy? Yes, But . . . ." *Energy and Buildings* 41, no. 8: 897–905.

Office of the Mayor, City of Chicago. 2013. "Mayor Emanuel Announces Sustainable Chicago 2015 Action Agenda Makes Significant Progress in Year One." Press release. Accessed September 8, 2014. http://www.cityofchicago.org/city/en/depts/mayor/press_room/press_releases/2013/december_2013/mayor-emanuel-announces-sustainable-chicago-2015-action-agenda-m.html.

Pellow, David. 2004. *Garbage Wars: The Struggle for Environmental Justice in Chicago.* Cambridge, Mass.: MIT Press.

People for Community Recovery. 2014. "PCR's History." Accessed September 3, 2014. http://www.peopleforcommunityrecovery.org/history.html.

Rees, William, and Mathis Wackernagel. 1996. *Our Ecological Footprint: Reducing Human Impact on the Earth.* Gabriola Island, B.C.: New Society Publishers.

Saulny, Susan. 2010. "Chicago Is Mayor Daley's Kind of Town." *New York Times*, September 11.

Schwebel, Michael B. 2012. "How Can a Successful Multi-Family Residential Recycling Programme be Initiated within Baltimore City, Maryland?" *Waste Management and Research* 30, no. 7: 727–737

Taylor, Dorceta. 2014. *Toxic Communities: Environmental Racism, Industrial Pollution, and Residential Mobility.* New York: New York University Press.

Taylor, John, and Sarah Lovell. 2012. "Mapping Public and Private Spaces of Urban Agriculture in Chicago through the Analysis of High-Resolution Aerial Images in Google Earth." *Landscape and Urban Planning* 108, no. 1: 57–70.

U.S. Department of Energy. 2014. "City of Chicago—Green Permit and Green Homes Programs." Accessed September 6, 2014. http://energy.gov/savings/city-chicago-green-permit-and-green-homes-programs.

United Nations. 1992. *Agenda 21.* Report of the United Nations Conference on Environment and Development, Rio de Janeiro, Brazil, June 3–14. Accessed September 3, 2014. http://sustainabledevelopment.un.org/content/documents/Agenda21.pdf.

———. 2000. *Resolution 55/2: United Nations Millennium Declaration.* Accessed May 2, 2016. http://www.un.org/millennium/declaration/ares552e.htm.

Washburn, Gary. 1999. "At City Hall, a New Wearing of the Green." *Chicago Tribune*, August 14.

Washburn, Gary, with Sallie L. Gaines 1999. "ComEd Signs $1 Billion Power Pact with City." *Chicago Tribune*, March 24.

Washington, Sylvia Hood. 2005. *Packing Them In: An Archaeology of Environmental Racism in Chicago, 1865–1954.* Lanham, Md.: Lexington Books.

Wasserman, Kim. 2011. "Fighting for a Breath of Fresh Air." *Chicago Tribune*, November 30.

Wheeler, Stephen. 1998. "Planning Sustainable and Livable Cities." In *The City Reader*, ed. Richard Legates and Frederic Stout, 486–496. London: Routledge.

Wheeler, Stephen, and Timothy Beatley. 2009. "Chicago, IL." In *The Sustainable Urban Development Reader*, 2nd ed., ed. Stephen Wheeler and Timothy Beatley, 442–444. London: Routledge.

Whitehead, Mark. 2007. *Spaces of Sustainability: Geographical Perspectives on the Sustainable Society.* London: Routledge.

Zavestoski, Stephen, and Julian Agyeman. 2015. *Incomplete Streets: Processes, Practices, and Possibilities.* London: Routledge.

Zeemering, Eric S. 2009. "What Does Sustainability Mean to City Officials?" *Urban Affairs Review* 45, no. 2: 247–273.

CHAPTER 5

Sports and Blue-Collar Mythology in Neoliberal Chicago

SEAN DINCES AND CHRISTOPHER LAMBERTI

Despite the decades of factory shutdowns, union busting, and stagnating or declining wages that have become part and parcel of the neoliberal assault on American cities, Chicago remains a blue-collar town—that is, if you ask the journalists and athletes who make up the city's professional sports scene. Seemingly at every opportunity, the local sports pages celebrate the Bears, Blackhawks, Bulls, and White Sox as "blue-collar team[s] in a blue-collar town with a blue-collar history" (Vancil 2013).

At first glance, such descriptions may seem entirely at odds with a postindustrial Chicago that has seen its manufacturing sector gutted since the end of World War II and with a sports industry in which athletes and coaches earn multimillion-dollar salaries. However, as we argue below, the language of blue-collar fans and athletes—a language that, at least in Chicago, has enjoyed growing popularity in recent decades—is perfectly consistent with the politics and history of American neoliberalism. In particular, it offers an often overlooked example of how the pro sports business—leagues, teams, and media—has played an important role in what critics of neoliberalism such as Henry Giroux (2006) describe as a larger project of masking, justifying, and profiting from intensified economic inequality.

We develop this argument in three parts. The first part zeroes in on the mainstream sports media's celebration of Chicago's allegedly blue-collar fans. More specifically, it details the obvious but rarely acknowledged irony that this rhetoric coincides with a Chicago in which the actual supply of blue-collar jobs—that is, positions in manufacturing or analogous sectors that pay relatively good wages—has dwindled to an alarmingly low level. We contend that the ongoing insistence of journalists that local fan bases are blue collar has come to function as a distraction from efforts by Chicago's sports franchises to price live games at levels that working people cannot afford and to erect increasingly high cost barriers to watching games on television. In short, asserting the persistence of a blue-collar fan base diverts attention from how teams have bolstered a model of urban leisure that caters to elites at the expense of regular Chicagoans.

The second part shifts the focus to the history of Chicago sportswriters describing professional athletes as blue collar. We show that this practice became popular only in the latter decades of the twentieth century, at the same time that usage of the term declined in U.S. popular culture more broadly. In other words, as deindustrialization undermined the material basis for traditional understandings of blue-collar identity, mainstream sports journalism preserved, and at the same time redefined, the language of blue collar by applying it to wealthy athletes.

Finally, we discuss how the explosion of commentary about "blue-collar" players precisely at the moment when pro athletes entered the ranks of the rich reflected a broader shift in American politics and media away from talking about social class as a matter of material circumstance and toward talking about it as a matter of behavior or even lifestyle. These "blue-collar" pros, glorified by the press for their "work ethic," have emerged as the poster boys for a society that sanctions profound economic inequality, provided that those at the top refrain from looking down their noses at the masses.[1]

Imagining the Blue-Collar Fan in Postindustrial Chicago

Given the opportunity, Chicago's pro athletes will tell you they play for blue-collar people in a blue-collar city. Bulls guard Jimmy Butler, for example, calls Chicago a place where "everyone has that blue-collar work ethic" (Cowley 2013). Perhaps this sentiment is strongest among White Sox players, who take the field on the city's South Side, once home to some of the nation's largest factories. Recently, White Sox centerfielder Adam Eaton called his ball club "a hard-nosed team on the blue-collar side of town" (McGrath 2014). Jake Peavy, who spent several seasons pitching for the White Sox, claimed to "love" the fans, whom he described as "blue-collar, good ol' hard-working people" (Haugh 2012).

One does not have to look far to find examples of the local or national sports media characterizing Chicago and its sports fans in the same way. In 2013, an *ESPN Chicago* reporter described White Sox first baseman Paul Konerko as

"'The Man' of the blue-collar White Sox fan base" (Levine 2013). That same year, a *Chicago Tribune* sports columnist wrote with satisfaction that Chicago was a "blue-collar town" (Haugh 2013). A senior writer at *Bleacher Report* suggested around the same time that Chicago embodied "blue-collar grit" (Rang 2013). The *CBS Sports* website celebrated its "blue-collar nature" (MacNamara 2010), and so on.[2]

The problem with the characterization of Chicago sports fans as blue collar is that it is an anachronism, if it was ever accurate. According to the Oxford Dictionaries website, "blue collar" is a category that traditionally refers to social class and to "manual work or workers, particularly in industry." There was a time when throngs of these workers toiled in Chicago, when the city was a major manufacturing hub. As the first half of the twentieth century progressed, Chicago's economy grew to support hundreds of thousands of jobs in meat packing, steel production, consumer products assembly, and processed food production.

By the second half of the 1900s, however, things had started to change. From 1967 to 1982, the city lost 250,000 jobs, and a quarter of Chicago's factories closed in the 1970s (Pacyga 2009, 366). In 1950, 37 percent of employed Chicago residents worked in manufacturing; by 1990, that number had dwindled to 19 percent (U.S. Census Bureau 1956, 1994). This reflected a larger national trend, as the migration of domestic investment to other sectors of the economy (e.g., services) and the proliferation of international free trade agreements marked the death knell of industrial growth in the American Rust Belt.

As shown in Map 5.1, every part of the city felt the effects of deindustrialization from 1970 to 2000. Of the 871 of 872 census tracts for which data is available for this period, the number of residents holding manufacturing jobs decreased in 848. The decline exceeded 50 percent in 625 tracts. While the process spared few neighborhoods, it hit hardest on Chicago's South and West Sides.

In the new millennium, manufacturing jobs in Chicago have continued to fall precipitously. Just under 12 percent of Chicago residents held manufacturing jobs in 2002, and that number dropped to 7.5 percent in 2011. Over this time span, no other sector of the local economy experienced such a dramatic decrease in its share of the work force living in Chicago. In fact, retail trade; professional, scientific and technical services; educational services; health care and social assistance; accommodation; and food services now each account for a higher share of jobs than manufacturing (U.S. Census Bureau n.d.a).[3]

Even on Chicago's South Side, home of the White Sox and (supposedly) the home of the bluest of Chicago's blue-collar fans, manufacturing jobs are scarce. In the area covered by the zip codes south of the Chicago River that divides the North and South Sides, manufacturing work accounted for only 8.5 percent of the total number of jobs residents held in 2011. That was lower than the rate in

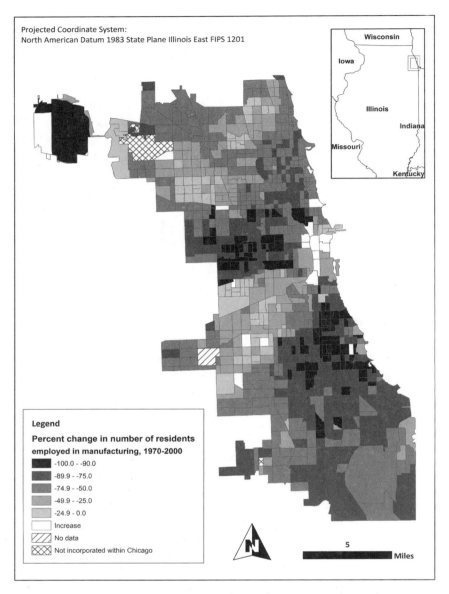

Map 5.1. Percentage change in number of manufacturing employees by census tract, City of Chicago, 1970–2000. Sources: City of Chicago (2015); US2010 Project (2012).

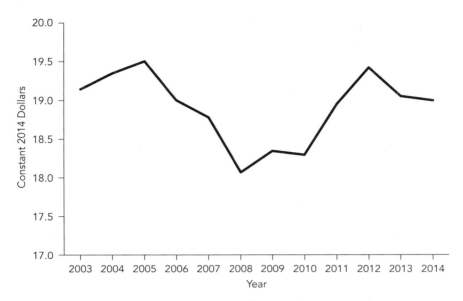

Figure 5.1. Annual average hourly earnings for manufacturing employees, Chicago-Naperville-Arlington Heights, Illinois, metropolitan division. Source: U.S. Bureau of Labor Statistics (n.d.b; n.d.c).

the Chicago metro area (10.4 percent manufacturing workers) and the state of Illinois (10.9 percent). Despite Chicago's reputation, the South Side, Chicagoland, and Illinois do not rate well regionally. As a point of comparison, in Wisconsin and Indiana the rate of manufacturing jobs among employed residents was 18 and 17.9 percent, respectively, in 2011 (U.S. Census Bureau, n.d.a).[4]

Characterizing Chicago as a blue-collar sports town deserves scrutiny not simply because of the dwindling numbers of actual blue-collar Chicagoans. The description is also problematic because it obscures the fact that fewer and fewer blue-collar sports fans can afford to partake in the sports entertainment experience. In the postwar era, blue-collar work was a ticket to a middle-class material existence, as high union density in the American industrial sector made factory jobs among the highest paid in the private sector. But the offshoring of unionized industrial plants, investment in manufacturing facilities offering lower paying and non-union jobs in the American South and "right-to-work" states, automation, and increased unemployment have led to the reduction or stagnation of manufacturing wages (Tankersly 2013). Indeed, the Bureau of Labor Statistics numbers in Figure 5.1, which show average hourly earnings for manufacturing workers in Chicagoland from 2003 to 2014, indicate that in terms of wages, blue-collar employees have been falling behind or at best treading water in recent years.

While manufacturing workers in Chicago have found it more difficult to make ends meet, Chicago sports team owners have indulged in dramatic game-day price increases. Long gone are the days of a century ago when admission cost 25¢ at Comiskey Park, the old home of the White Sox (Farrell 1998). These were modest prices even by early twentieth-century standards.[5] By contrast, the cost of entertaining a family of four at the various stadiums and arenas in Chicago in 2014–2015 ranged from $210 to $597 (Fort 2015).[6] According to estimates derived from the 2012 Consumer Expenditure Survey, the average household expenditures on fees and admission charges for spectator sports in the U.S. amounted to about $65 (U.S. Bureau of Labor Statistics 2014). It is fair to infer, then, that the aforementioned prices put live professional sporting events beyond the reach of most contemporary wage earners and their families.

Data on fan demographics included in team brochures produced by the White Sox and Blackhawks in order to attract sponsors confirm thoroughly white-collar game-day crowds. The Blackhawks cite a 2007 study of NHL fans that found an average household income of $103,825 among ticket buyers (Chicago Blackhawks n.d.). A brochure recently published by the White Sox boasts that their attendees "are 38% more likely to have a household income of $150,000-$250,000 than the average Chicagoan" (Chicago White Sox 2014). Compare these figures to the median household income of $47,831 (in 2014 dollars) in the city of Chicago, as estimated by the U.S. Census Bureau (n.d.b) based on American Community Survey data for 2010–2014.

The displacement of working-class fans from live games in Chicago is part of a much larger trend within the professional sports business over the last twenty to thirty years. As the economist Robert Baade (1996) points out, the growing income inequality that accompanied the halt of wage growth for American workers pushed major-league franchises to refocus their marketing and sales efforts on expanding the base of fans who want and can afford luxury experiences. This has meant the expansion of "premium" tickets for sky boxes and club sections, which have typically displaced more affordable seats. Thus, luxury seating and associated amenities have become increasingly central to a neoliberal growth strategy in the pro sports business that caters to urban elites' desire for exclusivity at the expense of the common fan (Lamberti 2013, Dinces 2014).

Even seats that remain outside of expanding premium sections have, in the last quarter-century or so, become a luxury that most working families cannot afford. In 1985, the average, inflation-adjusted cost of a non-premium White Sox ticket was $12.69 (2014 dollars). In 2014, the average White Sox ticket price was $26.05. Admission to a Bears game was $31.90 (2014 dollars) in 1985, but in 2014, it was $108.44, a 240 percent increase in real terms (Fort 2015). These are not isolated examples: in recent decades, all of Chicago's teams have imposed steep price increases. Figure 5.2 shows the real change in ticket prices for the

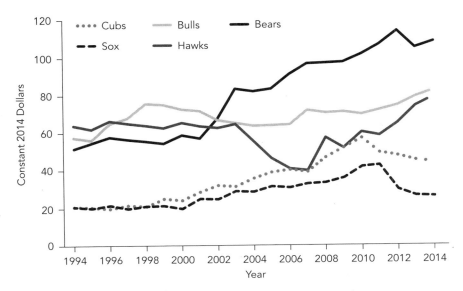

Figure 5.2. Weighted average ticket prices for Chicago's Major League sports franchises, 1994–2014. Source: Fort (2015); U.S. Bureau of Labor Statistics (n.d.b).

five major sports teams since 1994 in constant 2014 dollars. Ticket prices have dropped in particular years due to poor team performance, lockouts, or economic downturns, but overall the average stadium admission price has risen much faster than inflation since 1994.[7]

The cost to fans of following professional sports via television broadcasts has also risen significantly in Chicago and across the United States. This owes much to cable and satellite affiliate fees paid to national and regional sports networks, which are passed on to household subscribers. For example, ESPN alone costs consumers over five dollars a month in affiliate fees (per-customer charges for certain channels included in one's overall cable bill) (Thompson 2013). Comcast SportsNet Chicago (CSN; 80 percent of which is owned by the Bulls, the Blackhawks, the Cubs, and the White Sox) is the city's regional sports network and major broadcaster of Cubs, Whites Sox, Bulls, and Blackhawks games. In 2012, CSN Chicago's monthly affiliate fee was $2.75 and rising (Ozanian 2013). Because of increases in sports broadcast and other programming fees, the cost of cable has outpaced the rate of inflation by 47 percent since 1998 (Zara 2014).

These fees may seem insignificant. However, marketing research on Chicago-area sports fans suggests that such charges have resulted in an overrepresentation of wealthy fans among those who view games on cable. Survey estimates by Scarborough Research (see Figure 5.3) indicate that in 2011, while residents

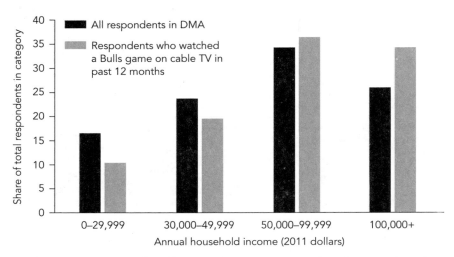

Figure 5.3. Percentage of residents in Chicago Designated Market Area (DMA) having watched a Chicago Bulls game on cable television in the past year, 2011. Source: Brad Sherer, e-mail correspondence with Sean Dinces, March 19, 2012; Scarborough Research (2012).

whose annual household income exceeded $100,000 made up about 26 percent of respondents from the Chicago Designated Market Area, or DMA, residents from this category made up 34 percent of those who reported having watched a Chicago Bulls cable broadcast in the previous twelve months. Conversely, residents whose annual household income amounted to less than $30,000 made up between 16 and 17 percent of total respondents, but only about 10 percent of respondents who reported having taken in a game on a cable network (Brad Sherer, e-mail to Sean Dinces, March 19, 2012).

It would appear, then, that even within the confines of Chicagoans' living rooms, watching pro sports has become an increasingly elite endeavor. Nevertheless, the rhetoric of so-called blue-collar fans continues unabated. Chicago's teams may still enjoy a large following of wage-earning devotees, but they have nonetheless done much to marginalize them as spectators. Whether intentionally or not, the purveyors of this rhetoric have directed attention away from this marginalization, and distraction of this type has real stakes. In particular, it minimizes the scrutiny directed toward major-league franchises that secure massive public subsidies and political favoritism by arguing that they help foster a unique sense of civic pride and community cohesion. It has made more palatable the ongoing efforts by Chicago's major-league franchises to displace actual blue-collar fans from the ranks of those who are welcome as full-fledged consumers within Chicago's postindustrial entertainment economy.

The Rise of the "Blue-Collar" Athlete in Chicago

The journalists, players, and team officials who conjure up images of Chicago's blue-collar fans rarely go into much detail about the types of jobs these fans hold. This sidestepping makes sense, given that the most visible fans (i.e., those regularly attending actual games) are elite. Delving into any detail about their actual occupations might draw attention to the hollowness of the rhetoric.

At present, one of the few jobs actually discussed in commentators' celebrations of Chicago's alleged blue-collar identity is playing (or coaching) a professional sport. A recent *Tribune* retrospective on the career of Chicago Bear Brian Urlacher insisted that the linebacker "ideally fit an image immediately embraced by our big, blue-collar town. . . . Urlacher looked like a meat packer and worked as if he signed a time card instead of autographs" (Haugh 2013). This is not unique to football. A *Tribune* piece on the 2013 Chicago Blackhawks earnestly referred to team members as "blue-collar workers" who "get physical" (Hamilton 2013). Not to be outdone, a 2014 article on the Comcast SportsNet Chicago website reminded readers that the "Chicago Bulls are known as a blue-collar team with a blue-collar head coach who demands the absolute best night-in and night-out. . . . The team is filled with hard-nosed players who leave it all on the floor, especially two-time All-Star center Joakim Noah" (Comcast SportsNet Chicago 2014). All of this may come as a surprise, given the fact that most of the athletes on any of Chicago's major league rosters are millionaires. However, as we detail below, the increasing promotion of professional athletes as blue-collar icons of the city is the logical outcome of a broader shift in popular conceptions of class in the United States.

Regular use of the modifier "blue-collar" to describe professional athletes by Chicago's popular press began just as its use within broader American popular and intellectual culture declined. When we conducted a systematic search of the digitized books in American English that help make up the larger Google Books corpus (using Google's Ngram Viewer), we found that writers hardly ever used the expression before 1950, but that by the late 1950s they were beginning to do so more frequently. In the 1960s, appearances of the term "blue collar" in books continued to increase. Usage peaked in the mid-seventies, and since then it has plummeted.

It would appear, then, that the rise and fall of "blue collar" as a component of the American lexicon coincided more or less with rise and fall of the economic fortunes of the U.S. working class. Such a pattern makes sense. In the quarter-century of boom times that followed World War II, American wage earners shared in an era of "unprecedented affluence" characterized not simply by widespread unionization and higher incomes but also by widespread (government-subsidized) homeownership, strong purchasing power, and the promise that parents could send their children to college and toward a life of upward mobility. Moreover, relatively high union density gave workers a meaningful political voice; the Democratic Party in the immediate postwar period catered to the working class more than at any time in history (Schulman 2001). In other words, the lived experience of wage earners emerged in the minds of many as cause for celebration, and the cultural embrace of terms such as "blue collar" reflected the rising fortunes of wage earners within American society.

By the 1970s, the lived experience of being blue collar had begun to lose its luster. Stagflation and the significant advances made by movement conservatism in the United States readied the American political landscape for what social critic Mike Davis (1986, 157) describes as the "seismic shift rightward . . . at every level of American politics." The oncoming neoliberal onslaught would ultimately bring American organized labor to its knees, mercilessly squeeze wages by prioritizing anti-inflationary monetary policy, and shift public investment away from basic social programs toward military spending and corporate welfare. That there have been few causes for celebration for workers amid the unmitigated political and economic disaster of the last forty years makes it understandable that usage of "blue collar" has declined significantly. Moreover, the institutions that went hand in hand with its definition—unions and a relatively progressive system of economic redistribution—have withered, leaving the term with little resonance in twenty-first-century America.

How strange, then, that sportswriters started to use "blue collar" in reference to athletes (or quote athletes using the phrase in reference to themselves) only after its wider usage began to wane. The research for this chapter included systematic searches for the phrases "blue-collar" or "blue collar" in conjunction with either "Bears," "Blackhawks," "Bulls," or "Sox" in the *Chicago Tribune*, the only local newspaper that has a comprehensive, searchable database covering the entirety of the twentieth century. Bob Logan, beat writer for the Bulls for much of the 1970s, appears to have been the first to talk about pro athletes in Chicago as "blue collar." During the 1974 season, Logan (1974) described "just an ordinary, workmanlike Chicago Bulls team back on the job . . . a bunch of blue-collar lunch pail toters who hammer out . . . victories on an assembly line." It would be several years before sportswriters at the *Tribune* adopted variations of this ode as standard practice. In fact, in the case of the Bulls, Logan appears to have given it up after that first over-the-top effort. Bob Sakamoto eventually resurrected and made prolific use of it during the mid-1980s to describe unheralded Bulls players such as Gene Banks and Charles Oakley as "blue collar workers" or "blue-collar overachievers" (Sakamoto 1986, 1987a).

Discourse around other local teams followed a similar chronological trajectory. Bob Verdi, who covered the White Sox for the *Tribune*, first referred to the team as a "blue-collar gang" in articles appearing in the late 1970s (Verdi 1977a, 1977b). It wasn't until the 1990s, however, that in any given year readers could encounter a new generation of Sox writers labeling the squad a bunch of "blue-collar guys" or quoting players such as Lance Johnson describing themselves as "blue collar" and claiming to "punch in every day, play hard and hustle" (Jauss 1991; Holtzman 1992).

A handful of *Tribune* articles on the "blue-collar Bears" appeared between 1979 and 1985, but it wasn't until Bears coach Mike Ditka famously declared, "We're a Grabowski" when describing his team to the press in January 1986 that the local media pounced on "blue collar" as a descriptor for the hometown football team. As one reporter put it immediately in the wake of Ditka's statement, "Grabowski" was a synonym for "the shot-and-a-beer, hard-hat, lunch-bucket guy who gets his muscles through toil" (Myslenski 1985; Galloway 1986). Since then, it has been standard operating procedure in all mainstream Chicago papers to let readers know that the "blue collar still fits" Bears players. Even in an era when athlete salaries have reached Himalayan heights, so they tell us, we should listen to and take seriously statements from the likes of tight end Martellus Bennett that "I'm a blue-collar player, and that's what I always will be" (Verdi 1992; Jahns 2013).

Descriptions of hockey players as blue collar appeared as early as the late 1970s in the *Tribune*, but they did not become de rigueur in the paper's sports coverage until the beginning of the 1990s, when Blackhawks beat writer Mike Kiley made it a centerpiece of his coverage (Verdi 1978). By that point, Kiley wasn't the only one touting the "blue-collar career" of players such as wing Dirk Graham or likening other Hawks to "blue-collar, crew-cut plumber[s] who expect a full day's pay for a full day's work" (Kiley 1994, 1992). Hockey coverage in the *Sun-Times* followed a similar pattern, advertising the Blackhawks as "blue collar guy[s]" who "roll up [their] sleeves" and "give you a full day's work, and often more, for a full day's pay" (Gould 1993).

What did these writers actually mean when they talked about athletes as blue collar? Certainly it had little to do with their class position as measured by income. By the mid-1980s, mean salaries in MLB, the NFL, and the NBA all reached well into six figures, while average "total money income" for U.S. households barely topped $30,000 (Staudohar 1998; U.S. Census Bureau 1988, 8).

Instead of signaling income or job category, "blue collar," when used to characterize pro athletes, has indicated a broad range of behavioral attributes. Some of these are sports-specific. Dedication to the unglamorous art of defense, for example, has proven a quick way for a player or team to earn the blue-collar badge. "You see," wrote Bulls beat writer Sam Smith in 1995, "defense is associated with . . . digging in and all the good clichés of sport," or in other words, with "that blue-collar Chicago ethic" (Smith 1995).

Sportswriters have also equated blue collarness with traditionally masculine traits such as aggressiveness, toughness, and a willingness to sacrifice one's body in the name of victory. A recent post on the website of Comcast SportsNet Chicago carried the title "The 'Blue Collar' in these Blackhawks." It explained, "While they still may lose some of the physical numbers that are totaled up on the stat sheet, their willingness to pay the price in attacking the net . . . has provided the definition of toughness this team really needs" (Boden 2013).

Much more than specific references to defense or toughness, though, sportswriters in Chicago have designated pro athletes as blue collar when they demonstrate a strong work ethic or a commitment to hard work. Pick out any Chicago sports article containing the term "blue collar," and chances are you will also find the phrases "work ethic," "hard work," or some variant thereof. A 2000 *Tribune* retrospective on former White Sox catcher Carlton Fisk lauded his "gritty, blue-collar work ethic." A similar piece in a 1997 edition of the *Sun-Times* celebrated former Blackhawks Jeremy Roenick and Ed Belfour for their "work ethic and blue-collar style" (Reynolds 2000; Leptich 1997). The list of pieces like these goes on and on.

Professional Sports and the Neoliberal Redefinition of Social Class

One interpretation of the proliferation of references to blue-collar fans, athletes, coaches, and teams in postindustrial America is that it embodies the growing fixation on personal responsibility at the heart of neoliberal ideology. Indeed, the obsession with the term "work ethic" in local sports coverage often seems to be cut straight from the rhetorical playbook Ronald Reagan developed in the late 1970s. As social critic David Sirota (2011, 58) explains, acolytes of the Reaganite world view have "been banging the American Dream's drum about a country where there are supposedly no economic or racial barriers" for those willing to roll up their sleeves and engage in "a little hard work." According to Sirota, the "Just Do It" philosophy popularized in the 1980s—not just in political discourse but also in the lionization of African American superstar athletes such as Chicago Bull Michael Jordan—has left many convinced that "the difference between success and failure is individual desire and willingness to persevere through impossible trauma." Incessant talk of athletes as "hard workers" by sportswriters, it would seem, became an ideal vessel for such rhetoric, since it spotlighted this so-called desire and perseverance while conveniently passing over an outside world in which the economic policies popularized by Reagan—not to mention New Democrats such as current Chicago mayor Rahm Emanuel—have radically reduced social mobility in the United States.

No doubt there is some truth in this reading, but it is important not to overstate it. As sports historian Allen Guttmann (1978) points out, notions of meritocracy and individual achievement through hard work have permeated modern sport for centuries. Moreover, much of the blue-collar rhetoric enveloping athletes in cities like Chicago has placed their efforts in the context of teamwork—a concept at odds with the hyperindividuality that neoliberal ideologues glorify (Sirota 2011).

The relatively recent rise of the so-called blue-collar athlete as a rhetorical device is important to an understanding of the history of neoliberalism for a different reason: it sheds light on how conversations about sport have emerged as a forum for undoing the presumed link between one's class and access to economic resources and for redefining class in terms of culture—that is, in terms of behavioral norms. Just as striking as how often Chicago sportswriters have linked athletes' supposed blue collarness to their work ethic is how frequently they describe it in terms of "approach," "attitude," "mentality," or "style." Bears great Walter Payton won over fans with his "blue-collar mentality" (Sherman 1999). Blackhawk fans "appreciate the blue-collar approach of white-collar players" (Kiley 1989). "Chicagoans turned out in record numbers" in 1987 "to savor the Bulls' blue-collar, work-ethic style of basketball" (Sakamoto 1987b). These formulations, all of which refer to players earning six- or seven-figure salaries, invariably uproot working-class identity from the realm of economic status and power and relocate it squarely within the context of image and demeanor.

That many if not most Americans have, in the last thirty to forty years, come to understand class in cultural terms rather than economic ones is not a new observation. The consensus among historians such as Jefferson Cowie (2012) and David Farber (1994) is that Richard Nixon's successful "blue-collar strategy" in the 1968 and 1972 elections marked the pivot point of this transformation. Nixon's appeals to white working-class voters on the basis of patriotism and traditional morality offered them solace in the face of feeling "forgotten" amid the Civil Rights movement, anti-war activism, and second-wave feminism. According to Cowie (2012, 164–165), these appeals ultimately "helped to push the concept of 'worker' out of the realm of production and helped drive a long process of deconstructing the postwar worker as a . . . materially based concept." Detached from the "realm of production"—that is, from a world in which the descriptor "working-class" unambiguously signaled one's identity as a wage earner—a modifier like "blue-collar" was up for grabs in a way it had not been previously. In reviving "blue-collar" as a way to talk about professional athletes, Chicago sportswriters have played an overlooked role in the larger reappropriation of language traditionally used to denote someone's place in the capitalist hierarchy for use in describing personality or image.

This phenomenon also tells us much about how neoliberal rhetoric around class has worked to legitimate profound material inequality. As Walter Benn Michaels (2006) argues, for some time public debate in the United States has avoided acknowledging economic inequality as an ethical and political problem in and of itself. Instead, such debate has moralized about the importance of being sensitive to the "diversity" of class backgrounds from which people come. The "problem" of class, in other words, has been redefined as a "'condescension' problem," with journalists and intellectuals insisting that "what's wrong with elite institutions is the way they make poor people feel their poverty," as opposed to their role in perpetuating poverty itself (Michaels 2006, 95).

This perverse philosophy of justice is either implicitly or explicitly at play in almost all of the journalistic references to "blue-collar" athletes. For sportswriters, what makes these "hard-working," "gritty," "tough" millionaire athletes palatable—and, indeed, respectable—is their refusal to act spoiled or superior to fans even when, in economic terms, they *are* superior. By highlighting the fact that major-league players embrace or even embody the cultural mores and behavioral norms of less privileged fans, sports pages in cities such as Chicago have sent the message that obscene disparities in wealth are acceptable so long as the haves refrain from "looking down" on the have-nots (Michaels 2006, 103).

There is something more at work, however, behind the language of "blue-collar" fans, athletes, and coaches than the erasure of class as a material reality or a political problem. Its use has also emerged as an important marketing tool for those involved in the professional sports business. In Chicago, this was made clear in 1987, when Mike Ditka recorded a music video in which he and a handful of hand-picked Chicagoans (including a former police officer and a sewer worker) performed the "Grabowski Shuffle." The lyrics accompanying the "30-minute romp highlighted by a 5-minute 'polka-funk' dance number" tapped into Ditka's self-styled blue-collar identity. "We like to work, we love to play," Ditka and his backup "Grabowskis" sing. "We do them both, about the same way!" Apparently, the message resonated with Christmas shoppers in Chicago. One local woman who purchased a copy for her father explained, "My dad's a big fan of Ditka's. . . . He's a blue-collar guy. He likes Ditka's work ethic." According to the producer, the "Grabowski Shuffle" sold 50,000 copies by the end of the year (Obejas 1987; Found Footage Festival 2013; Kogan 1987).

While the "Grabowski Shuffle" was not an official Bears endeavor, by the last two decades of the twentieth century, officials from all of Chicago's pro franchises had come to understand the cultivation of a blue-collar image as a crucial part of their marketing toolbox. In 1990, the *Tribune* described how Blackhawks coach Mike Keenan very consciously pushed players to cultivate a working-class identity in order to sell more tickets. "If the Hawks would just submit to a lunch-bucket mentality, Keenan figured, they'd have the local folk eating out of their hand," the paper explained. "His assessment was accurate," the article continued. "The Hawks have sold out 29 straight home games" (Kiley 1990). More recently, the White Sox developed the "Grinder Rules" and "Back to the Grind" ad campaigns, which, according to the *Tribune*, "play[ed] off the team's blue-collar image" (Meyer 2007).

Players have also learned to market themselves to fans and sponsors using the same language. White Sox players such as Adam Eaton and Jake Peavy have readily adopted "blue-collar speak." Bulls guard Kirk Hinrich is another local sports pro who has developed into a consummate self-promoter in this regard, broadcasting his belief that he was "kind of meant to play in Chicago. . . . The city is blue-collar. It's how I play. I'm a guy willing to do the little things" (Smith 2004). Some player-related merchandise even contains imagery that refers to players' alleged blue collarness (Cubby Tees 2014).

All of this—the promotion by merchandisers, team officials, and players themselves—captures the degree to which the sports business has transformed the idea of class into a commodity. It is not simply that professional sport in the United States has helped divorce definitions of class from the realm of production; it has incorporated new cultural conceptions of class into its contemporary growth strategy.

As local athletes and teams have harnessed the rhetorical power of a widely appealing "blue-collar" aesthetic and leveraged their influence in the realm of popular culture in order to cash in on it, the increasingly precarious position of Chicago's wage earners has receded from public view. Part of this owes to the fact that the healthy base of relatively well-paid manufacturing workers that the city once incubated has shrunk drastically over the last half-century. Another part owes to the fact that the low-paying, hyper-exploitative service jobs that have largely replaced an older generation of relatively well-compensated, unionized jobs in manufacturing are poorly suited to the journalistic romanticism at the heart of conversations about so-called blue-collar fans. That major-league athletes themselves have become, if we are to believe the local sports pages, the standard bearers of Chicago's blue-collar identity exemplifies the degree to which neoliberalism has obscured the notion of social class as an indicator of one's position in the economic hierarchy.

Notes

The authors wish to thank Vaneesa Cook and Elena McGrath for their assistance with copy-editing and footnote checking for earlier drafts of this chapter.

1. Chicago is not the only city in which the papers fawn over so-called blue-collar fans and athletes. Other notable sports towns such as Detroit, Indianapolis, and Pittsburgh have incubated the same rhetoric. However, the local concentration of teams and news outlets make Chicago a prime case study for our analysis.

2. Cubs fans are the lone exception to this trend, and the difference is geographic: followers of Chicago's North Side baseball team stand in contrast to their South Side rivals. In a newspaper interview during the run-up to a crosstown Cubs–White Sox series in 2008, sports historian Richard Davies described tensions between Chicago baseball fans: "What you have is the upper-middle-class professional group who is located near Wrigley Field on the North Side of town and are Cubs fans.... And on the South Side you have minorities, ethnics and working-blue-collar folks who root for the White Sox" (Friedman 2008). According to this common sense, the Cubs are the exception that proves the rule that Chicago is a blue-collar sports town.

3. Data generated from the U.S. Census Bureau's On the Map website, which draws from the Longitudinal Employer-Household Dynamics Origin-Destination Employment Statistics (LODES). The specific figures in this paragraph are derived from a "Home Area" analysis of "Primary Jobs" for "Chicago city IL." "Home area" indicates that the job numbers are for Chicago city residents (whether or not they work inside city limits), and "primary job" indicates the highest-paying position held by each resident (U.S. Census Bureau n.d.a).

4. Data generated from the U.S. Census Bureau's On the Map website by conducting a "Home Area" analysis of "Primary Jobs" in the "Manufacturing" industry sector for "Chicago city IL," Wisconsin and Indiana, and Zip Codes 60616, 60609, 60632, 60638, 60653, 60615, 60621, 60636, 60629, 60652, 60620, 60637, 60619, 60649, 60617, 60628, 60643, 60655, 60633 and "Home Area Profile Analysis: Chicago-Joliet-Naperville, IL-IN-WI from Metropolitan/Micropolitan Areas (CBSA), Detailed Report" (U.S. Census Bureau, n.d.a).

5. According to the Bureau of Labor Statistics (n.d.a) online "CPI Inflation Calculator," a 25-cent ticket in 1913 would be the equivalent of $5.98 in 2014 dollars.

6. "Cost of entertaining" based on *Team Marketing Report*'s "Fan Cost Index" (FCI), which includes the cost of four average-priced tickets, four small soft drinks, two small beers, four hot dogs, two programs, parking, and two of the cheapest adult-size caps. The 2014–2015 FCI's for Chicago teams are as follows: 2014–2015 Blackhawks, $463.20; 2014 Bears, $596.76; 2014–2015 Bulls, $477.32; 2014 Cubs, $304.64; and 2014 White Sox, $210.18 (Fort 2015).

7. Averages weighted by number of seats at each price level, excluding premium seating (i.e. club seats and luxury boxes).

Bibliography

Baade, Robert. 1996. "What Explains the Stadium Construction Boom?" *Real Estate Issues* 21, no. 3: 5–11.

Boden, Chris. 2013. "The 'Blue Collar' in these Blackhawks." *CSNChicago.com*, February 26. Accessed August 11, 2014. http://www.csnchicago.com/blue-collar -these-blackhawks.

Chicago Blackhawks. n.d. "A New Era: 2008–2009 Sponsorship Opportunities." Accessed August 10, 2014. http://blackhawks.nhl.com/ext/sponsorbrochure.pdf.

Chicago White Sox. 2014. "Chicago White Sox Corporate Partnership Opportunities." Accessed August 10, 2014. http://chicago.whitesox.mlb.com/cws/components /sponsorship/y2014/brochure.pdf.

City of Chicago. 2015. Boundaries—City. *City of Chicago Data Portal.* Accessed May 26, 2015. https://data.cityofchicago.org/Facilities-Geographic-Boundaries /Boundaries-City/ewy2–6yfk.

Comcast SportsNet Chicago. 2014. "Prefer the Blue-Collar Bulls or the Superstar-Laden Heat?" Accessed August 10, 2014. http://www.csnchicago.com/bulls/prefer-blue -collar-bulls-or-superstar-laden-heat.

Cowie, Jefferson. 2012. *Stayin' Alive: The 1970s and the Last Days of the Working Class.* New York: New Press.

Cowley, Joe. 2013. "Firm Belief in Butler." *Chicago Sun-Times,* January 28.

Cubby Tees. 2014. "Clock-Punching Taj." Accessed August 11, 2014. http://www .cubbytees.com/ShirtPages/LunchPail.html.

Davis, Mike. 1986. *Prisoners of the American Dream: Politics and Economy in the History of the U.S. Working Class.* London: Verso.

Dinces, Sean. 2014. "Fanfare without the Fans." *Jacobin* 15–16 (Summer).

Farber, David. 1994. "The Silent Majority and Talk about Revolution." In *The Sixties: From Memory to History,* ed. David Farber, 291–316. Chapel Hill: University of North Carolina Press.

Farrell, James T. 1998. *My Baseball Diary.* Carbondale: Southern Illinois University Press.

Fort, Rodney. 2015. *Rod's Sports Business Data.* Accessed May 2, 2015. https://umich .app.box.com/s/41707f0b2619c0107b8b.

Found Footage Festival. 2013. "The Making of the Grabowski Shuffle." Accessed August 11, 2014. http://www.foundfootagefest.com/2013/05/the-making-of-the -grabowski-shuffle/.

Friedman, Emily. 2008. "Cubs-Sox Feud: Healthy Competition or Class War?" *ABC News,* July 30. Accessed May 30, 2015. http://abcnews.go.com/Sports/story? id=5482372.

Galloway, Paul. 1986. "Grabowski Town." *Chicago Tribune,* January 19.

Giroux, Henry. 2006. *Stormy Weather: Katrina and the Politics of Disposability.* Boulder, Colo.: Paradigm.

Gould, Herb. 1993. "Chelios Deal Included Marketing Provision." *Chicago Sun-Times,* November 23.

Guttmann, Allen. 1978. *From Ritual to Record: The Nature of Modern Sports.* New York: Columbia University Press.

Hamilton, Brian. 2013. "Blue-Collar Workers." *Chicago Tribune,* June 3.

Haugh, David. 2012. "At Last, Peavy Enjoying View." *Chicago Tribune,* May 4.

———. 2013. "Like Jordan, Urlacher Symbolized Chicago." *Chicago Tribune,* May 23.

Holtzman, Jerome. 1992. "Johnson's a 'Blue-Collar' Player." *Chicago Tribune,* March 27.

Jahns, Adam. 2013. "Bennett Can Do Super Brawl Scuffle." *Chicago Sun-Times,* August 3.

Jauss, Bill. 1991. "Sox Power Show Sinks Indians." *Chicago Tribune,* September 1.

Kiley, Mike. 1989. "Hawks Gaining Salvation." *Chicago Tribune*, April 26.

———. 1990. "Keenan Creates a Big Red Machine." *Chicago Tribune*, April 1.

———. 1992. "Belfour Gives All vs. Best." *Chicago Tribune*, January 19.

———. 1994. "Injured Graham Realizes Goals Aren't for Him." *Chicago Tribune*, February 20.

Kogan, Rick. 1987. "A Ceramic Jaunt Down Lill Street." *Chicago Tribune*, December 20.

Lamberti, Christopher. 2013. "Rich Man's Game: Rising Ticket Prices in Taxpayer Funded Facilities." *Chicago Sport & Society*, May 9. Accessed August 9, 2014. http://www.chicagosportandsociety.com/2013/05/09/rich-mans-game-rising -ticket-prices-in-taxpayer-funded-facilities/.

Leptich, John. 1997. "Roenick Backs Ex-Teammate." *Chicago Sun-Times*, February 4.

Levine, Bruce. 2013. "Konerko Return Would Not Be a Surprise." *ESPN Chicago*, September 29. Accessed May 30, 2015. http://espn.go.com/blog/chicago/white -sox/post/_/id/17611/konerko-return-would-not-be-a-surprise.

Logan, Bob. 1974. "Bulls Give New Jazz the Blues." *Chicago Tribune*, November 13.

MacNamara, Dylan. 2010. "Bears vs. Packers Monday Night Football: Live Reaction to the Games Biggest Stories." *Bleacher Report*, September 27. Accessed May 30, 2015. http://bleacherreport.com/articles/475256-packers-vs-bears-monday-night -football-live-reaction-to-games-biggest-stories/.

McGrath, Dan. 2014. "Adam Eaton: A Strong Serving of Grit." *Chicago Sun-Times*, April 1.

Meyer, Gregory. 2007. "Mending Holes in the Sox." *Crain's Chicago Business*, August 20.

Michaels, Walter B. 2006. *The Trouble with Diversity: How We Learned to Love Identity and Ignore Inequality*. New York: Henry Holt and Company.

Myslenski, Skip. 1985. "John Madden Rolls through Life, Football." *Chicago Tribune*, November 19.

Obejas, Achy. 1987. "Waiting for Grabowski." *Chicago Reader*, August 6.

Ozanian, Mike. 2013. "Chicago Blackhawks Stanley Cup Win Will Add $50 Million to Team's Value." *Forbes*, June 25. Accessed May 30, 2015. http://www.forbes.com /sites/mikeozanian/2013/06/25/chicago-blackhawks-stanley-cup-win-will-add -50-million-to-teams-value/.

Pacyga, Dominic. 2009. *Chicago: A Biography*. Chicago: University of Chicago Press.

Rang, Rob. 2013. "Finding the Fits: Enigmatic Wilson Could Surprise for Gambling Bears." *CBSSports.com*, May 27. Accessed May 30, 2015. http://www.cbssports .com/nfl/draft/nfl-draft-scout/22311596/finding-the-fits-enigmatic-wilson-could -surprise-for-gambling-bears.

Reynolds, Bill. 2000. "Boston's Prodigal Son Returns." *Chicago Tribune*, September 10.

Sakamoto, Bob. 1986. "Banks' Attitude Spurs Bulls." *Chicago Tribune*, March 13.

———. 1987a. "40-Victory Season Just 'Incredible' for the Bulls." *Chicago Tribune*, April 19.

———. 1987b. "Bulls Have Backs Against Cozy Walls." *Chicago Tribune*, April 28.

Scarborough Research. 2012. "Methodology." *Nielsen Media Research*. Accessed May 3,

2015. http://en-us.nielsen.com/sitelets/cls/documents/scarborough/Scarborough
-Methodology-2012.pdf.

Schulman, Bruce. 2001. *The Seventies: The Great Shift in American Culture, Politics
and Society*. Cambridge, Mass.: Da Capo Press.

Sherman, Ed. 1999. "City Mourns Its 1st Best Ever." *Chicago Tribune*, November 7.

Sirota, David. 2011. *Back to Our Future: How the 1980s Explain the World We Live
in Now*. New York: Ballantine Books.

Smith, Sam. 1995. "Bulls Forced to Go On the Offensive." *Chicago Tribune*, January 3.

———. 2004. "Fearless Hinrich Plays Like Sloan Clone." *Chicago Tribune*, February 14.

Staudohar, Paul. 1998. "Salary Caps in Profession Team Sports." *Compensation and
Working Conditions* (Spring): 3–11.

Tankersly, Jim. 2013. "As Manufacturing Bounces Back from Recession, Unions Are
Left Behind." *Washington Post*, January 16.

Thompson, Derek. 2013. "Mad About the Cost of TV? Blame Sports: Television
Economics Are Sports Economics, and Sports Economics Are Television Economics." *The Atlantic*, April 2. Accessed August 14, 2014. http://www.theatlantic
.com/business/archive/2013/04/mad-about-the-cost-of-tv-blame-sports/274575/.

US2010 Project. 2012. Longitudinal Tract Data Base. LTDB Downloads. Accessed
May 26, 2015. http://www.s4.brown.edu/us2010/Researcher/LTBDDload/DataList
.aspx.

U.S. Bureau of Labor Statistics. 2014. "Table 1101. Quintiles of Income before Taxes:
Average Annual Expenditures and Characteristics." 2012 Consumer Expenditure
Survey Prepublication Tables. Data tables provided to Sean Dinces via e-mail by
Aaron Cobet, Bureau of Labor Statistics.

———. n.d.a. "CPI Inflation Calculator." Databases, Tables & Calculators by Subject.
Accessed May 2, 2015 from http://www.bls.gov/data/inflation_calculator.htm.

———. n.d.b. "Series ID CUUR0000SA0,CUUS0000SA0." Databases, Tables & Calculators by Subject: Prices. Accessed May 1, 2015. http://www.bls.gov/data/#prices.

———. n.d.c. "Series ID SMU17169743000000008." Databases, Tables & Calculators by Subject: Employment. Accessed May 1, 2015. http://www.bls.gov/data
/#employment.

U.S. Census Bureau. 1956, 1994. *County and City Data Book*. Washington, D.C.:
Government Printing Office.

———. 1988. *Money Income of Households, Families, and Persons in the United States:
1986*. Washington, D.C.: Government Printing Office.

———. n.d.a. "Longitudinal-Employer Household Dynamics Program." Accessed
May 1, 2015. http://onthemap.ces.census.gov/.

———. n.d.b. *QuickFacts: Chicago City, Illinois*. Accessed March 30, 2016. http://
www.census.gov/quickfacts/table/PST045215/1714000.

Vancil, Mark. 2013. "MJ at 50: Focused on the Moment." *Southtown Star*, February 17.

Verdi, Bob. 1977a. "Sox Are Flip over High Altitude." *Chicago Tribune*, July 25.

———. 1977b. "Sox Feed Royals to the Lions." *Chicago Tribune*, July 30.

———. 1978. "Night After Night, Marks Does a Vital, Glamorless Job." *Chicago Tribune*, November 7.

———. 1992. "Bears' Waddle: Blue Collar Still Fits." *Chicago Tribune*, August 4.

Zara, Christopher. 2014. "Cable Bills Rising: Amid Comcast-TWC Merger Scrutiny, FCC Media Bureau Report Shows Pay-TV Price Hikes Outpacing Inflation." *International Business Times*, May 20. Accessed May 30, 2015. http://www.ibtimes.com/cable-bills-rising-amid-comcast-twc-merger-scrutiny-fcc-media-bureau-report-shows-pay-tv-1587304.

PART III

NEOLIBERAL SPACES

Neoliberal Chicago is most evidently a city of new spaces: neighborhoods, public venues such as parks and transit facilities, and individual buildings. In their contributions to *Neoliberal Chicago*, Carrie Breitbach, Alex Papadopoulos, and Yue Zhang examine three characteristically neoliberal spaces. Breitbach's study of the far South Side Lakeside development contrasts the old—sprawling steel mill complexes and adjoining working-class residential areas—and a projected new—lakefront commercial and recreational facilities and upscale residential communities. Two uncertainties have shadowed the Lakeside project. In the first instance, will the memory of the old Southeast Side, an iconic part of "smokestack Chicago," be entirely effaced? And second, could the almost preposterously ambitious Lakeside scheme—encompassing many hundreds of acres located miles from the remainder of upscale Chicago, and in a city that has not especially prospered in the wake of the 2008 economic crash—ever be realized? In the short run, the latter uncertainty seems to have been resolved: in early 2016 the development partnership advancing the Lakeside plan collapsed.

Alex Papadopoulos's account of the formation of "Boystown" represents a long arc neighborhood history that, over the last quarter-century, has paralleled the emergence of neoliberal Chicago. While as social scientists we rarely use terms such as poignance to characterize events or trends, there is an undercurrent of poignance to Papadopoulos's neighborhood "morphology." Just as Chicago gays established a welcoming space on the city's North Side, the very success of that effort generated a wave of new investment that has both upscaled local real estate and diluted its character as a gay-friendly neighborhood.

Yue Zhang's retrospective analysis of the events leading to the preservation of the Medinah Temple and Tree Studios complex focuses on a complicated planning challenge. Is historic preservation merely a matter of saving physical structures or is it a broader project to preserve meaningful components of a city's social and physical heritage? In the case of the Medinah Temple/Tree Studios block, the much more limited aim of physical preservation was achieved. Zhang's view is that neoliberalism characteristically privileges physical revitalization centered on fiscal return over more place-sensitive strategies that highlight and extend a city's social and cultural heritage.

CHAPTER 6

Remaking Chicago's Industrial Spaces

CARRIE BREITBACH

If the dreams of a prominent Chicago developer come to fruition, the former U.S. South Works complex—which has been described as "once . . . the industrial anchor of Chicago's Southeast Side, a steelmaking complex with a dozen product mills spread over 650 lakefront acres" (Goozner 1991a)—will be transformed in a way that would have been unimaginable to its once-huge work force. The project is not simply a matter of land use conversion, as advocates of the proposed Lakeside development anticipate that it "will not only redevelop and re-purpose a former steel mill but it will also rebuild the entire southeast lakefront and offer a new way for people to live, work, shop and play" (PR Newswire 2012).

The deindustrialization of key sites of the Fordist economy, such as Chicago's steelmaking region, is a pivotal indicator of the neoliberal turn. While the narrative of deindustrialization has been told in numerous accounts (see Bensman and Lynch 1987; Bluestone and Harrison 1982), the story of what comes next for the landscapes of former industrial spaces is still being told. The remaking of former industrial landscapes, like deindustrialization itself, is always place specific and a product of struggle and negotiation. The transformation of about 600 acres of lakefront land in southeast Chicago that extends from U.S. Steel's South Works plant to Lakeside is so far more rhetoric than reality. Despite the incomplete physical redevelopment of a site that was once Chicago's largest employer (Maclean 1992) into a "new, dynamic and diverse community" (McCaffery Interests n.d.), there is much to learn from this piece of land about industrial redevelopment in Chicago and about the city itself. What the ongoing narrative of the redevelopment of South Works suggests most strongly is the way a neoliberal vision of the city—the "new way" as proposed above—has risen to dominance over the past two decades, making any alternative ideas about the way this land should be redeveloped increasingly unfeasible. The shifting plans for remaking the South Works site reflect the solidification of neoliberalism into a seemingly inevitable doctrine dictating the form of the city. Today it is no surprise that in a place where steel manufacturing created an anchor not just for Chicago's Southeast Side but also for the city and country as a whole, the proposed Lakeside redevelopment has no place for industrial production or, quite likely, for the city's current working class. The characteristics of new places "for people to live, work, shop and play" are both ubiquitous and expected. And yet this vision of what the city can and should be like has taken hold only in the two decades since the last South Works steel plant closed in 1992. Further-more, neither its inevitability nor its desirability are, in reality, complete. In this chapter I seek to dissect the trajectory of the rise of neoliberalism in Chicago by recounting the story of redevelopment efforts at South Works. My goal is to describe space and opportunity for alternatives, showing the city as indeed a continuing work in progress rather than a foregone conclusion.[1]

Lakeside's Future Vision

On a sunny day in August 2013, a line of people stood outside the Lakeside Chicago Marketing Center waiting to board a tour bus. A crowd of perhaps a hundred people had turned up to see what was behind the high concrete wall dividing the old South Works property from the community surrounding it. Some of those people were old enough to know what once took place at the South Works site or were even former steelworkers, but there was also a large group of high school students among the visitors who could never have seen the much longer lines of people who once streamed in to work at that site. Every fiscal quarter, McCaffery Interests, a co-developer of the site with property owner United States Steel Real Estate, invites the public to tour the emerging Lakeside development.[2] As evidenced by the crowd, which we were told was expanding with each tour offered, the public is eager to see what is happening at the old South Works site.

The marketing center is at 86th Street and Green Bay Avenue, about twelve miles south of Chicago's Loop, in a building dating from 1917 that once housed the credit union of U.S. Steel South Works. McCaffery has remodeled the build-ing into a U.S. Green Building Council certified (LEED silver) office that show-cases the company's plans for the site, which are projected to take around forty years to complete. A three-dimensional model of the planned development is prominent as one enters the office and aerial photos line the floor along the walls, showing off the bright blue water of Lake Michigan that edges the property.

The marketing office where tour seekers gather also features local art, locally made cookies (as we were told), and a small bookshelf of academic literature on southeast Chicago. A few aesthetically charming relics from South Works' industrial past decorate the office: a giant maintenance log book, a South Works clock, and an 1881 (rebuilt in 1900) cornerstone cement block outside. The center and its surrounding gardens are beautifully landscaped, and information on the building's environmental merits abounds on signs throughout the building and garden: for example, "92% of stormwater recharged back into Lake Michigan."

Throughout the tour of the proposed Lakeside, project manager Nasutsa Mabwa repeatedly stressed McCaffery's interest in involving the local community in the new development beyond incorporating local cookies and art. In a question-and-answer session, some tour goers asked about the jobs that might be available to them at Lakeside. In response, Mabwa stressed that McCaffery made every effort to hire locally for construction. She said that the "door is always open" and that the "whole purpose was to bring community in and through the site," especially to access the lake shore that had been cut off from public access for more than a century. She urged residents to talk about Lakeside with others, stressing that the project would be more successful as more people know about it and support it. As evidence of the developers' commitment and enthusiasm, we were told that all the McCaffery representatives that were there to show us around were volunteering their time that day. Banners hanging on the fence surrounding the marketing center reinforced the message McCaffery was advertising. "Lakeside: Committed," one declared, with a picture of a bulldozer. The message conveyed through the tours and McCaffery's media output was that visitors and investors are encouraged to trust McCaffery's vision, good will, and ability to be the ones that will finally make good on this unique, if challenging, property.

The proposed Lakeside Development covers an area more than twice as large as Chicago's Loop. The plan includes 15,000 residential units, more than 17 million square feet of restaurants and retail, commercial, institutional, and research facilities; a 1,500 slip marina; and a new high school. The 3-D model in the Marketing Center features flagged "Live/work residences" next to a "Technology Park," a "Medical Research Park," and a "BioMedical Park" and windmills extending into Lake Michigan. All this creates an image of the "new way" of life being proposed at Lakeside, which was perhaps most succinctly summed up in an online promotional video provided on McCaffery's website and on YouTube and other sites titled "Imagine: Chicago Lakeside Development" (Chicago Lakeside Development 2013). In the video, Clayton McCaffery described Lakeside as "nearly utopian. You can be walking distance to the park, walking distance to your boat, a ten-minute drive to downtown, and walking distance to all of your shopping and daily needs" (viewed on http://chicagolakesidedevelopment

.com/videos, September 17, 2013). In McCaffery's words, what is being planned at South Works is "a global initiative for innovative living," "a home to progressive thinkers and doers," and "a catalyst for a 'New Chicago.'" The utopian vision of life at Lakeside is part of a grander idea of "the good life," both in Chicago and globally, that weds "clean and green" urban living with high paid jobs in flourishing sectors of the economy. This vision gained global recognition when Lakeside was awarded the 2012 Sustainia Community Award for innovation in sustainable city planning, presented by Arnold Schwarzenegger in Copenhagen. When Chicago Lakeside was named to the "Sustainia 100" list, which was announced at the Rio + 20 UN conference in Brazil, the plan was heralded as "provid[ing] a new way of living based on 21st century infrastructure and technologies." In Brazil and Denmark, Chicago Lakeside is seen as "a transformative model for U.S. city planning and could upend the traditional thinking of how people live and work in Chicago and across the U.S." (PR Newswire 2012; Skidmore Owings & Merrill 2012). In Chicago, the reality of Lakeside is more complex.

The beautifully designed Marketing Center and the tiny version of "utopian" Lakeside that it presents are all the more remarkable because of their surroundings. Since the last plant at South Works closed in 1992, the site has been separated from the communities known as the Bush and South Chicago by a concrete wall that is now crumbling and marked with graffiti. Not surprisingly, the adjoining neighborhoods have visibly declined as people have left the area and as buildings have been vacated. The South Chicago Community Area, which surrounds the South Works site, had lost nearly 33 percent of its 1980 population by the 2010 U.S. Census (a loss of 15,224 people). In the period 2007–2011, approximately 31 percent of the population of the community area was living below the federal poverty line, compared to about 21 percent for the city of Chicago as a whole (Clary 2013). Brandon Avenue, which fronts the site, is lined with vacant lots and boarded-up buildings. Many of the buildings that once housed U.S. Steelworkers are in poor repair, and many of the businesses that once catered to steelworkers and their families are closed. The site itself is currently a dusty, weedy expanse, covered with cottonwood and sumac trees that have grown tall in the two decades since the many buildings and the internal rail lines of the U.S. Steel complex were removed. The ground is composed of slag, a waste by-product of the steel-making process that was dumped into the lake beginning in the late nineteenth century. Within the slag, extending down to fifty feet below the surface, are foundations of the many buildings that U.S. Steel built at South Works. The only visible features that remain from the site's industrial past are two long, massive concrete ore walls, which line the slip of lake water cutting into the site and were once used to hold deliveries of iron ore. In McCaffery's vision of Lakeside, these ore walls will be artistically reworked into the new landscape, providing the same kind of aesthetic interest that the old U.S. Steel clock contributes to the Marketing Center.

As of the summer of 2013, work on the site had been largely limited to four projects. First, in April 2004, a joint state of Illinois and federal government project called Mud to Parks sponsored a delivery of 232,000 tons of sediment dredged from the Illinois River near Peoria to the South Works site in order to begin creating soil on the slag foundation. Nearly four years later, the Chicago Park District created the somewhat odd Park Number 523, located along the lakefront around 87th Street. Renamed Steelworkers Park in 2014 and wholly funded by $676,000 drawn from the South Works industrial tax increment financing (TIF) district, the park is landscaped in native plants with benches and paths, all lit by functioning street lights. The Chicago Park District website announces it is open from 6 a.m. to 11 p.m. (Chicago Park District 2014). The park is odd because, as we were informed by McCaffery's spokesperson on our 2013 tour, it is located on land within the former South Works site that was given to the park district by U.S. Steel but that was cut off from public roads so that the public could not actually go there. A more accessible, though also incomplete facility located on the South Works site is the Chicago Velo Campus, a project initiated by a bicycling enthusiast who is hoping to raise significant funds to build a stadium-sized indoor velodrome, a steeply banked arena for track cycling. Founder Emanuele Bianchi imagines the Chicago Velo Campus as a major national cycling center that would also integrate programs to train local youth in bicycle maintenance and riding. A temporary velodrome was constructed in the summer of 2011 on the former South Works parking lot at South Burley Avenue and 87th Street. The last major project is a rerouting of U.S. Highway 41, which is Lake Shore Drive to the north and has been renamed, at McCaffery's insistence, South Lake Shore Drive instead of Avenue O, as the prior street grid would predict. The eastward relocation of U.S. Highway 41 connects the former South Works site to the city, making the temporally utopian "ten-minute drive to downtown" possible. The project has been planned since at least 1999, but it was not begun until April 2012, as part of Building a New Chicago, a $7 billion, three-year infrastructure co-project of the city and the state. In October 2013, the South Lake Shore Drive extension opened, making Park No. 523 accessible to the public. The opening of South Lake Shore Drive was marked with a 5K run and a cycling race at an event attended by city and state elected officials and developer Dan McCaffery—and by a small group of "protesters . . . chanting 'Jobs, not condos'" (Ali 2013).

The contrast between this reality—a massive empty site with a hodgepodge of seemingly uncoordinated projects surrounded by struggling neighborhoods—and the future world of shoppers, boaters, and "progressive thinkers and do-ers" that McCaffery projects through its models and imagery in the gleaming Marketing Center, is stark. Nonetheless, the "utopian" development is alluring, especially for former workers and community residents who have been faced with what is essentially a hole in their neighborhood for over twenty years and for the teenagers whose only vision of the steel industry is the mess it left behind. After our bus tour, I chatted with a woman who was also on the tour as we stood waiting for the restroom, next to a giant projection of the future Lakeside in the Marketing Center. Lakeside was in equal parts impressive and hard to believe, she said, but still she thought that the potential of the development might persuade her husband to stay in the area instead of getting out, as he had been wanting to do for so long. This woman wanted to be a part of that new way of life being advertised at Lakeside. Its utopian imagery was indeed appealing, and in McCaffery's presentation Lakeside was feasible enough to generate some hope. But exactly who and what is this redevelopment for, and what else could it be?

Building Southeast Chicago

To answer these questions, it is useful to examine the history of the site and its role in the community and the city. Steelmaking began near the current site in 1857, and by 1889 the Illinois Steel Company had built the first plant at the South Works site. In 1901, U.S. Steel incorporated and took over the Illinois Steel Company. In the years leading up to its productive and employment peak during World War II, U.S. Steel followed the path of many steel companies by fighting with its workers over pay, hours, and union representation. In 1937, U.S. Steel agreed to recognize the Steel Workers Organizing Committee, ushering in an era of unionization at the company. Gradually, wages and conditions at the plant improved in Southeast Chicago, as they did across the U.S. manufacturing belt, allowing steelworker communities to thrive. While recognizing that employment at a steel plant was difficult and dangerous, many accounts of the mill communities of Southeast Chicago note the stability that relatively well-paid and secure union jobs brought to the region. In her account of her own family's roots in Southeast Chicago, anthropologist Christine Walley (2013, 55) argues that the steel industry's postwar success allowed the immigrants and native poor who sought work in the mills to achieve "stable, almost middle-class prosperity."

This middle-class prosperity was made manifest in the neighborhoods themselves, as a great majority of the workers at South Works and the other nearby mills lived close to work in Southeast neighborhoods such as the Bush, South Chicago, or East Side. In their photo book of Chicago's Southeast Side, Rod Sellers and Dominic Pacyga (1998, 27) note that "the major banks, theaters, restaurants, and stores that served Southeast Chicago were all located here." They show images of the bustling streets, transportation points, and entertainment venues that thrived on the wages of steelworkers. In the *Chicago Tribune* eulogies for the plant, a former South Works employee recalled that "on paydays in the '60s the bars outside the gates had $60,000 to $70,000 to cash paychecks"

(Maclean 1992a). Steelworker families were the lifeblood of local churches, ethnic community centers, and political organizations, and the plants supported various sports teams, charity groups, and even music clubs (Sellers and Pacyga 1998). "At one time South Works supported a softball league with 63 teams, a bowling league with 90 teams and a golf league with 54 foursomes," noted *Chicago Tribune* reporter John Maclean as he chronicled the plant's closing in 1992 (Maclean 1992a). While the jobs were still dangerous and the pollution significant, South Works and the other steel plants in the area supported Southeast Chicago's working-class population in a functional community both financially and socially:

> The intense personal bonds of trust forged in the workplace provided the basis for a host of local institutions—ethnic clubs, church groups, and political associations. This dense web of interconnections has made Southeast Chicago the kind of community that people cling to, despite its antiquated streets and sewers, despite the pollution and the grime. (Bensman and Lynch 1987, 21–22)

This period was short lived, however. By the end of the 1970s, U.S. Steel had stopped investing in South Works. In the 1970s, facilities such as an alloy bar mill (1975) and a foundry (1978) were closed, and by 1980, with the closure of a blast furnace, employment was down to about 3,500 people. Maclean reports that these disinvestments reshaped Southeast Chicago: "The neighborhood began to change, commercially and racially. Stores along 79th Street and Commercial Avenue were shuttered. Quality specialty stores vanished" (Maclean 1992a). In the early 1980s, a proposal by U.S. Steel to build a new rail mill at South Works brought hope for renewal to the community. After the company was awarded concessions from both the city and the union, though, it withdrew the rail mill plan when the United Steelworkers refused further concessions that would have allowed half of the work force at South Works to be non-union. Employment was down to about 800 people by 1983. U.S. Steel claimed that foreign competition, new technologies, and non-union mini-mills were cutting into its profits. It shifted steel investment to its Gary Works plant, across the state border in Indiana (Bensman 1983). By 1986, U.S. Steel had diversified into oil and other industries and had become USX, a company that no longer was weighed down by the "industrial anchor" of places such as South Works.

Closure of South Works

Recognizing that USX had "no interest in running that plant," South Works' remaining employees began research into technologies and financial plans that might save their jobs and allow the foundation of their community to survive (Goozner 1991a). They found that modernization would cost $200 million, and

650 union employees began setting aside 50 cents an hour from their paychecks to fund a possible employee buyout. Explaining the workers' efforts, despite the apparent futility, Steelworkers Local 65 president Willie Ross said that he "believes it is important to keep good-paying steel jobs on the Southeast Side. 'Come down here and look at the devastation,' he said. 'If you lived down here, you'd want to see it stay open and keep jobs around, too'" (Goozner 1991b). Though the final tab for modernization was lowered to between $100 and $140 million, in November 1991 the union announced that it could not raise sufficient funds, and the buyout plan was scrapped.

Community organizations had already begun to consider options for the next life of the South Works site, even before U.S. Steel announced the final closure of the plant. Representatives of the United Neighborhood Organization (UNO), a prominent voice for Chicago's Latino populations, and the Southeast Chicago Development Commission, were quoted in the *Chicago Tribune* as thinking ahead for the site: "I don't think the plant has a future as a steelmaking facility. . . . but perhaps as something else [said Lynne Cunningham of the Southeast Chicago Development Commission]. . . . No matter what happens, we as a community want to be involved [added Maria Elena Montes of UNO]" (Yates 1991). The earliest ideas centered on contemporaneous proposals for locating a third Chicago airport in the Calumet region. Perhaps the South Works site could be built up to support that, speculated some residents. However, as plans for the airport met with strong opposition from environmental and other local groups, new ideas for South Works were needed.

In January 1992, USX announced it would close the final facilities at South Works in April of that year. Though the years of disinvestment in steel had changed the composition of the neighborhood, as the plant finally closed, Southeast Chicago was still organized and outspoken on behalf of the place that was its "anchor." Of primary concern was the need for jobs: "Us older guys will be okay," a 53-year-old resident was quoted as saying, "But there won't be jobs for the young ones" (Hanna 1992). But many community members and organizations were also looking for an opportunity to address the environmental legacy of Southeast Chicago's industrial foundation and to remake their part of the city with some of the assets found in other neighborhoods. UNO, for example, argued for "a string of beaches and parks similar to those on the city's North Side" (Oloroso 1992).

In the months following the plant's closure, plans for South Works' future seemed to be moving quickly. In January 1993, Southeast Chicago was in competition with locations in Texas and Pennsylvania to be the site of a stainless steel mini-mill, and the City of Chicago had "offered tax abatements and other financial inducements" (Lashinsky 1993a). The plan fell through, though, as the stainless steel company failed to raise necessary venture capital to move forward.

Residents who were greatly in need of the proposed 400 to 500 jobs the plant had offered were especially disappointed.

Even as the final plant at South Works closed, U.S. Steel Group was announcing its own plans to commission a private study to determine the best use of its 585-acre property. A U.S. Steel spokesperson expressed the company's view: "We want to get value from the facilities. . . . The mill is one direction. Real estate and development is another direction" (Maclean 1992b). Less than a year after the stainless steel plan dissolved, USX announced the results of its study, which included three proposals combining residential, commercial, and industrial uses and a plan for a "gambling riverboat-anchored theme park" (Lashinsky 1993b). In any of its iterations, the redevelopment would be "the biggest development project in the city of Chicago since the World's Fair of 1933," according to local 10th Ward Alderman John J. Buchanan (Lashinsky 1993b).

Community organizations, which had not been a part of the planning, reacted to USX's announcements with displeasure. Despite the identification of several local community groups in the heavy media coverage of South Works' closure, the company seemed to not realize that these groups were a necessary part of the redevelopment project. As a USX spokesperson acknowledged, "We haven't had a lot of meetings with community groups" (Elstrom 1994). UNO's director argued, "That land is privately held, but it holds a tremendous public interest. . . . The community wants to be at the table." Concerns from residents centered on fears of being cut off from the redevelopment by new roads or isolated from public transit stations. People also wondered whether the environmental problems of the site would be truly remediated. UNO's spokesperson asked, "Are we going to have a highway over our heads?," no doubt referring to the Chicago Skyway that was controversially built over the communities of South Chicago and the East Side in the late 1950s. Community members were keenly aware of the danger of a new development that would require Southeast Chicago to bear the costs of benefits delivered outside the community. The city of Chicago did not want to alienate Southeast residents, despite its support for the USX plans, and these factors further stalled the redevelopment of South Works.

Redevelopment Delayed

"For seven years now, Chicago's last, largest stretch of developable lakefront property has lain dormant behind a fence of chain link, mute testimony to a lack of civic imagination and the lassitude of absentee corporate ownership" (*Chicago Tribune* 1998). So editorialized the *Chicago Tribune* in January 1998, as the former South Works site, priced at $85 million, was languishing on the market. The problems causing the lack of redevelopment, according to the *Tribune*'s editors, were USX's reluctance to foot the bill, a lack of initiative within the administration of Chicago mayor Richard M. Daley, and attributes of the site itself, including the unappealing "dowdy, working-class neighborhood" that surrounded it. Though likely not goaded into action by the *Tribune*'s comments, the city's Department of Planning did increase its activities on behalf of South Works in 1998, when it both contracted with consultants and held workshops with community members "to gauge their expectations" (Crown 1998). The city published a document in April 1998 called "South Works: A Community Vision for Future Development" that summarized the input of various residents and groups gathered through workshops. What community members wanted was "a lakefront park, a tranquil neighborhood and a job-producing industrial park" consisting of non-polluting industries (Martin 1998). These would be the assets that would allow the people who lived there to stay in their neighborhoods and improve their quality of life.

While USX's listing of the property for sale signaled its own disinterest in funding redevelopment of the South Works property, the company did complete a $10 million environmental remediation project that earned the site a "No Further Remediation" letter from the Illinois EPA and cleared the way for residential, not just industrial use. USX's next step was to appoint a development management consultant, the Chicago firm Walsh, Higgins & Company, to "work with city officials who have an understandable interest in what becomes of the parcel." Walsh, Higgins & Company's principals were "staunch Daley allies and fundraisers," and the company was reported to be well connected to other Chicago developers (Gaines 1998). Since it did not have offers to buy the property for the $85 million it was asking, USX seemed resigned to the need for help from the city administration and its allies.

The city released its proposal for the South Works site in September 1998, beginning with a symbolic show of allegiance by unveiling the plan to Southeast Chicago residents first. The plan recommended a first phase that would include a mixed-use development of park space, residential housing, and an industrial park at the south end of the property. Overall, the plan closely mirrored the vision put forth in the community-generated "Vision for Future Development," and it specified that it would remain flexible to changing market conditions. While perhaps amenable to many residents living near the site, the plan received a less favorable reaction from *Chicago Tribune* architectural critic Blair Kamin, whose long opinion piece epitomized a shift in predominant ideology about the nature of local redevelopment. Kamin's primary argument was that the city's plan was not bold enough. He described the South Works site as "a vast canvas on which to paint a masterly vision of public space" that would help establish Chicago as a "global cultural city" and would "capitalize on a new trend in leisure time" (Kamin 1998). Praising the transformation of Bilbao, Spain, epitomized by the Frank Gehry–designed Guggenheim Museum, Kamin argued that "cities can create wealth by importing tourists as well as exporting widgets." In Kamin's vision, industry was part of a past age that had been replaced by "the Information Age." Kamin recognized the significance of the industrial anchor that had built Southeast Chicago, especially the importance of organized labor, and he argued that the cultural attractions in the region should reflect the history of steel. Kamin spoke favorably of a proposal for a National Heritage Area that had been advanced by Illinois Congressman Jerry Weller. Instead of providing employment through new facilities, in Kamin's vision the role of manufacturing should be to provide an "industrial flavor" to new developments catering to culture seekers and tourists (Kamin 1998).

While certainly reflecting a widespread shift in thinking about what cities are and should be (and the place of manufacturing in a global city; for a critique, see Curran and Hanson 2005), Kamin's view was not the guiding principle behind South Works redevelopment efforts. USX had not yet abandoned efforts to profit on some of the industrial capital it still had sunk at South Works, and in December 1998 the company was considering the possibility of becoming an independent power producer by converting the natural gas power plant that remained on the property to a coal-fired generator (Arndt 1998). This scenario did not come to fruition. While in the short term the power plant continued to produce energy that was used at USX's Gary Works facility, it was eventually razed, clearing the way for new land use.

In early 1999, the city released a more detailed redevelopment plan that would "bring new life to Chicago's Southeast Side," specifying the cost of needed infrastructure improvements as $200 million "to be raised from state, federal and local sources" (Washburn 1999). City planners announced that they would seek city council approval for a tax increment finance (TIF) district to fund development, both for the South Works site and the surrounding South Chicago community. With this announcement, two prospective plans were released. One version included an industrial-commercial park on the south portion of the parcel, as had long been planned. This iteration of the plan also included a recreational marina at the slip that once brought raw materials to the steel plant and, surrounding the marina, an expanded area of loft housing, shops, and arts and cultural facilities. This first version brought praise from the *Tribune*'s Blair Kamin, who declared that "culture can correct the imbalance between the lakefront's overwhelmed North Side and its underachieving South Side" (Kamin 1999). In the second version of the plan, the industrial park expanded north of the slip, the marina was excluded, and an office park and small residential area filled the remaining space.

Speaking for local community opinion on the plans, Southeast Chicago Development Commission president Lynne Cunningham said, "I think the city is on target with how they are reading the community's hopes for the site. . . .

Whenever you talk to people here, they say, 'We need more jobs.'" Despite her endorsement of the city's efforts, Cunningham added that "we believe the city needs to be aggressive in forcing something to happen," expressing a fairly widespread opinion that the city of Chicago should purchase all or some of the land to dilute the corporate interest of U.S. Steel's real estate group. However, the *Chicago Tribune* reported that Mayor Richard M. Daley "steadfastly has rejected that approach as too costly," instead preferring to use funding mechanisms such as TIFs. City Planning Commissioner Christopher Hill was quoted as saying that "market demand will be the primary factor shaping ultimate land use" (Washburn 1999).

After eight years of shifting plans and little action that was no doubt extremely frustrating to the people living next to the weedy ruins of their former industrial anchor, in June 1999 an announcement brought real hope to residents of Southeast Chicago. Solo Cup Company, a locally based manufacturer of disposable products, had agreed to "purchase and develop a big chunk of the acreage" of South Works (Gaines 1999). The deal happened because Solo Cup was threatening to move its two Chicago operations to a new site in Indiana. To prevent the loss, the state of Illinois and the city of Chicago agreed to cooperate on a package of benefits that would entice Solo Cup to stay in the state. State funds would be used for infrastructure improvements that would facilitate truck access to the site, and the city promised $15 million in TIF funds. USX was to get $6.5 million for 107 acres of its parcel, much less than the $85 million asking price for the entire lot, and Solo Cup projected it would be hiring 200 additional workers, plus construction jobs. The new facility would open in 2001. Mayor Daley saw the deal as ushering in "a new era for the people of South Chicago and the region, where new space, jobs and also mixed income housing will be enjoyed for generations to come" (Green 1999). With Solo Cup slated to be a new anchor, the planning process moved through the city's legislative processes. The South Works Industrial TIF was approved in November 1999 and, in conjunction with the Solo Cup deal, in February 2000 Mayor Daley announced the creation of the city's first all-residential TIF district in South Chicago, abutting the South Works site. The South Chicago TIF, which was officially designated in April 2000, would be used to finance repairs and upgrades for local residences, spurring the mayor's vision of "the South Chicago neighborhood . . . coming alive with new development and growth" (Strausberg 2000). This neighborhood vision clearly encompassed future industrial development tied to the deal with Solo Cup and the prospect that it would soon entice more manufacturers to come to the South Works site.

But it was not to be. In 2005, four years after the slated opening of its new facility, Solo Cup announced what many had already surmised in the absence of any construction activity: it would not be opening a new facility at the South

Box 6.1: Norfolk Southern and Englewood

In the early 2000s, Englewood residents noticed something unusual happening in their South Side Chicago neighborhood: buildings were being demolished. The community was no stranger to demolitions of wooden-frame and derelict buildings, but their sense was that a new class of property was being targeted, including corner stores and solid brick homes. Rumors were that a nearby community college needed a residential campus, that a homebuilder was redeveloping the neighborhood, or that the area was being cleared in anticipation of the city winning its Olympic bid.

In September 2011, the transportation company Norfolk Southern addressed the rumors with a public meeting that announced its proposed expansion into the neighborhood. Hundreds of families would be displaced and approximately eleven square blocks, including a small public housing project, would be razed in order to significantly enlarge the company's intermodal freight yard located just north of the neighborhood.

The expansion of the yard, which facilitates the movement of shipping containers between trucks and trains, was fueled by the dramatic expansion of intermodal shipping-container traffic over the last thirty years. Transportation companies have invested billions of dollars to meet this changing system. These investments have often been sited on the edge of urban centers in order to avoid the notorious delays caused by urban rail networks. In this case, Norfolk Southern is expanding its Chicago yards alongside publicly funded rail infrastructure projects designed to reduce rail traffic congestion in the city.

While no direct city funding is scheduled to support the project, Mayor Rahm Emanuel's administration supports the rail expansion and has urged the Chicago City Council and relevant administrative boards to support the project through the sale of city-owned lots, tax increment financing modifications, and other changes. To that end, one of the mayor's press releases on the expansion states that "in reinforcing Chicago's transportation infrastructure, this project will help local manufacturers, distributors, and other companies that depend on cost-effective and convenient options to ship and receive goods." Mayor Emanuel asserted in particular that this "means more efficiency for local businesses and more jobs for area residents."

As with other major resident relocation programs, including the recent elimination of nearly all of the city's high-rise public housing, concerns abound regarding the location of displaced residents. Norfolk Southern and, when relevant, the Chicago Housing Authority have provided moving assistance for neighborhood residents. Still, many residents worry about their reception in new neighborhoods and the evaporation of their previous support networks. No significant group has arisen to reduce the negative effects of displacement, although a local environmental coalition won some concessions to protect those who will remain in the shadow of the expanded yard.

Works site. The company had spent about $13 million in site preparation, but instead of breaking ground on a new plant it was focusing on its other locations and its recent acquisition of former competitor, Sweetheart Cup (Roeder and Newbart 2005). This was more than thirteen years after the closure of the last South Works plant, and it was the apparent end of plans for manufacturing at the site.

From Industrial Anchor to Cultural Venue

The next major event at the South Works property came in 2011, when the former steel mill site hosted a three-day Dave Matthews Band Caravan concert. For many, especially young Chicagoans, this was an opportunity for a first glimpse of the site that had been off limits to the public for nearly twenty years. While a great deal of debris had to be cleared to prepare for the concert, the site was appealing because, as a concert tour manager said, "There's plenty of room to work with," and "parking won't be a problem." Hosting the concert brought some temporary jobs to local residents, but 7th Ward Alderwoman Sandi Jackson and other political leaders hoped the larger effect would be to encourage outsiders to see the place in a new way. Steve Johnson of the *Chicago Tribune* summarized this view: "[They] don't think the concert alone will change things, but what it will do is mark the area on Chicago's map in vivid highlighter, maybe make people notice a location they hadn't before, maybe get them to think about moving into one of the nice new homes that are supposed to start going up next year" (Johnson 2011a). Concert planners (and McCaffery Interests) agreed with the idea of the event as a way to remake the image of the South Works site.

"The Dave Matthews Band is into greening and sustainability, and this was an opportunity to take an old steel mill and green the site," said concert planner Jerry Mickelson, who also referred to the site as a "hidden gem." The "greening" included hauling away "59 tons of debris . . . most of which was recycled" (Conner 2011). This effort certainly helped transform the property now called Lakeside, not South Works, into "literally a blank slate," as the parcel was referred to in articles in both the *Chicago Tribune* and *Sun-Times*. McCaffery Interests CEO Dan McCaffery described Lakeside as "a beautiful, beautiful piece of land . . . and what's great about it is just how absolutely virgin it is" (Johnson 2011a).

Concertgoers were mostly from outside the Chicago area, and evaluations following the concert suggested it was largely a success. There were some reports of transportation problems as concertgoers made their way home. One pair chronicled their "urban adventure" through the South Chicago neighborhood for the *Tribune*. They were escorted by the police for safety as they made their way to the El. Steve Johnson wrote, "You should have seen some of the looks we got" (Johnson 2011b). While Southeast Chicago's 10th Ward Alderman John Pope hoped for a booth at the festival that might remind concertgoers that "the site you're standing on once employed 20,000 people," the only evidence of the former identity of the place was in the name "South Works" that was given to one of the concert stages set up for bands (Johnson 2011b; Conner 2011).

From South Works to Lakeside

In the more than twenty years since South Works' closure, there have been many ideas about what this lakefront land should become. While Lakeside is certainly far from a built reality, it is the currently prevailing vision, and it is a significant transformation from its past. South Works was a place built by U.S. Steel, but through the organizing work of its employees and their families, it came to be a foundation for a vibrant working-class community. The earliest versions of redevelopment at the property included an industrial economic base to allow some kind of continuity for that working-class community, but this is not retained by Lakeside. The "live/work" jobs being promoted at Lakeside are not for the working class, nor are the homes with adjacent private boat slips. As a requirement of receiving TIF funding, the Lakeside development plan includes 20 percent of its housing units to be available at affordable prices. However, the definition of affordable housing, which is based on a percentage of the Chicago Metropolitan Area's median income, makes its actual cost well above what is affordable for a family earning close to South Chicago's median income of about $31,000.[3] This means that the opportunities for the working class in Lakeside are either as low-wage retail or service employees or as shoppers and public space users.

Just as members of the working class were able to use their wages and build on their social connections to develop Southeast Chicago as a livable working-class community, it is likely that the class of people who are able to move into the new Lakeside will leverage their incomes and connections to rebuild Southeast Chicago as a gentrified community. This, clearly, is the reason "No condos" protesters appeared at the opening of the South Lake Shore Drive extension and signs were put up that read "No Lakeside" and "No Displacement Zone" on boarded-up houses in the streets immediately outside the Lakeside Marketing center that I saw as I left the tour of the planned development. Lakeside's planners describe the future development as an "example . . . for how to best live and work within a vibrant walkable community that connects seamlessly to the South Side," but in reality the contrast between "utopian" Lakeside and the existing Southeast Side is so jarring that the only way for Lakeside to be seamlessly integrated is to remake the Southeast Side in Lakeside's image (Skidmore Owings & Merrill 2012).

Remaking this portion of Southeast Chicago from an industrial anchor into "a developer's tabula rasa dream," as the site was described in accounts of the Dave Matthews Caravan's visit, has been the work of two decades of neoliberal ideas and practices that have shifted the dynamics and landscapes of class in Chicago and elsewhere. Neoliberalism is, in short, "a class project" to restore the upper classes to power following the brief rise of working-class power made possible during the era of Fordism that, in effect, built Southeast Chicago (Harvey 2009). This project is "masked," according to geographer David Harvey, by rhetoric about individual freedom and the free market. In the case of Lakeside, the rhetoric that masks the class project is also about sustainability, "innovative living," and the inevitable demise of an industrial age. But the story of the transformation of South Works to Lakeside shows that the class project of neoliberalism is more complex than a simple power grab by a developer. McCaffery is not so apparently the representative of a class at war. Nonetheless, a series of changes in ideas about and policies toward urban development and a broader economic shift from industrial to real estate capital have negated the possibility of a meaningful working-class presence at South Works. The example of South Works shows how a confluence of city policies, ideological shifts, and a reorientation of capital play out in a particular landscape.

One clear place to see the neoliberal turn is in U.S. Steel. In addition to being a class project, neoliberalism is a movement to "free" capitalism from the geographical and regulatory strictures that threatened profit rates. This is just what U.S. Steel sought to do as it moved investment from plants such as South Works to Gary Works or away from steel altogether. Its transformation from industrial capitalist to real estate and conglomerate capitalist was the most immediate cause of South Works' closure. However, just as important was a change in city government in Chicago, which followed other major U.S. cities in turning away from support for manufacturing (and the people who relied on its wages) in favor of real estate and other tertiary economic sectors. In research profiling the rise and decline of the Chicago Association of Neighborhood Development Organizations (CANDO), a citywide coalition of local neighborhood groups working for economic development, Dan Immergluck (2005) argues that a key turning point for Chicago's manufacturing base was the start of Richard M. Daley's mayoral term in 1989: "Because of Daley's ties to industrial landowners who wanted to convert their property into residential developments, he was not viewed as an advocate for industrial retention policies." This meant that organizations such as those in Southeast Chicago that were seeking to retain or rebuild decimated manufacturing economies had a much less supportive partner in city government than they had under previous administrations. The power of CANDO further declined throughout the 1990s, as access to city-level funding and planning that had previously been within reach of community organizations was devolved to the ward level and therefore subject to aldermanic discretion. "At the same time," Immergluck (2005) argues, "improvements in the business services sector and the highly visible downtown gentrification made city officials less concerned about neighborhood economic development." The time period of this shift in the 1990s parallels the long hiatus in development at South Works. Immergluck asserts that an increasingly antagonistic relationship with the city and the ongoing decline of manufacturing jobs contributed to the fragmentation of many once-influential community organizations.

Though they may be fragmented, community organizations in Southeast Chicago are neither absent nor silent about the future of their neighborhoods. Peggy Salazar of the Southeast Environmental Task Force is one of many residents and activists who is skeptical about the notion that Lakeside will be a savior of the area. What is missing, according to Salazar, is a comprehensive plan to remake not just the property but also the community (interview with the author, July 2013). She wants to see businesses that are good neighbors in terms of both their environmental impact and their employment practices, and she wants government support for such businesses at all scales.

McCaffery's announcement of its withdrawal from the Lakeside Project in February 2016 (Gallun 2016), which it ascribed to U.S. Steel's inadequacy as a real estate developer, is yet another setback for residents such as Salazar. This latest failure of redevelopment at the former South Works also shows the deep challenges to a neoliberal model that relies solely on market demand and profitability to rebuild viable and vibrant neighborhoods and workplaces for people left behind by deindustrialization. Market demand and profitability are simply not reliable as a motivation or a source of funds for the kind of comprehensive plan that the people of Southeast Chicago need and deserve.

In a feature article for *Green Building & Design*, Timothy Schuler (2013) begins his discussion of the transformation from South Works to Lakeside with a vision of the future:

> In 2050 few Chicagoans remember the steel plant at Seventy-Ninth Street. Residents of Lakeside, the city's newest neighborhood built on the site of the old mill, ignore the placards in their apartment buildings, which state that for almost a century U.S. Steel's South Works plant produced the steel that became the backbone of their city. . . . Those whose families are from the Great Lakes states hear over and over that no one expected Chicago to become a global hub of clean energy development or Lakeside to become the economic driver the area lost when the steel mill was razed in the 1990s. They have trouble imagining why. To them, it is a given that the world's innovators migrate to Lakeside, to this peninsula bulging out into Lake Michigan, to the city built on last century's industrial waste.

If Lakeside is fully realized according to some version of Schuler's vision, it will indeed be a draw to "the world's innovators." But in order for the current population of underemployed former steelworkers and the people who moved to Southeast Chicago because of its affordability to have a place in the new Lakeside beyond employment as poorly paid service workers, these people and their children need opportunities built on more than increasing property values and new shopping options. What they demand, and have demanded for the last two decades, is genuine participation in planning the future of their community. There are many competing visions for the future of Southeast Chicago, and it is worth seeking out those of the city's working class so they do not become merely the subject of memorial placards or consigned to "last century's industrial waste."

Notes

1. Filmmaker David Granskog's *South Chicago: In Progress* documents the ongoing negotiations of the remaking of the South Works site.

2. In late February 2016, several Chicago media outlets announced that McCaffery had pulled out of the Lakeside project, stating that partner and landowner United States Steel was not in a position to be a real estate developer (Gallun 2016).

3. The Chicago Metropolitan Area median income for a household of four in 2012 was $73,600 (City of Chicago 2010–2014.)

Bibliography

Ali, Tanveer. 2013. "Lake Shore Drive Southern Extension Officially Opens." *DNAinfo Chicago*, October 26. Accessed November 12, 2013. http://sankofaonline.com /archives/11744.

Arndt, Michael. 1998. "U.S. Steel Plant May Add Muscle: Plan Considered to Increase South Works Electricity Output." *Chicago Tribune*, December 18.

Bensman, David. 1983. "Concessions at South Works: What Price a Rail Mill?" *Labor Research Review* 1, no. 2. Accessed December 4, 2013. http://digitalcommons.ilr.cornell.edu/lrr/vol1/iss2/6/.

Bensman, David, and Roberta Lynch. 1987. *Rusted Dreams: Hard Times in Steel Community*. Berkeley: University of California Press.

Bluestone, Barry, and Bennett Harrison. 1982. *The Deindustrialization of America*. New York: Basic.

Chicago Lakeside Development. 2013. "Imagine: Chicago Lakeside Development." Accessed September 17, 2013. http://chicagolakesidedevelopment.com/new-2013-chicago-lakeside-development-video.

Chicago Park District. 2014. "Steelworkers Park." Accessed February 27, 2016. http://www.chicagoparkdistrict.com/parks/steelworkers-park-/.

Chicago Tribune. 1998. "Get Going on South Works." *Chicago Tribune*, January 18.

City of Chicago. 2010–2014. "Area Median Income (AMI) Chart." Accessed December 4, 2013. http://www.cityofchicago.org/city/en/depts/dcd/supp_info/area_median_incomeamichart.html.

Clary, Jennifer. 2013. *Chicago Neighborhood Indicators, 2000–2011*. Chicago: Social Impact Research Center, Heartland Alliance. Accessed March 4, 2016. http://www.ilpovertyreport.org/sites/default/files/uploads/Chicago_Neighborhood_Indicators_00–11_130109.pdf.

Conner, Thomas. 2011. "Dave Matthews Band Caravan Rolls into South Works." *Chicago Sun-Times*, June 30.

Crown, Judith. 1998. "City Studies Options for South Works." *Crain's Chicago Business,* April 27.

Curran, Winifred, and Susan Hanson. 2005. "Getting Globalized: Urban Policy and Industrial Displacement in Williamsburg, Brooklyn." *Urban Geography* 26, no. 6: 461–482.

Elstrom, Peter J.W. 1994. "South Works Plan Stalls: Locals Want More Say in Redevelopment." *Crain's Chicago Business*, September 5.

Gaines, Sallie L. 1998. "USX Open to Ideas on Former Mill Site: Developer to Advise on Options for South Works." *Chicago Tribune*, August 26.

———. 1999. "South Works Deal Got Heavy Help: Tax Increment Financing and Infrastructure Improvements May Strengthen the Price Foundation for the Remainder of the vast USX Site." *Chicago Tribune*, June 11.

Gallun, Alby. 2016. "South Works Redo Melts Down as Partners Split." *Crain's Chicago Business*, February 29.

Goozner, Merrill. 1991a. "Last Chance for a Rusty South Works." *Chicago Tribune*, February 5.

———. 1991b. "South Works Buyout Effort a Bold Gamble." *Chicago Tribune*, May 5.

Green, Hurley. 1999. "Kick-Off New South Works Development Project." *Chicago Independent Bulletin*, June 17.

Hanna, Janan. 1992. "South Works Eulogies Have Family Themes." *Chicago Tribune*, January 10.

Harvey, David. 2009. "Is This Really the End of Neoliberalism?" *Counterpunch*, March

13–15. Accessed December 6, 2013. http://www.counterpunch.org/2009/03/13/is-this-really-the-end-of-neoliberalism/.

Immergluck, Dan. 2005. "The Power of a Community-Based Development Coalition: Lessons from the Demise of the Chicago Association of Neighborhood Development Organizations." *National Housing Institute Shelterforce Online* 141 (May–June). Accessed December 6, 2013. http://www.shelterforce.com/online/issues/141/CANDO.html.

Johnson, Steve. 2011a. "Field of Dreams." *Chicago Tribune*, June 29.

———. 2011b. "Smooth Music, Rocky Environs at Caravan." *Chicago Tribune*, July 11.

Kamin, Blair. 1998. "A Landmark of Labor." *Chicago Tribune*, November 2.

———. 1999. "South Works Heading in New Direction." *Chicago Tribune*, February 15.

Lashinsky, Adam. 1993a. "S. Works Bidder Surfaces: Group Eyes Stainless Venture." *Crain's Chicago Business*, January 4.

———. 1993b. "New Plan to Reforge S. Works." *Crain's Chicago Business*, November 1.

Maclean, John. 1992a. "A Mighty Engine Expires: An Industrial Epoch Passes with South Works Demise." *Chicago Tribune*, January 10.

———. 1992b. "Study to Examine Options for South Works' Next Life." *Chicago Tribune*, April 10.

Martin, Andrew. 1998. "South Works Neighbors Have Big Hopes." *Chicago Tribune*, April 24.

McCaffery Interests. n.d. "Lakeside." Promotional flyer in author's possession.

Oloroso, Arsenio. 1992. "South Works after Steel." *Chicago Tribune*, January 27.

PR Newswire. 2012. "Chicago Lakeside Shortlisted for the Sustainia Award." September 24. Accessed December 6, 2013. http://www.prnewswire.com/news-releases/chicago-lakeside-shortlisted-for-the-sustainia-award-170989861.html.

Roeder, David, and David Newbart. 2005. "Solo Cup Drops Plans for South Side Plant." *Chicago Sun-Times*, June 14.

Schuler, Timothy A. 2013. "Chicago's Final Frontier." *Green Building & Design*, May–June. Accessed July 18, 2014. http://gbdmagazine.com/2013/lakeside-development/.

Sellers, Rod, and Dominic A. Pacyga. 1998. *Images of America: Chicago's Southeast Side*. Charleston, S.C.: Arcadia Publishing.

Skidmore Owings & Merrill. 2012. "Chicago Lakeside Shortlisted for Sustainia Award." Sept. 21. Accessed August 12, 2013. http://www.som.com/news/chicago_lakeside_shortlisted_for_sustainia_award.

Strausberg, Chinta. 2000. "Mayor Creates South Chicago TIF District." *Chicago Defender*, February 17.

Walley, Christine. 2013. *Exit Zero: Family and Class in Postindustrial Chicago*. Chicago: University of Chicago Press.

Washburn, Gary. 1999. "South Works Plan Has Price: City Adding Details, Costs, for Developing Former Steel Plant." *Chicago Tribune*, February 12.

Yates, Ronald. 1991. "South Works Area Looking for Options." *Chicago Tribune*, November 14.

CHAPTER 7

Becoming "Boystown" in Neoliberal Chicago

A Critical Urban Morphology of the North Halsted–Broadway Corridor

ALEX G. PAPADOPOULOS

Hailed by the *Huffington Post* in 2013 as the world's most desirable LGBT community, Boystown, or the core of it, the North Halsted Street–Broadway Corridor, is the geographic focus of this critical urban morphologic study.[1] I trace urban morphological change in the corridor, starting in the 1960s, before the 1969 Stonewall riot. I mark the significance of the festival redevelopment of North Halsted Street in 1997–1998 and finish with the emergence of the corridor as a target of investment interest at the local, metropolitan, regional, and national scales. The study of the corridor's urban morphological development in the context of broader urban change in Chicago's North Side helps us understand aspects of the mobility, entrepreneurship, and place making of Chicago's LGBT community and, most important, the way that Boystown, Chicago's gay village, arose in the city in the era of neoliberalism.

The transformation from roughly 1970 to 2000 of East Lakeview, a neighborhood in relative decline after World War II, into a LGBT bright-lights district and residential neighborhood with a substantial LGBT population was a process of gradual and often contentious urban collapse and disinvestment, changes in building and land use, reinvestment, and gentrification.[2] During this period the city and neighborhood experienced changes that reflected a hard-fought rollback of discrimination on many fronts, including housing, and a rollout of entrepreneurial opportunity, community media, and political participation, all of which made it possible for the LGBT community to augment and consolidate its village-building potential in East Lakeview. At roughly the same time, a neoliberal rollback of regulation and the social state at all levels—national, regional, and local—was paired with the rollout of neoliberalization, which normalized market forces as the preferred means of urban change.[3] An important part of this story is how these seemingly unconnected developments were in the end very much connected and contributed to the making of Boystown.

The rollout of neoliberalization produced expanded urban markets and credit in the 1980s and 1990s, bringing new capital and vigor in historic neighborhoods of the North Side, including Lincoln Park, Lakeview/Boystown, Edgewater, Bucktown, and Wicker Park. The refashioning of the historic street north of Belmont Avenue into a quasi-ethnicized LGBT festival district came after decades of antagonistic politics with city and police establishments. Importantly, it marks the formal integration of Chicago's most significant gay neighborhood into the city's global city tourism and entertainment brand.[4] Marks of neoliberalism—such as the penetration of national and global commercial brands into the neighborhood's commercial structure—are unmistakable. The residential "village" and special-purpose commercial district, which primarily served the LGBT community in its early incarnation, has become increasingly integrated into the city's neoliberal economy.

By the start of the new millennium, significant gentrification marked East Lakeview's neoliberal economic alignment and in important, symbolic terms, the "de-queering"/mainstreaming of the corridor. That trend is not unique to Chicago, and it may have been caused by more than neoliberalism and urban mobility. In writing about the onset of a "post-mo" era in Toronto, geographer Catherine Nash suggests that intergenerational differences within the LGBT community account for the different ways identities are forged and transacted across urban space (Nash 2013). Although gay villages such as Boystown may remain the epicenters of LGBT life and enterprise, the spatially fixed village appears to be increasingly understood as an artifact of historic activism. If that is the case, it is ironic that the much-lauded "gaying-up" of North Halsted Street in 1997–1998 associated with the North Halsted Street beautification project coincides with the sunsetting of gay villages across the United States.[5] Amin Ghaziani's extensive ethnographic work on Boystown, the Castro, and New York's West Village points to the emergence of a post-gay era in which "post-gays obsess over being perceived as normal and respectable, and as they abandon the gayborhood, more straights move in and stumble through challenges of their own. Once they arrive, for example, some prefer to say that they live in a 'diverse neighborhood' rather than a 'gay neighborhood'" (Ghaziani 2014, 52).

The generation that grew up with *Ellen*, *Will & Grace*, and the fight for marriage equality knows places such as the Castro, West Hollywood, Provincetown,

Palm Springs, and Chicago's Boystown as places of LGBT pride, community, celebration, and commerce. Understood as quasi-ghettos, "villages," or "communities," their histories and geographies are not fully explored. I explore here the beginnings and development of Chicago's North Side LGBT communities, which culminated in the making of Boystown as the epicenter of LGBT life beginning in the 1970s. There is no foundation myth to uncover here, since it is the mobility of early LGBT communities that ultimately defined the location of Boystown and the process of village making. Moreover, while the importance of the political struggle for equal rights cannot be understated, I write counter to the classic heroic discourse of gay pioneers renewing the city by pointing instead to the strategic (and pragmatic) nature of the efforts of place entrepreneurs in the LGBT community who leveraged the bounty of Lakeview's urban morphology to build a symbolically significant LGBT place, a residential village, and a high-value specialized economic area in the city.

Studying Gays in the City

In the 1970s, gender and sexuality studies in geography gave rise to the subfield of feminist geography, which came into being at the same time as the second-wave feminist movement. In the 1980s and 1990s, sexual minorities became the subject of systematic geographic analysis (starting with Levine 1979; Castells and Murphy 1982; Ley 1984; and Wilson 1987). There are growing literatures on the making of gay villages, ghettos, and communities and various constructions of LGBT spaces (Bell and Valentine 1995; Valentine 1996; Knopp and Brown 2002; Reed 2003; Brown 2008; Browne and Bakshi 2011; Bell and Binnie 2004). Of importance here is scholarship on the role LGBT persons play as agents of urban change with special reference to land markets (Lauria and Knopp 1985; Knopp 1990, 1997; Bouthillette 1994; Ruting 2008). This literature largely analyzes "the urban," although it does not substantially analyze urban morphology.

The Sources

Gays and lesbians first declared themselves visible in politics in Chicago in 1924 through the Society for Human Rights, the oldest organization of its kind in the United States. In the 1960s and early 1970s, the Chicago chapter of the Mattachine Society, Mattachine Midwest, was a critical agent for civil rights and a catalyst for community building in Chicago and the broader region.[6] Published statements by the organization about incidents of harassment, entrapment, arrest, and physical assault and the adjudication of such incidents provide further insight about the locations of the spaces gays and lesbians inhabited. Geographic information appeared in calls for meetings, announcements of social and cultural events and activist gatherings, and business advertisements and directories. In the mid-1960s, crudely drawn advertisements in mimeographed pamphlets located at least a few of the LGBT businesses on the North Side map. These sketches gave way in the 1970s to lengthy listings of LGBT businesses and services in the gay press and ultimately to glossy bound business directories by the end of the 1980s. Social geographies sometimes emerged out of such listings. In the 1970s directories, gay businesses in Chicago's South Side were often not listed by street address but by intersection. This geographic ambiguity suggests social distance between the mostly white North Side LGBT communities (or at least the LGBT press) and mostly minority-based LGBT communities in the South Side.

Following the mobility of LGBT entrepreneurship through business directories across the North Side is an important dimension of this story of village building in the era of neoliberalism. Drawing on communication streams by organizations such as Mattachine Midwest and pamphlets, magazines, and news publications such as *Mattachine Midwest, One* (Chicago), *GayLife, Counter-Clout,* and the *Windy City Times,* I construct aspects of the temporal and spatial contours of gay Chicago on the North Side, including the outlines of Boystown, an incipient gay village or "ghetto" north of Clark Street and Diversey Parkway.

Ambiguous Demography

Historic trends for East Lakeview's LGBT population are difficult to pin down since direct questions about same-sex households were not included in census surveys until the survey that covered the 2010–2012 three-year cycle. And because households were the focus, the count did not come close to capturing the full demographic footprint of the LGBT community. For the preceding decades, a probable LGBT population geography can be gleaned with modest confidence by cross-referencing census data with non-census-based sources, mostly in the gay press.

From 1960 to 1980, population densities in Chicago's lakefront neighborhoods north of the river decreased considerably, in part because of the general trend of suburbanization after World War II and in part as a result of anti-blight campaigns, urban clearance, and revitalization strategies that were underwritten by down-zoning and rising land values.[7] In the same period, spatial sorting of racial/ethnic groups produced white supermajorities in most census tracts north of the Chicago River and along the lakefront, with the exception of the Cabrini-Green public housing district. Although densely populated Lakeview lost some population, there was a significant surge in the numbers of the 25–34 and 35–44 age cohorts. The community's narrative spoke of East Lakeview as a stronghold of the young, organized overwhelmingly in nonfamily households.

In the quote that follows, the *Chicago Tribune* may have been indulging in double-speak about the gays of the area then widely known as New Town, but the description of the neighborhood in 1973 is still instructive:

> When night falls, New Town springs to life. Cars—hunting for nonexistent parking spaces—cruise congested streets. Young singles spill out of bars. Suburban tourists and part-time street-freaks wander around, mingling with the neighborhood residents who congregate on Broadway. . . . [After] the decline and fall of Old Town, where increasing crime and skyrocketing rents forced Chicago's nomadic singles to find another "in" place to live, they chose New Town. (Lauerman 1973, 55)

Ten years later, it seems to have been acceptable to write openly, albeit still with derision, about gays:

> It is Saturday midnight at the corner of Broadway and Clark Street. Streams of men, clad in Levi 501 button-fly jeans and rainbow-hued shirt collars jutting out from black leather jackets, pour into Chicago's newest multimillion-dollar disco. . . . A few blocks west, a handful of women make their way out of a church basement where they have spent the evening sipping hot cider and herb tea, while listening to ancient folk songs updated to omit any references to men. . . . Is Chicago ready for gay rights? . . . Politicians have no choice but to turn an ear toward the outcries of some 200,000 potential voters, and retailers must cater to the buying power of Chicago's free-flowing gay dollar. (Mahany 1983)

In this leering and sneering piece, every gay and lesbian stereotype was used to typecast gays' and lesbians' cultural distinctiveness as sexual while grudgingly acknowledging their rising political and economic profile as a coming reality. Rightfully, reporter Barbara Mahany draws the vital connection between Chicago's allegedly large LGBT population and its latent political and economic agency and power. Mahany outlined the findings of a recently conducted marketing study that questioned 1,275 men in eleven markets across the country. The survey found that gay men were more likely to be affluent, were more likely to be employed in administrative/managerial professions, and were active voters and contributors to electoral campaigns (Mahany 1983). It would be reasonable to speculate that this population contained place entrepreneurs who possessed surplus capital that would potentially find its way to the local real estate development market.[8]

Mapping percent change in nonfamily households from 1960 to 1980—the time frame for the movement of LGBT persons north from Old Town—identifies significant growth across all census tracts associated with the early establishment of the gay village around Diversey Parkway and Clark Street and its recrystallization around Belmont and Broadway in 1980 (see Maps 7.1 and 7.2). Of course,

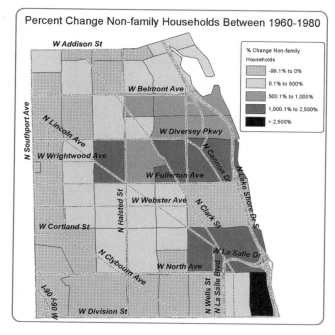

Map 7.1. Percent change nonfamily households, 1960–1980.

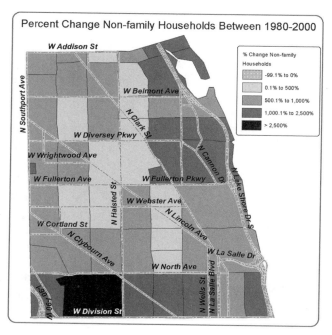

Map 7.2. Percent change nonfamily households, 1980–2000.

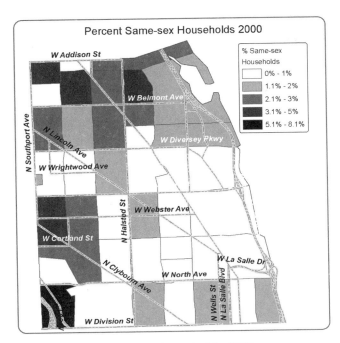

Map 7.3. Percent same-sex households, 2000.

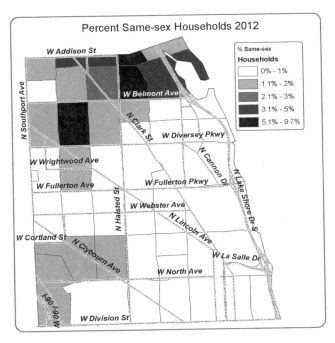

Map 7.4. Percent same-sex households, 2012.
Source: Created by Nadnhini Gulasingam, Social Science
Research Center, DePaul University, February 2014.

there is no way to know how many of these nonfamily households represented LGBT residents. By 2012, the local concentrations of nonfamily households had shifted to the north, approaching Addison Street (Maps 7.3 and 7.4). Percent change in the 25–34 cohort for the period from 1960 to 1980 is very significant and exceeds 100 percent in the census tracts east of Broadway. Then, from 1980 to 2000 the age profile of the near-lakefront areas shifted upward (Maps 7.5 and 7.6). Since census classifications and data before 2010 did not specifically count the demographics of the LGBT community in East Lakeview or elsewhere in the United States, one needs to draw upon community narratives. For example, in an advertisement for the Chicago-based LGBT community publication *All Together Journal* that appeared in the *Chicago Gay Crusader* in 1976, a young man mused: "I am a very independent, single, working male in the ripe old age of 27. I do not intend ever to be 'legally' married or to have my own natural children. I expect to find life a bit rough in spots because of my lifestyle. That's why I joined ALL TOGETHER . . . maybe you should too."[9]

Mirroring trends in other historic LGBT villages in the United States, such as the Castro, the West Village, and Chelsea, by 2000 East Lakeview and Boystown in particular had become destinations for affluent, straight, nonfamily house-holders. At the same time, census tracts associated with Boystown persist in the American Community Survey of 2012 as strongholds of same-sex households.[10] In the 2000 census and the 2012 *American Community Survey* data, tracts north of Diversey Parkway and especially north of Belmont exhibit concentrations of same-sex households. Tract 0620, Boystown's geographic epicenter, exhibits the highest or one of the highest concentrations in Chicago's North Side. The operative question, which cannot be answered, is how these numbers relate with any degree of confidence to earlier profiles of nonfamily household status and age. By the time we can confidently map same-sex households in East Lakeview, Boystown as a gay residential village and even more so as a gay "ghetto" may have been evaporating.

Mobility as Destiny in the Making of Boystown

The starting point here is the northbound displacement of gays from the Near North and Old Town neighborhoods to New Town and East Lake View in the 1950s.[11] I suggest that the combination of the traditional animus of the state toward sexual minorities and urban renewal and development north of the Gold Coast was primarily responsible for the expulsion of gays to the north. Broad structural changes in the way the state managed the containment of urban blight and plans for urban development in the 1950s produced demographic shifts and changes in the land market and altered land uses. These trends were

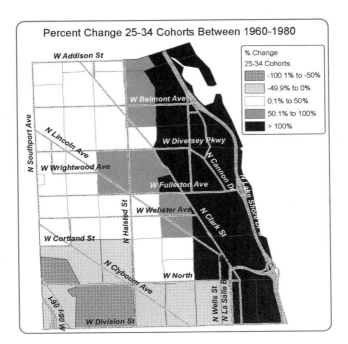

Map 7.5. Percent change 25–34 cohort, 1960–1980.

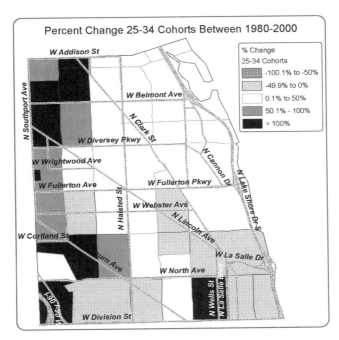

Map 7.6. Percent change 25–34 cohort, 1980–2000.
Source: Created by Nadnhini Gulasingam, Social Science
Research Center, DePaul University, February 2014.

hostile to the alternative businesses that defined the bright lights and commercial character of the early LGBT urban nodes in the North Side. This accounts for the gradual move north, across Lincoln Park and into East Lake View, in the period 1950 to 1970.[12]

The Boystown "gayborhood" came together gradually in demographic and business terms during the 1970s, in spite of the city's surveillance and disciplining of gays through police entrapment, bar raids, false arrests, intimidation, and denial of equal access to the local economy. Public queer lives were lived behind tinted bar and tavern windows, although the neighborhood ground plan— North Halsted, Broadway, Pine Grove, and the latticework of their tributary streets and alleys—was bravely queered day and night by people looking for sex, love, or community. If the Stonewall Inn riot of 1969 was the beginning of a LGBT revolution, the HIV-AIDS epidemic that broke out in the early 1980s dramatically changed the national conversation on LGBT rights and produced a politically muscular community, including in Chicago. The social disapproval of gay lives lived openly, however, was a stumbling block to full membership in Chicago's public life until a number of protective ordinances were passed in the 1980s and 1990s. As a generation of gay men was being lost to AIDS, gay villages such as Boystown became ever more important as service centers, places of refuge and solidarity, and geographic hubs of political activism at the local, state, and national levels.[13] The urban implications were considerable. A new broad spectrum of social organizations and services and political agents, activists, and leaders sprang into being with Boystown (and to a lesser extent Edgewater and Rogers Park) as the epicenter.

These structural changes were recorded in the changing ground plan (the street and the block), built forms, and land uses of the North Side and helped reveal stories of LGBT mobility, entrepreneurship, and residential settlement. The parameters of LGBT geographic incidence exhibit a great deal of complexity. In the 1960s and 1970s, Chicago's gay space was polycentric with two significant nodes, one in the central business district and the surrounding frame and skid row, which I call Queer Bohemia,[14] and a second one in New Town that extended north from Old Town and the long-gone "Towertown" village to the Lake View–Buena Park boundary on Irving Park Road (Papadopoulos 2006).[15] Less dense nodes on the South Side and in Uptown-Edgewater complete the location geography (Maps 7.7 and 7.8).[16] The geographical distributions of LGBT bright lights, commerce, and social/community organizations, each surrounded by a 400-yard walkable buffer, can give us the trace of a lesbi-gay functional area and may reveal some of the residential geography of gays and lesbians.

I suggest that there is a vital link between the two nodes. The New Town village absorbed and concentrated LGBT populations and enterprises that had been expelled, mainly by gentrification, from Queer Bohemia. The geographic

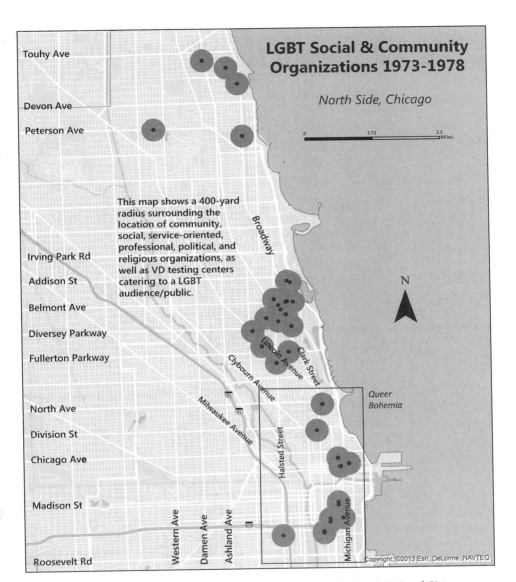

Map 7.7. LGBT social and community organizations in the North Side of Chicago, 1973–1978.

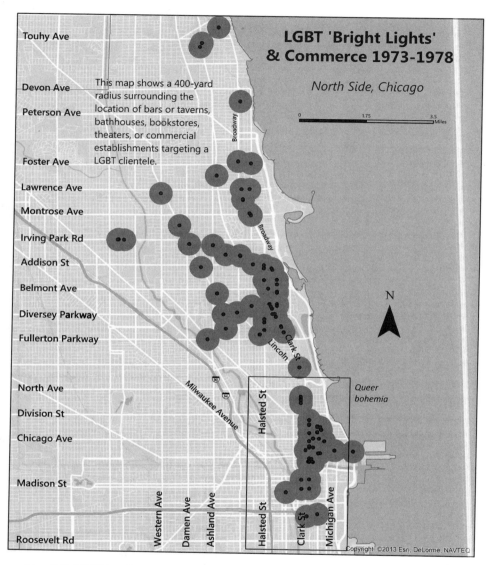

The following labels appear on the map:

Touhy Ave

Devon Ave

Peterson Ave

Foster Ave

Lawrence Ave

Montrose Ave

Irving Park Rd

Addison St

Belmont Ave

Diversey Parkway

Fullerton Parkway

North Ave

Division St

Chicago Ave

Madison St

Roosevelt Rd

Western Ave

Damen Ave

Ashland Ave

Halsted St

Clark St

Michigan Ave

Milwaukee Avenue

Broadway

Lincoln

Halsted St

LGBT 'Bright Lights' & Commerce 1973-1978

North Side, Chicago

0   1.75   3.5 Miles

This map shows a 400-yard radius surrounding the location of bars or taverns, bathhouses, bookstores, theaters, or commercial establishments targeting a LGBT clientele.

Queer bohemia

N

Copyright ©2013 Esri, DeLorme, NAVTEQ

Map 7.8. LGBT bright lights and commerce, North Side, Chicago, 1973–1978.
Source: Created by the author.

mobility and the community potential of these two significant LGBT spatial concentrations needs to be understood in the context of Chicago's urban governance and planning practices.

"Boystown":
From Automotive Row to Gay Village

The area and the limits of gay New Town changed over time. North Halsted Street, located between Irving Park Road to the north and Belmont Avenue to the south, has been Boystown's signature commercial corridor since the mid-1980s.[17] The Northalsted Business Alliance and the East Lakeview Chamber of Commerce list 197 and 416 businesses, respectively (there is some overlap), which are very much skewed toward dining, entertainment, shopping, and personal services.[18] Surveys of historic LGBT business directories show that gay bars did not relocate north of Belmont to Halsted Street until the early 1980s. There were, of course, exceptions. The renowned Little Jim's Tavern (located on the corner of Halsted and Cornelia) opened its doors to gay patrons in 1975.

The gay community started shedding its Old Town and Lincoln Park posts in the 1970s. Until 1978, the geographical center of New Town's LGBT business community was located east of Halsted Street and south of Belmont. In the 1980s it redeployed and recrystallized north of Belmont Avenue (today the de facto southern boundary of Boystown), establishing North Halsted Street between Belmont Avenue on the south and Irving Park Road to the north as its newest and most significant bright-lights ribbon.

Importantly, the gay village in Lakeview went beyond replicating the bright lights and social and civil services geographies of Queer Bohemia. Inside the limits of this plastic urban quarter of an incipient gay village, queer space was constructed both overtly (think post-Stonewall pride parades, which started in 1970) and covertly (for example, queering the street through cruising or watching others walk by behind the smoked glass windows of bars and taverns). Queer space was both ephemeral (think the duration of a gay group's town hall meeting in a church hall) and spatially fixed, as in the case of gay commercial enterprises, the location and lifespan of which were contingent not only upon the vagaries of the market but upon the attitudes and tactics of the police.

In the period 1960–1970, North Halsted Street reached the nadir of urban morphological transition. Severe blight of the physical plant in the blocks that lined its length in Lake View, building vacancies, a high incidence of violent crime, and business disinvestment produced a deep trough in land rents. The crisis did not end until the 1980s were well under way. Kerrie Kennedy writes that when bar owner Jim Ludwig purchased the property that would become Roscoe's, the vacant building was serving as a gang headquarters, with a Puerto

Table 7.1. Land uses on North Halsted Street, early 1950s

Number	Building/Land Use
13	Garage/parking
10	Auto/tire/body repair
9	Auto sales (new and used)
6	Metal products manufacturing/sheet metal works/ornamental wrought iron/tin shop
6	Paint shop
	Hotels/rooming houses
4	Filling station
4	Laundry/dry cleaner
4	Drug store
4	Printing/typesetting
3	Auto greasing
3	Cabinet shop/Woodworking
2	Candy factory
2	Cobbler
2	Plumbing
2	Upholstery
2	Bakery
2	Lodge Hall/Club house
1 (each)	Auto washing, plastics factory, lunch box factory, ice factory, furniture warehouse, contractor supplies, electrical supplies and storage, tractor parts, machine shop, store fixtures, mill construction, catering, dance hall, theater, church, parochial school, sign shop, junk

Source: Sanborn Fire Insurance Atlases 1930–1951.

Rican gang in front and a Mexican gang in back. Not exactly a comforting thought for the man who planned to turn it into a gay bar. "I had to take on the persona of a hard-ass guy, with a full beard, cowboy hat and boots," recalls Ludwig. "The gang members eventually left, but it was years before the neighborhood lost its gritty edge" (quoted in Kennedy 2005). In 1951, however, this was still a vibrant, albeit decayed, working-class neighborhood. Drawing on *Sanborn Fire Insurance Atlas* maps for Lake View (1930–1951, vol. 9), we can account for the full population of listed businesses that lined North Halsted Street between Irving Park Road to the north and Wrightwood Avenue to the south.[19] The represented buildings and land uses conjure a workmanlike urban landscape thickly smeared in automotive oil and machine grease (see Table 7.1).

The mixed land-use pattern is not surprising, although it postdates the Chicago zoning ordinance of 1923 that sought to spatially segregate "objectionable buildings and uses" from residences. The assumption guiding the ordinance was that the presence of negative externalities depressed land values in residential areas. The presence of light manufacturing on North Halsted Street and especially the broad spectrum of automotive service facilities that were woven spatially

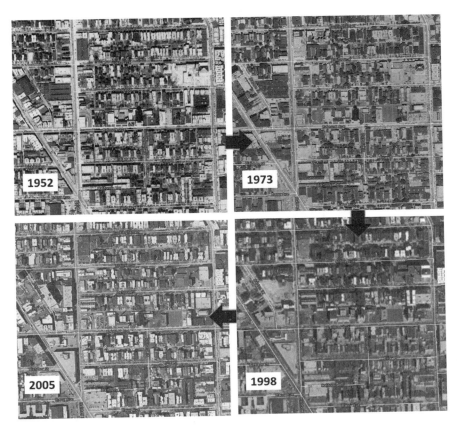

Figure 7.1. North Halsted Street's physical evolution.
Source: Created by the author.

into the mainly residential built environment would have, understandably, been found to be in violation of the 1923 ordinance. However, grandfather clauses abounded in the ordinance, and for a considerable time the status quo ante of 1923 must have held across the city (McMillen and McDonald 1999). The San-born atlas data suggest that at least until 1951, mixed land use was the norm in the study area. Moreover, it is clear from the specific assemblage of automotive land uses that North Halsted Street, at least at this latitude, enjoyed important agglomeration economies. Garage and light industrial uses were clearly located in special-purpose built forms.

These are easily identifiable along the short course of North Halsted Street in the 1952 aerial photograph centered on the Halsted-Belmont-Clark intersection (see Figure 7.1). The expectation would be that in spite of the 1923 zoning ordinance's tolerance for nonconformity, either the zoning ordinance of 1957 or land markets would eventually spatially sort out offending building and land uses, in effect sequestering them in special districts. It would be reasonable to hypothesize, then, that from 1951 to the time investment capital was again introduced in critical volume, land rents on North Halsted Street would trend lower as one by one the nonconforming enterprises either failed or left, adding to the rate of vacancy. Moreover, the significant reduction in population density in Lakeview from 1960 to 1980 likely further depressed local markets and contributed to the neighborhood blight regularly reported in the press.

From a morphological standpoint, the spatial structure of street blocks to the east and south of the North Halsted Street ribbon was stable. The ground plan appeared to be largely in the state in which it had been platted, with little evidence that lots had been either assembled or subdivided since the area's building boom of 1889 to the 1920s.[20] Built forms as represented by their footprints were consistent with prevalent forms of the period 1880–1930. This kind of built environment stasis or fallow state is often indicative of low levels of capital circulation and investment.

The building and land uses that characterize North Halsted Street were also present along Broadway north of Diversey, but less frequently so. It would be proper to characterize Broadway and the street blocks lining it as a zone of transition from mixed land use with a light manufacturing component to a higher-value mixed commercial-residential zone (see Figure 7.2). In contrast, and as expected, the dominant building and land uses on the tributary streets east of Broadway and the street blocks between Broadway and the lake were a mix of residential (multifamily and single-family units) and other land uses such as religious or governmental buildings. The dominant built forms were mid-rises, which graduated into taller volumes approaching the lakefront.

Clearly, North Halsted Street was a special-purpose district with strong automotive and small-manufacturing components. Bright lights burned only on the one dance hall and the Vogue Theater (which was demolished after a fire in 1958). In contrast, North Broadway was substantially denser and more residential. The area of built lots increased considerably east of the Broadway streetscape, creating opportunities for substantial residential and institutional blocks. Commercial nodes were a short distance away, to the north at the terminus of North Halsted Street, to the west at the intersection of Belmont and Clark, and to the southeast at the intersection of Diversey, Clark, and Broadway.

Twenty years later, a 1973 aerial photograph of the same quadrangle reveals that the cadastre and built volumes were largely intact. There was some evidence of clearance but little indication of significant morphological turnover. While it is entirely possible that some or all of these built volumes were occupied, there is significant narrative evidence that vacancy and dereliction were commonplace. It is unclear whether the negotiation and passing of the 1957 Chicago

Figure 7.2. A new commercial building, currently occupied by a Gap store, has replaced a Broadway garage built in 1936. Source: Copelin Commercial Photographers, 1965 photo of Broadway garage building.

zoning ordinance precipitated greater anti-blight activism in Lakeview and elsewhere, but from mid-decade on, alarms against blight were ringing and special-purpose associations were formed to fight blight. Coincidentally, a public discourse was constructed to bring significant change to the community area by clearance and reinvestment, by targeting specific issues (such as parking), and by pursuing architectural conservation status for key parts of Lakeview. The *Chicago Tribune* noted that in Lakeview, "commercial blight [is] listed as a main problem facing the community, is scattered[,] and is caused by the area being overbuilt with store front buildings, many of which have been allowed to decay. . . . Obsolete strip commercial areas which should be considered for clearance include portions of Clark Street, Broadway, and Lincoln and Belmont avenues" (Chicago Tribune 1961). Photographs of streetscapes and buildings in decline taken by the Department of Streets and Sanitation from 1940 to 1960, some of them executed by Copelin Commercial Photographers, are an invaluable resource; they provide information on built form, land use, and the state of repair of buildings.

There is strong evidence that by the late 1970s the physical plant of the neighborhood was substantially obsolete. North Halsted Street was strewn with the building and business carcasses of an older Chicago. Decay of North Halsted Street's built environment and business failure and flight became spatial-economic opportunities for the LGBT entrepreneurial class. Gentrification was already transforming Lincoln Park to the south, but in the colonization of the North Halsted Street land-rent canyon, the LGBT business pioneers of Lakeview had the advantage of a geographically proximate clientele that was committed to LGBT businesses.

By the beginning of the 1980s, the LGBT business community was transitioning to North Halsted Street, north of Belmont Avenue, gradually taking over the empty stores and filling the business vacuum. Comparisons of historical aerial photographs suggest that by 1998 (and probably by the late 1980s) significant morphological changes were occurring in the study area. Aided by zoning provisions for planned developments, the spatial scope of new projects increased. The ground plan was changing with a strong trend toward lot consolidation. The LGBT community was not a lone actor in the gentrification of East Lakeview, but it undoubtedly was an important one and the *most* important one in the redevelopment of North Halsted Street north of Belmont Avenue. It is fair to say that over a period of twenty years, it transformed this area—one storefront at a time—into a special-purpose LGBT bright-lights district.

Geographer Larry Knopp's work on potential alliances between gay and nongay urban developers and speculators is key here. In his study of gentrification of the Marigny district in New Orleans, he observed the crafting of cross-cultural (gay and nongay) and cross-class alliances (Knopp 1990). If the nongay population experienced any social disapproval about collaborating with members of the local gay community, it was trumped by a desire to profit. In the Chicago case, the temporal dimension is critical to understanding gentrification and commercial business entrepreneurship in the North Halsted–Broadway Corridor in the 1980s and later: LGBT business entrepreneurs chronologically precede non-LGBT place entrepreneurs. That is especially true of non-LGBT structural speculators who began introducing urban projects of greater financial and geographic scope to the neighborhood in the 1990s, as neoliberal policies rolled out a broad spectrum of business investment instruments. I suggest that the window of LBGT entrepreneurial dominance over the corridor opened and then closed in the period 1980–1998. The latter date signals the arrival of national (and in some cases international) investment capital in the corridor and the broader East Lakeview district.

Redevelopment of North Halsted Street as Neoliberal Denouement

The transformative power of the Stonewall Inn riot of 1969 cannot be underestimated. After Stonewall, gays and lesbians lived increasingly public lives and came together to create a robustly led, politically activist, entrepreneurially vibrant collective, a gay village or "ghetto." Large, diverse cities such as Chicago became destinations for LGBT persons from less urbane and tolerant places (truly, it was Oz!), contributing to the regionalization of LGBT demography and political and economic power.

By 1980, although the visibility of Chicago's LGBT community had increased greatly, its leaders had secured only modest political and legal gains. The first municipal anti-discrimination ordinance was proposed in July 1973, but it was not approved until 1988. Post–Richard J. Daley relations between the community and the police improved slowly, and by the late 1970s, overt and systematic police harassment of LGBT businesses had declined substantially. New Town's LGBT businesses, press, and social and community organizations multiplied and thrived as the spatially dynamic "village" became the preferred destination for the region's LGBT population. North Halsted Street's low rents and the morphological character of the broader area provided the structural basis for the northward mobility of LGBT enterprises and their relatively brief market dominance along the North Halsted–Broadway Corridor. That privileged state ended with the arrival of structural speculators from outside.

Gay pride parades became a metaphor for the urban mobilities of the community as they etched paths across areas of the city that were claimed actually or figuratively by and for the LGBT community. The first, on June 28, 1970, drew 150–200 attendees, and the eighth, on June 26, 1977, drew 3,000. The seventeenth parade, on June 29, 1986—at the height of the HIV/AIDS epidemic—attracted 40,000 attendees, and the twenty-ninth, in 1998, which coincided with the inauguration of the redeveloped North Halsted Street, was attended by more than 200,000. The forty-third gay pride parade, held on June 24, 2012, which featured as grand marshal Evan Wolfson of Freedom to Marry, drew 850,000 attendees. The 2013 parade topped the 1 million mark. The changing geography of the parades validated community mobility claims. In 1970, it started in the Near North's Washington Square and terminated downtown in Daley Plaza. The second one started closer to the new home of the community, at Diversey Harbor, marched west to Clark Street, and then turned south to end at the Free Forum on LaSalle Street. The *Chicago Tribune* described the 1998 parade as stepping off "at 2 p.m., heading north on Halsted Street at Belmont Avenue with 10 mounted Chicago police officers keeping people on the sidewalks over the two-mile course. It ended some three hours later at Diversey Parkway and

Sheridan Road with a crowd so large that traffic was being halted many blocks from the intersection" (Galloway 1998).

The previous year, the City of Chicago had approved a $3.2 million redevelopment of six street blocks along North Halsted Street north of Belmont Avenue. It was one of several commercial district beautification and infrastructure improvement projects the Daley administration undertook, but this one was in a neighborhood that was distinguished by its sexual identity politics rather than its ethnic heritage. In fact, one of the controversies was the city administration's equation of sexuality with ethnicity. The bulk of the funds were earmarked for the design and execution of new electrical infrastructure, high-quality hardscapes and urban fixtures, and the planting of 180 trees. Only a small percentage of the funds was allocated to beautification, which ultimately took the shape of twenty-two art deco–inspired, rainbow ring–encircled pylons erected along the six street blocks of North Halsted Street. A loud public debate ensued, with critics claiming that a line was about to be crossed. They were correct.

Minneapolis's *Star Tribune*, a regional paper owned by the Tribune Corporation, laid it bare: "Chicago celebrates gay, lesbian neighborhood; North Halsted Street has been at the center of homosexual life in Chicago for more than a decade, transforming a down-at-the-heels, gang-ridden place into a prosperous district" (Johnson 1997). It took almost twenty years to complete the urban morphological and demographic transformation of the North Halsted–Broadway Corridor into a model gentrified Chicago quarter.

The important story, therefore, had been developing in plain sight but outside public discourses about the LGBT community's right to the city. The key story was the importance of the alliance between the Democratic Party and LGBT elites. Mayor Richard M. Daley's decision to finance the Halsted Street redevelopment project was clearly payback for the loyalty of the LGBT community to his version of local Democratic Party politics. Timothy Stewart-Winter remarks that "Daley, who did not have funds for schools and who secured huge federal grants to transform, through demolition, the city's public housing, found a relatively modest sum of city money to spend on strengthening his ties to the gay community." In fact, the LGBT community courted mayoral favor systematically from the 1970s, but it was only with the election of Harold Washington that the LGBT community started gaining political traction. Stewart-Winter continues that "the Boystown streetscape renovation project illustrates that gay clout was intertwined with pro-growth development policies and with the neoliberal fashioning of urban space through capital improvements that distribute only basic facilities to poorer areas and more elaborate developments to more prosperous neighborhoods" (2016, 221). Although that was the case by the late 1990s and is still true in the 2010s, for the decades that the LGBT community was politically marginalized, urban renewal, real estate, business entrepreneurship, and gay place making were carried out largely by LGBT agency and with LGBT capital. The neoliberal turn occurred only after the clout of the queer community became clear.

Commercial mortgage data from 2013–2014 suggests that the types of capital and the geographic origins of investors engaged in real estate development projects in Lakeview have expanded. As geographer Larry Knopp (1990) suggests in his study of the gay Marigny Quarter of New Orleans, the prospect of accumulation animates capitalists and promotes real estate speculation and makes partners of unlikely bedfellows. A survey of commercial mortgages granted in 2013–February 2014 for projects located in the urban quarter defined by Diversey Parkway to the south, Irving Park Road to the north, Clark Street to the west, and Lake Michigan to the east—essentially, the area that the gay village had occupied since 1970—reveals the significance and degree of penetration of nonlocal investment capital in the era of mature neoliberalism. The evidence supports the hypothesis that Boystown and its immediate hinterland have increasingly become integrated into regional and national circuits of capital. When one takes into consideration the geographies of the banking institutions involved in these transactions, the global connection is revealed. Local, regional, and national and international banks, such as Bank of America and Citicorp, have extended commercial mortgages to East Lakeview's corporate place entrepreneurs, many of whom can be characterized as structural speculators, given the scope of projects and the size of commercial mortgages. City-based investors lead with approximately 50 percent of a total of $87,839,861 in commercial real estate debt (Table 7.2). Nationally situated investors rank second with approximately 22 percent of the value of commercial mortgages, and Lakeview-based investors rank third with 20 percent. Chicago metropolitan area and Illinois investors trail with 5.9 percent and 2 percent of the value of commercial mortgages in the district, respectively (Figure 7.3). The change in source and magnitude of business and real estate development capital since the early 1980s (the beginning of investment on North Halsted by LGBT entrepreneurs) is quite stark.[21] Politicians, the police, and the general public may have historically disapproved of LGBT persons, but investors originating from all geographical scales saw the potential for great profit in Lakeview, at least by the end of the millennium.

The political alliance between Chicago Democratic and LGBT elites that had been constructed since 1989 and Richard M. Daley's first mayoral victory was consolidated and augmented in his five subsequent reelections. The North Halsted Street Redevelopment Project and Daley's appointment of an LGBT liaison with City Hall stand among his most significant contributions. His successor, Rahm Emanuel, has taken a page from the Daley political playbook and is a strong supporter of popular LGBT aspirations such as marriage equality and the passage of the Employment Non-Discrimination Act (ENDA). However, fiscal

Table 7.2. Pattern of real estate investment in Boystown

Borrower	Borrower Profile	Lender	Amount (USD)	Geography
Frank Christ Buildings, LLC	Urban development corporation based in Lakeview, Chicago	Standard Bank & Trust	2,500,000	District
Frank Christ Buildings, LLC	Urban development corporation based in Lakeview, Chicago	Standard Bank & Trust	9,573,000	District
Frank Christ Buildings, LLC	Urban development corporation based in Lakeview, Chicago	Standard Bank & Trust	1,826,765	District
4021 Broadway, LLC	Corporation based in Lakeview, Chicago	American Chartered Bank	360,000	District
3731 N Clark Street, LLC	Corporation based in Lakeview, Chicago	Amalgamated Bank Chicago	1,250,000	District
3740 N Clark Street, LLC	Media corporation based in Lakeview, Chicago	Small Business Growth Corp	587,000	District
Clark Buckingham, LLC	Corporation based in Lakeview, Chicago	State Bank of Countryside	1,500,000	District
			17,596,765	Subtotal 1
LPAC Broadway Building LLC	Urban development corporation based in Chicago	Citibank, NA	15,368,421	Chicago
618 Roscoe, LLC	Real estate development corporation based in Chicago; incorporated in 2010	Jefferies Loancore LLC	17,000,000	Chicago
Halsted Belmont, LLC	Corporation based in Chicago	Bank Financial FSB	2,350,000	Chicago
851 W Belmont, LLC	Corporation based in Chicago	North Shore Community Bank & Trust	3,075,000	Chicago
3301 N Clark Street, LLC	Corporation based in Chicago	Belmont Bank & Trust Co.	1,800,000	Chicago
3418 Halsted Street, LLC	Corporation based in Chicago	Bridgeview Bank Group	1,600,000	Chicago
Eddy Clark, LLC	Corporation based in Chicago	Somercor 504 Inc.	1,498,000	Chicago
3524 N Clark Street, LLC	Corporation based in Chicago	Cole Taylor Bank	1,353,000	Chicago
			44,044,421	Subtotal 2

Borrower	Borrower Profile	Lender	Amount (USD)	Geography
Park Place Garage, LLC	Corporation based in Northbrook, IL	First Eagle Bank	1,700,000	Chicago-Metro
3445 N Halsted Street, LLC	Corporation based in Rolling Meadows, IL	Gold Coast Bank	802,400	Chicago-Metro
Cimpar Investments, LLC	Corporation based in Melrose Park, IL	Bancorp Bank	1,479,875	Chicago-Metro
Cimpar Investments, LLC	Corporation based in Melrose Park, IL	Bancorp Bank	1,183,900	Chicago-Metro
			5,166,175	Subtotal 3
Chicago Title Land Trust Company	Leading Illinois land trustee	Lakeside Bank	1,100,000	Illinois
2845 N Clark Street, LLC	Corporation based in Winthrop Harbor, IL	Lake Forest Bank & Trust Co.	680,000	Illinois
			1,780,000	Subtotal 4
ASP Realty, Inc	A subsidiary of New Albertson's, Inc., an operator of grocery and drug stores in the Northwest and West Coast based in Spokane, WA.	Bank of America	6,000,000,000 (outlier; excluded from calculation)	National
Store Master Funding V, LLC	Corporation based in Scottsdale, AZ; incorporated in 2013	Citibank, NA	2,050,000	National
Fog Bs, LLC	Petroleum firm operating gas stations based in Atlanta, GA	Lakeside Bank	1,732,500	National
G&A Properties, LLC	Operator of nonresidential buildings; incorporated in 2008 in Montana	North Shore Community Bank & Trust	1,100,000	National
G&A Properties, LLC	Operator of nonresidential buildings; incorporated in 2008 in Montana	North Shore Community Bank & Trust	1,200,000	National
3175 Broadway Street, LLC	Corporation based in Los Angeles, CA	Bank of America	2,950,000	National
Sp Belmont, LLC	Corporation based in Wilmington, DE	Lake Forest Bank & Trust	1,820,000	National
2927 Halsted Street, LLC	Corporation based in Juneau, AK	Albany Bank and Trust Co.	1,235,000	National
Gramar, LLC	Corporation registered in Park Ridge, IL (multiple national locations)	Gold Coast Bank	4,925,000	National
Gramar, LLC	Corporation registered in Park Ridge, IL (multiple national locations)	Gold Coast Bank	2,240,000	National
			19,252,500	Subtotal 5
			87,839,861	TOTAL

Source: *Crain's Chicago Business* 2009.

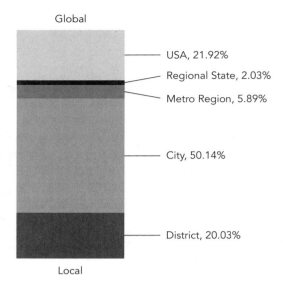

Global

USA, 21.92%

Regional State, 2.03%

Metro Region, 5.89%

City, 50.14%

District, 20.03%

Local

Figure 7.3. Geographic origin of commercial
mortgage value in study area. Sources: "Chicago
Real Estate Daily," *Crain's Chicago Business.*

stress and financial instability caused, in part, by the global financial crisis of
2008 provided Emanuel with a context (perhaps a pretext) for making deep cuts
to the city's budget, including significant reductions to contributions to community organizations. Forty-five percent of nonprofit entities—including ones
that serve the LGBT community—have annual budgets of less than $100,000,
and the reductions in city contributions are causing significant strains in social
service agencies (Simonette 2013). One such nonprofit community organization,
Night Ministry, which serves LGBT homeless youth, notes the double challenge of reduced resources and hostility from the neighborhoods where they
are located (read gentrified Lakeview) (Simonette 2014). As a gay wonderland
and historic community hearth, Lakeview draws this vulnerable population,
but much of neoliberal Boystown is less than welcoming. However, the city's
public image vis-à-vis the gay community remains untarnished. Under Rahm
Emanuel's leadership, Chicago has been distinguished as one of the most LGBT-
friendly cities in the United States, scoring 100/100 in the 2013 Human Rights
Campaign's Municipal Equality Index (Demarest 2012).[22] Perhaps undeservedly,
the city received bonus points for its care for vulnerable LGBT groups.

From the 1950s, City of Chicago redevelopment priorities pushed new investment north of the main branch of the Chicago River and along the lakefront.
Aggressive policing, gentrification, and urban morphological renewal in the

form of large-scope projects such as Carl Sandburg Village gradually expelled LBGT businesses and the population they serve from Old Town's Queer Bohemia, their historic hearth in the Near North Side and Old Town. Drifting north, the LGBT community established a commercial and services node first around the Lincoln Park–Lakeview border and then farther north in the heart of Lakeview, where it established Boystown as a gay village. The North Halsted–Broadway Corridor's low rents and the morphological character of the deteriorated broader area provided a structural opportunity for the northward-bound LGBT enterprises. LGBT place entrepreneurs capitalized on their local knowledge and market dominance to establish control of the market along the North Halsted–Broadway Corridor for a brief period in the 1980s to mid-1990s, before structural speculators from outside arrived.

Political gains that followed the Stonewall revolt paralleled the onset of neoliberalism in Chicago. The becoming of Boystown coincided with the advent of neoliberalism and what Peck, Theodore, and Brenner (2009) call rollback regulation-corrosive mechanisms and rollout market-consolidating mechanisms. While deregulation and privatization were becoming the new normal, Chicago's LGBT community was marshaling its electoral and economic capital to secure its right to the changing city. On first observation, the rollback of anti-gay discrimination and the rollout of gay political and economic influence appear to be unconnected to the rollback of the local state and the rollout of market-driven urban governance. However, in the case of East Lakeview and Boystown, the growing debility of the local state made new, LGBT-inclusive political alliances necessary, not unlike what happened in the Marigny Quarter in New Orleans. Less a paradox and more a case of political-economic expediency, neoliberalism accelerated the crystallization of Boystown as a mature gay village and a special commercial district with a strong LGBT character. However, the gay village is no longer a gay ghetto. Both the national respectability the Chicago LGBT community earned through its civil and political struggles, notably as a result of cross-race and cross-class alliances with African Americans and straight lakefront progressives, and the allure of profitable gentrification attracted non-LGBT real estate capital and developers. The greenback and the "pink dollar" are equally welcome in this era of acceptance of same-sex difference. In the era of neoliberalism, the North Halsted–Broadway Corridor became the target of, first, city-based capital and then regionally and nationally situated capital. The growing presence of deep-pocketed national and international commercial brands has been squeezing out (or at least crowding out) LGBT enterprises since the turn of the millennium, transforming the commercial streetscape of Halsted and Broadway and undermining its historic queer sense of place. Boystown's gay village ontology has been gradually rescripted, substantially commodified, and markedly dequeered while retaining a bright and celebratory LGBT façade.

Notes

I would like to thank Nandhini Gulasingam of DePaul University's Social Science Research Center for her significant assistance with the census data visualizations. I am grateful for the access to material I was granted by the Gerber-Hart Library and Archives and for Lucas McKeever's assistance there.

1. Urban morphology studies cadastral (having to do with the ground or town plan, including streets, street blocks, plots/lots and their subdivisions), built environment (often described as "urban tissue"), and building- and land-use change at different scales, starting with the urban plot or lot. Morphology is interested in the forms and the processes that produce and are produced by urban generation and development, collapse, and redevelopment. Initially animated by a desire to understand the historic cores of European cities for the purpose of preservation planning, urban morphology adapted well to the study of cities in the era of advance finance capitalism. Critical urban morphology uses the forensic tools of the method, such as time-series plans, maps, and landscape photography, to explain spatial pattern changes and interrogate power relations that produce and change urban space.

2. I use the term bright lights here in two ways: as an entertainment district and, drawing on the migration literature, as an idealized destination for those who saw in the bright lights of the city the prospect of a better, freer existence. As Timothy Stewart-Winter (2016) notes, Chicago drew gay migrants from across the Midwest. The broader subject of gay rural-to-urban and urban-to-urban migrations remains a relatively unexplored subject in the LGBT literature.

3. Here I am adapting Peck, Theodore, and Brenner's ideas of the neoliberal rollback and rollout of regulation: successive rollbacks of the state, followed by successive insertions of markets and "market-think." They write that "concrete programs of neoliberal restructuring tend to combine the rollback of oppositional institutional forms through the dismantling of collectivist, progressively redistributionist systems and the contradictory deregulation of economies, along with the rollout of new modes of institutional regulation and new forms of statecraft" (Peck, Theodore, and Brenner 2009, 55).

4. Browne and Bakshi (2011) go a long way toward demolishing the stereotype that LGBT people socialize primarily in LGBT spaces, although I would argue that before key civil rights were attained, the "gay ghetto" and its bright lights provided much-needed security from harassment and violence. If we follow their argument, however, the city's and the community's decision to crystallize North Halsted Street as "gay street" which was decorated with art deco–inspired, rainbow-girded decorative pylons along its length is part of a narrative that sees gays as urban builders.

5. I use the term sunsetting to describe the gradual decline in the visibility of LGBT populations in gay villages, such as Chicago's Boystown and San Francisco's Castro, that may represent a reduction in LGBT population in these neighborhoods as this demographic is increasingly geographically integrated into the metropolitan region in an era of increased rights and acceptance. Even in cases when the raw numbers of LGBT residents has not decreased (or in fact may have increased) the rate of growth of that demographic is less than the rate of growth of often-affluent non-LGBT populations. Sunsetting was evident in the Castro as early as 2007 (Buchanan 2007).

6. The Mattachine Society, the first national gay rights organization, was formed in 1951.

7. Down-zoning is a change in the zoning classification of a land parcel that is intended to reduce the building-to-land ratio, hence reducing the density in that parcel. It is often considered a controversial strategy because it limits the development potential of land parcels. Cities use down-zoning to reduce population density, relieve pressure on urban infrastructure, and support land values.

8. The marketing survey Mahany refers to is not available. In that same year, however, the *New York Times* provided similar findings: "Most decisions and assumptions about the market can be traced back to readership surveys done for The Advocate in 1977 and 1980 by the Los Angeles marketing firm of Walker & Struman Research Inc. The survey's 1,100 respondents were predominantly professional men residing in urban areas. Seventy percent of them were between the ages of 20 and 40, and their annual median income in 1980 was $30,000. By comparison, the national median income for the select group of men between the ages of 35 and 44—traditionally, a period of peak earning power—was $21,776. What is more, 28 percent of the respondents earned over $40,000 in 1980, while nationally, the number of men earning over $35,000 was only 6.9 percent" (Stabiner 1982).

9. "You Need All Together" (advertisement), *Chicago Gay Crusader*, April 1976.

10. American Community Survey is an online data depository of the U.S. Census Bureau; see https://www.census.gov/programs-surveys/acs/data.html.

11. At the time of its incorporation into Chicago in 1889, the community place name was Lake View. Both Lake View and Lakeview are in use, although the latter is more current.

12. Gay life in Chicago's South Side, which centered mostly on the Hyde Park and South Shore neighborhoods, deserves careful treatment and falls outside the scope of this chapter.

13. The impact of the HIV/AIDS epidemic on the building of cross-community alliances (especially between gay men and lesbians) and in changing the functional and demographic character of villages such as Boystown is worthy of close consideration and study elsewhere.

14. "Queer Bohemia," a term I have coined, was Chicago's proto– and informal gay ghetto in Chicago's North Loop and River North areas. Starting at the time of the Great Depression and continuing during World War II, disinvestment and physical plant obsolescence in Chicago's central business district created a classic mid-century blighted quarter. Overt and covert lesbi-gay business establishments (gay bars and taverns, bathhouses, blue movie theaters, and gay bookstores, among others) and a few social and community organizations filled a niche in the commercial structure of the Near North and incubated an early version of a Chicago gay village or ghetto. Combining elements of skid row and a zone of transition, the polygon defined by the North Loop (to the south), Wells Street (to the west), LaSalle (to the east), and North Avenue (to the north) became the target of massive land clearance in the 1950s and early 1960s, followed by significant gentrification. Starting in the late 1950s, most of the LGBT business and population, exiled by urban renewal, moved north to East Lakeview.

15. Chicago School sociologists have gathered ethnographic evidence that there was significant co-location of bohemians and sexual minorities in the neighborhoods north of Water Tower (Heap 2003).

16. Address data for the mapping of commercial and social organization entities were taken from business directories published in the *Gay Chicago* and *Lavender Defender* magazines for the period 1973–1978.

17. Halsted Street terminates at its intersection with North Broadway. Two blocks to the north of that intersection, North Broadway and then Clarendon Street connect the north terminus of Halsted Street to Irving Park Road. In the LGBT community's imaginary, Irving Park Road is the northern limit of Boystown, even though North Halsted Street falls somewhat short of it.

18. External sources of investment notwithstanding, it appears that significant investment capital cycles inward: "Halsted corridor[,] [which] serves as the backbone of the Boystown business district[,] has become even more stable as the 'vast majority' of bar and nightclub owners bought their properties. [Roscoe's bar owner] Ludwig noted that by doing so, the bar owners aren't chased away by higher rents and can plow their profits into upgrading their buildings" (Guy 2013).

19. The Sanborn Fire Insurance Atlases, also known as the Sanborn Maps, can be accessed through the Library of Congress at https://www.loc.gov/rr/geogmap/sanborn/.

20. Lake View Township was incorporated into Chicago in 1889. It quickly became the most densely populated community area in the city.

21. Historical data on commercial mortgages in East Lakeview for the period 1980–1990 is difficult to procure. I relied on gay press coverage of business ventures and launches in this period to support my assertion that a substantial proportion of real estate development capital on North Halsted Street was raised both locally and from within the LGBT community.

22. The first Municipal Equality Index report was released in November 2012. It rated 133 cities on a scale of 0–100 on a number of categories of LGBT rights and services. Eleven cities including New York and San Francisco received perfect scores.

Bibliography

Bell, David, and Jon Binnie. 2004. "Authenticating Queer Space: Citizenship, Urbanism and Governance." *Urban Studies* 41, no. 9: 1807–1820.

Bell, David, and Gill Valentine, eds. 1995. *Mapping Desire: Geographies of Sexualities*. London: Routledge.

Bouthillette, Anne-Marie. 1995. "Gentrification by Gay Male Communities." In *The Margins of the City: Gay Men's Urban Lives*, ed. Stephen Whittle, 65–83. Aldershot, UK: Ashgate.

Brown, Gavin. 2008. "Urban (Homo)sexualities: Ordinary Cities and Ordinary Sexualities." *Geography Compass* 2, no. 4: 1215–1231.

Browne, Kath, and Leela Bakshi. 2011. "We Are Here to Party? Lesbian, Gay, Bisexual and Trans Leisurescapes beyond Commercial Gay Scenes." *Leisure Studies* 30, no. 2: 179–196.

Buchanan, Wyatt. 2007. "S.F.'s Castro District Faces an Identity Crisis: As Straights Move In, Some Fear Loss of the Area's Character." *SFGATE*, February 25. http://www.sfgate.com/news/article/S-F-s-Castro-district-faces-an-identity-crisis-2615423.php.

Castells, Manuel, and Karen A. Murphy. 1982. "Cultural Identity and Urban Structure: The Spatial Organization of San Francisco's Gay Community." In *Urban Policy under Capitalism*, ed. Norman Fainstein and Susan Fainstein, 237–260. Beverly Hills, Calif.: Sage Publications.

Chicago Tribune. 1961. "Report Cites Store Blight in Lake View: Citizens' Council Lists Plans." October 19. Accessed May 3, 2016. http://archives.chicagotribune.com/1961/10/19/page/109/article/report-cites-store-blight-in-lake-view.

Crain's Chicago Business. 2009. "Chicago Real Estate Daily." Accessed May 3, 2016. http://interactive.chicagobusiness.com/closer/commercial-mortgages/full/.

Demarest, Erica. 2012. "HRC Unveils Municipal Equality Report." *Windy City Times* (online edition), December 5.

Galloway, Paul. 1998. "Pride on Parade: Chicago's Annual Procession, Once Spurned by the Straight World, Is Becoming The Place To See And Be Seen." *Chicago Tribune*, June 29. Accessed April 4, 2016. http://articles.chicagotribune.com/1998–06–29/features/9806290090_1_lesbian-pride-parade-lesbian-officers-gay-children.

Ghaziani, Amin. 2014. *There Goes the Neighborhood?* Princeton, NJ: Princeton University Press.

Guy, Sandra. 2013. "Gay beyond Boystown." *Chicago Sun-Times* (online edition), August 9. Accessed April 4, 2016. http://www.suntimes.com/news/metro/21487290–418/gay-beyond-boystown.html.

Heap, Chad. 2003. "The City as a Sexual Laboratory: The Queer Heritage of the Chicago School." *Qualitative Sociology* 26, no. 4: 457–87.

Johnson, Dirk. 1997. "Chicago Celebrates Gay, Lesbian Neighborhood: North Halsted Street Has Been at the Center of Homosexual Life in Chicago for More Than a Decade, Transforming a Down-at-the-Heels, Gang-Ridden Place into a Prosperous District." *Star Tribune*, August 31. Accessed April 4, 2016. http://www.highbeam.com/doc/1G1-62615357.html.

Kennedy, Kerrie. 2005. "Boy's Town Tries to Maintain Its Identity as Popularity Brings Higher Prices, New Residents and a Shrinking Gay Population." *YoChicago*, April 1. http://yochicago.com/boys-town-tries-to-maintain-its-identity-as-popularity-brings-higher-prices-new-residents-and-a-shrinking-gay-population/3/.

Knopp, Larry. 1990. "Some Theoretical Implications of Gay Involvement in an Urban Land Market." *Political Geography Quarterly* 9, no. 4: 337–352.

———. 1997. "Gentrification and Gay Neighborhood Formation in New Orleans." In *Homo Economics*, ed. Amy Gluckman and Betsy Reed, 45–64. New York: Routledge.

Knopp, Lawrence, and Michael P. Brown. 2002. "We're Here! We're Queer! We're Over There Too! Queer Cultural Geographies." In *The Handbook of Cultural Geography*, ed. Kay Anderson, Mona Domosh, Steve Pile, and Nigel Thrift, 460–481. New York: Sage.

Lauerman, Connie. 1973. "New Town: A Night Place." *Chicago Tribune*, May 6.

Lauria, Mickey, and Larry Knopp. 1985. "Towards an Analysis of the Role of Gay Communities in the Urban Renaissance." *Urban Geographies* 6, no. 2: 152–169.

Levine, Martin P. 1979. "Gay Ghetto." In *Gay Men: The Sociology of Male Homosexuality*, ed. Martin P. Levine, 182–204. New York: Harper and Row.

Ley, David. 1984. "Inner City Revitalization in Canada: A Vancouver Case Study." In *Gentrification, Displacement, and Neighborhood Revitalization*, ed. Bruce London and J. John Palen, 186–204. Albany, N.Y.: State University of New York Press.

Mahany, Barbara. 1983. "Dollars, Votes Promote Gay Power." *Chicago Tribune*, March 4. Accessed May 3, 2016. http://archives.chicagotribune.com/1983/03/04 /page/93/article/dollars-votes-promote-gay-power.

McMillen, Daniel, and John F. McDonald. 1999. "Land Use before Zoning: The Case of 1920's Chicago." *Regional Science and Urban Economics* 29: 473–489.

Nash, Catherine J. 2013. "The Age of the 'Post-Mo'? Toronto's Gay Village and a New Generation." *Geoforum* 49 (October): 243–252.

Papadopoulos, Alex. 2006. "From 'Towertown' to 'Boystown' and 'Girlstown': Chicago's Gay and Lesbian Geographies." In *Chicago's Geographies: Metropolis for the 21st Century*, ed. Richard P. Greene, Mark Jansen Bouman, and Dennis Grammenos, 232–241. Washington, D.C.: Association of American Geographers.

Peck, Jamie, Nik Theodore, and Neil Brenner. 2009. "Neoliberal Urbanism: Models, Moments, Mutations." *SAIS Review of International Affairs* 29, no. 1: 49–66.

Reed, Christopher. 2003. "We're from Oz: Marking Ethnic and Sexual Identity in Chicago." *Environment and Planning D: Society and Space* 21, no. 4: 425–440.

Ruting, Brad. 2008. "Economic Transformations of Gay Urban Spaces: Revisiting Collins' Evolutionary Gay District Model." *Australian Geographer* 39, no. 3: 259–269.

Sanborn Fire Insurance Atlases. 1930–1951. https://www.loc.gov/rr/geogmap/sanborn/.

Simonette, Matt. 2013. "Human Rights Panel Looks at Challenges and Rewards." *Windy City Times* (online edition), December 16.

———. 2014. "Homeless Agency Looks at Increasing Needs." *Windy City Times* (online edition), April 16.

Stabiner, Karen. 1982. "Tapping the Homosexual Market." *New York Times Magazine*, May 2. Accessed July 14, 2016. http://www.nytimes.com/1982/05/02/magazine /tapping-the-homosexual-market.html?pagewanted=all.

Stewart-Winter, Timothy. 2016. *Queer Clout. Chicago and the Rise of Gay Politics*. Philadelphia: University of Pennsylvania Press.

Valentine, Gill. 1996. "(Re)Negotiating the 'Heterosexual Street': Lesbian Production of Space." In *Bodyspace: Destabilizing Geographies of Gender and Sexuality*, ed. Nancy Duncan, 145–154. London: Routledge.

Wilson, David. 1987. "Urban Revitalization: The Case of Chelsea in New York City." *Urban Geography* 8: 129–145.

CHAPTER 8

Historic Preservation in a Neoliberal Context

From the Medinah Temple to Bloomingdale's

YUE ZHANG

If you walk around the Near North Side of Chicago, one of the hottest spots of real estate development in the city, a block on State Street between Ontario and Ohio Streets will undoubtedly catch your eye. On the eastern half of the block is the Medinah Temple, a large Middle Eastern–style structure with colorful ornaments and onion domes that looks like a mosque (Figure 8.1). On the western half of the block is the Tree Studios, three two-story buildings faced in handsome Roman brick that make up a U-shape complex (Figure 8.2). In the forest of high-rises and concrete-and-glass structures of the Near North Side, this block stands out because of the unique architectural styles of the buildings it houses. Looking closely, you will find something more interesting: the exterior of the Medinah Temple is decorated with black banners that announce that Bloomingdale's is located there and the ground level of the Tree Studios is covered in a cast-iron arcade and is occupied by trendy retail stores.

What is the story of this block? How did the Medinah Temple and the Tree Studios survive the real estate boom in downtown Chicago without being demolished to make space for high-rises? How did Medinah Temple become a Bloomingdale's? Were the Tree Studios built to be a space for retail? This chapter answers these questions through an investigation of the history and redevelopment of the block. The Medinah Temple was built by the Shriners in 1912 as a civic space to accommodate conventions, circuses, and concerts; the

Figure 8.1. The Medinah Temple building, viewed from across the intersection of Wabash Avenue and Ohio Street. Source: Photo by Larry Bennett.

Figure 8.2. The north façade of the Tree Studios, viewed from across Ohio Street. Source: Photo by Larry Bennett.

Tree Studios complex was constructed between 1894 and 1913 and was for a time the oldest artist enclave in the United States; its bylaws required its owners to support working artists. After a recent preservation and redevelopment project, the physical forms of the buildings are largely saved but their functions are completely changed. By examining the policy process of the redevelopment project, this chapter reveals the mechanisms and consequences of adaptive reuse of historic structures and sheds light on the complex and contested nature of historic preservation in a neoliberal era.

The chapter is divided into two main sections. The first section examines the impacts of neoliberalism on historic preservation. In particular, it discusses how adaptive reuse has become an increasingly prevalent approach to historic preservation in the neoliberal era and the inherent problems such an approach produces. The second section is a detailed case study of the preservation and redevelopment of the Medinah Temple and the Tree Studios in Chicago. It discusses the history of the buildings, the controversies about their landmark status, and the process and results of redevelopment. It also offers a critical evaluation of the consequences of adaptive reuse and its implications for historic preservation. Before examining these two principal topics, I briefly outline how neoliberalism reshapes urban space.

Neoliberalism is a theory and practice of political economy that demands a reduction in government provision of services and advocates for the primacy of the private market. At the center of neoliberal ideology is the belief that open, competitive, and unregulated markets, liberated from all forms of state interference, are the optimal mechanism for economic development (Harvey 2005). Although the intellectual roots of this "utopia of unlimited exploitation" (Bourdieu 1998) can be traced to the postwar writings of Friedrich Hayek and Milton Friedman, neoliberalism first gained widespread prominence during the late 1970s and early 1980s as a strategic political response to the sustained global recession of the preceding decade (Harvey 2005). In the neoliberal context, culturally and socially oriented policies have lost their primacy.

Neoliberalism has profound impacts on urban policies and reshapes urban space in distinct ways. Borrowing Joseph Schumpeter's famous expression, Neil Brenner and Nik Theodore (2002) describe the impact of neoliberalism on urban space as "creative destruction." Moments of destruction include the elimination and/or intensified surveillance of urban public spaces, the destruction of traditional working-class neighborhoods in order to make way for speculative redevelopment, and a retreat from community-oriented planning initiatives. At the same time, neoliberal ideology produces a new spatial order in cities through the creation of privatized spaces of elite/corporate consumption; the construction of large-scale megaprojects intended to attract corporate investment and reconfigure local land-use patterns; the creation of gated communities, urban enclaves, and other "purified" spaces of social reproduction; the "rolling forward" of the gentrification frontier and the intensification of social and spatial segmentation; and the adoption of the principle of "highest and best use" as the basis for major land-use planning decisions.

Adaptive Reuse: Historic Preservation between Public Good and Private Benefit

Historic preservation is defined as the act or process of applying measures to sustain the existing form, integrity, and material of a building or a site (Murtagh 2006). It has a long history that dates back to the days of the Roman Empire, when historic monuments were carefully maintained for future generations in order to provide them with a tangible form of connection to the past (Zhang 2013). In the modern era, the subject of historic preservation has expanded from historic monuments to vernacular architecture and neighborhoods, so-called urban texture. While these buildings are occupied by different people, they collectively constitute the architectural profile and the cultural memory of the community and the city. By providing a collective identity or cultural experience for urban dwellers, historic preservation has become a public good.

In a neoliberal city, architectural heritage is increasingly understood in terms of its monetary potential and profitability rather than its historic, cultural, or social values. To obtain the economic value of historic buildings, local officials and developers have employed adaptive reuse as a major approach in preservation practice. The National Trust for Historic Preservation defines adaptive reuse as "the process of converting a building to a use other than that for which it was designed, e.g., changing a factory into housing. Such conversions are accomplished with varying alterations to the building" (Murtagh 2006, 99).

Economic incentives are the driving force behind the adaptive reuse of historic buildings. From the 1966 National Historic Preservation Act to the 1976 Tax Reform Act and the 1981 Economic Recovery Tax Act, a series of national statutes have provided tax incentives for property owners and developers to rehabilitate historic buildings (Frank 2002). Meanwhile, tax increment finance (TIF) districts have become a popular tool local governments can use to route property tax revenue to real estate developers to stimulate adaptive reuse of historic buildings and the redevelopment of "blighted" historic districts. Thanks to these policies, developers have realized that preserving and reusing historic buildings can be more profitable than tearing them down. Collectively, these policies have created a unique economy of historic preservation in American cities, in which historic preservation has become a strategic device for increasing land value and managing property taxes (Barthel 1996; Fitch 1982; Reichl 1997).

As a particular type of preservation practice, adaptive reuse is a clear step forward from the massive demolition of historic buildings that was prevalent during the postwar era. However, there are two problems inherent in adaptive reuse. First, the physical structure of the preserved buildings usually needs to be altered in order to accommodate new functions, and this practice often compromises the historic fabric, thus destroying a building's historic character. To maintain the historic integrity of preserved buildings, alterations should be kept to a minimum. However, neither the National Trust for Historic Preservation nor the National Park Service has specific regulations about how to define or maintain historic integrity of buildings (Murtagh 2006). In their rush to turn a profit, developers often appear insensitive to the historic fabric of a building. Churches and theaters are particularly vulnerable because adaptive reuse seldom allows for the survival of the large interior space found in such buildings. Their unbroken interior space is usually divided, and the original fabric is lost to accommodate more economically viable activities.

The second problem of adaptive reuse is how it changes the function of preserved buildings. More often than not, culturally and socially oriented functions are replaced by more profit-driven, market-oriented ones. As a structure's function changes, the particularities of its history are muted and the users of cultural heritage change. As new, market-oriented functions have arisen, cultural heritage has been pushed from its social context and turned into an expression of prevailing political and economic interests. In this process, historic buildings are repackaged and marketed as a good or commodity whose purpose is to cater to social elites who are capable of paying for the consumption of the good, thus subordinating the commitment to providing a collective identity or cultural experience to the general public. In a word, by recycling historic structures to fulfill new functions, adaptive reuse risks sacrificing the public value of cultural heritage for private benefit.

Underlying these two problems are the challenging decisions related to how to successfully implement adaptations for economic viability and still preserve the quality of historicity for which the building is being kept. In the context of neoliberalism, however, economic logic often overrides the concern for historic integrity or cultural value. Architectural heritage has increasingly become an instrument for making profit and increasing the economic competitiveness of cities. The next section discusses the adaptive reuse of Tree Studios and the Medinah Temple. As two of Chicago's most salient examples of adaptive reuse in recent years, the stories of the two building complexes demonstrate how historic preservation is used by public and private actors as a strategic device for fulfilling economic interests in a neoliberal city.

Box 8.1: The South Loop Entertainment District

In May 2013, DePaul University, a private higher education institution, announced a multimillion-dollar agreement to construct a 10,000-seat basketball arena in the South Loop. DePaul is partnering with the City of Chicago, the Metropolitan Pier and Exposition Authority (MPEA), and Marriott Hotels to develop an entertainment district in the blocks just west of the city's huge convention complex, McCormick Place. In addition to the arena, which was initially estimated to cost $173 million and will also be used for concerts and other public events, the development plans included two hotels, one with 500 rooms, the second with 1,200, to anchor the redeveloped blocks. Initially, the financing of the stadium called for $70 million from DePaul, $55 million via increment financing (TIF), and the balance from MPEA. Soon after these details were announced, the Chicago City Council approved eminent domain powers to acquire the necessary parcels.

Critics argued that the city's use of TIF for the privately controlled arena was inappropriate and was particularly galling as it coincided with the closure of fifty Chicago public schools and cuts in school funding. Residents of adjoining neighborhoods, whose concerns centered on the prospects of increased traffic and the erection of architectural monoliths that would stunt street life, organized a protest demonstration. DePaul students formed the Coalition for an Alternatively Funded Arena (CAFA) to challenge the arena's construction and financing. University faculty members also questioned the financing arrangement, contending that DePaul's contribution to the project could be better spent on student scholarships, among other things. Faculty also expressed concern that the project came at time when salaries were frozen and part-time instructors were facing layoffs. In February 2014, DePaul's administration and the Emanuel administration announced that no TIF dollars would be used to directly fund the stadium. However, $55 million in TIF funds would still be allocated to the project, primarily to finance land acquisition for hotel construction.

As of late 2014 the estimated cost of the DePaul arena had increased and its construction timeline had been pushed back one year, but even so, changes to the original design scheme—which included setting the floor of the arena below street level—were under consideration. Still unaddressed by project proponents were the widely circulated views that an entertainment district adjoining McCormick Place was unlikely to rejuvenate the struggling convention complex and, conversely, that there was little chance that the episodically busy convention center would provide a sufficient volume of patrons to support commercial establishments in this lightly populated section of the South Loop.

The Redevelopment of an Oasis in the Concrete Forest

The Tree Studios were built between 1894 and 1913 by philanthropist Judge Lambert Tree and his wife, Anna Magie Tree. Impressed by Parisian ateliers they had visited, the Trees wanted to create an affordable workspace for artists. The original Tree Studios building had thirty-four studios and was located in the 600 block of North State Street, right behind the Trees' mansion on Wabash Avenue. It was built in 1894 to entice out-of-town artists working at the World's Columbian Exposition to stay in Chicago. Two annexes that were added on Ohio and Ontario Streets in 1912 and 1913 completed the Tree Studio Complex; the final total was fifty loft-studios (Richards 1998).

The original building was designed by the architectural firm of Parfitt Brothers and the annexes by architects Hill and Woltersdorf (Sinkevitch 2004). All of the buildings are framed in steel and are two stories high. The U-shape plan of the complex encloses an open courtyard. The ground level of the west façade is covered in a cast-iron arcade and was designed as storefronts, while the second story is covered in Roman brick and is designed to serve as artist studios with large windows that allow natural light to enter. Commercial space on Ohio Street generated revenue that subsidized rents for the artists, who worked in the units on the second floor and along the inner courtyard.

Lambert Tree set up a legal trust that allowed only artists, who would pay moderate rents, to reside in the Tree Studio Complex. Thanks to the legal trust, the Tree Studios became the oldest artists' colony in the United States. Throughout the years, Tree Studios was home, and even muse, to more than 600 artists. John Singer Sargent painted in its courtyard. James Allen St. John illustrated Edgar Rice Burroughs's Tarzan stories there. For a time, Academy Award nominees Burgess Meredith and Peter Falk lived at the studios. Those artists, whether avant-garde or classical, bourgeois or starving, notable or unknown, were drawn to the studios and struggled there before finding their true calling. The Tree

Studios provided a rare space for a diverse and lively artist community to form and grow in downtown Chicago (Briggs 2005).

After the death of Lambert Tree in 1910, the Trees' mansion was sold to the Ancient Arabic Order of Nobles of the Mystic Shrine, a fraternal club popularly known as the Shriners. The Shriners razed the house and used the land to build the Medinah Temple in 1912 as a meeting place and convention center for their members (Stevens 2010).

Designed by two Shrine architects, Harris Huehl and Richard Gustave Schmid, the Medinah Temple is one of the country's best examples of Islamic Revival architecture. It has horseshoe-shaped arches, geometric decoration, ornamental grills, and onion domes, all of which give it the unique look of a mosque. The temple took up half the block and contained an auditorium that seated 4,200 people and a banquet hall with room enough for 2,300. Although the temple was the home to a private and exclusive organization, many events were open to Shriners' families and some were open to the greater public. The temple's ornate auditorium was one of the best in the city and contained an Austin Organ Company pipe organ that was installed in 1915. The acoustics of the auditorium were so good that the Chicago Symphony Orchestra recorded over 100 performances, including many of its most famous recordings, at the temple from the late 1960s to the 1980s (Stevens 2010).

The Historic Block Becomes Contentious

In 1959, the Tree Studios complex was sold to the Medinah Temple Association. The Shriners thus became the owner of the entire block. According to the Tree Studios' later residents, the building had been poorly maintained for some time: roof repairs were made at the cost of destroying the hallway skylights and an administration wing the Shriners built took over part of the courtyard (Brotman 1985). The studios still maintained a high proportion of artist residents, but the "artist only" clause of the trust was no longer enforced. Residents claimed that over time rent increased from $400 to $1,200 per month, too expensive for many artists to afford (Richards 1998).

The block occupied by the Tree Studios and the Medinah Temple had become increasingly contentious space when the topic of landmark designation appeared on the agenda. The Tree Studios complex was listed on the National Register of Historic Places in 1974 and on the Illinois Historic Preservation Agency's Register of Historic Places in 1987. After the building was placed on the state's Register of Historic Places, a designation that requires a negotiation process before an owner may alter the property, the Shriners filed a lawsuit challenging the constitutionality of the Illinois Historic Places statute (Huebner 2001). In 1982, the Commission on Chicago Landmarks recommended that Tree Studios be designated a city landmark, a move that could prevent the building from being demolished. The Medinah Temple Association opposed the designation, emphasizing that the Tree Studios was an asset they had purchased and retained for benefit of their use, not as an artists' colony. The ensuing fifteen-year battle ended with a hearing in 1997 at which the Chicago City Council, which can vote down any landmark designation, thwarted the recommendation of the Commission on Chicago Landmarks to designate all of the Tree Studios and listed only the front façade and the roof line on State Street (Huebner 2001). In contrast to the disputes about the landmark status of the Tree Studios, the Medinah Temple was never considered for landmark designation, even though it has long been rated among the city's 200 most significant buildings. Anyone buying the property could have legally ripped down the Moorish Medinah Temple and most of the Tree Studios.

The entire block of the Tree Studios and the Medinah Temple became endangered in the late 1990s when the Shriners decided to sell the structures. The Shriners initially agreed to a $21 million deal with developer Steven Fifield, who wanted to tear down the temple and build a parking garage and a 49-story condominium tower (Greising 1998). The plan was subject to intense attack from artists inhabiting the Tree Studios, other members of the local art community, preservationists, and concerned citizens. Artist and Tree Studios resident Barton Faist and other Tree Studios supporters organized a letter-writing campaign. They sent over 1,200 letters to the Chicago Landmarks Commission to urge the city to save the buildings. The World Monuments Fund, a New York–based preservation organization, named the Tree Studios Complex and the Medinah Temple one of the world's 100 most endangered landmarks, in the company of Machu Picchu in Peru and the Valley of the Kings near Luxor, Egypt (Rozhon 1999).

Under the barrage of media coverage and intense public pressure, the city began to take a more proactive approach to saving the Tree Studios and the Medinah Temple. The local alderman, who had backed the studios' significantly reduced landmark designation, proposed new hearings to include the rest of the complex. Mayor Richard M. Daley also announced that the Medinah Temple should be saved (Washburn 1999). Fifield claimed that if he had to save both the studios and the temple, the property would be worth much less than $21 million. Seeing the potential for their interest to be undermined, the Shriners threatened to sue the city.

After a nine-month moratorium, Mayor Daley's administration rejected Fifield's plan and negotiated a new deal with developer Albert Friedman, who had already renovated several historic buildings in the River North and Near North Side neighborhoods. Friedman's plan was to save the exterior of the Medinah Temple and the Tree Studios and rehabilitate nearly all of the complex's interior.

Friedman paid $21 million for the properties. The Daley administration created a TIF district on the entire block that would generate real estate tax revenue of $14 million to be used for the renovation of the historic complex (Briggs 2005). The project also received $2 million in Illinois FIRST funding (see Illinois Government News Network 2001). To work out the rest of the renovation cost, Friedman proposed to Bloomingdale's parent company, Federated Department Stores, that the Medinah Temple be turned into a home furnishings store. It was an unlikely gambit, considering the retailer's reputation as a bastion of Manhattan chic, but Federated went for it, perhaps because the many condominium towers rising on adjoining blocks gave the store a built-in market of new homeowners (Kamin 2003).

In light of the previous plan to demolish the historic temple, the new plan of saving the building for adaptive reuse was undoubtedly preferable. However, the public still questioned the new plan because of its threat to the historic integrity and original functions of the temple. It was criticized as "a surgical procedure that removes all of the organs and leaves just the sagging skin" (Mendell 2000). The opponents suggested the city government ask voters to approve a bond issue to purchase the temple and use it for cultural activities, but the city did not consider this idea. Instead, city officials defended the compromise deal as the only economically viable solution that could save the buildings from becoming yet another Near North Side high-rise. "It was critical that we came up with a solution that met the owner's price or all of the Medinah Temple would be lost," said Alicia Mazur Berg, deputy commissioner of the city's Planning Department. She also emphasized that the city was "saving as much as possible." Alderman Burton Natarus of the 42nd Ward, where the Medinah Temple and the Tree Studios are located, maintained that "it's easy to give speeches and talk about preserving culture. The project is not perfect . . . but the fact of the matter is, this is private property, and we stopped the Shrine from selling it to a high-rise developer" (Mendell 2000).

Adaptive Reuse of the Historic Block

In 2001, the Medinah Temple was granted historic landmark status. In 2003, the renovation was completed, and the temple was reopened as the new home to the 120,000-square-foot, four-level Bloomingdale's home furnishings store. The renovation of the Medinah Temple was done by Chicago architect Dan Coffey and New York architect James Harb. Some historic features of the building are gone because of the renovation, including the theater's balconies and sloping floors and the organ pipes. To meet the need of the retailer, the architects inserted a four-level interior within the historic context, essentially a building within a building.

Figure 8.3. A ceramics display in the Bloomingdale's home furnishings store, with one of the Medinah Temple's historic windows visible in the background. Source: Photo by Larry Bennett.

Despite the alteration to the historic structure, the project has received positive feedback from architects and preservation professionals. Comparing a number of designs in Chicago that strive to give new life to old buildings, the *Chicago Tribune* architecture critic Blair Kamin (2003) maintained that the Medinah project "occupies the brighter side of this spectrum": more gut rehab than fine-grained redo, the project largely succeeds at enhancing the historic identity of the ninety-year-old building while meeting modern commercial needs (Figure 8.3).

The renovation of the adjacent Tree Studios was completed in 2004 and cost about $70 million (Briggs 2005). Like the Medinah Temple, the interior of the studios has been largely redesigned to accommodate new functions. The redevelopment plan gutted all seven sculpture studios on the ground level to accommodate shops, and it removed all of the kitchens and bathrooms from the studios in the State Street wing. A basement has been excavated under the courtyard to provide more retail space. Four studios were lost in order to make the building code-compliant, handicap accessible, and wired for the Information Age; that space is now occupied by elevators, bathrooms, airshafts, and electrical rooms.

What has been changed is not only the physical character of the buildings, but also their existence as the oldest artist colony in the United States (Osgood 2001). While about twenty-five artists lived in the Tree Studios before the renovation, no one is allowed to live there anymore. Artists who want to rent a studio must exceed a very high bar; not many of them can afford both a living space and a second commercial space. Under the $14 million TIF agreement with the city, Friedman agreed to lease 25 percent of the space to artists at below-market rates, although only for ten years, and the below-market-rate units are supposed to be offered first to artists who were forced out of the building. According to the deal, the City's Cultural Affairs Department, an artist chosen by the department, and the developer determined which artists would be allowed into these units when the project was finished. But the agreement also specified that if this committee could not find "qualified" artists, the owners could lease the units to arts-related businesses (Huebner 2001). There is little information about who was chosen as "qualified" artists, if an effort was ever made to select such artists. The result is that none of the tenants who were forced out of the building moved back. Many of them confessed that they could not afford the rents of the renovated units, so they had to relocate to neighborhoods with cheaper rents (Briggs 2005).

The twenty-six studios are re-leased as artist workspaces or as office space for art-related businesses. The current tenants are mostly painters, but they also include architects, fashion and interior designers, graphic artists, and photographers. Rents at the Tree Studios had always been modest because the studios' bylaws required its owners to support working artists (Chandler 2000). Today, however, the former haven for artists has become an exclusive space for those who are financially well off. Meanwhile, the expansion of the art-related businesses has caused the Tree Studios to increasingly drift away from its original purpose of nurturing the local artist community.

Gone with the art community are local businesses. There were previously eleven small businesses on the street level of the studios, including Jim Romano's antique store, Brudnos Art Supply, Quintessence frame shop, and a barbershop where hair had been cut since "day one" in 1894. Some of the longtime businesses had deep ties both to the local area and to the larger art community. After the renovation project, those eleven small businesses were replaced by six large ones, including a champagne bar, a men's clothing and accessory store, an antique store, a teashop, a bed store, and a beauty salon, all of which tend toward the luxury end of the retail spectrum. The studios' North Annex and South Annex (eight large annex apartments, including the "Tarzan studio") were restored and leased to Metropolitan Capital Bank and to the furniture store Design Within

Reach, respectively. In the eyes of locals, the fact that the preceding retailers were pushed out is a loss to the community. As preservationist Anna Weaver put it before the studios were renovated, "It's not as though [the retailers] are people working at a shopping mall. There's a village-like sensibility" (quoted in Chandler 2000).

An Outcome to Be Celebrated?

The renovation of Medinah Temple and the Tree Studios has received positive evaluation from architecture and preservation professionals. According to David Bahlman, executive director of the Landmarks Preservation Council of Illinois (LPCI, also known as Landmarks Illinois), the compromise that preserved the historic block is a success. Bahlman says that although adaptive reuse is not a perfect solution, it allows more modifications and the best chance for saving the building. He also emphasizes that "the Landmarks Preservation Council is not for preserving culture, it's for preserving buildings." Lisa DiChiera, director of advocacy at the LPCI, says her organization is "thrilled" with the renovation. "Compromise is what historic preservation is all about," she said, "Lifestyles change, neighborhoods change, economics change. You cannot freeze a building in time" (Briggs 2005). The restoration project received the President's Award from the LPCI in 2007. It is considered a national model for how public-private partnership can be used to enable preservation (see Landmarks Illinois 2010).

In contrast to the praise from architects and other designers, many from the local community, especially former artist and business tenants, criticize the renovation project. They call the renovation a tragedy and lament that although the buildings have been saved from the wrecking ball, they have permanently lost their socially and culturally oriented functions. The community that gave the historic block its unique charm is gone. The Medinah Temple, one of the finest examples of a Middle Eastern–style Shrine temple in America, is gutted in favor of a national retailer. The Tree Studios, the nation's oldest enclave for working artists, has become retail space and an exclusive "artsy" spot for those who are economically well off.

To be fair, the Tree Studios had already lost much of the feel of the original artists' community after it was sold to the Shriners in 1959. Although artists still occupied the majority of the units, the building was no longer restricted to artists who were highly recommended and had a portfolio of work. According to a *Chicago Tribune* article published in 1998, the fifty studio lofts also were home to lawyers and small business owners who lived alongside the artists (Richards 1998). Some artists consider the renovation project to be the last blow to their ability to find space where they can work and live. James Stola, a member of the board of the Chicago Artists' Coalition, notes that many artists "cannot afford separate spaces to live and work. . . . And eliminating that working and living space is really sending a message to artists to get out of town" (Huebner 2001).

It is important to note that the charm of the historic block lies not only in the buildings but also in the inhabitants and the urban life. The artists, local businesses, and people who randomly visited the block had created a community there. They provided the kind of "street ballet" of urban life that Jane Jacobs (1961) described so enthusiastically. While the renovation project has maintained most of the physical form of the buildings, it did nothing to preserve the community inside the buildings or the dynamic city life on the historic block. City officials emphasize that they have saved "as much as possible" of the buildings, but the question is whether saving as much as possible of the physical form is the only thing that matters for historic preservation. Public officials should recognize the value of the lively urban community that lies behind the façade of such buildings.

The case of the Medinah Temple and the Tree Studios also shows the city government's insufficient and ineffective involvement, or *inaction*, in historic preservation. Both the Medinah Temple and the Tree Studios lacked adequate legal protection over the years. Although the Medinah Temple has long been rated among Chicago's most significant buildings, it was not considered for landmark status until the Shriners decided to sell it to the developer who wanted to demolish the building. While the Tree Studios received landmark designations from both the federal and state governments, it did not receive that designation from the city until 1997, fifteen years after the Landmarks Commission recommended that the city give it landmark status. In addition, the city protected only a portion of the building. As the evidence shows, the effort the city made to preserve the buildings was reactive, making one wonder whether the result would be different if the city had taken action to protect the buildings earlier when the real estate market was down and before physical deterioration was so far advanced.

The Medinah Temple and the Tree Studios are not the only buildings that have experienced the city government's inaction in historic preservation. The previous preservation ordinance permitted the city council to leave proposed landmarks in a legal limbo, where they were protected from demolition temporarily but were denied permanent landmark status. This was the case with twenty-nine buildings and districts. New York, for example, sets a 120-day limit for its legislative body to take up such matters, but in the 1990s there was no such mandate in Chicago, and the waiting period could go on interminably. In the mid-1990s, some of the proposed designations had been awaiting a city council vote for at least five years (Kamin 1996). In 1996, the city council passed a new law requiring that landmark recommendations be approved within a year, but it failed to mandate that the council vote on the issue. The result is that some buildings are automatically denied landmark status one year after landmark recommendations were made. This arrangement prompted architecture critic Kamin (1996) to comment that what the aldermen did was to "replace an old landmarks law that was bad with a new one that is worse." He pointed out that the danger of the new preservation ordinance was that "aldermen can consign buildings to the graveyard without signing their names on the death warrant." Preservationists also challenge the new law as "part of a plot by some aldermen to foil proposed landmark designations they have long opposed" (Kamin and Fegelman 1996).

The city government's inaction on historic preservation can be partially justified by the difficulty of balancing the different interests involved in preservation. There is no doubt that historic preservation is a highly contentious process due to the diverse and sometimes conflicting interests and preferences of the relevant actors. Among the major actors are property owners. In Chicago, although the city's landmark ordinance does not require an owner's consent to the designation of his property, some aldermen, including Alderman Natarus of the Medinah Temple and Tree Studios struggle, have long made such consent a prerequisite for designation (Kamin 1996). In the face of demand from the public to designate the Medinah Temple and the Tree Studios as local landmarks, Natarus emphasized that the buildings were private properties, implying that the city council could not unilaterally approve the designation without trampling on the rights of the property owners.

The case of the Medinah Temple and the Tree Studios shows that even a minority of objecting owners in a district or building is enough to stall designation, leaving historic buildings in danger of dilapidation or demolition. Thus, while it is important to protect private property rights, it is equally important to recognize the public good that results from saving historic buildings. In any urban context, protecting the past means finding a way to balance the clashing interests of private property rights and the public good that results from saving historic buildings. To successfully achieve that balance, public officials should be more proactive in recognizing and protecting the public good instead of using private property rights as an excuse for their insufficient support of historic preservation.

The story of the Medinah Temple and the Tree Studios reveals the tremendous power of local aldermen in historic preservation. According to the legal procedure of landmark designation in Chicago, the city council has the final say after the Commission on Chicago Landmarks recommends a building, site, or district for landmark status. But more important, city council members normally defer to the local alderman when they vote on the landmark status of a building or district in his or her ward. The power of aldermen to initiate or block city council or city government actions concerning their own wards is called aldermanic prerogative, a longtime tradition in Chicago politics. This prerogative is particularly influential in land-related issues, including historic preservation, zoning, and redevelopment (Zhang 2013). Since aldermen tend to placate the wishes of the developers who often finance their campaigns, the exercise of aldermanic prerogative increases the influence of developers in historic preservation and urban development.

The redevelopment of Medinah Temple and the Tree Studios clearly demonstrates the dominant role of developers in the preservation process. A letter from a reader published in the *Chicago Tribune* puts it this way: "The situation involving Medinah Temple and Tree Studios is a reflection of the fact that developers are the de facto urban planners for the city of Chicago" (Weaver 1999). This statement perfectly illustrates the dynamics of historic preservation and urban planning in a neoliberal city. It would be unfair and unrealistic to ask private developers to change their nature and stop trying to maximize profit. Therefore, as the experiences from other cities show, the government should play a more active role in regulating the behaviors of private developers and mitigating the negative impacts of the market. This is the key for more socially responsible and human-scaled historic preservation and urban planning. The implication for Chicago is that implementing a more centralized approach in historic preservation by eliminating the veto power of aldermen and empowering city-level government agencies on historic preservation might be a possible way to mitigate the influence of real estate developers and achieve a more balanced preservation policy.

Preservation as a Public Good

In the neoliberal era, many cities are using economic incentives to foster historic preservation and adaptive reuse of historic buildings. From tax credits to TIF districts, those policies have helped property owners make ends meet and encouraged real estate developers to redevelop instead of demolishing historic buildings. Municipal leaders have realized that historic preservation does not necessarily mean economic hardship. Adaptive reuse is no doubt an advance compared to the practice of wholesale demolition of historic buildings that prevailed in the postwar urban renewal era. However, as this chapter shows, when both public officials and private developers focus on the economic feasibility and profitability of redevelopment plans, the historic integrity of the buildings—both physical and social—may be lost, to the detriment of both the local community and the city at large.

To avoid those problems, we need to remember that preservation is a public good that provides a collective identity and gives cultural depth to our society. While it is important to balance different interests and take into account changing times and a changing social environment, giving old buildings new life does not require that we convert historic structures into cash machines. It is critical for policy makers and planners to protect local communities and their ways of life behind the façades of buildings. We should respect and support the socially and culturally oriented functions that many such structures were intended to house. Otherwise we might sacrifice not just a vibrant urban life; we might also lose ourselves in the ever-accelerating neoliberal era.

Bibliography

Barthel, Diane. 1996. *Historic Preservation: Collective Memory and Historical Identity*. New Brunswick, N.J.: Rutgers University Press.

Bourdieu, Pierre. 1998. *Acts of Resistance: Against the Tyranny of the Market*. New York: Free Press.

Brenner, Neil, and Nik Theodore. 2002. "Cities and the Geographies of 'Actually Existing Neoliberalism,'" *Antipode* 34, no. 3: 349–379.

Briggs, Johnathon E. 2005. "Historic Tree Studios Survives Redo, But Homes for Artists Don't." *Chicago Tribune*, August 24.

Brotman, Barbara. 1985. "Where Art and Artists Still Reside." *Chicago Tribune*, November 28.

Chandler, Susan. 2000. "Renovation Leaves Tree Studios Retailers Unsure." *Chicago Tribune*, December 23.

Fitch, James Marston. 1982. *Historic Preservation: Curatorial Management of the Built World*. New York: McGraw-Hill.

Frank, Karolin. 2002. *Historic Preservation in the USA*. Berlin and New York: Springer.

Greising, David. 1998. "Tree Studios Could Be Sapped of Its Real Life." *Chicago Tribune*, October 28.

Harvey, David. 2005. *A Brief History of Neoliberalism*. New York: Oxford University Press.

Huebner, Jeff. 2001. "Hollow Tree Promises." *Chicago Reader*, November 1.

Illinois Government News Network. 2001. "$2 Million in Illinois FIRST Funding for Medinah Temple Renovation." Press release. Accessed February 27, 2016. http://www3.illinois.gov/PressReleases/ShowPressRelease.cfm?SubjectID=3&RecNum=741.

Jacobs, Jane. 1961. *The Death and Life of Great American Cities*. New York: Vintage.

Kamin, Blair. 1996. "Chicago Landmarks: Tumbling Legacy." *Chicago Tribune*, March 10.

———. 2003. "A Splendid Survivor." *Chicago Tribune*, February 6.

Kamin, Blair, and Andrew Fegelman. 1996. "Council Glitch Puts Landmark Sites in Danger." *Chicago Tribune*, February 9.

Landmarks Illinois. 2010. "President's Award: Medinah Temple/Tree Studios Block, Chicago." Accessed February 27, 2016. http://www.landmarks.org/awards_2007_2.htm.

Mendell, David. 2000. "Artists of Tree Studios Fighting to Keep Homes." *Chicago Tribune*, September 6.

Murtagh, William J. 2006. *Keeping Time: The History and Theory of Preservation in America.* Hoboken, N.J.: John Wiley & Sons.

Osgood, Charles. 2001. "It's a Change of Season for Tree Studios." *Chicago Tribune*, June 24.

Reichl, Alexander J. 1997. "Historic Preservation and Progrowth Politics in U.S. Cities." *Urban Affairs Review* 32, no. 4: 513–535.

Richards, Cindy. 1998. "Artists Fear the End Is Near For Tree Studios." *Chicago Tribune*, July 11.

Rozhon, Tracie. 1999. "Turf; Chicago Artists Battle the Clock." *New York Times*, September 16.

Sinkevitch, Alice. 2004. *AIA Guide to Chicago.* Orlando, Fla.: Harcourt.

Stevens, Caroline Nye. 2010. "The Medinah Temple." *Blueprint: Chicago,* August 11. Accessed July 16, 2014. http://www.blueprintchicago.org/2010/08/11/the-medinah -temple/

Washburn, Gary. 1999. "Daley Fights for Medinah Temple." *Chicago Tribune*, April 28.

Weaver, Anna. 1999. "Urban Planning." Letter to the editor. *Chicago Tribune*, March 13.

Zhang, Yue. 2013. *The Fragmented Politics of Urban Preservation: Beijing, Chicago, and Paris.* Minneapolis: University of Minnesota Press.

PART IV

NEOLIBERAL PROCESSES

Neoliberal Chicago is shaped by an array of broad social forces and by the chains of decision making we conventionally label public policy. Martha Martinez's analysis of the varied neighborhood impacts of the 2008 real estate crash highlights how national-level deregulation of financial institutions produced devastating and highly uneven local consequences. The saga of police surveillance Rajiv Shah and Brendan McQuade present clearly combines elements of the local and nonlocal: technological developments and evolving policy thinking that promote increasingly intrusive electronic surveillance at the national and international scales and adaptation of new technologies in alignment with a particular view of local policing priorities. Larry Bennett, Michael Bennett, and Stephen Alexander examine the local politics of a trademark and globally encompassing neoliberal policy inclination: the promotion of mega-events as prime generators of urban economic growth.

As with other aspects of neoliberal Chicago, these processes routinely produce (or reproduce) familiar inequalities: income and wealth inequality and inequalities in the conditions of neighborhood life. These processes are also profoundly alienating. Olympic salesman portray a bright future to audiences of community residents who cannot begin to imagine how their day-to-day lives will be improved through Olympic hosting. Homeowners who have attempted to pursue the American dream are wiped out in the wake of unforeseen macro-economic and public policy breakdowns. And even as new surveillance technologies promise to yield a safer Chicago, some portions of the city remain unabated crime hotspots.

CHAPTER 9

Neighborhood Impacts of the Foreclosure Crisis

MARTHA MARTINEZ

Homeownership both symbolizes and embodies key elements of the neo-liberal policy agenda. At the same time, it demonstrates the limits of neoliberalism and the failure of markets to substitute for government-based public policy. Homes occupy an intermediate space between consumer goods and investments (Dietz and Haurin 2003). Although houses very clearly satisfy the need for shelter and they deteriorate over time because of this use, with proper maintenance they have historically (the recent housing crisis notwithstanding) retained and even increased their value over time. Owner-occupied dwellings have played a pivotal role as funding for retirement, particularly as older citizens sell their family homes and downsize to smaller and cheaper properties. Home equity is a sizable part of American family wealth, accounting for 25 percent as of 2011. However, the most recent housing crisis demonstrated once again that investments in housing are anything but safe. In fact, the drastic reduction in the median net worth of American households during the recent recession, from $106,000 in 2005 to only $68,000 in 2011, can be attributed almost exclusively to the loss of home equity and the reduction of housing prices (Gottschalck, Vornovytskyy, and Smith 2013).

Homeownership is also clearly connected to the more subtle symbolic components of neoliberalism, especially the proposition that markets are a source of social virtues. The neoliberal assumption is that private ownership of homes, in contrast to renting, will provide incentives for individuals to maintain their properties and cooperate with their neighbors to increase general levels of social capital and, in turn, achieve a higher quality of life for the whole community

(DiPasquale and Glaeser 1999). The assumptions are that a higher level of political participation, investment in local amenities, and positive maintenance of properties will lead to better communities (Rohe, Van Zandt, and McCarthy 2002). From this point of view, homeownership can be viewed as a substitute for government intervention to solve a host of social problems, from insufficient retirement incomes, high crime rates, and low school quality to deficits in individual "social investment" (Dietz and Haurin 2003). In addition, homeownership is assumed to have positive effects on social mobility by improving the behavioral metrics of children, including lower school dropout and teen pregnancy rates among the offspring of homeowners (Green and White 1997).

For a variety of reasons, researchers have not been able to conclusively prove or disprove the assumed social benefits of homeownership (Engelhardt, Eriksen, Gale, and Mills 2010), let alone compare them to its potential costs such as reduced labor mobility (Oswald 1996; Rohe and Stewart 1996). Regardless, the neoclassical logic of this viewpoint presumes that high levels of homeownership are ideal. For society to benefit from homeownership, a high proportion of the general population must have access to the tools that permit widespread home purchasing. In public discourse this belief took the form of policies by President George W. Bush to promote an "ownership society" (Becker, Stolberg, and Labaton 2008). However, three factors make the neoliberal dream of universal homeownership almost impossible in a city such as Chicago: the return of the upper middle class to the inner city, the global nature of urban real estate markets, and stagnating incomes of families in the middle to lower level of the income distribution.

An important source of contemporary demand in urban housing is the return of the professional and "creative classes" to urban centers (Florida 2002). Professionals not only settle in cities at the start of their careers, but in ever-growing numbers they are staying to raise their children. Many of Chicago's long-standing working-class neighborhoods are now dominated by a returning upper middle class. Although gentrification has been more pervasive on Chicago's North Side, even ethnic neighborhoods on the South and West Sides are experiencing settlement by new residents with higher incomes. The South Loop, Bronzeville, Pilsen, and Chinatown are becoming destinations for the children and grandchildren of immigrants and working-class ethnic families who have achieved social mobility through education. Although these individuals and families often move into such areas in an effort to maintain or recapture their individual and neighborhood ethnic identities, the improvement in services and amenities they create also attracts prosperous whites. Eventually, lower income ethnic residents are priced out of the area. Stagnant wages at the lower occupational levels and income inequality compound the problem. Chicago, according to a recent report by the Brookings Institution, is the eighth most unequal city in the country: the 95th percentile of income earners makes around

$200,000 a year and the bottom 20th percentile makes only around $16,000, a more than tenfold gap (Berube 2014).

These local dynamics are exacerbated by the mobility of capital, which has transformative consequences in urban real estate markets that affect both demand and supply. One such effect is the increasing importance of foreign direct investment and foreign companies on the U.S. real estate market, both in financing new construction and in buying financial instruments based on aggregated mortgages (Gotham 2006). Despite the potential for investment in real estate created by global capital flows, the globalization of real estate finance means that local housing needs become secondary to profit taking. When directly involved in construction projects, holders of global financial capital are more likely to concentrate on fulfilling the needs of global elites, a class of people whose incomes and expectations are so far removed from local interests that they can be described as "super-gentrifiers" (Butler and Lees 2006). Although the effect of global capital in the housing market in Chicago may not be as substantial as it is in New York City, for example, the reality is that a regulatory and policy environment more responsive to the needs of capital and more concerned with maintaining an attractive global city have contributed to making the most desirable locations in Chicago unaffordable for anybody but the very prosperous.

In various ways, the competition between local and global elites and the urban poor contradicts the rhetoric of an extended homeownership society. Increased competition for space means that the urban poor are outbid for an increasing proportion of desirably located neighborhoods, the process widely known as gentrification. Thus, extensive homeownership for groups of limited or moderate income is imperiled by a lack of affordable housing options. The communities that remain affordable are usually those that offer the fewest economic opportunities. Chicago neighborhoods with higher gentrification levels, which include much of the North Side, the South Loop, Humboldt Park, Logan Square, and Bronzeville, are strategically located near the core of the city, provide the best job opportunities, and have the best public transportation. While easy public transportation is a convenience for the rich, it is a necessity for the poor, who often have to travel great distances to find jobs.

The crisis of affordability yields a striking conundrum for the neoliberal approach to housing. Any mechanism or policy that interferes with the market in a way that may alter the quality and pricing of the supply is seen as suspicious. Therefore, policies such as subsidizing or requiring the construction of affordable new properties are out of the question. Direct government involvement in the housing sector in the form of financing for housing projects is also an ideological sin. How then is a neoliberal regime supposed to achieve near-universal homeownership in the face of prices that are unaffordable for a large portion of the population?

The answer to this question is the expansion of credit. As the stimulation of demand became more important for capitalism during the twentieth century, credit became a key tool for propping up consumption (Watkins 2000). Despite its bad reputation in the wake of the recent Great Recession, credit has been one of the most important tools for improving the standard of living in industrialized economies. Instead of saving for extended periods of time before enjoying the benefits of expensive commodities such as cars and houses, consumers can possess these goods while still paying for them. The philosophy of credit as social policy and a primary lever for increasing homeownership was especially promoted via modifications to the Community Reinvestment Act (1977), which put pressure on the secondary-market mortgage buyers, the Federal National Mortgage Association (Fannie Mae) and the Federal Home Loan Mortgage Corporation (Freddie Mac), to support increased lending to low-income and minority families. Fannie Mae and Freddie Mac are government-sponsored entities that Congress created to provide financial services and increase the flow of mortgage credit. Although neither of these companies directly lends to prospective homeowners, they buy mortgages from the original lenders. They then aggregate the cash flows mortgage payers produce into financial instruments that can be sold to investors anywhere in the world and that can then be retraded endlessly in open markets. These instruments increase the capacity of original lenders to offer home loans, as they can replenish their own capital to finance mortgages. In the 1990s and thereafter, amendments to the Community Reinvestment Act and the Clinton and George W. Bush administrations' unflinching commitment to expanding homeownership directed Freddie Mac and Fannie Mae to support lending to minority and low-income families. For example, in 2000, the Department of Housing and Urban Development required Fannie Mae to dedicate 50 percent of its business to moderate- and low-income families by 2010. Concurrently, trends in the banking industry reduced the share of mortgage lending subject to Community Reinvestment Act regulations intended to reduce risk, and a new generation of non-bank lenders began to target minority and low-income families with subprime loans. By the early 2000s Freddie Mac and Fannie Mae had become a prop for this rapidly growing housing submarket through their purchase and resale of mortgages (Immergluck 2009; Katz 2009).

This is the point at which the desire for an "ownership society" collided with market dynamics and individual motivations. Credit is itself a commodity that can be bought and sold, having both a price and return on investment in the form of interest. A second effect of global capital invested in real estate is that it increases the demand for real estate "transactions" that can be both easily commoditized and transformed into liquid assets to be traded in financial markets. Securities separate actual physical assets (which are too specific and difficult to trade) from the profits they would generate over time in the form of interest rates or rents. In short, globalization connects the local mortgage market to the more unstable international financial markets (Ashton 2009).

Because of the demand for mortgage-backed securities, which before the recent financial crisis were considered a very safe and profitable product, banks were incentivized to increase the number of mortgages they provided in order to create more securities so they could sell them to avid investors. These dynamics were presumed to harness the market in order to significantly increase the level of homeownership. To protect their own bottom lines, Freddie Mac and Fannie Mae became aggressive purchasers of subprime mortgages, which they securitized and resold to global investors (Becker, Stolberg, and Labaton 2008). These subprime securities were incorrectly rated as low risk (AAA). The combination of (apparent) low-risk and high returns on investment made these instruments extremely popular among investors, which created more incentive for mortgage lenders to sell subprime mortgages. The expansion of mortgage lending was made possible by the loosening of credit requirements. The risk of default and foreclosure was increased, but ratings were never adjusted for the new conditions (Ashton 2009). Moreover, credit default swaps were tied to the mortgage-backed securities. A credit default swap is a financial instrument for which the buyer pays a certain amount of money to the seller; in the event of defaults in the underlying, securitized loans, the buyer receives the value of the security. This instrument has an obvious speculative element, as the buyer is betting on loan defaults.

The push toward broader securitization of mortgages and the growth of credit default swaps happened at the same time that the financial industry was substantially deregulated. In 1999, Congress approved the Financial Services Modernization Act, which repealed the Glass-Steagall Act of 1933 (Katz 2009). The new act allowed financial institutions to function simultaneously as investment banks, consumer banks, and insurance companies. As such, they could promote the consolidation of financial institutions and—in the now-notorious expression—permit them to become "too big to fail." It also systematized conflicts of interest that magnified market risks instead of spreading and diversifying them. The Financial Services and Modernization Act further specified that credit default swaps were unregulated products and as such, were not subject to government oversight.

While financial deregulation and the expansion of global capital hungry for investment opportunities played a role in transforming the foreclosure mess into a global financial crisis, the root of the problem was the assumption that any credit, no matter how expensive, can solve problems of affordability, particularly in global cities. The usefulness of credit as a tool of social change depends on two different characteristics: availability and affordability. The biggest mistake of neoliberal policies on housing was that they confused one with the other. While both public officials and banking institutions worked very hard to make mortgages available, they did not ensure that they were affordable. In fact, availability was increased only by the expansion of riskier, less affordable loans.

The expansion of mortgage availability was achieved by two strategies. First was the transformation of underwriting practices and the expansion of alternative types of loans. In response to the Clinton and Bush administrations' push to increase homeownership and more broadly, to the deregulation of the financial sector, many lenders transformed their underwriting requirements with the following types of prospective buyers in mind: those with low (or no) credit scores, those who were unable to make the traditional down payment of 20 percent, and those without traditional income sources. These problems were characteristic of the urban poor, but they also characterized the situation of the nation's growing immigrant population (including undocumented immigrants). These underwriting changes included not requiring at least two years' employment, not penalizing borrowers for job changes, allowing higher debt-to-income ratios, permitting small down payments, and recognizing nontraditional credit sources (life insurance policy payments, school tuition programs, remittances, etc.).

However, for many borrowers, the availability of credit came with a high price. Much of the expansion in credit came from the subprime market. Subprime loans are characterized by relaxed underwriting policies, and because they are considered riskier than regular loans, banks levy substantially higher interest rates. A loan that charges 1.5 percentage points above rate is considered subprime, but many mortgages issued in the early 2000s were more costly than that. In 2004, 42 percent of all U.S. subprime loans for site-built houses charged interest rates that were 4 percentage points above the prime rate, and 15 percent of them charged more than 5 percent higher than the prime rate. These loans became very common across the United States: from 1998 to 2006, subprime mortgage originations grew from 10 to 23 percent of total mortgages issued. In Chicago, in 2004, 11 percent of all first-time mortgages were subprime, and minorities were more likely to get them. In that year, 24 percent of first mortgages for Latinos in the city were subprime (Martinez 2007). The irony embodied by the emergence of the subprime mortgage bubble was that it did, after a fashion, respond to the historical exclusion of racial and ethnic minorities from mortgage credit. However, it did so by creating a system of racial exploitation, through which minorities were given credit only at an unreasonable and unsustainable price (Ashton 2012).

Subprime loans are accompanied by nontraditional loan arrangements. A traditional loan is a 15- or 30-year commitment with a fixed interest rate for the duration of the loan. Some alternatives to fixed rate loans include:

- No-down-payment loans, in which the down payment is financed by a second loan instead of using the borrower's savings. However, borrowers have to pay higher interest rates on the second loan, as it is considered riskier. They are also required to purchase mortgage insurance, which presumably covers the risk of default.
- No-interest loans, in which for a fixed period of time (on average two years) the borrower only makes a portion of the normal monthly payment, corresponding to the principal. Interest payments are higher, though the loan is more affordable in the first few years. However, interest accumulates to the total debt during this initial period, and borrowers eventually have to make significantly higher monthly payments to make up for the difference.
- Adjustable rate mortgages (ARMs), which provide low introductory interest charges that last for an average of two years. After this introductory period, interest rates are adjusted to higher levels.

These alternative types of loans address the problem of affordability for a short time but then make mortgages much less affordable, particularly for individuals with limited opportunities to significantly increase their income. When these alternative loan forms were created, they were intended for people with higher levels of income. However, in the years preceding the mortgage crisis, financial institutions with no incentive to make sure the loans were sustainable relentlessly marketed these products to the poor and racial minorities (Katz 2009).

Short-term affordability can work when there is high demand and increasing prices. Many borrowers were told that given market trends, they could expect high appreciation in their properties and that they could use the newly gained equity to refinance and acquire lower-interest, traditional fixed-rate loans. This was a self-fulfilling prophecy, at least in the short term, as the easy availability of credit artificially inflated demand for housing and created what economists call a bubble. However, the fact that new credit policies were developed with the idea of helping low-income and minority families does not mean that they were the only ones benefiting. Higher income families used the new credit standards to buy bigger properties, second homes, and investment properties. By doing so, they put even more pressure on real estate prices, which made home purchase a riskier proposition for low-income and minority families. As access to credit loosened, properties became even less affordable and homeownership risk was increased for low-income and minority families.

This conjunction of public policies and new financing mechanisms expanded the availability of mortgage credit in the short run, including for low-income and ethnic minority families, but this access to credit was not sustained over time, culminating in foreclosures, bankruptcies, and the erosion of the homeownership gains achieved in the previous ten years. Homeownership expansion was an initial, short-term success followed by a deceleration of prices and credit accompanied by increasing foreclosures, particularly in neighborhoods with lower median incomes and higher proportions of ethnic minorities. A few years later, the final stage of catastrophic disinvestment arrived, wiping out all of the progress in homeownership growth during the preceding decade.

In the remainder of this chapter I examine the consequences of this arc of overheated investment and subsequent property value loss. The Great Recession was a global catastrophe, but depending on which neighborhood in Chicago happened to be "your home," the impacts of this global crisis were very different.

The Foreclosure Crisis in Chicago

Table 9.1 shows the percentage of mortgaged properties (or parcels) from 2005 to 2012 in several neighborhoods across Chicago.[1] These neighborhoods were selected to illustrate the different effects for communities with particular ethnic compositions and levels of gentrification. In this sample, as is generally true for Chicago, white neighborhoods are located on the North Side, while neighborhoods with majorities of African Americans are located on the South and West Sides of the city (see Chapter 2). Table 9.2 provides the ethnic composition of these neighborhoods, using the categories of white, black, and Hispanic, which, of course, are not in every case mutually exclusive.

The data indicate that in 2005, mortgage originations were prevalent in most neighborhoods and that the city average was 31 percent of parcels. Surprisingly, mortgage levels were actually higher in Austin, Oakland, Englewood, and Logan Square. The first three neighborhoods are predominantly African American, and Logan Square is heavily Latino. Richer, whiter, and more gentrified areas, such as Lincoln Park and North Center, had relatively lower levels of mortgages. However, the high levels of mortgage credit were not sustainable. By 2012, the levels of mortgage were much reduced. Although all neighborhoods were affected, the most dramatic transformation occurred in the neighborhoods that had the highest mortgage levels in 2005. In fact, the concentration of mortgaged properties in all neighborhoods with a strong African American presence fell to the single digits. In the mostly Latino neighborhood of Logan Square, mortgage levels fell comparatively less, to a still-low 17.5 percent. In contrast, South Lawndale, which includes the mostly Hispanic neighborhood of Little Village, had only 3.8 mortgages per 100 properties. The difference between South Lawndale and Logan Square can be attributed to variation in the gentrification process; more highly gentrified neighborhoods (such as Logan Square) experienced a lower reduction in the number of mortgages.

The collapse of credit was the result of the housing crisis after the market bubble created by the high level of unsustainable credit burst. Bubbles are severe

Table 9.1. Mortgages per 100 residential parcels by community area, Chicago, 2005–2012

	2005	2006	2007	2008	2009	2010	2011	2012
Lincoln Park	28.9	24.5	24.3	19.8	20.4	17.7	15.5	20.0
Portage Park	32.1	28.2	20.7	11.9	10.2	8.9	8.1	10.8
Austin	40.0	38.0	25.6	12.7	8.7	6.1	4.8	6.4
South Lawndale	29.9	24.9	18.5	8.5	4.1	3.2	2.7	3.8
Oakland	42.1	32.0	25.1	10.3	9.4	6.2	6.1	8.6
South Chicago	31.7	31.1	19.3	9.6	6.1	4.6	3.5	3.4
Englewood	40.7	34.0	24.8	12.0	6.8	5.1	3.4	3.7
North Center	34.0	32.4	29.7	25.7	24.0	22.5	20.4	26.2
Logan Square	36.8	34.5	27.9	19.2	14.8	13.1	12.7	17.5
City of Chicago	31.3	28.1	22.3	14.4	12.1	9.9	8.5	11.5

Sources: Institute for Housing Studies, DePaul University; data from Cook County Recorder of Deeds.

Table 9.2. Racial composition and median income of selected Chicago neighborhoods, 2005 and 2011*

	% White		% Black		% Hispanic		Income
	2005	2011	2005	2011	2005	2011	2011
North Center	84.6	87.2	2.4	2.5	13.3	11.8	$87,500
Lincoln Park	85.6	86.5	5.0	4.6	5.1	5.8	$87,500
Portage Park	65.7	64.0	1.7	2.0	34.5	38.7	$62,500
Logan Square	58.7	74.8	7.2	6.7	53.5	49.1	$42,500
Austin	8.2	8.2	85.1	85.6	8.3	8.8	$30,000
South Lawndale	37.0	56.0	14.3	12.6	81.6	83.0	$30,000
Oakland	3.4	4.9	92.4	92.0	2.7	3.4	$20,000
South Chicago	11.1	15.9	71.5	74.1	26.4	22.3	$30,000
Englewood	0.7	1.1	98.8	98.0	0.4	0.5	$20,000

Source: Social Science Research Center, DePaul University; data from American Community Survey.
* This tabulation reflects some double-counting across racial/ethnic categories.

market disruptions characterized by a relatively short period of rapid price escalation followed by a sudden crash in asset values due to a sharp decrease in demand. The housing bubble was created from 2000 to 2005 because of expanding mortgages and historically low interest rates for fixed loans with prime rates, creating a high demand for houses that translated into price increases of around 10 percent a year. For example, the median sales price in the Chicago neighborhood of Logan Square moved from around $120,000 in the year 2000 to a peak of $336,000 in 2007. Prices in the neighborhood of Englewood, which has one of the lowest median incomes in the city, increased from around $60,000 in 2000 to $140,000 in 2007.[2]

However, the fact that conventional interest rates were relatively low does not mean that the actual loans provided were affordable or cheap. In fact, by 2006 it was very clear that many of the subprime loans were not sustainable and would go into foreclosure. One explanation for the disappearance of mortgages would be that owners were selling their property. Any such transactions, given the retightening of mortgage underwriting that occurred in 2008, would almost certainly be at a loss and for cash that may or may not have covered the loan. A second explanation is that a bank seized the property. Seized properties are put into a public auction. Properties that are not successfully auctioned become real estate owned (REO), which basically means that they become the property of banks and lenders (and probably will be put up for sale at a later date). Table 9.3 reports the percentage of properties for which foreclosures were filed and the percentage of properties that could not be sold at auction and became bank property. The African American neighborhoods of Austin, South Chicago, and Englewood experienced the highest levels of both foreclosure filings and REOs, and the mostly white communities of Lincoln Park and North Center had the lowest levels of both. Mostly Latino and mixed-race neighborhoods occupied a midpoint between the other neighborhoods, although they experienced relatively high levels of both foreclosure procedures and REOs. The one exception to high foreclosure rates in a mostly African American community was Oakland, an indicator that black-led gentrification had already gone some distance in transforming the neighborhood.

The data underscore the point that when borrowers take a mortgage, there are two types of risk. The first risk pertains to their individual finances and the conditions and events that may lead to foreclosure. The second is a community risk that is related to how many properties in the area concurrently fall into foreclosure and the desirability of the neighborhood. For neighborhoods, families, and even lenders, selling a property before foreclosure is the best-case scenario even when it is done at a loss. Families are able to eliminate or reduce their debt without losing the potential for future credit, neighborhoods are not affected by long-term vacancies that may cause blight, and banks do not have to manage severely depreciating assets with which they have no direct experience. In a city as highly segregated as Chicago, the mortgage risks for ethnic and racial minorities (caused by expensive and disadvantageous credit) is compounded by their close geographical proximity to other individuals of the same group. In addition to the individual's higher probability of falling behind on mortgage payments, if others in the neighborhood are trapped in a similar situation, it becomes more difficult or almost impossible to sell properties at all, let alone at a price that may cover the value of the original mortgage. Although Latinos are in general more dispersed across Chicago than African Americans (see Chapter 2), both groups are sufficiently segregated to experience the compounding of mortgage crisis-induced negative effects.

Table 9.3. Cumulative percentage of
foreclosures, 2005–2013

	Filings	REOs
Lincoln Park	4.7	1.5
Portage Park	17.7	6.6
Austin	30.7	15.2
South Lawndale	22.3	8.8
Oakland	21.2	8.2
South Chicago	30.8	17.3
Englewood	43.0	28.3
North Center	6.4	2.1
Logan Square	15.0	6.0
City of Chicago	17.8	8.2

Source: Institute of Housing Studies, DePaul University; data from Cook County Recorder of Deeds.

Individuals and families in mostly white, high-income neighborhoods were able to sell properties before foreclosure was finalized, and even when they were not able to do so, the bank was able to sell these properties at auction. The glut of properties in low-income, mostly black and Latino neighborhoods that were not sold either by their owners or the bank have made it more difficult for remaining homeowners to sell their properties at reasonable prices. Such neighborhoods deteriorate for lack of occupancy. In Chicago, the foreclosure crisis became so severe that prices fell to levels that predated prices at the beginning of the bubble in 2000. For example, Logan Square median prices in 2010 reached a low of $120,000, while Englewood's reached a low of $23,000 in 2009.[3]

The vicious cycle of bad credit, foreclosures, and lower prices was completed by a tightening of credit standards. Banks basically stopped providing credit to anyone but the most qualified buyers and have reinstituted the "old" standards. It was mainly buyers with large amounts of cash who were able to take advantage of the more affordable prices created by crisis. Figure 9.1 presents data on Chicago-area mortgage applications and denials. From 2004 to the evident start of the housing crisis in 2008, loan applications dropped by 54 percent, and the rate of loan denial increased from 36 percent to 53 percent. From this low point, mortgage credit has slowly increased by 25 percent from 2008 to 2012, and the rate of denials has decreased to 29 percent. However, some types of loans are more likely to be granted than others. Figure 9.2 separates mortgage loans into three categories: home purchase, which includes all first-time buyers; refinances, which can include moving from one home to another or simply redoing the original loan to take advantage of lower interest rates; and home improvement loans, which usually take home equity so that homeowners can do repairs and upgrades. First-time loans for home purchases remained at very low level at 59,000 in 2012, a huge reduction from the peak of 226,000 first-time mortgages

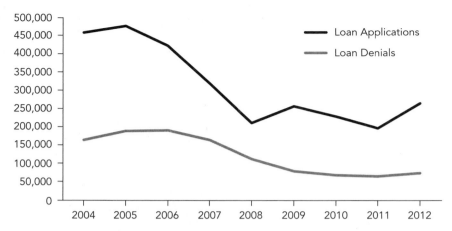

Figure 9.1. Loan applications and loan denials, Chicago metropolitan area, 2004–2012. Source: Home Mortgage Disclosure Act data for Chicago Metropolitan Area.

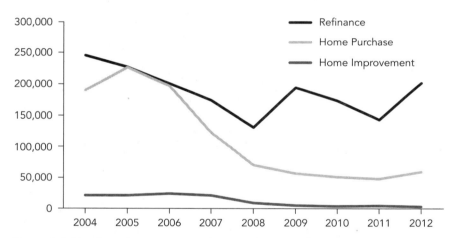

Figure 9.2. Number of mortgage applications by type of loan, 2004–2012. Source: Home Mortgage Disclosure Act data for Chicago Metropolitan Area.

issued in 2005. Most of the mortgages banks provided in 2012 were refinances, which have no direct effect on homeownership levels.

This reduction of credit is not neutral. It affects precisely those individuals that the Community Reinvestment Act was designed to help: low-income and minority individuals looking to become homeowners. Although Latinos and African Americans have always been underrepresented as loan recipients in

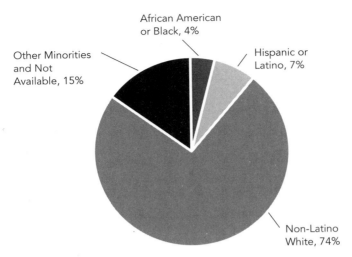

Figure 9.3. Percentage of mortgage applications by ethnicity, Chicago Metropolitan Area, 2012. Source: Home Mortgage Disclosure Act data for Chicago Metropolitan Area.

Chicago (Martinez 2009), their access to mortgages was particularly inhibited after the crisis. Figure 9.3 indicates that African Americans received only 4 percent and Hispanics only 7 percent of all loans given in the Chicago Metropolitan Area in 2012, even though these populations constituted 17.1 percent and 20.7 percent of the area population, respectively.[4]

How do foreclosures, mortgage levels, and credit availability translate into homeownership? For some neighborhoods the housing crisis seems to have had a relatively modest effect, while others faced more negative consequences. Table 9.4, drawn from the American Community Survey, offers summary data for the seventy-seven community areas of the City of Chicago and for the sample of neighborhoods I have examined. The data show strong reductions in occupancy levels in South Chicago and Englewood, both predominantly African American neighborhoods. Because these large reductions in occupancy are not accompanied by similar reductions in owner-occupied homes, this data suggests that many of the mortgages that went into foreclosure were investment properties that were bought by other investors who could produce cash. The other neighborhoods in the table experienced small decreases in the level of occupied properties. The number of owner-occupied households increased in North Center and Lincoln Park, the whiter and more gentrified areas, indicating that individuals seized the opportunity offered by lower prices to buy in these areas. An increase in the occupancy levels in Oakland suggests that African

Table 9.4. Percentage of occupied and owner-occupied properties in selected Chicago neighborhoods

	% Occupied		% Owner Occupied	
	2005	2011	2005	2011
North Center	89.0	89.2	51.8	53.1
Lincoln Park	89.0	88.7	50.1	56.3
Portage Park	90.7	89.6	58.4	56.2
Logan Square	90.3	89.9	38.3	37.0
Austin	85.6	83.0	42.6	41.0
South Lawndale	80.9	79.0	41.5	37.7
Oakland	83.6	88.1	24.0	24.8
South Chicago	83.5	77.5	44.1	42.8
Englewood	74.2	69.6	32.3	32.7
Chicago Average	86.9	86.1	42.4	40.6

Source: Social Science Research Center, DePaul University; data from the American Community Survey.

Americans took advantage of low prices, just as whites did in Lincoln Park and North Center. The neighborhoods of Portage Park, Logan Square, and South Lawndale experienced reductions in owner occupancy that exceeded reductions in the overall level of occupancy, suggesting that foreclosed properties were snatched by investors rather than by prospective homeowners.

Broadening Homeownership through Markets and Policy

While no one can deny the vital role of credit in increasing the standard of living and even wealth, two clear lessons can be gleaned from the recent housing crisis. First, markets are not good tools for solving problems stemming from social inequality. In fact, unbridled markets exacerbate inequality instead of reducing it. More marketization, whether it is expressed in the easier movement and investment of global capital or the higher availability of credit, cannot by itself solve social problems. The institutions driving global capital movement do not prioritize solving the problem of affordable housing for the poor and members of the working class. Risk-priced credit designed to service the interests of profit-hungry investors cannot solve the issues of affordability in modern global cities. Second, markets without proper regulation are likely to create more problems than they solve. Opportunism and fraud accompany many financial services innovations, destroying both individual lives and communities. The policy commitment to increasing credit without regulating the conditions of such credit expansion was naïve. In terms of homeownership in Chicago, the

Box 9.1: Anti-Foreclosure Activism in Chicago

Community organizing has long been a fixture of civic life in Chicago. The anti-foreclosure movement has been inspired by the work of pioneers such as Fred Hampton and Gale Cincotta, who helped pave the way for the recent wave of community organizing. Their work on housing during the 1960s and 1970s has inspired grassroots organizers to take direct action against banks in order to address foreclosures and the further erosion of communities. Following the collapse of the housing market in 2008, many distressed homeowners realized that they could not rely on the government or large financial institutions to protect their communities. Instead, they turned to grassroots organizations and pursued various strategies to prevent foreclosures and evictions. These have included blockades, camp-outs, sit-ins, petitions, and protests.

Groups such as the Chicago Anti-Eviction Campaign (CAEC) are among the leaders in this united resistance against foreclosures. The CAEC is a grassroots organization that seeks to enforce the human right to housing. It has adopted Alinsky-style community organizing to keep families inside their homes and to challenge the policies that produce foreclosures and evictions. The CAEC is renowned for guerrilla tactics such as its "move back" strategy, which moves families back into their homes after sheriffs have evicted them. The strategy was initiated after the CAEC witnessed how banks evicted families in foreclosure, leaving perfectly good homes vacant and ripe for damage by vandals and thieves. CAEC also has joined a coalition of groups across the Midwest in a series of actions against foreclosure. In the summer of 2014, the CAEC joined a coordinated day of action alongside the Centro Autonomo of Albany Park/Casas del Pueblo Community Land Trust, Occupy Homes Minnesota, Communities United Against Foreclosure and Eviction, Detroit Eviction Defense, and around thirty homeowners facing foreclosure actions in Chicago, Detroit, and Minnesota. These partners brought their fight against foreclosure to the front lawn of the suburban River Forest home of the regional director of the Federal National Mortgage Association (Fannie Mae). Housing activists were demanding that Fannie Mae and the other government-sponsored enterprises buttressing the housing market place a moratorium on eviction and foreclosure in an effort to keep families in their homes.

Meanwhile, some federally certified housing counseling agencies have sought to differentiate themselves from their contemporaries by using a community organizing model to empower distressed homeowners and provide a direct support network in the community. On March 16, 2011, the Northwest Side Housing Center took a busload of incensed homeowners to the Bank of America building in the downtown Loop and refused to leave until they had met with the bank's vice-president of loss mitigation. The homeowners were upset by the fact that the staff of the loss-mitigation team was not adhering to federal guidelines that govern the loan modification process, and as result they were being wrongfully denied a five-year fixed modification. In response to the protest, the Housing Center was granted a meeting with bank executives and was able to establish and implement a best-practice model for modification procedures.

neoliberal approach to expanding homeownership proved to be a fool's errand. All the gains in homeownership that occurred in the 1990s and early 2000s had been lost by the end of the latter decade.

The failure of the neoliberal homeownership policy does not mean, however, that homeownership should be rejected as a family and a public goal. Homeownership may not be the high-yield investment that it appeared to be during the housing bubble, but it is a form of long-term savings and can leverage the passing of wealth across generations. The housing crisis also does not mean that mortgages have no role to play in strengthening urban communities. However, they cannot do so in the absence of clear government regulation and, to some degree, public financial support. Credit needs to be both available and affordable. Furthermore, mortgages for low-income and minority families need to be designed with their interests in mind, not those of global financial investors.

Alongside the subprime loans that contributed to the 2008 crash was an unheralded parallel program that used mortgages to increase homeownership in urban and rural areas. The Home Investment Partnerships Program (HOME) of 1990 (National Low Income Housing Coalition 2015) provides federal block grants to states and local communities to create affordable housing. States and counties have a variety of options in using this funding. Some local entities such as the Chicago Housing Authority, the Illinois Housing Development Authority, and Neighborhood Housing Services of Chicago use the money to fund programs that mirror changes in the mortgage industry. Their programs ease many underwriting requirements and reduce the minimum down payment to 3 percent of the property value and accept alternative documentation for credit and income. However, these relaxed standards have avoided the looseness of the subprime sector of the private market, and homeowners were not charged a premium interest rate. These loans are usually provided by private mortgage lenders, and they always have fixed and low interest rates. These programs require extensive financial education and housing counseling to help families increase their likelihood of maintaining ownership. Accompanied by the American Dream Down Payment Assistance Act of 2003, which provides a maximum of $10,000 in assistance for closing costs and down payments, this program makes mortgages a real option for low-income individuals.

Although these programs still use mortgages, through local organizational collaborators the government absorbs some of the costs and risks embedded in any loan. These programs rely on private capital much less than subprime mortgages do, and they seek a carefully targeted group of prospective consumers. From a policy perspective, relying on market dynamics and greed was a shortcut to fast and relatively easy social change. However, one must remember that structural changes such as the redistribution of wealth cannot be accomplished without a profound and sustained social investment. Markets, particularly underregulated markets, are not good substitutes for public policy.

Notes

1. This figure represents all properties with mortgages at that particular time, regardless of when these mortgages were issued.

2. Prices are estimates obtained from real estate company website Trulia, located at http://www.trulia.com/real_estate/Englewood-Chicago/2905/market-trends/#qma _median_sales_price_chart_container for Englewood and http://www.trulia.com /real_estate/Logan_Square-Chicago/2927/market-trends/ for Logan Square.

3. Source of data is again Trulia, same websites as in previous footnote.

4. Data obtained from "Chicago-Naperville-Joliet, IL-IN-WI Profile: Summary," diversitydata.org, accessed May 3, 2016, http://diversitydata.org/Data/Profiles/Show .aspx?loc=308.

Bibliography

Ashton, Phillip. 2009. "An Appetite for Yield: The Anatomy of the Subprime Mortgage Crisis." *Environment and Planning A* 41, no. 6: 1420–1441.

———. 2012. "'Troubled Assets': The Financial Emergency and Racialized Risk." *International Journal of Urban and Regional Research* 36, no. 4: 773–790.

Becker, Jo, Sheryl Gay Stolberg, and Stephen Labaton. 2008. "White House Philosophy Stoked Mortgage Bonfire." *New York Times*, December 20.

Berube, Alan. 2014. "All Cities Are Not Created Unequal." Metropolitan Opportunity Series no. 51. Washington, D.C.: The Brookings Institution. Accessed August 5, 2014. http://www.brookings.edu/research/papers/2014/02/cities-unequal-berube.

Butler, Tim, and Loretta Lees. 2006. "Super-Gentrification in Barnsbury, London: Globalization and Gentrifying Global Elites at the Neighbourhood Level." *Transactions of the Institute of British Geographers* 31, no. 4: 467–487.

Dietz, Robert D., and Donald R. Haurin. 2003. "The Social and Private Micro-Level Consequences of Homeownership." *Journal of Urban Economics* 54, no. 3: 401–450.

Dipasquale, Denise, and Edward L. Glaeser. 1999. "Incentives and Social Capital: Are Homeowners Better Citizens?" *Journal of Urban Economics* 45, no. 2: 354–384.

Engelhardt, Gary V., Michael D. Eriksen, William G. Gale, and Gregory B. Mills. 2010. "What Are the Social Benefits of Homeownership? Experimental Evidence for Low-Income Households." *Journal of Urban Economics* 67, no. 3: 249–258.

Florida, Richard. 2002. *The Rise of the Creative Class: And How It's Transforming Work, Leisure, Community and Everyday Life.* New York: Basic Books.

Gotham, Kevin Fox. 2006. "The Secondary Circuit of Capital Reconsidered: Globalization and the U.S. Real Estate Sector." *American Journal of Sociology* 112, no. 1: 231–275.

Gottschalck, Alfred, Marina Vornovyskyy, and Adam Smith. 2013. *Household Wealth in the U.S.: 2000 to 2011.* Washington, D.C.: U.S. Census Bureau. Accessed July 28, 2014. http://www.census.gov/people/wealth/files/Wealth%20Highlights%20 2011.pdf.

Green, Richard K., and Michelle J. White. 1997. "Measuring the Benefits of Homeowning: Effects on Children." *Journal of Urban Economics* 41, no. 3: 441–461.

Immergluck, Dan. 2009. *Foreclosed: High-Risk Lending, Deregulation, and the Undermining of America's Mortgage Market.* Ithaca, N.Y.: Cornell University Press.

Katz, Alyssa. 2009. *Our Lot: How the Real Estate Industry Came to Own Us.* New York: Bloomsbury.

Martinez, Martha A. 2007. "Promoting and Maintaining Household Ownership among Latino Immigrants." South Bend, Ind.: Institute for Latino Studies, University of Notre Dame.

———. 2009. *The Housing Crisis and Latino Homeownership in Chicago: Mortgage Applications, Property Foreclosures, and Property Values.* South Bend, Ind.: Institute for Latino Studies, University of Notre Dame. Accessed March 4, 2016. https://latinostudies.nd.edu/assets/95319/original/martinez_housingcrisis.pdf.

National Low Income Housing Coalition. 2015. "HOME Investment Partnerships Program." Accessed January 31, 2015. http://nlihc.org/issues/other/HOME.

Oswald, Andrew J. 1996. "A Conjecture on the Explanation for High Unemployment in the Industrialized Nations: Part 1." Warwick Economic Research Papers No. 475. Coventry, UK: University of Warwick.

Rohe, William M., and Leslie S. Stewart. 1996. "Homeownership and Neighborhood Stability." *Housing Policy Debate* 7, no. 1: 37–81.

Rohe, William M., Shannon Van Zandt, and George McCarthy. 2002. "Homeownership and Access to Opportunity." *Housing Studies* 17, no. 1: 51–61.

Watkins, John P. 2000. "Corporate Power and the Evolution of Consumer Credit." *Journal of Economic Issues* 34, no. 4: 909–932.

CHAPTER 10

The Chicago Bid to
Host the 2016 Olympics
Much Promised, Little Learned

LARRY BENNETT, MICHAEL BENNETT,
AND STEPHEN ALEXANDER

If the essential features of neoliberal urban policy are typically presumed to be a preference for public-private partnership with private-sector actors assuming the leading role, the winding down of "social welfare state" government functions, and a core priority of economic growth, then the effort Chicago's business, civic, and governmental elites mounted from 2006 to 2009 to host the 2016 Olympic Games was a characteristic neoliberal economic development initiative. Even so, the particular variety of neoliberal initiative the Chicago 2016 Olympic bid represented, in some crucial respects, deviated from the approaches other host city candidates have adopted and the evident expectations of many International Olympic Committee (IOC) members. One way to understand the failure of Chicago's 2016 Olympic bid is to view it as case study of clashing neoliberalisms.

Our exploration in this chapter of why and how Chicago's elites organized the city's bid to host the 2016 Olympics—which is in part based on interviews with civic and community leaders who were active in promoting, discussing, and in some cases opposing the Olympic bid—reveals a second striking insight: influential Chicagoans, including some who threw their time and reputations into the Olympic bid campaign, were not especially conversant with crucial features of the Olympic bid.[1] Indeed, after failing to win the host city designation for the 2016 games, Chicago's leadership seems to have engaged in very little reflection concerning either the possible deficiencies of the city's bid or, more broadly, the hazards of devoting substantial local resources to economically dubious spectacular event hosting. We argue that for many leading Chicagoans, support for the 2016 Olympic bid was more an act of faith than a product of rational, empirically grounded calculation.

Finally (some would assert predictably), Chicago's 2016 Olympic bid generated substantial political discord. We devote attention to how the Chicago 2016 Committee reached out to Chicago's public and to its interactions with targeted neighborhood constituencies. We also discuss the organic counter-neoliberalism that emerged in response to the Olympic plan the Chicago bid's proponents advanced.

Our account begins with a chronology of Chicago's Olympic bid. We then turn to analyses of the Chicago 2016 Committee's composition, structure, and operations; the Chicago bid's physical and financial plans; and the committee's community outreach efforts. We emphasize the obvious dissonance between Olympic proponents' and many neighborhood activists' perception of the Chicago Olympic plan. We conclude by discussing how the Chicago 2016 Olympic bid grew out of the local neoliberal political regime orchestrated by Richard M. Daley that was fully realized in the last several years of his mayoralty. We emphasize how extremely tenuous the empirical assumptions and policy logic driving Chicago's Olympic proposal were.

The Chicago 2016 Olympic Bid: Who, How, and When

In the summer of 2005, the Chicago press reported that Mayor Richard M. Daley's administration was considering whether to support an Olympic host city bid. Only the year before Daley had publicly dismissed the Olympics as a "construction industry," complaining of the expenditure required merely to formulate and submit a bid to the IOC (Washburn 2005). Obviously something had changed the mayor's mind, and the most likely lever of change was Chicago's business and civic elite, who would become highly vocal supporters of the Chicago bid. In May 2006, Daley announced the formation of the Chicago 2016 Committee to plan and promote Chicago's bid to host the 2016 Olympics. The committee was headed by retired insurance executive Patrick Ryan, and Daley served as the committee's honorary chairman.

In the early fall of 2006, the Chicago 2016 Committee announced its decision regarding the first major infrastructure hurdle: the general plan for and location of the Olympic Stadium. This would be a temporary structure (with a seating capacity of 80,000, as mandated by the IOC) located in Washington Park on the city's mid-South Side. Ultimately, the Chicago 2016 Committee planned to site a large share of the Olympic venues in public open spaces such as Washington Park. In January 2007, the committee submitted its "bid book" to the United States Olympic Committee (USOC), which would determine which, if any, U.S. city would tender a bid to the IOC. In the bid book, the Chicago 2016 Committee proposed to locate the Olympic Games' residential quarters (the "Olympic village") on a site overlooking the Near South Side lakefront that adjoined the McCormick Place convention center. At that point, Chicago's principal competitors for the USOC endorsement were Los Angeles and San Francisco.

In April 2007, the USOC selected Chicago to be the U.S. nominee for host city of the 2016 Olympic Games. Over the course of that year the Chicago 2016 Committee refined its bid, which was submitted to the IOC in early 2008 in what might be considered second draft form as its official Applicant File. In June 2008, the IOC announced the four finalist cities: Chicago, Madrid, Rio de Janeiro, and Tokyo. In the latter months of 2008, the Chicago 2016 Committee modified its physical plan for the 2016 games by, among other things, relocating its swimming complex from Douglas Park on the West Side to Washington Park on the South Side (Chicago 2016 Committee 2008b). Also, at the end of the year, Lori Healy, a veteran of the Daley administration, was appointed president of the 2016 Committee and charged with overseeing the committee's day-to-day operations. Almost at the same time, the 2016 Committee released its commissioned economic impact study (Tootelian and Varshney 2008).

The committee submitted its finalized 2016 Olympic bid, its revised bid book, to the IOC in February 2009. In April 2009, IOC representatives arrived for their official inspection tour of a Chicago that had not yet fully emerged from the rigors of midwestern winter. The IOC delegates also encountered anti-Olympics protesters as they inspected prospective Olympic venues. The opposition had two principal sources: first, an organization called No Games Chicago that drew on generalized antagonism to the Olympic Games and critics of the Chicago effort (who, as a rule, anticipated insider deals, profit-taking, and cost overruns that would be borne by the public); and second, neighborhood activists—mainly from the city's South Side—who distrusted the Chicago 2016 Committee's pledges to support sustainable economic development and who feared Olympics-generated gentrification. In early spring 2009, the committee announced that it had signed a memorandum of understanding (MOU) with a coalition of neighborhood organizations, labor unions, and businesses (Peterson, Scott, and Healy 2009). The MOU set goals for local hiring and affordable housing to be achieved by Olympic-related construction and games operations.

In the months to follow, what had seemed to be a civic consensus in support of the Olympic bid threatened to unravel. Members of the Chicago City Council, under heavy pressure from the mayor, grudgingly approved an IOC-mandated commitment to publicly fund any 2016 Olympics operating deficit. The Daley administration acquired property adjoining the originally designated Olympic village site, which generated new concerns about Olympic-induced gentrification of the South Side. In the summer of 2009, the 2016 Committee organized public hearings in each city council ward. The turnout for these events was often impressive, but for many observers, their stage management was equally impressive. Chicago 2016 Committee representatives rebuffed critical commentary their audiences offered. A widely circulated rumor suggested that the Daley administration "bused in" Olympics "supporters" to round out local audiences (Bennett, Bennett, Alexander, and Persky 2011). In any event, Chicago's Olympic dreams for 2016 were dashed in Copenhagen, Denmark, on October 2. In spite of Barack and Michelle Obama's presence—indeed, even despite the presence of Chicago's leading booster celebrity, Oprah Winfrey—Chicago was eliminated from the competition to become the 2016 Olympic host city in the first round of IOC voting. With the subsequent eliminations of Tokyo and Madrid, the IOC chose Rio de Janeiro as host city for the 2016 Olympics.

The Chicago 2016 Committee

The Chicago 2016 Committee was the face of the Chicago campaign to host the 2016 Olympic Games. The committee included a roster of more than 300 business, governmental, civic, and other community leaders. It did not function as an actual decision-making body. The core Chicago 2016 Committee decision makers were its Board of Directors and senior management staff. Each of these groups numbered slightly more than a dozen. The board was sprinkled with leading civic figures such as Chicago's former city planning commissioner, Valerie Jarrett, and financier John W. Rogers Jr. Both are more than leading Chicagoans; Jarrett and Rogers have for many years been close friends of Barack and Michelle Obama.[2] Senior management staff included executives seconded from local corporations and administrators who had moved from the Richard M. Daley administration to the Chicago 2016 Committee. Another source of board members and senior staff was former Olympic athletes and individuals with experience with the IOC or the USOC, or who had worked on other cities' Olympic hosting bids.

The Chicago 2016 Committee created seventeen advisory councils to "provide feedback to Chicago 2016 management and the board on pertinent aspects of the bid" (Chicago 2016 Committee 2008a). Members of the advisory councils were largely drawn from the 300 or so individuals that constituted the "at-large" 2016 Committee. It also appears that the operations of the advisory councils varied substantially. One of our interviewees was very enthusiastic about the work of his advisory council, which he expected to have an impact on future local public policy even though Chicago did not win the 2016 competition. In contrast, another Chicago 2016 Committee member said in reference to a different advisory council: "We were never asked for any input. Instead, [the Chicago 2016 Committee staff] would tell us about what they were doing" (Bennett, Bennett, Alexander, and Persky 2011, 4–5).

The Proposed Physical Plan

The physical plan for the Chicago 2016 Olympics clustered sports venues and the proposed Olympic village in central Chicago. As the committee's candidature file highlights publication noted:

> The Games will be staged in and around five historic parks that have been preserved for more than 100 years right in the center of the city. This spectacular setting—on the beautiful shores of Lake Michigan and under the city's iconic skyline—forms a natural Olympic Park that will generate dramatic television imagery. By integrating the venues into the parks and lakefront, Chicago 2016 has put the sport competitions in the midst of the accommodations, celebration sites, museums, concert halls, dining, music, theater, shopping and nightlife that make Chicago so vibrant. (Chicago 2016 Committee 2009, 33)

The Chicago 2016 Committee anticipated the use of several existing facilities: the McCormick Place convention and trade-show complex, the United Center indoor sports arena (home to the Chicago Blackhawks and the Chicago Bulls), and the UIC Pavilion (a multipurpose indoor arena on the campus of the University of Illinois at Chicago). The major construction projects that would directly serve the Olympics were the Olympic village (which would cost approximately $1.1 billion) on the Near South Side adjoining McCormick Place; the Olympic stadium ($400 million) in Washington Park; and the aquatics center ($125 million), also in Washington Park.

The logics that drove this basic physical model were easy enough to discern and, for the most part, quite candidly enunciated by local Olympic supporters. Concentrating activities in this fashion would show off Chicago to the best effect and reduce the logistical challenges of moving athletes to the various sports venues. Using existing facilities such as McCormick Place and situating many activities in public parks would reduce construction costs and the complications of site acquisition. Yet the Chicago 2016 Committee boxed itself into a promotional paradox with its claim that the economic benefits of hosting the games would be immense even though one of the sure ways to substantially transform the city—investments in large-scale infrastructure such as public facilities and improvements in mass transit—was virtually absent from the plan for the Olympics. Indeed, the commitment of public spaces to games venues, notably the heavily used Washington Park—actually generated substantial neighborhood-level opposition to the Chicago 2016 Committee's plans. And finally, residents of neighborhoods such as Woodlawn on the South Side and East Garfield Park on the West Side viewed the Olympics the committee sold to the world as "right in the center of the city" as something else entirely. In the minds of many, the Olympic bid represented the local elite's newest campaign to push residential gentrification out from the near-Loop neighborhoods to adjoining communities that were poorer and home to mostly racial minority populations.

The Fiscal Plan and Economic Impact

By the standards of recent summer Olympics such as the Athens (2004), Beijing (2008), and London (2012) games, the Chicago 2016 Committee proposed a very modestly funded Olympic extravaganza. The operating budget was set at $3.8 million and capital expenditures were estimated at slightly more than $1 billion. Chicago's projected operating budget did exceed those of its three competitors to host the 2016 Games, in each instance by approximately $1 billion. However, the Madrid, Tokyo, and Rio de Janeiro capital budgets ranged from $3.4 billion to more than $11 billion (Bergen, Hersh, and Avila 2009).[3]

As trumpeted in a 2007 *Chicago Tribune* headline, Chicago 2016 Committee and Daley administration officials repeatedly asserted that the "Olympics won't cost taxpayers" (Washburn 2007). This claim was rhetorical rather than factual. Had Chicago won the competition to become host city, there would have been some direct governmental expenditures on various Olympic venues, notably by the Chicago Park District, but as Mayor Daley pointed out to a reporter in September, 2009, "the new Olympic facilities would remain as recreation amenities long after the games end" (Mihalopoulos 2009a). In addition, tax increment finance (TIF) district allocations would have supported construction of the Olympic village, and the original source of these funds is, of course, local property taxes (Cohen and Bergen 2009b).[4] The Chicago 2016 Committee projected that approximately 60 percent of revenue for the operations budget would come from international and local games sponsorships and ticket sales. The funds the IOC would generate and reallocate to the Chicago games would constitute a little less than 20 percent of the operating revenue. A variety of smaller sources would account for the remaining 20 percent of operating revenue. In the summer of 2009, the Civic Federation, a local organization that functions as a watchdog on public finance, released a report that judged the Chicago 2016 Committee's revenue estimates to be "fair and reasonable" though "several line items [are] projected at the optimistic end of reasonable ranges" (Civic Federation 2009, 11).

Of the capital budget expenditures the Chicago 2016 Committee projected, undoubtedly the most curious was the $400 million Olympic stadium. This was to be a temporary facility; once the games were completed, the enormous stadium would be largely dismantled, leaving a smaller venue with the seating capacity of a few thousand that could be used for local (for example, high school) sporting events. The Chicago Olympic stadium plan followed from the IOC requirement that host cities stage major ceremonies and track/field events in a facility with a seating capacity of at least 80,000. Chicago's largest outdoor arena, the lakefront Soldier Field, seats only 67,000. The plan to build the temporary facility in Washington Park seemed to respond to the dictates of cost containment, reduced inconvenience for the nearby residents who used Washington Park for day-to-day recreational purposes, and providing a "legacy" amenity for the park (and its local users). However, no temporary stadium of this scale has ever been constructed (and dismantled), so one must assume that the Chicago 2016 Committee's cost estimate for this project was highly speculative.

The other major capital expenditure associated with the Chicago bid was for the proposed Olympic village, which was not included in the Chicago 2016 Committee's budget. This residential development would have the capacity to house more than 15,000 athletes and other Olympic personnel and would be converted to permanent, private housing once the games were completed. The Daley administration and the Chicago 2016 Committee anticipated that private developers would finance and construct the village. Certainly the location of the Olympic village, near both downtown Chicago and the Near South Side lakefront, would make it an attractive site for prospective renters and home purchasers. But this scenario further agitated residents in adjoining neighborhoods who were already fearful of Olympic-driven gentrification (Gallun 2008).

Although it did not constitute a formal component of any of the versions of Chicago's bid to host the 2016 Olympics, the findings of the Chicago 2016 Committee's commissioned economic impact study were aggressively used to build local public support for Chicago's Olympic bid. The economic impact analysis, which was produced by a California-based firm, Tootelian & Associates (Tootelian and Varshney 2008, 6), projected an extraordinary statewide economic impact of $22.5 billion (over eleven years). Independently conducted analyses of the games' economic impact produced much less robust results, such as the Anderson Economic Group's $4.4 billion estimate of "total likely economic impact" for Chicago and Cook County (Watkins and Anderson 2009, 2). However, debate over just how large the economic impact of the Chicago Olympics would be never occurred. Indeed, when he was asked to comment on the discrepancy between the Tootelian & Associates and Anderson Economic Group economic impact estimates, Mayor Daley quipped that the latter, a Michigan-based firm, was envious: "They wish they had the Olympics" (Epstein 2009). In the summer and fall of 2010, when we interviewed twenty civic, political, and community leaders and inquired about the strengths and weaknesses of the failed Chicago Olympic bid, the Chicago 2016 Committee's highly suspect economic impact projections were rarely mentioned (Bennett, Bennett, Alexander, and Persky 2011).

Community Outreach

In 2007, representatives of the Chicago 2016 Committee began to meet with neighborhood leaders and organizations in the areas of the city that would host Olympic events. These meetings were often hosted by "park advisory councils," groups of neighborhood residents appointed by the Chicago Park District to advise district staff on local park policy and operations. Early on in this process, there were signs of discontent with the Chicago 2016 Committee's plan to use public open spaces for Olympic venues. For example, in August 2007 the local advisory council passed a resolution opposing the Chicago 2016 Committee's plan to build a field hockey arena in Jackson Park on the South Side (Joravsky 2007). The difficulties the Chicago 2016 Committee experienced as it pushed ahead with its community outreach efforts were the product of a complicated array of factors, which, given the basic aims of the Chicago 2016 Committee and the composition of 2016 Committee leadership and staff, yielded a fundamental division between Olympic bid proponents and many neighborhood activists that was unresolvable in the short term. The IOC precluded what might have constituted the long term—achieving some degree of equitable community development attributable to the games through the impact of the MOU signed in the spring of 2009—on October 2, 2009. The legacy of the 2016 Olympic Games outreach process is another stratum of mistrust between neighborhood and community activists and members of city government and the downtown elite, a geology of conflict running back to the urban renewal era of the 1950s and 1960s.

One of our 2010 interviewees, who was an at-large member of the Chicago 2016 Committee, offered this strikingly pragmatic depiction of the community outreach process:

> It's important to separate the bid from Chicago's plan for the Games. The latter is hard to discuss, because its development had to wait for the selection process. The community meetings that were held were mainly to give people a voice. But you didn't get to subjects like the improvements that would be made along Garfield Boulevard [near Washington Park]. We just didn't get there. Community development was dealt with in very broad strokes. The 2016 Committee and the City focused on the bid. . . . The choice was made to wait

for the bid to be approved. This was one wild card they didn't want to deal with. Everyone knows that the IOC monitors local media. One noisy public meeting at which people complain about displacement could get the IOC's attention. So the decision was made to defer these issues. (Bennett, Bennett, Alexander, and Persky 2011, 5)

In other words, and just as critics of the Chicago 2016 Committee asserted, the Olympic outreach efforts were largely promotional. The point was not to discuss in detail the range of impacts that would follow from a particular neighborhood's hosting this or that Olympic venue (or, for that matter, alternative approaches to venue or community development). Instead, the 2016 Committee staff came to sell the games to local audiences. For example, following the 2016 Committee's setback of August 2007, the Park District pledged specific physical improvements once the games concluded, and based on this commitment and other concessions, the Jackson Park advisory council reversed itself and endorsed the field hockey arena project (Joravsky 2007).

The locus of grassroots opposition to the 2016 Olympics was the string of South Side neighborhoods between the proposed Olympic village site and the areas adjoining Washington Park. Though there is considerable socioeconomic diversity to be found in this group of neighborhoods—the southern portion of Kenwood and most of Hyde Park are prosperous, racially diverse areas—much of this section of Chicago (for instance, Grand Boulevard, Oakland, and Woodlawn) is very poor and heavily African American. Were there—as many Olympics proponents asserted—wild-eyed intransigents who would descend on community hearings in some of these South Side neighborhoods and who would never be convinced that the Olympics could help arrest the downward spiral of neighborhoods that had suffered decades of overclearance, disinvestment, abandonment, and inadequate city services? There certainly were, and there were also longtime, experienced community activists who were deeply skeptical of the Olympic initiative. On the one hand, this was due to the outreach approach 2016 Committee staff adopted, as described above by our 2016 Committee informant. On the other hand, the skepticism of these clear-eyed activists was an outgrowth of their having observed many iterations of failed neighborhood development activity and many experiences of attempting to influence an often unresponsive city government.

In spite of the huge socioeconomic and conceptual gaps that divided Chicago 2016 Committee and staff from many South Side neighborhood activists, in the early months of 2009 Fourth Ward alderman Toni Preckwinkle brokered the MOU that would have constituted the "community benefits agreement" governing Olympics hiring and contracting and Olympic village development (Cohen and Bergen 2009a). The MOU was another curious aspect of the Chicago Olympic bid in that it could be construed as an agreement between the Chicago 2016 Committee and itself. This is because the co-signers of the MOU were Lori Healy, 2016 Committee president, and Terry Peterson and Michael Scott, co-chairs of the 2016 Committee's Outreach Advisory Council. Affiliates of the Outreach Advisory Council included an array of neighborhood organizations (such as the Kenwood-Oakland Community Organization and the Washington Park Advisory Council), labor groups (the Chicago Jobs Council, the Chicago Federation of Labor), and local firms (Azteca Foods, Harris Bankcorp, Inc.). The MOU, among other commitments, set targets of 30 percent for contracts with businesses owned by minorities and disabled people, 10 percent for women-owned contractors, and an affordable housing target within the Olympic village, once it was converted to private housing, of 30 percent (Peterson, Scott, and Healy 2009).

Among the organizations deeply involved in monitoring Olympic planning that did not sign on to the MOU was the Communities for an Equitable Olympics (CEO), which was formed by activists from several South Side neighborhoods. In April 2009, the Chicago City Council approved the MOU, though this affirmative vote in no way made the city government a guarantor of MOU implementation. Groups such as CEO felt that the MOU's contracting, hiring, and affordable housing targets were set too low. Other individuals and groups viewed the MOU more positively. Indeed, one of our informants described the process of developing the MOU as "democracy in action" (Bennett, Bennett, Alexander, and Persky 2011, 11). What will never be known is whether or not the Chicago 2016 Olympic MOU would have been a practical, enforceable tool for channeling business and employment opportunities toward struggling venue neighborhoods on Chicago's South and West Sides.

The 2016 Olympic Bid, Spectacular Event Hosting, and Chicago Neoliberalism

For Chicago's leadership, more devastating than the IOC's selection of Rio de Janeiro to host the 2016 Olympics was Chicago's elimination in the first round of voting on October 2, 2009. In the words of one our informants, the local elite experienced a "psychic trauma." The explanations of what happened have been numerous. One explanation claims that the IOC is resolutely committed to promoting its brand in rising economic powers such as Brazil (and thus in 2009 Chicago "never had a chance"). Others claim that Chicago 2016 Committee representatives mishandled the intricacies of internal IOC politics. The leader of No Games Chicago has asserted that his group persuaded a substantial number of IOC members that Chicago would be a poor choice to host the 2016 games (Bennett, Bennett, Alexander, and Persky 2011, 12; Perlstein 2013, 14).

Among the Chicago 2016 Committee members and staff that we interviewed, we routinely encountered characterizations such as "a quality bid" or "a technically superior bid" to describe the Chicago Olympic proposal (Bennett, Bennett, Alexander, and Persky 2011, 12). What we did not encounter was anything approaching the recognition that Chicago's low-budget, limited-infrastructure-development approach to hosting the Olympics might have struck many IOC members—especially in the wake of the 2008 Beijing extravaganza—as just not spectacular enough to project the "Olympic movement" in the way that movement wishes to be projected around the world (Broudehoux 2007). In essence, the neoliberalism of Chicago's highly privatistic Olympic bid seems to have lost out to the better funded—in large part due to more concerted state involvement—neoliberalism of the bids from Brazil, Japan, and Spain (Lenskyj and Vagg 2012; Boykoff 2014).

The Olympic bid advocates we interviewed also seemed blissfully immune to critical examination of questionable aspects of the Chicago bid such as the temporary stadium proposal or the Chicago 2016 Committee's highly optimistic economic impact claims (Bennett, Bennett, Alexander, and Persky 2011, 18–22). Nor did these bid advocates perceive grassroots opposition to the bid as signaling that there may have been substantive weaknesses in Chicago's Olympic plans. Instead, most expressed some version of the view that the Chicago 2016 Committee had not effectively explained the Olympic plan, and that if it had (or if it had had more time to do so), most neighborhood activists would have fallen in line with the supporters of the bid. The consensus among these Chicago 2016 Committee members and staff was that Chicago had produced a sensible Olympic plan, and that if Chicago had hosted the games, the benefits for the city and region would have been substantial.

In fact, opponents of the Olympic bid were offended as much by the 2016 Committee's mode of outreach as they were by the bid's content. Many neighborhood activists viewed the placement of Olympic events and facilities as the first wave of a longer-term effort to gentrify their communities. This concern—which in many instances was a presumption—was amplified by the highly orchestrated, "one way" tenor of local public hearings. As a rule, the Chicago 2016 Committee's viceroys to the neighborhoods were men and women in suits who were ready at a moment's notice to deploy stunning visual presentations but were carefully noncommittal when queried by their audiences. This neoliberal policy discourse encountered an organic counter-neoliberalism built upon innate skepticism about the Olympic proposal, aggravation in the face of the bid advocates' resolute commitment to salesmanship (rather than two-way dialogue), and a history of poor relations between neighborhoods and city government.

The Chicago bid to host the 2016 Olympics was the last gasp of Mayor Richard M. Daley's governing coalition. Bolstered by favorable economic trends throughout the 1990s and the first half of the succeeding decade, Daley had emerged as both a locally commanding figure and a municipal leader whose vision and approaches to day-to-day governance earned him national recognition. Daley was widely admired not just by the city's business titans but also by the leaders of many civic and philanthropic groups (Bennett 2010; Koeneman 2013). This admiration was confirmed by both the monetary support directed to the Chicago 2016 Committee, which raised more than $70 million to finance its efforts, and by the near-unanimity of support for the Olympic proposal among Chicago's civic groups, foundations, and other major nonprofit organizations. This unanimity of support clearly signaled a buy-in to the bid's underlying premises that Olympic hosting would be good for all Chicagoans, and in a variety of ways, and that mounting the Olympics could be accomplished in large part via the private sector, with municipal leaders steering activities without becoming the principal implementers of the Olympic plan.

Just as Chicago mounted its campaign to host the 2016 Olympics, the Great Recession of 2008 (and the years thereafter) struck. Although Chicago's real estate sector was not as devastated as the boomtown economies of several Sunbelt metropolises, the local foreclosure crisis especially punished the city's mainly African American and Latino neighborhoods (see Chapter 9). In the early fall of 2010—and much to the surprise of many local political observers—Richard M. Daley announced that he would not seek reelection in the upcoming 2011 mayoral contest. As discussed in Chapter 3 of this volume, Daley's successor as mayor, Rahm Emanuel, has adopted a policy program even more single-minded in its neoliberalism than his predecessor's. Mayor Emanuel's administration has pursued a diverse array of "hosting opportunities"—which, in turn, have been billed as major economic stimulants—with unusual enthusiasm. These have included events of presumably great consequence, such as the 2012 NATO summit, but just as often, they constitute minor episodes in the ongoing global entertainment extravaganza, such as the 2015 and 2016 National Football League player drafts (Pearson and Mack 2012; Hopkins 2015).

Strikingly absent from local public discourse has been any serious debate about the actual benefits (or costs, or even risks to the city's reputation) derived from making short-term hosting a key element of the city's efforts to reanimate its economy. In light of our research on the very substantial effort to organize and promote the 2016 Olympic bid, this quiescence should not be a surprise. Chicago's civic memory presumes that the bid constituted a terrific campaign that fell "just short," and subsequently there was very little reflection on the sources or implications of the Olympic quest's failure. The large majority of city council representatives, key players in the mayoral administrations of both Richard M. Daley and Rahm Emanuel, business leaders, and leading civic figures and organizations have settled on a narrative that emphasizes Chicago's enduring magnetism as a tourist and entertainment destination. A crucial component of this civic consensus on tourism, entertainment, and economic development is the value of short-term hosting. Whether or not the hosting economy really benefits most Chicagoans is not addressed. Even less salient to this policy consensus is the question of whether or not neighborhood development across the city can be advanced in any meaningful way via event hosting, tourism, and entertainment promotion.

Notes

1. For details regarding these interviews, see Bennett, Bennett, Alexander, and Persky (2011), esp. Appendix A.

2. Jarrett, in addition, has been one of President Obama's principal advisors.

3. The formal Olympic budget proposed by each host city candidate does not include expenditures for infrastructure (such as public transit improvements) that may serve but is not solely dedicated to Olympics use. Chicago's 2016 bid was very parsimonious both in terms of Olympic venue investment (as enumerated in its Olympic budget) and other infrastructure expenditures.

4. Less than a month before the IOC made its choice for 2016 host city, Chicago's City Council bowed to the IOC's expectation that it pass an ordinance obligating the city government to fund any deficit generated by hosting the games (Mihalopoulos 2009b).

Bibliography

Bennett, Larry. 2010. *The Third City: Chicago and American Urbanism*. Chicago: University of Chicago Press.

Bennett, Larry, Michael Bennett, Stephen Alexander, and Joseph Persky. 2011. *The Chicago Bid to Host the 2016 Olympic Games: A Civic Post-Mortem*. Chicago: Egan Urban Center, DePaul University.

Bergen, Kathy, Philip Hersh, and Oscar Avila. 2009. "Chicago's Olympic Rivals." *Chicago Tribune*, April 17.

Boykoff, Jules. 2014. *Celebration Capitalism and the Olympic Games*. New York: Routledge.

Broudehoux, Anne-Marie. 2007. "Spectacular Beijing: The Conspicuous Construction of an Olympic Metropolis." *Journal of Urban Affairs* 29, no. 4: 383–399.

Chicago 2016 Committee. 2008a. *Our Team*. Accessed July 8, 2008. http://www .chicago2016.org/bidinformation/Pages/ourteam.aspx.

———. 2008b. "Chicago Unveils Enhanced Games Plan." Press release, December 12.

———. 2009. *Reaching for a Better World: Candidature File Highlights*. Chicago: Chicago 2016 Committee.

Civic Federation. 2009. *Chicago 2016 Olympic Bid Review: Summary Findings*. Chicago: The Civic Federation. Accessed March 4, 2016. https://www.civicfed.org /sites/default/files/Chicago%202016%20Olympic%20Bid%20Review.pdf.

Cohen, Laurie, and Kathy Bergen. 2009a. "Minorities Seek Olympics Share." *Chicago Tribune*, January 9.

———. 2009b. "Finance Committee OKs 2016 TIF Funds." *Chicago Tribune*, January 13.

Epstein, David. 2009. "Financial Risks Loom as Chicago Awaits Olympic Fate." *SI.com*, September 30. Accessed July 20, 2013. http://www.si.com/more-sports /2009/09/30/chicago-olympicbid.

Gallun, Alby. 2008. "Lake Meadows Residents Criticize Redevelopment Plan." *Crain's Chicago Business*, February 20.

Hopkins, Jared S. 2015. "NFL Draft Got Free Use of Grant Park." *Chicago Tribune*, May 28.

Joravsky, Ben. 2007. "A Promise Made to Be Broken." *Chicago Reader*, October 4.

Koeneman, Keith. 2013. *First Son: The Biography of Richard M. Daley*. Chicago: University of Chicago Press.

Lenskyj, Helen Jefferson, and Stephen Wagg, eds. 2012. *The Palgrave Handbook of Olympic Studies*. Houndmills, UK: Palgrave Macmillan.

Mihalopoulos, Dan. 2009a. "Daley Trumpet Pros of Landing '16 Games." *Chicago Tribune*, September 2.

———. 2009b. "Council Backs the 2016 Bid." *Chicago Tribune*, September 10.

Pearson, Rick, and Kristen Mack. 2012. "Hopes High, So Are Risks." *Chicago Tribune*, May 17.

Perlstein, Rick. 2013. "Chicago Rising: A Resurgent Protest Culture Takes on Rahm Emanuel's Austerity Agenda." *The Nation*, July 22–29.

Peterson, Terry, Michael Scott, and Lori T. Healy. 2009. "Memorandum of Understanding." Chicago, March 26. In authors' possession.

Tootelian, Dennis H., and Sanjay B. Varshney. 2008. *Chicago 2016 Economic Impact Analysis: The Expected Incremental Economic Impact of Chicago Hosting the 2016 Olympic and Paralympic Games*. Report for the Chicago 2016 Committee, December. In author's possession.

Washburn, Gary. 2005. "Daley Considering Bid to Get the 2016 Olympics." *Chicago Tribune*, July 27.

———. 2007. "Olympics Won't Cost Taxpayers, City Says." *Chicago Tribune*, March 9.

Watkins, Scott D., and Patrick L. Anderson. 2009. *The Likely Economic Impact of a Chicago 2016 Summer Olympics*. Chicago: Anderson Economic Group. Accessed February 27, 2016. http://www.andersoneconomicgroup.com/Portals/0/upload /AEG_chicago_olympics_final.pdf.

CHAPTER 11

Surveillance, Security, and Intelligence-Led Policing in Chicago

RAJIV SHAH AND BRENDAN MCQUADE

In July 2003, the Chicago Police Department (CPD) initiated Operation Disruption, a program intended to monitor gangs and reduce drug trafficking in high-crime areas (Heinzmann 2003; Theodore, Martin, and Hollon 2006). It was the first time police in the United States used high visibility cameras to deter street crime. At a cost of $16,000 each, the city purchased thirty specially designed cameras constructed of lightweight bulletproof materials, equipped with a flashing blue light at the top, and sporting the trademark checkerboard markings of the CPD. The cameras can zoom and rotate 360 degrees, record in night vision, and operate twenty-four hours a day in all weather conditions. The highly visible cameras communicated to the public that the area around them was under police surveillance. The cameras transmitted video instantly to portable terminals equipped with a monitor and joystick that enabled police officers in the field to manipulate the cameras from remote locations. With the joystick, officers could pan 360 degrees and zoom in on suspicious activity. Rejecting the accusation that the cameras brought Orwellian surveillance to Chicago's streets, Mayor Richard M. Daley mockingly told reporters, "[A] police officer is Big Brother, Big Sister. . . . Having a camera on a street corner is no different than having a police officer on a street corner" (Heinzmann 2003).

The blue-light cameras quickly became emblematic of surveillance in Chicago. Although some residents complained about the cameras, officially known as Police Observation Devices or PODs, typically these complaints were about distractions caused by the flashing blue lights or that the presence of cameras stigmatized neighborhoods. With little popular resistance to the cameras or to police surveillance more broadly, the city had added another fifty cameras by the end of 2003 (Washburn 2006; Chicago Police Department 2013a). By 2014, there were over 20,000 cameras (Schwartz 2013; see Map 11.1). Some of these were operated by the police and others were privately owned but connected through the police network to a state-of-the-art data analysis "fusion center," the Crime Prevention and Information Center (CPIC) the Chicago Police Department operates at 3510 S. Michigan Avenue. These developments put Chicago at the cutting edge of urban surveillance. "I don't think there is another city in the U.S.," stated former secretary of Homeland Security Michael Chertoff in 2010 "that has as an extensive and integrated camera network as Chicago has" (Associated Press 2010).

The PODs provide surveillance capabilities that since 2003 have led the CPD to reshape its practices toward the development of high-technology, data-driven, intelligence-led policing (ILP). More than a mere matter of changing policy, ILP and related police surveillance constitute a broader political project to make municipal government more cost effective and to "secure" Chicago as a site of consumer-driven accumulation. Echoing neoliberal admonitions to cut budgets, increase managerial control over labor, and privatize the public sector, Chicago alderman Isaac Carothers, who represented the heavily African American 29th Ward on the city's West Side from 1999 to 2010, explained, "It's easier to put a camera up to watch over a neighborhood than it is to put a police officer on the corner. . . . Not that it's necessarily more effective. But it is less expensive." A CPD officer, calculated Carothers, cost "at least $100,000 a year, a sum that includes training, salary, and benefits. A surveillance camera costs about $13,000" (quoted in Isackson 2009). During this period of ILP and growing POD use by the CPD, the number of employees in the second largest municipal police force in the United States declined by 13 percent from 14,736 total employees in 2007 to 12,766 in 2012 (Federal Bureau of Investigation 2007, 2012).

Intelligence-Led Policing

The development of policing is often told as a story of gradual professionalization through a progression of distinct eras: 1) political (1840s–1890s); 2) reform (1890s–1960s); 3) community policing (1960s–early 2000s); and 4) homeland security (the present) (Kelling and Moore 1988; Oliver 2006). This discourse of professionalization, however, obscures the wider politics of policing and masks connections across policing eras, their representative policing techniques, and other aspects of civil administration. The discretionary power of the police extends as an unbroken thread from the early modern period to the present.

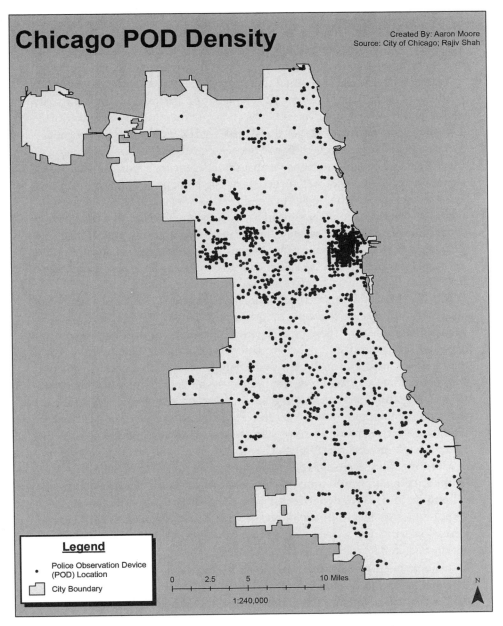

Chicago POD Density

Created By: Aaron Moore
Source: City of Chicago; Rajiv Shah

Legend

• Police Observation Device
(POD) Location

City Boundary

0   2.5   5   10 Miles

1:240,000

N

Map 11.1. Chicago POD density. Source: City of Chicago; Rajiv Shah.

As Mark Neocleous (2008, 108), a critic of state security measures, explains, "An object of police governance is either a resource for the welfare of the community or a threat to that welfare. The job of the police is to classify everyone and everything properly, and to treat each object according to its classification."

While policing retains a certain fundamental character, the specific way police power is organized and operates has changed significantly. In the last twenty years, neoliberal urban governance has become increasingly reliant on ILP. A practice that accelerated after the World Trade Center attacks of 2001, ILP focuses on collaboration within and between local and national law enforcement, intelligence, and emergency management agencies. It reorganizes policing around intelligence and uses surveillance, big data, geographic information systems, and other technologies to monitor urban areas and target "chronic offenders" (Peterson 2005). Organizationally, policing is no longer a public good monopolized by the national state but is rather a commodity provisioned by a diffuse network of private and public actors. Temporally and practically, police are now considered to be less concerned with controlling and prosecuting crime than with preempting potential risks and minimizing future loss.

Indeed, ILP is more than a mere policing doctrine. It is a component of the larger political project of neoliberal urban governance. ILP reorganizes police agencies around "a top-down management approach" of data-driven control. Proponents describe ILP as a "business model and managerial philosophy where data analysis and crime intelligence are pivotal to an objective, decision-making framework that facilitates crime and problem reduction, disruption and prevention through both strategic management and effective enforcement strategies that target prolific and serious offenders" (Ratcliffe 2008, 87, 6). Thus, ILP brings neoliberal reorganization to the policing sector by making staff reductions possible through increased administrative control over public sector workers.

More broadly, ILP changes the organization and operation of political power, shifting the relationships among citizens, police authority, and the state. Local politics and police departments are now heavily invested in surveillance technologies to ensure future order, or what Michel Foucault (2009, 10–11) terms "security." The work of security is always unfinished because the inherent unpredictability of what lies ahead can never be fully secured. Thus, a perpetual demand for security can be made, necessitating constant surveillance, investment, and technological advancement. This contemporary merging of data, surveillance, intelligence, and policing is thus integral to the construction of a neoliberal order. French sociologist Loïc Wacquant (2009) identifies two responses to increased social insecurity that have formed the neoliberal state: 1) the growth and veneration of the police, the courts, and the penitentiary; and 2) restrictive "workfare" and expansive "prisonfare" policies. In this neoliberal context, ILP and the expansion of surveillance entail "not just the *maintenance* or *reproduction* of order" but "its *fabrication*" (Neocleous 2000, 5, italics in original). This is how technologies of surveillance and the related application of police power purportedly produce ordered urban spaces.

Understood within this theoretical framing, the police and the wider criminal justice system are the primary institutional mechanisms of civil administration. They are the enforcers of capitalist social relations. In the current neoliberal moment, their work expands from ensuring the primacy of private property to producing privatized public spaces in which individuals are able to appropriately consume urban lifestyles. This neoliberal era is marked, therefore, by a devil's bargain in which a large proportion of the public and the media agree to accept surveillance and monitoring in return for the promise of safety. After the high crime rates of the later twentieth century and the shock of 9/11, concepts of contemporary citizenship (which include access to consumer lifestyles) have been renegotiated to include a broad mandate for authorities to engage in electronic surveillance and record keeping. In Chicago, however, this was not a wholly new phenomenon.

Intelligence-Led Policing in Chicago

Police surveillance in Chicago began in the late nineteenth century when the CPD aggressively targeted suspected anarchists and labor activists after the 1886 Haymarket bombing. Over the next 100 years, Chicago police surveilled and infiltrated a variety of social and political groups, such as the American Civil Liberties Union (ACLU), the League of Women Voters, the National Association for the Advancement of Colored People, the National Lawyers Guild, the National Council of Churches, and Operation PUSH. The internal CPD group responsible for these efforts, the Subversive Activities Unit, was colloquially known as the Red Squad (Donner 1990). By 1960, the CPD held surveillance files on approximately 117,000 Chicagoans, 141,000 out-of-towners, and 14,000 organizations (Storch 2004). In 1974, a lawsuit was filed against the CPD on behalf of fifteen organizations, four churches, and eighteen individuals. Eleven years later, a court decision ended the CPD's Subversive Activities Unit. As a temporary measure, a consent decree provided rules for and limits on the CPD's investigation of activities protected by the First Amendment. In 2001, however, lawyers for the city and the police department were successful in having the consent decree modified, and in 2009 the consent decree was dissolved (Mihalopoulos 2009).

The consent decree brought a series of professionalizing reforms to the CPD that, in effect, enhanced the surveillance capacities of police while tightening managerial control over police labor. One of the first of these initiatives was the computerization of databases through development of the Criminal History Records Information System (CHRIS). The CHRIS database, co-developed with Oracle, moved the CPD away from cumbersome handwritten reports to a Web-based interface. The resulting system, known as Citizen Law Enforcement Analysis and Reporting (CLEAR), was launched in 2000 (Pastore 2004). CLEAR epitomizes the technological approach of ILP. It allows police out on patrol to access criminal and case histories, outstanding warrants, 911 calls, crime scenes, license plate data, suspect details, police booking photographs, and geographical crime data. CLEAR currently contains over 10 million individual data sets and grows daily (City of Chicago, Department of Police 2007).

The computerization of records led to larger reforms that reorganized the CPD around command centers that made the data-driven managerialism associated with ILP possible. During the 1990s, Chicago was struggling to manage emergency calls; operators answered only about half of 911 calls within twelve seconds or less (Martin 1996). This delayed response led the city to build the Chicago Emergency Communications Center (CECC) in 1995 in the West Madison Street facility of the Office of Emergency Management and Communications. This consolidated emergency communications for police, fire, and emergency medical services. After the new CECC went on line, over 90 percent of 911 calls were answered within 1.2 seconds (Martin 1996). Enormous quantities of data and information are transmitted throughout Chicago through over 1,000 miles of the city-owned fiber optic network (Isackson 2009). In the 2000s, as POD camera surveillance spread, personnel in the CECC gained access to their video feeds. By the mid-2010s, the city expanded the CECC to incorporate the Operations Center, which monitors a variety of systems from cameras to traffic management; the City Incident Center, which monitors traditional infrastructure; and the Joint Operations Center, which coordinates with all emergency and command personnel (Careless 2007).

In 2007, the CECC was supplemented by the Crime Prevention and Information Center (CPIC). As one of seventy-eight fusion centers recognized and partially funded by the Department of Homeland Security (DHS), the CPIC has a potentially limitless mission of "all crimes, all threats, all hazards." It operates twenty-four hours a day from police headquarters and has a regular staff of thirty to thirty-five people. Personnel from the FBI, the DHS, and the Illinois State Police are assigned full time to the CPIC, along with representatives from other agencies that include the Illinois Department of Corrections, Cook County Sheriff's Police, the U.S. State Department, the Metra (commuter rail system) Police, DHS Customs and Border Protection, the U.S. Secret Service, the U.S. attorney's Northern District of Indiana, and the Transportation and Security Administration. Various suburban police departments also contact the CPIC as needed (Chicago Police Department 2013b). While the CECC monitors traffic flow and manages emergency services, the CPIC is an information clearinghouse that analyzes long-term trends, monitors the "threat environment" to achieve real time "situational awareness," and provides tactical case support. In the latter capacity, the fusion center monitors crime in real time, identifies crime patterns, continually assesses available resources, automatically constructs police deployments to prevent retaliatory violence, and provides instant access to background data on persons of interest (Government Accountability Office 2007, 70). Together, the CECC and the CPIC, information-driven command-and-control centers within the CPD, have created the institutional framework that supports ILP. They provide police commanders with the necessary information to preemptively manage crime and other disturbances while allowing for the most efficient deployment of police resources.

The Expansion of Chicago's Surveillance System

The computerization of records and the creation of the CECC and the CPIC developed hand in hand with the expansion of Chicago's surveillance system. The second generation of PODs added new features. The new cameras are movable and wireless (City of Chicago, Department of Police 2007). Some second-generation PODs include gunshot detection; these were designed by Safety Dynamics and were expanded in a 2007 pilot program called ShotSpotter. These PODs detect gunfire and transmit gunshot alerts directly to the CECC and, after 2007, the CPIC. Given its expense, the ShotSpotter technology is concentrated in the downtown Loop area rather than throughout Chicago (Delgado 2012). The placement of these gunshot detectors thus does not correspond with the areas of highest gun violence. Instead, they are part of a wider effort to secure downtown as a safe site.

The use of new technologies became a hallmark of Chicago's ILP, and government officials from around the world came to study the city's program. The promise of camera surveillance led Mayor Daley to say that by 2016, "we'll have [cameras on] almost every block" (Spielman 2006). In 2005, the CPD began installing smaller "hybrid" PODs. Still marked by a CPD star, checkerboard, and flashing blue lights, these hybrid PODs could be controlled by operators in the CECC and, later, the CPIC, who could start or stop the flashing blue light atop the devices at any time. A year later, the CPD began using wireless micro-PODs that had no CPD markings but could be fitted with flashing blue lights. Micro-PODs weighed just fifteen pounds (compared to the 100 pound first-generation PODs) and cost just $6,000 each. Easily movable and designed to look like streetlights, micro-PODs have zoom lenses, night-vision capability, and can rotate 360 degrees. The majority of the outdoor cameras currently in use in Chicago are micro-PODs.

The changing design of PODs reflects the CPD's changing surveillance strategy. The initial PODs installed in 2003 were highly conspicuous cameras that announced a police presence and were intended to deter criminal activity. Newer cameras, by contrast, inconspicuously blend into the background. As surveillance became increasingly normalized on Chicago streets, the city's surveillance network became ever more integrated. Along with the increase in CPD surveillance POD cameras, after 2008 the CECC gained access to cameras located in the city's airports, parks, and McCormick Place, and further, the 5,000 cameras housed in public schools (Spielman 2008; Schwartz 2013). By 2013, the Chicago Transit Authority had integrated the cameras in its stations, buses, and elevated rail cars with this expanding surveillance network (Schwartz 2013; Hilkevitch 2013). The CPIC was thus able to access almost 25,000 cameras throughout Chicago (Chicago Police Department 2013a). Although the initial focus of city government was to install and monitor its own cameras, by the second half of the 2000s, the owners of private cameras, such as those monitoring the Willis Tower skyscraper, were encouraged to join its surveillance network (Cullotta 2009). As of 2014, over 100 private entities allow the city to access their camera networks (Hall 2013).

This expansive and integrated camera network is increasingly subject to automated data analysis, which makes operating the system less labor intensive. Video analytic software now dissects the surveillance camera data. This software takes over the routine monitoring of surveillance cameras, alerting police personnel when incoming data merit further scrutiny. The software's object detection features establish a spatial trip wire that functions like a virtual fence. At the Union Station rail terminal, for example, a virtual fence has been created that detects any cars that park in front of the building. When the software detects a car, a message notifies the camera operator that someone is parking and human observation is in order. Police can use video analytic software to analyze hundreds of hours of camera surveillance footage. Journalist Noah Isackson (2009) cites a particular instance of this application: the CPD received a report that an individual had buried something in a park. Video analytics was used to review months of footage in search of a shovel, but ultimately none was found.

In 2013, the city began using facial recognition software (Main 2013a). The city has access to 4.5 million photos of previously arrested crime suspects. With facial recognition software, police can compare these photos to those in video footage, with the promise of identifying individuals via the camera lens. This was accomplished in 2013 when the CPD successfully used facial recognition technology to identify a robbery suspect. This individual's face had been recorded by a CTA surveillance camera (Stroud 2014). A more common use of surveillance technology and video analytic software is license plate recognition (LPR), which can identify 3,600 license plates per hour. Data collected from PODs includes license plate images (and time and location information). By 2012, the city had scanned over 500 million license plate images, making it possible to track cars and drivers within its boundaries.

Red-light cameras, which were introduced in 2003 and were promoted as a cost-effective, labor-saving means of monitoring traffic violations, quickly induced controversy. "A police officer would no longer have to be present to nab drivers," explained journalist Jon Hilkevitch (2003). "The cameras record the violation, the vehicle's rear license plate, speed of the vehicle and the date, time and location. The ticket is sent to the vehicle's registered owner along with a photo showing the red-light violation and the vehicle's license plate." After Redflex Traffic Systems and Affiliated Computer Services delivered 384 cameras attached to traffic lights across the city, Chicago became the leading user of red-light cameras in the United States. Despite the promise that these cameras would reduce traffic accidents, it is unclear whether the reduction in traffic accidents since 2003 can be attributed to their presence. Just as plausible a cause was the reduction of car use during this span of time (Shah 2010). In fact, an investigation by the city's Office of the Inspector General subsequently found that no metrics had been developed to ensure that cameras were placed where they were most needed (Office of Inspector General, City of Chicago 2013).

Such findings and related questions about the revenue derived from the LPR red-light cameras led the Schaumburg Freedom Coalition, the National Motorists Association, and the ExpiredMeter blog to question their purpose. With almost five million tickets issued since 2007, the cameras have generated $500 million in revenue for the city (Brockway 2014). In addition, financial malfeasance is associated with red-light cameras in Chicago. The *Chicago Tribune* found that a city official had improperly received payments and gifts from Redflex, and a former Redflex employee disclosed that the firm routinely offered bribes to municipal officials in return for contracts. These allegations led to firings and Chicago's cancellation of its contract with Redflex (Kidwell and Chase 2014).

The red-light cameras remain, however, and even in the face of data demonstrating that accidents due to excessive driving speed typically occur in other locations, in 2011 Mayor Rahm Emanuel advocated adding cameras that would be triggered by cars exceeding the speed limit near schools and parks (Secter, Heinzmann, and Rust 2011; Spielman 2013). Critics continued to argue that the city's enthusiasm for LPR was principally a function of its capacity to generate revenue. This sentiment was reinforced when cameras were placed on six street sweepers to identity and ticket cars (*Chicago Tribune* 2008). Although the "Sweepercam" experiment seemed operationally plausible, the complexities of Chicago's parking rules and signage led to the project's demise when the city failed to develop a standard set of protocols to be used across Chicago.

Evolving Techniques in Police Practice

The accumulation of years of data has allowed the CPD to use predictive analytics to identify criminal activity hotspots. In Chicago, crime hotspots that constitute 2 percent of the geographic area account for 10 percent of the city's crime (Main 2013b). Given this insight, the CPD targets greater resources in these locations. As crime hotspots move over time, predictive analytics are also used to identify neighborhoods and locations where crime is likely to increase in the future. Using the increased capacity of software to process real-time data, predictive analytics even purports to allow the prediction of specific crimes before they occur. *Chicago Sun-Times* reporter Frank Main (2011) describes an event in October 2010 when the CPD's Predictive Analytics Group analyzing 911 calls was able to anticipate a shooting on the city's South Side three minutes before it happened.

Another use of predictive analytics is to identify people at risk using social network analysis to study the connections between people. Analyzing the social networks related to homicides in several cities including Chicago, sociologists Andrew Papachristos, Anthony Braga, and David Hureau (2013) found strong connections between shooters and shooting victims (see also Moser 2013). The CPD's use of this type of data analysis, funded by a National Institute of Justice grant and implemented by the CPIC (Flannery 2014), has placed 420 people on a "heat list" of individuals who are "500 times more likely than average to be involved in violence" (Gorner 2013). Derived from data that includes a person's previous arrests, parole or warrant status, and weapons or drug arrests; the arrest histories of the person's acquaintances; and whether they have been the victim of a shooting, the CPD project, officially called Two Degrees of Association, began in 2013. The CPD identifies and then visits people on the heat list based on the proposition that taking these steps will prevent shootings. Police official Debra Kirby told a reporter (Gorner 2013): "What we're trying to figure out now is how does that data inform what happens in the future."

Impact on Crime

The millions of dollars spent on intelligence-led policing, technological surveillance, and fusion centers typically have a twofold justification. First, the data so collected is presumed to aid investigations. For example, police circulated surveillance footage of suspected attackers after the 2013 Boston Marathon bombing (Federal Bureau of Investigation 2013), yet whether these camera images were actually instrumental to solving this case is unclear (Warrick, Finn, and Nakashima 2010). Second, it is argued that the presence of cameras reduces or prevents crime. This argument presumes that a rational criminal is likely to avoid committing a crime in the presence of cameras because of the perceived risk of identification. Overt camera configurations—such as Chicago's original Operation Disruption—are a characteristic application of what is termed situational crime prevention (Ratcliffe 2006). Cameras are also supposed to reduce crime by acting, in the words of former Chicago police official Ron Huberman, as a "force multiplier" (Buchanan 2003). Cameras are analogized to eyes, allowing the same number of police officers to monitor a more expansive area (Cameron, Kolodinski, May, and Williams 2008).

In his exploration of Chicago's crime trends, however, community policing expert Wesley Skogan (2007) concludes that technology has not been a significant factor in reducing crime rates. Rather, changing demographics and incarceration rates seem to be more significant. Further, a recent examination of Chicago's camera surveillance program found that although highly visible cameras placed in high crime areas are effective crime deterrents, cameras located elsewhere had little effect on reducing crime: "Diffusing a large number of cameras throughout a city does not appear to be effective in reducing crime. Instead, the targeted use of a smaller number of cameras in high crime areas is much more effective" (Shah and Braithwaite 2013, 422; also see La Vigne et al. 2011). This limited crime-fighting utility suggests that security cameras may ultimately serve another purpose. They communicate to the public that the area is a safe playground for consumers. They disperse "the mythical entity called 'security' through civil society" (Neocleous 2011, 200).

Civil Liberties Concerns and Grassroots Responses

Although a 2006 poll found that 58 percent of the respondents supported Chicago's video security network (UPI 2006), these ILP programs and the city's network of surveillance POD cameras have provoked a variety of civil liberties concerns. For example, it is unclear how long the city retains surveillance footage; the length of time often is dependent on the type of camera. Some broadcast directly to the CECC, while others have a local digital video recorder. The Local Records Commission in Cook County sets a 30-day limit for how long such public records can be kept, yet despite this standard the city has stated that it keeps LPR data for seven weeks, or longer if the license plate has been "flagged" (Shah 2014).

Consequently, the ACLU of Illinois has called for stricter controls on the use of surveillance data, describing the surveillance network as "poorly regulated" and a "threat to our privacy" (ACLU of Illinois 2011). Even though the ACLU has persuaded the CPD to limit the use of PODs to locations "where no legally protected reasonable expectation of privacy exists" and affirm that racial profiling cannot occur, the CPD can still engage in "automatic vehicular tracking" and both "magnify anyone" and "small objects at great distances" without a warrant (Schwartz 2013). Further, Adam Schwartz of the ACLU (American Civil Liberties Union 2013, 50–51) observes that "no public information [is] available regarding the total number of cameras, the location of most cameras, the total amount of money spent on the cameras, and the sources of that money."

In addition to the ACLU, a number of grassroots organizations based in Chicago are also agitating for change. Going beyond the consideration of surveillance as a narrow issue with relevance to civil liberties questions, organizations such as We Charge Genocide (WCG) call for more comprehensive changes. A radical collective of police and prison abolitionists, WCG takes its name from a 1951 report presented to the United Nations that cited lynching, legal discrimination and disenfranchisement, police brutality, and systemic public health inequalities to make that the case the United States was engaged in a genocide against African Americans. In September 2014, WCG (2014) submitted a report to the United Nations Committee against Torture detailing the Chicago police's systemic harassment and abuse of minority communities, the failure of existing redressive mechanisms, and the resultant impunity of the Chicago police. Two months later the UN Committee against Torture (2014) denounced U.S. government torture, issuing a fifteen-page report that included a section on the Chicago Police Department. Since then, WCG has mounted a series of protests against police violence and in support of reparations to compensate victims of torture at the hands of infamous Chicago police detective John Burge.

While WCG, like many organizations of its kind, struggles to enunciate clear middle-term goals as steps toward realizing a revolutionary change in policing and criminal justice, other grassroots organizations are pushing for community control of the police. The Chicago Alliance Against Racist and Political Oppression (n.d.) is organizing a drive to pass legislation that would create a Civilian Police Accountability Council with powers to appoint the police commissioner, rewrite the police rule book, investigate police shootings, and otherwise oversee the police department. From a variety of perspectives, policing is one of Chicago's most vexing public policy challenges. WCG and other grassroots groups seeking to reshape local policing have been emboldened by the 2012 Chicago Teachers Union strike and national movements such as Occupy Wall Street and Black Lives Matter. Nevertheless, issues such as citizen surveillance and police conduct in racial minority neighborhoods have yet to receive the political attention that they merit, and it remains to be seen how local movements seeking to address these matters and reframe public policy will reach a wider public or an elite audience.

The Future of Chicago Police Surveillance

In the short term, it appears that the institutionalization of surveillance in the name of security is a fixture of urban life in the United States. Since 2003, there has been the rapid growth to over 25,000 cameras available to Chicago's city government. But cameras are only part of the surveillance arsenal. Myriad other technologies exist, including video analytics, license plate recognition, facial recognition, red-light cameras, and speed cameras. Hand in hand with these technologies is the use of new data analysis techniques such as predictive hot-spot and social networking analysis. For much of the public, police surveillance and its associated technologies are uncontroversial. In effect, these techniques secure spaces for consumption while quarantining social depredation in a belt of high-crime neighborhoods running from the West Side into the mid-South Side. Although the application of these strategies has generated some controversy, it remains to be seen whether the civil liberties–oriented program of groups such as the ACLU will align with the community-derived concerns of groups such as WCG to produce a forceful and widely acknowledged critique of the policing/surveillance regime that constitutes one of the key pillars of neoliberal Chicago.

Bibliography

ACLU of Illinois. 2011. *Chicago's Video Surveillance Cameras: A Pervasive and Unregulated Threat to Our Privacy.* Chicago: ACLU of Illinois.

American Civil Liberties Union. 2013. "You Are Being Tracked: How License Plate Readers Are Being Used to Record Americans' Movements." Accessed February 27, 2016. https://www.aclu.org/feature/you-are-being-tracked.

Associated Press. 2010. "Cameras Make Chicago Most Closely Watched US City." *Fox News,* April 6. Accessed February 20, 2015. http://www.foxnews.com/us/2010/04/06/cameras-make-chicago-closely-watched-city/.

Brockway, Mike. 2014. "Red-Light Camera Tickets Drop for Fifth Straight Year as Drivers Hit Brakes." *DNAinfo Chicago.* Accessed July 24, 2014. http://www.dnainfo.com/chicago/20140324/chicago/red-light-camera-tickets-drop-for-fifth-straight-year-as-drivers-hit-brakes.

Buchanan, Andrew. 2003. "On Chicago Streets, Cameras Are Watching." *Christian Science Monitor,* July 30.

Cameron, Aundreia, Elke Kolodinski, Heather May, and Nicholas Williams. 2008. *Measuring the Effects of Video Surveillance on Crime in Los Angeles.* Sacramento: California Research Bureau. Accessed February 27, 2016. https://www.library.ca.gov/crb/08/08-007.pdf.

Careless, James. 2007. "Emergency Management Chicago Style." *EMS World,* May 1. Accessed July 24, 2014. http://www.emsworld.com/article/10321936/emergency-management-chicago-style.

Chan, Sewel. 2007. "Why Did Crime Fall in New York City?" *New York Times.* Accessed July 22, 2014. http://cityroom.blogs.nytimes.com/2007/08/13/why-did -crime-fall-in-new-york-city/?_php=true&_type=blogs&_r=0.

Chicago Alliance Against Racist and Political Repression. n.d. *The People's Guide to an Elected Civilian Accountability Council.* Accessed February 28, 2015. http:// naarpr.org/wp-content/uploads/2014/12/Cpac-Pamphlet_2sided.pdf.

Chicago Police Department. 2013a. "Police Observation Devices (PODS)." Chicago Police Department. Accessed July 22, 2014. https://portal.chicagopolice.org/portal /page/portal/ClearPath/About%20CPD/POD%20Program.

———. 2013b. "Crime Prevention and Information Center (CPIC), Special Order S03– 03–06." Chicago Police Department. Accessed February 28, 2015. http://directives .chicagopolice.org/lt2014/data/a7a57bf0-13ed7140-08513-ed71-4cecd9c378c05dec .html.

Chicago Tribune. 2008. "Smile, You're on the Street Sweeper Cam." July 10.

City of Chicago, Department of Police. 2007. *Technology Update.* Summer. Accessed July 24, 2014. https://portal.chicagopolice.org/portal/pls/portal/!PORTAL .wwpob_page.show?_docname=522702.PDF.

Committee against Torture. 2014. "Concluding Observations on the Third to Fifth Periodic Reports of the United States of America." November. Accessed February 28, 2015. http://tbinternet.ohchr.org/Treaties/CAT/Shared%20Documents/USA /INT_CAT_COC_USA_18893_E.pdf.

Cullotta, Karen Ann. 2009. "Chicago Links Street Cameras to Its 911 Network." *New York Times,* February 20.

Delgado, Jennifer. 2112. "Cops Using Sensors to Pick Up Gunshot Sounds in 2 Locations on South, West Sides." *Chicago Tribune,* October 26.

Donner, Frank. 1990. *Protectors of Privilege: Red Squads and Police Repression in Urban America.* Berkeley: University of California Press.

Federal Bureau of Investigation. 2007. Table 78. Illinois: Full Time Police Employees by City. Accessed March 26, 2015. https://www2.fbi.gov/ucr/cius2007/data /table_78_il.html.

———. 2012. Table 78. Illinois: Full Time Police Employees by City. Accessed March 26, 2015. http://www.fbi.gov/about-us/cjis/ucr/crime-in-the-u.s/2012/crime-in- the-u.s.-2012/tables/78tabledatadecpdf/table-78-state-cuts/table_78_full_time _law_enforcement_employees_illinois_by_city_2012.xls.

———. 2013. "Surveillance Video Related to Boston Bombings." Accessed March 17, 2015. http://www.fbi.gov/news/updates-on-investigation-into-multiple-explosions -in-boston/surveillance-video-related-to-boston-bombings.

Flannery, Mike. 2013. "Police Narrow Focus to 450 Criminals Responsible for the City's Violence." *Fox 32,* July 11. Accessed February 28, 2104. http://www.myfoxchicago .com/story/22820740/police-narrow-focus-to-450-criminals-responsible-for- citys-violence.

Foucault, Michel. 2009. *Security, Territory, Population: Lectures at the Collège de France 1977–1978.* New York: Macmillan.

Gorner, Jeremy. 2013. "Chicago Police Use 'Heat List' as Strategy to Prevent Violence." *Chicago Tribune*, August 21.

Government Accountability Office. 2007. *Homeland Security: Federal Efforts Are Helping to Alleviate Some Challenges Encountered by State and Local Information and Fusion Centers*. Washington, DC: United States Government Accountability Office. Accessed February 28, 2015. http://www.gao.gov/new.items/d0835.pdf.

Hall, Charlie. 2013. "Watch Dogs: Invasion." *Polygon*, October 16. Accessed March 17, 2015. http://www.polygon.com/features/2013/10/16/4817988/watch-dogs-invasion.

Heinzmann, David. 2003. "City to Put 'Gotcha' Cameras on Crime." *Chicago Tribune*, July 11.

Hilkevitch, Jon. 2003. "For Drivers Who Can't See Red, City Has Just the Ticket." *Chicago Tribune*, May 16.

———. 2013. "CTA Adding Cameras to Older Rail Cars." *Chicago Tribune*, February 9.

Isackson, Noah. 2009. "Can Cameras Replace Cops?" *Chicago Magazine*, March. Accessed April 15, 2015. http://www.chicagomag.com/Chicago-Magazine/March-2009/Can-Cameras-Replace-Cops/.

Kelling, George, and Mark Moore. 1988. "The Evolving Strategy of Policing." *Perspectives on Policing* 4 (November): 1–15.

Kidwell, David, and John Chase. 2014. "Charges Filed against Ex-City Hall Manager of Red-Light Camera Program." *Chicago Tribune*, May 14.

La Vigne, Nancy G., Samantha S. Lowry, Joshua A. Markman, and Alison M. Dwyer. 2011. *Evaluating the Use of Public Surveillance Cameras for Crime Control and Prevention*. Washington, D.C.: Urban Institute Justice Policy Center and Community Oriented Policing Services, U.S. Department of Justice. Accessed February 26, 2015. http://www.urban.org/research/publication/evaluating-use-public-surveillance-cameras-crime-control-and-prevention/view/full_report.

Main, Frank. 2011. "Police Sensing Crime before It Happens." *Chicago Sun-Times*, February 22.

———. 2013a. "Chicago Police Go High-Tech with Facial Recognition Software." *Chicago Sun-Times*, August 15.

———. 2013b. "Cops on Overtime Help Drive down Murder Rate in City's 'Hot Zones.'" *Chicago Sun-Times*, March 3.

Martin, Andrew. 1996. "Some 911 Calls Fail To Make It Through." *Chicago Tribune*, February 27.

Mihalopoulos, Dan. 2009. "'Red Squad' Decrees: Federal Judge Dissolves Restrictions Linked to Chicago Police's 'Red Squad.'" *Chicago Tribune*, June 9.

Moser, Whet. 2013. "The Small Social Networks at the Heart of Chicago Violence." *Chicago Magazine*, December.

Neocleous, Mark. 2000. *The Fabrication of Social Order: Critical Theory of Police Power*. London: Pluto Press.

———. 2008. *Critique of Security*. Edinburgh: Edinburgh University Press.

———. 2011. "'A Brighter and Nicer New Life': Security as Pacification." *Social & Legal Studies* 20, no. 2: 191–208.

Office of Inspector General, City of Chicago. 2013. *Red-Light Camera Installation Audit*. Chicago: Office of Inspector General. Accessed February 27, 2015. http://chicagoinspectorgeneral.org/wp-content/uploads/2013/05/Red-Light-Camera -Audit-Final1.pdf.

Oliver, Willard. 2006. "The Fourth Era of Policing: Homeland Security." *International Review of Law, Computers & Technology* 20, nos. 1–2: 49–62.

Papachristos, Andrew V., Anthony Braga, and David Hureau. 2013. "The Corner and the Crew: The Influence of Geography and Social Networks on Gang Violence." *American Sociological Review* 78, no. 3: 417–447.

Pastore, Richard. 2004. "Chicago Police Department Uses IT to Fight Crime, Wins Grand CIO Enterprise Value Award 2004." CIO, February 15. Accessed March 17, 2015. http://www.cio.com/article/2439813/it-organization/chicago-police -department-uses-it-to-fight-crime--wins-grand-cio-enterprise-value-aw.html.

Peterson. Marilyn. 2005. *Intelligence Led Policing: The New Intelligence Architecture*. Washington, DC: U.S. Department of Justice, Bureau of Justice Statistics.

Ratcliffe, Jerry. 2006. "Video Surveillance of Public Places." Washington, D.C.: Community Oriented Policing Services, U.S. Department of Justice.

———. 2008. *Intelligence-Led Policing*. Cullompton, UK: Willan Publishing.

Schwartz, Adam. 2013. "Chicago's Video Surveillance Cameras: A Pervasive and Poorly Regulated Threat to Our Privacy." *Northwestern Journal of Technology & Intellectual Property* 11, no. 2: 47–60.

Secter, Bob; David Heinzmann, and Max Rust. 2011. "Would Speed Cameras Really Save Lives?" *Chicago Tribune*, November 6.

Shah, Rajiv. 2010. "Effectiveness of Red Light Cameras in Chicago: An Exploratory Analysis." June 17. Accessed July 24, 2014. http://www.thenewspaper.com/rlc/ docs/2010/il-chicagostudy.pdf.

———. 2014. "License Plate Recognition (LPR) in Chicago." January 19. Accessed July 24, 2014. http://eyeingchicago.com/blog/2014/1/19/license-plate-recognition- lpr-in-chicago.html.

Shah, Rajiv, and Jeremy Braithwaite. 2013. "Spread Too Thin: Analyzing the Effectiveness of the Chicago Camera Network on Crime." *Police Practice and Research* 14, no. 5: 415–427.

Skogan, Wesley G. 2007. "Reflections on Declining Crime in Chicago." Unpublished report. Accessed July 24, 2014. http://skogan.org/files/Skogan.Crime_Drop_in _Chicago.April_2007.pdf.

Spielman, Fran. 2006. "Daley: By 2016, Cameras on 'Almost Every Block.'" *Chicago Sun-Times*, October 12.

———. 2008. "Daley Unveils Plans to Increase School Security." *Chicago Sun-Times*, March 6.

———. 2013. "Speed-Camera Tickets Coming in September." *Chicago Sun-Times*, June 22.

Storch, Randi. 2004. "Red Squad." *Electronic Encyclopedia of Chicago*. Chicago Historical Society. Accessed February 27, 2016. http://www.encyclopedia.chicagohistory.org/pages/1049.html.

Stroud, Matt. 2014. "Did Chicago's Facial Recognition System Catch Its First Crook?" *The Verge*, August 8. Accessed February 27, 2016. http://www.theverge.com/2014/8/8/5982727/face-wreck-how-advanced-tech-comes-up-short-for-police.

Theodore, Nik, Nina Martin, and Ryan Hollon. 2006. "Securing the City: Emerging Markets in the Private Provision of Security Services in Chicago." *Social Justice* 33, no. 3: 85–100.

UPI. 2006. "Chicago Voters Don't Mind Surveillance." February 16. Accessed July 22, 2014. http://www.upi.com/Top_News/2006/02/18/Chicago-voters-dont-mind-surveillance/UPI-71851140313814/.

Wacquant, Loïc. 2009. *Punishing the Poor: The Neoliberal Government of Social Insecurity*. Durham, N.C.: Duke University Press Books.

Warrick, Joby, Peter Finn, and Ellen Nakashima. 2010. "Times Square Bombing Attempt Reveals Limits of Video Surveillance." *Washington Post*, May 4.

Washburn, Gary. 2006. "City Sold on Video Security." *Chicago Tribune*, February 18.

We Charge Genocide. 2014. *Police Violence against Chicago's Youth of Color*. Chicago, September. Accessed February 28 2015. https://chicagopatf.org/2016/01/04/police-violence-against-chicagos-youth-of-color-by-we-charge-genocide/.

Conclusion

Beyond Neoliberal Chicago

LARRY BENNETT, ROBERTA GARNER,
AND EUAN HAGUE

As we began planning *Neoliberal Chicago*, one of our first points of debate was whether to characterize Chicago as *the* neoliberal city—an urban center whose social structure, policies, and practices exemplify the essential, defining features of neoliberalism—or whether the more plausible interpretation would peg Chicago as *a* neoliberal city. With several years of editorial exchange and the solicitation, drafting, and editing of chapters behind us, we have concluded that the most apt characterization of Chicago is as a *paradigmatic* neoliberal city, not unique in its approach and character, but characteristic of an important variety of neoliberal urbanism.

As such, what kind of neoliberal city is Chicago? We think that we can best approach that question by beginning with another characterization: What kind of global city is Chicago? In our view, Chicago can be grouped with the class of cities that includes Amsterdam, Frankfurt, Paris, Rio de Janeiro, and Sydney whose global functions are multiple but whose centrality and breadth of connections do not match Saskia Sassen's (2001) famous trio of New York, London, and Tokyo. Chicago is of global significance because of the scale of its metropolitan region and regional economy and because of the corporate "weight" of its metropolitan region. Among the city's strong points are its finance sector and its concentration of business services expertise, and not inconsequentially, the global reach of its museums, professional performance ensembles, and elite universities.

At the same time, Chicago's position as a key global city is not invulnerable. Electronic trading has decentered commodities markets and poses a threat to Chicago's exchanges. The rise of Las Vegas and Orlando as convention cities has forced significant changes in management and labor relations at Chicago's huge McCormick Place convention complex, which for many years had been the premier convention and trade-show host in the United States. Moreover, contemporary Chicago's business and civic leaders are well aware of their hometown's long slide from the top of the hill as the leading U.S. manufacturing center. Chicago is a global city whose local elites constantly fret over the prospect of the loss of corporations through outside acquisition or relocation, the hollowing out of once-key local economic sectors, or, very simply, bad publicity. This nervous, global Chicago is a city whose elites are, for example, prone to overselling the expected economic and community development boost to be derived from hosting mega-events such the Olympic Games.

This nervous global Chicago elected a New Democrat mayor in 2011, Rahm Emanuel, whose intellectual inclination and business contacts prompted him to seek a local economic fix to the Great Recession by reconceiving a corporate-dominated promotional group, World Business Chicago, as the city's economic development think tank. Politics is the hinge that links global Chicago and neoliberal Chicago. In various ways Chicago's situation can be aligned with broader currents of public opinion and public policy fashion. As a New Democrat, Mayor Emanuel is a member of the cohort that two decades ago rebranded the ideological profile of the national Democratic Party and in so doing made a substantial contribution to the scaling back of the already limited U.S. welfare state. Another salient component of the broader context is the withering of working-class consciousness in the United States and the decline of union affiliation. This means that a self-styled education reformer such as Mayor Emanuel can presume that if a teachers' union can be incapacitated, then voilà, student performance will be turned around.

Yet neoliberalism is more than a toolkit of market-inflected policy prescriptions. That toolkit is encompassed by a world view that privileges competition and hyperindividualism, celebrates financial acumen above all other human pursuits, disparages governmental efforts to serve less-advantaged members of society, and assumes that *consumption*—of products, of experiences, even of *memory*—is society's fundamental connective tissue. This neoliberal cultural envelope shapes public policy in very distinctive ways. As Michael Lorr argues, it pushes the City of Chicago's environmental/sustainability policy in the direction of "smart consumption." Yue Zhang, in turn, demonstrates how neoliberalism's pinched sense of cultural value restricts the city government's historic preservation agenda to a highly selective application of physical design protections, as opposed to a more broadly framed effort to save defining artifacts of Chicago's cultural heritage. Beyond the parameters of public policy, Sean Dinces and Chris Lamberti identify a neoliberal mindset in the marketing and journalistic coverage of local sports franchises and athletes as "blue-collar" that camouflages the social and economic distortions of contemporary professional sports with a set of agreeable (and largely obsolete) communal tropes.

Chicago's new reality is most palpably expressed through its transformed neighborhood spaces. The Lakeside development plan Carrie Breitbach describes, a characteristic early twenty-first-century vision of high-end dwellings, shops, and entertainment, anchored—so to speak—by ready access to Lake Michigan (especially for the boaters among Lakeside's prospective residents) exemplifies the new Chicago. Long gone—if Lakeside's sponsors had been able to push their project beyond planning and marketing—would be the working-class enclaves and social networks that once enlivened this corner of industrial Chicago. Alex Papadopoulos's account of the gentrification of East Lake View on the North Side, popularly known as Boystown, exposes one of neoliberal Chicago's intriguing paradoxes. On the one hand, contemporary Chicago is "gay friendly" in a way that would have been unimaginable a quarter-century ago. However, the real estate development that incessantly remakes the city's hot neighborhoods is beginning to dilute the Boystown neighborhood's distinctive ambiance.

Martha Martinez's neighborhood-level survey of the recent foreclosure crisis pinpoints one of neoliberalism's crucial attributes, the acceleration of social and economic inequality. In a number of Chicago neighborhoods with large African American and Latino populations, subprime lending in the early to mid-2000s produced a housing bubble that yielded devastating ripple effects after the 2008 crash, including housing abandonment, population loss, and increasing crime. Yet as of 2015, on Chicago's affluent North Side and in gentrifying portions of the Near South, Near West, and Northwest Sides, the aftereffects of the Great Recession are barely noticeable. And finally, Rajiv Shah and Brendan McQuade's account of police surveillance in Chicago communicates with crystalline clarity which parts of Chicago constitute the "wild city" (Castells 1975): the areas of the South and West Sides that have experienced disinvestment and population loss for decades and in the early twenty-first century are largely populated by African Americans.

Neoliberal Chicago is thus a very far cry from the "just city," as this concept has been developed by planning scholar Susan Fainstein. Fainstein identifies three core markers—equity, democracy, and diversity. Contemporary Chicago scores very badly in terms of equity, defined as "a distribution of both material and non-material benefits derived from public policy that does not favor those who are already better off at the beginning" (Fainstein 2010, 36). It also scores poorly on democracy, which is the openness of political institutions to public influence. Chicago *is* a diverse city, but its literal diversity is undercut by racial division and continuing spatial segregation. Across the civic and political arenas, elite recruitment and co-optation processes produce diversity in terms of race, ethnicity, gender, and sexual orientation among the city's institutional leadership without yielding parallel reductions in broader economic disparities and segregation. In short, there is much work to be done if Chicago is to become more like the just city we and our contributors would like to experience. In the remainder of this conclusion, we offer our thoughts on the challenges to making Chicago a more just city and how such a transformation might occur. We approach our topic from three perspectives: 1) the broader context that shapes Chicago and other neoliberal cities; 2) what we have elsewhere (in Chapter 10) called "organic counter-neoliberalism," current local efforts to stem the tide of neoliberalism; and 3) accepting the limits imposed by the broader context, a plausible first step toward a politics of local transformation.

Agency in the Face of Implacable Structure

First of all, things could be worse! Chicago remains a livable and affordable city for a large slice of its residents. It has not yet reached the levels of "plutocratization" that have been documented in many other global cities such as New York, San Francisco, and London. By plutocratization we mean the transformation of the central city into a *zone of concentrated advantage* in which only the wealthy can afford to live and buy homes and in which the choices of globally oriented elites guide development, often with disregard for local cultures and needs. Chicago still offers affordable housing (in a broad sense of the term) to a substantial portion of its residents. Thanks to the foresight of the enlightened and civic-minded Chicago bourgeoisie of the early twentieth century, its stunning lakeshore, parks, and beaches remain accessible to the public. Chicago offers dining, nightlife, theater, and music across a wide spectrum of tastes and incomes. Its economy remains diversified and consequently less ephemeral than that of other global cities; it is not overly specialized or focused only on financial services (Kotkin 2005). Many Chicagoans love their city, and it remains a powerful magnet for young people from the suburbs and the Midwestern heartland. Chicago retains many assets, a foundation on which a better city can ultimately be built.

But could Chicago be better? For us, "better" means a city that is less divided by class and race, a city with shrinking rather than growing disparities and inequalities. "Better" means a city that is less segregated, with fewer areas of racial isolation and fewer communities of concentrated disadvantage. For many observers, "better" would mean a more robust range of social services and an enhanced quality of life for all. These improvements should not be viewed as a zero-sum proposition. There are many benefits to the affluent as well as the poor in a city that is both egalitarian and rich in public amenities. As British scholars

Richard Wilkinson and Kate Pickett (2010, 177–178) argue, greater equality can mean a better life for all, the advantaged as well as the disadvantaged.

- A better city would offer quality education to all its children and youth, enabling all of them to complete secondary school and be prepared for success in universities or in skilled trades along the lines of the most effective European apprenticeship programs. Education would enrich cultural and political capacities above and beyond preparing young people for labor markets.
- A better city would provide job training to help workers move from sectors of declining employment into emerging sectors.
- A better city would work with unions to protect and expand workers' rights to safe working conditions, a living wage, reasonable hours, and job security.
- A better city would assure an adequate supply of affordable housing, with dispersion rather than concentration of low and moderate rental units in order to support economic and racial integration.
- A better city would be one that distributes health care and health-supporting amenities such as bike lanes and supermarkets evenly across its territory. It would offer incentives to providers of these goods and services who locate in underserved communities.
- A better city would energetically implement sustainable development and offer attractive mass transit options at affordable prices.
- A better city would have lower crime rates throughout its territory, and vulnerable communities would no longer have to bear the burden of the effects of mass incarceration.
- A better city would be one with a broader base of participation in governance and decision making, a city with an active political life in the neighborhoods, an engaged citizenry, and an ample supply of social capital, instead of one that is ruled narrowly and opaquely by government officials in crony-type relationships with developers.

The most dynamic and complete forms of the "better city" are impossible within the broad confines of neoliberalism. More analytically, one might say that the currently prevailing institutional structure of capitalist accumulation places sharp limitations on the progressive policies that could bring about the "better city." Political economist David Kotz (2003), among others, argues that it is unlikely that this structural/institutional barrier will change markedly in the near future. But within these confines, there is wiggle room, and cities can implement reforms that improve the lives of working people and enhance livability for all. Examples include the "municipal socialism" that Benjamin Goldfrank and Andrew Schrank (2009) have documented convincingly in the Latin American context and the progressive policies or "equity agendas" that a number of other urban policy analysts have identified in U.S. cities (Gendron and Domhoff 2008; Bennett and Giloth 2008). Three underlying preconditions could power a drive for socially just urban policy within neoliberalism: 1) low unemployment and underemployment—that is, tight rather than loose labor markets; 2) structures that promote coherent and coordinated collective action; and 3) an expansion of political consciousness to a larger public. At present, these conditions are absent or only weakly present, but current circumstances are not unalterable.

Tight labor markets and full employment in secure, well-paying jobs can be a fulcrum for accomplishing a local equity agenda, as Michael Bennett and Bob Giloth (2008) argue in their analysis of progressive urban governance in past decades. But after the crash of 2008, this prospect faded (some might say that it was in fact already weak by historical standards even in the boom years of the 1990s and the early 2000s), and it remains uncertain in the current phase of weak recovery in labor markets and wages. As long as unemployment rates remain high, worker solidarity (especially across racial lines) is undercut by a sense of competition for scarce jobs. The impact goes far beyond the situation of individuals and households because entire neighborhoods experience poverty, declining household incomes, and the psychological and material effects of exclusion from the economy. As noted in Chapter 1, these local and national economic conditions are closely linked to racial isolation and inequality. In a climate of insecurity in which households struggle to make ends meet, it is difficult for progressive forces to organize city residents to press for improved social services aimed at reducing inequality and realizing "the better city." The daily challenge of surviving on low wages or no wages at all drains time and energy from collective action. The economic situation is probably a major reason for the decline in political efficacy in African American community areas as the momentum of the civil rights movement and community organizing has been dissipated in a period of sustained job loss. High unemployment decisively shifts the class balance of forces because corporations and developers gain power both directly in their capacity as employers and indirectly as major organized players in the local political arena.

Collective action is necessary to bring the "better city" into being, and in Chicago and many other contemporary American cities collective action is weak and divided. Labor unions and workplace organizing are not well integrated with urban activism, neighborhood mobilization, and cultural contention. Andrés Walliser's (2013) account of the new urban activism in Spain makes clear—reading between the optimistic lines—that in both Europe and the United States, labor organizing is not effectively linked to neighborhood and cultural movements. There seems to be little overall vision and organization that can be tapped to channel activism into an effective reform agenda and focused policy initiatives. The apparent fading away of Occupy Wall Street, in such sharp contrast to the vigor, funding, and electoral success of the Tea Party (Skocpol and Williamson 2013), illustrates the economic, organizational, and ideological weakness of progressive currents which did not quickly gel into a strong, coherent movement. And despite the buzz about social media and Internet activism and the tempting parallels to the role of print in eighteenth- and nineteenth-century revolutions (see, for example, Castells 2012; Tarrow 1998) it remains to be seen whether hashtags and tweets can actually accomplish structural reform or regime change.

Finally, cultivating political consciousness within the neoliberal social structure of accumulation presents a major challenge to progressive activists. While millennials hold progressive views, they exhibit little passion for political engagement and are not easy to mobilize for voting, let alone for the hard organizational work needed to effect change. Paul Taylor (2014), reporting Pew Research Center studies, has documented this combination of progressive orientations and weak political participation among young people. The Occupy Wall Street story of meteoric rise and gradual waning exemplifies these organizational challenges. The Bernie Sanders presidential campaign and the emergence of Black Lives Matter suggest that the weak political engagement of millennials is not an unalterable condition, but these two mobilizations also illustrate a tendency toward fragmentation among progressive forces. As sociologist Richard Sennett (2000) has so poignantly argued, the institutions, technology, and labor relations characteristic of "flexible capitalism" (the economic grounding of neoliberalism) generate an atomistic ideology in which "we" is the forbidden pronoun, the individual's interests are believed to be antagonistic to those of the collectivity, government is seen as a negative and intrusive force, and problems are addressed by exit rather than by voice. The everyday life and lived experience of flexible, globalized, and financially driven capitalism has generated a matching atomistic ideology marked by low voter turnout and, more broadly, "the narrowing of civic life" (Skocpol 2004).

The Chicagoan Antisyzygy

In 1919, a year when race riots left thirty-eight people dead in Chicago, Scottish cultural critic C. Gregory Smith published an essay in which he described the national literature of his home country as exhibiting what he termed "the Caledonian antisyzygy." In its combination of polarized, contradictory extremes within a single entity, the Caledonian antisyzygy, Smith argued, exemplified Scotland's split personality of opposing tendencies fighting for supremacy. The trait is arguably best illustrated by Robert Louis Stevenson's title character in his 1886 *Strange Case of Dr. Jekyll and Mr. Hyde*. Smith's diagnosis comes to mind when looking at Chicago at the start of the twenty-first century: a city of the superrich and of extreme poverty, of food deserts and Michelin-starred restaurants, of the North Side and the South Side, the Loop and the neighborhoods, of white and black, immigrant and native born. It is a city, as the contributors to this collection demonstrate, that is becoming more divided; a Chicago where residents experience both greater surveillance and insecurity; a "city of neighborhoods" that in the past fifteen years have been simultaneously booming and busting due to processes of gentrification and foreclosure. This is the Chicagoan antisyzygy that neoliberalism has produced: a city in which polarities coexist, intersecting in urban space that has been turned inside out as public housing projects have been replaced by luxury condominiums and former industrial areas such as South Works are reimagined as high-priced mixed residential, office, and retail complexes.

This neoliberal path leads in one direction, toward further polarization, fragmentation, and disparity. If current trends continue, the poor and less fortunate will find that they can only afford to live in areas farther and farther to Chicago's west and south, with concomitant increases in the distances to jobs, support services, and educational and recreational opportunities. Already recognizing this unhappy scenario, thousands of Chicago residents are working every day to produce an alternative urban future. From groups that are transforming vacant lots into urban gardens to others that are occupying foreclosed homes and challenging the displacement caused by gentrification, community organizations and local neighborhoods offer a vision of Chicago that represents a direct challenge to the neoliberalism radiating from City Hall.

There is Growing Home, which provides jobs and training in urban agriculture for low-income and homeless people and sells the produce they grow at city farmers' markets. This is the model Sweet Beginnings follows, which is employing formerly incarcerated individuals and transforming vacant lots in North Lawndale into a home for honey-producing beehives. There are countless other projects in Chicago that integrate a vision of community, social and economic development, jobs, and environmental sustainability. Rank-and-file Chicagoans are producing their own stories about what the city should be. Groups such as Civic Lab (http://www.civiclab.us/) and the Million Dollar Blocks project (http://chicagosmilliondollarblocks.com/) are advocating change by using city data to demonstrate inequities in neighborhood funding and provision of services. Other groups are making use of data to highlight social and public policy injustices (which at one time were matters of only anecdotal knowledge) using maps, charts, and graphs. Such data can also be used to fortify the neighborhood and community plans that organizations regularly produce but are so often ignored by the city's political leadership.

Of course, getting the city's political leaders to engage with residents has proven historically difficult, and past efforts to engender citywide conversations have met with varying levels of success. In the 1980s, the city's myriad community organizations, a legacy of Saul Alinsky and his compatriots of two previous generations, came together to overcome racially motivated resistance and elect Harold Washington as mayor in 1983 and again in 1987. More recently, in 2006, Developing Government Accountability to the People (DGAP) brought together hundreds of people from over thirty community organizations, activist groups, and other neighborhood stakeholders to issue a State of the City report card (the city got a D!) and offer perspectives for change. In 2013, even the *Chicago Tribune* began to solicit reader suggestions for a "New Plan of Chicago" that could provide jobs, community development, and educational opportunities and reduce crime. Chicago appears to be ripe for an extended citywide conversation about its future.

To advance this conversation and achieve the necessary partnerships to enact such change, Chicago's schools, colleges, and universities must work with community organizations, activists, and others in collaborations that can directly challenge the existing spatial injustices of the city. Some such efforts are already under way. Chicago State University offers expert community support through its Neighborhood Assistance Center and seeks to combat food deserts and meet nutritional needs in low-income neighborhoods through an innovative aquaponics fish-farming facility. This initiative offers students the opportunity to learn about ecology and operates as a neighborhood cultural space. Our own DePaul University gives students and faculty the opportunity to collaborate with over 300 Chicago-area nonprofit organizations through its Steans Center for Community-based Service Learning.

To create the Chicago of the future that groups and institutions such as these are envisioning, and the ability to participate in it, the city must be open to and engage with all of its inhabitants. This means pursuing what celebrated urban theorist Henri Lefebvre (1996, 158, quoted in Purcell 2002, 102) calls "the right to the city . . . [and a] right to urban life" in which urban spatial, political, and social relationships are fundamentally restructured. Instead of simply polling a small fraction of the electorate once every four years, it means a Chicago that regularly listens to the voices of immigrants, non-U.S. citizens, the homeless, renters, and others who live and work in Chicago. It means spatially restructuring Chicago so that urban administrative space is innovatively re-imagined in a different model from the current one of a 100-year-old city boundary that divides Chicago from outlying communities and an internal division of the city into seventy-seven community areas crosscut by fifty wards,. Externally, Chicago must be recognized as influencing the fortunes of hundreds of suburban communities and governmental jurisdictions and that this necessitates stronger cooperation across jurisdictions. Within the city, community areas, wards, and other spatial divisions should be redrawn so that they no longer hinder effective

Box C.1: The Chicago Public School Teachers Strike of 2012

Running for mayor in 2011, Rahm Emanuel pledged that, if elected, he would make improvement of the beleaguered Chicago Public Schools (CPS) a top priority. In fact, the newly elected mayor seemed to make attacking the Chicago Teachers Union (CTU) one of his primary aims. Shortly after taking office, Emanuel directed the school board—in the interest of cost saving—to rescind a pay raise for CPS teachers. In addition, the mayor pledged to expand the number of charter schools in Chicago (charter school teachers typically do not have union representation), called for a longer school day without additional compensation for teachers, and pushed for teacher evaluations to be tied to students' standardized test scores. In the early months of his mayoralty, Emanuel also developed a notably hostile relationship with the president of the Chicago Teachers Union, Karen Lewis. The mayor (who is notorious for his use of profanities) was widely reported to have blurted at the close of one meeting with the CTU president, "Fuck you, Lewis."

Mayor Emanuel pressed his case with the Illinois General Assembly, which obliged by passing legislation authorizing the extension of the CPS school day, and mandated that the CTU would need 75 percent approval by its members to initiate a job action. Nonetheless, after six months of laborious negotiations to reach a new CPS/CTU contract, the union's leadership authorized a strike vote in the late spring of 2012. To the surprise of many observers, rank-and-file support for the CTU leadership was nearly unanimous. Over 90 percent of the union members supported a walkout. The strike action began on Monday, September 10, 2012, just a few days into the new school year. Mayor Emanuel and his allies on the school board and, more broadly, among charter school "reform" advocates, encouraged parent disapproval of the union's actions, but over the course of the week-and-a-half job action, neither widespread parental discontent nor internal division among CPS teachers was evident. On September 18, the CTU's House of Delegates approved a compromise contract offer that the union's membership subsequently endorsed. The three-year contract included annual salary increases for teachers, specified a phased-in process making test score performance just one component of teacher evaluation, and included provisions for staff programming during the extended school hours, giving priority to teacher rehires whose performance preceding termination had been positively evaluated.

The resolution of the CTU strike was widely viewed as a victory for the teachers and for union president Karen Lewis. Lewis's assessment of the strike surely captures the sentiment of most CPS teachers and many other Chicagoans: "The key is that we are trying to have people understand that when people come together to deal with problems of education, the people that are actually working in the schools need to be heard."

development. In sum, this means challenging the neoliberal Chicagoan anti-syzygy by finding, funding, and pursuing alternatives. These are not impossible tasks. Already many are hard at work in our communities, classrooms, and at the grassroots seeking ways to produce a spatially just, sustainable city, block by block, and neighborhood by neighborhood.

Toward a Transformed Chicago: The First Political Steps

In a much-discussed article that appeared in the May 2014 issue of *The American Prospect*, Harold Meyerson (2014; see also Edsall 2014) reported on the emergence of distinctly left-leaning political movements in Pittsburgh, Minneapolis, Seattle, and even Phoenix, Arizona. In the latter city, situated in what is seemingly the most florid of red states, Mayor Greg Stanton supports marriage equality, and the city council, whose majority bloc of five members are aligned with Stanton, has, in the face of contrary state government action, "directed Phoenix police not to hand over detainees to immigration agents for deportation." Meyerson's explanation for this upsurge of urban progressivism turns on demographics—cities as magnets for younger people, often people of color, and, of course, many immigrants—the growing recognition of income/wealth inequality as the fundamental domestic challenge in the United States, and the forging of politically efficacious local progressive coalitions. The latter have often been led by service-sector unions such as the Service Employees International Union and have drawn on various local grassroots networks, such as neighborhood organizations, advocates of local economic development and affordable housing, and immigrants' rights organizations.

Meyerson's article focuses on smaller and mid-sized cities even as he notes that New York mayor Bill de Blasio is cut from the same cloth as Greg Stanton and his peers (and, in a pointed aside, observes that Rahm Emanuel is not). There is a logic to Meyerson's focus on mid-sized cities. The governments of such cities are close enough to local electorates to absorb prevalent populist sentiment, but these cities are large enough to have an impact, through local public policies, on substantial populations. In addition, these cities' experiments in public policy innovation can serve as models for other communities and possibly, for more ambitious national-scale initiatives. Meyerson's view of these cities as "laboratories of democracy," in fact, mirrors an argument made many years ago by the noted political scientist Robert Dahl (1967) in his 1967 presidential address to the American Political Science Association.

Could Chicago join this list of contemporary progressive cities? Certainly its current demographic trajectory matches the trend Meyerson identifies. Chicago is a decisively majority-minority city, and the obvious dynamism of many near-downtown neighborhoods such as Wicker Park, Logan Square, the Near West Side, and the South Loop are the result, in large part, of an influx of young people in their twenties and thirties over the past two decades. Nor is Chicago lacking grassroots networks or labor unions, though, as in the cities profiled by Meyerson, local labor progressivism is the province of service-sector unions and some public-sector unions such as the Chicago Teachers Union (CTU). However, there is no question that *politicized* neighborhood activism in Chicago has waned since its high-water mark in the late 1970s and early 1980s, and in recent years no movement has reached out to the city's households with the emphatic message of campaigns such as New York's Working Families Party or Minneapolis's TakeAction Minnesota.

The sources of Chicago's political quiescence are clear enough: as many grassroots organizations that emerged in the 1960s and 1970s matured in the 1980s and 1990s, staff and funder priorities pushed against the sorts of politicized organizing that initially had brought many of these groups to life. There is a deep divide between local African American and Latino political elites that is overlaid with a racial divide that separates both from many white progressives. Then there is the "myth of the machine," as described in Chapter 4. Chicago is a one-party, low-voter-turnout city, and the press and many politically influential people assume that all important decisions are made behind closed doors and that in order to make one's way politically one must cut deals with those in power. This is a perfect combination that aggressive, well-funded, big-name figures such as Richard M. Daley and Rahm Emanuel have used to fill what would otherwise be a void in civic and political leadership.

Nevertheless, Chicago is one of the nation's most economically divided cities (in a recent Brookings Institution analysis [Berube 2014], it ranked eighth in the ratio of 95th percentile incomes to 20th percentile incomes) so there is fuel of the same sort that has fired campaigns for a higher minimum wage, tougher community benefit agreements with developers, and publicly financed universal preschool commitments in other cities. Nor, at this writing, has the late-2015 upsurge in grassroots indignation over local police shootings abated. The presumably easy way to jump-start a progressive political movement with broad popular appeal is to find a charismatic figure to lead the charge, a local Bill de Blasio, or better yet, a latter-day Harold Washington. In effect, this was the course taken in the 2015 mayoral election as community and labor activists recruited Cook County commissioner Jesus "Chuy" Garcia to challenge Rahm Emanuel's reelection bid (Bogira 2015; Kennedy 2015). Garcia's unsuccessful "Two Chicagos" campaign directed the public's attention to many of the issues we have discussed in this volume, but ultimately the 2015 mayoral election turned on matters of personal character and the city government's short-term fiscal options.

For community and labor activists, dissident Democrats, and other groups that aspire to achieve a better Chicago, more important than recruiting an appealing mayoral candidate is giving shape to a broad, sustainable popular movement. A dozen or so leading progressives, including representatives of unions such as SEIU and the CTU, three or four brave city council members (and possibly one or two suburban mayors), and key neighborhood activists must join together and convene a citywide convention to forge a program that recommits the City of Chicago and surrounding communities to sound public schools accessible to all, an increase in the *regional* minimum wage, truly improved police-community relations, and substantive reform of tax increment finance policy within the city. Ultimately, this coalition will need to launch a new political party. Our choice for its name: the New America Party (Chicago branch).

Bibliography

Bennett, Michael I. J., and Robert Giloth, eds. 2008. *Economic Development in American Cities: The Pursuit of an Equity Agenda.* Albany, N.Y.: SUNY Press.

Berube, Alan. 2014. *All Cities Are Not Created Unequal.* Metropolitan Opportunity Series no. 51. Washington, D.C.: The Brookings Institution. Accessed August 5, 2014. http://www.brookings.edu/research/papers/2014/02/cities-unequal-berube.

Bogira, Steve. 2015. "What Makes Chuy Run?" *Chicago Reader*, January 22.

Castells, Manuel. 1975. *The Wild City: An Interpretive Summary of Research and Analysis on the U.S. Urban Crisis.* Santa Cruz, CA: n.p.

———. 2013. *Networks of Outrage and Hope: Social Movements in the Internet Age.* Cambridge, UK: Polity Press.

Dahl, Robert A. 1967. "The City in the Future of Democracy." *The American Political Science Review* 61, no. 4: 953–970.

Edsall, Thomas B. 2014. "Will Liberal Cities Leave the Rest of America Behind?" *New York Times*, April 29.

Fainstein, Susan F. 2010. *The Just City*. Ithaca, N.Y.: Cornell University Press.

Gendron, Richard, and G. William Domhoff. 2008. *The Leftmost City: Power and Progressive Politics in Santa Cruz*. Boulder, Colo.: Westview Press.

Goldfrank, Benjamin, and Andrew Schrank. 2009. "Municipal Neoliberalism and Municipal Socialism: Urban Political Economy in Latin America." *International Journal of Urban and Regional Health* 33, no. 2: 443–462.

Kennedy, Scott. 2015. "Chicago Mayoral Results: A Tale of Two Cities." *The Illinois Campaign for Political Reform*. Accessed April 18, 2015. http://www.ilcampaign. org/wp-content/uploads/2015/04/2015-Chicago-Mayoral-Runoff-Election-Analysis-ICPR_Kennedy.pdf.

Kotkin, Joel. 2005. "The Rise of the Ephemeral City." Accessed March 31, 2016. http://www.metropolismag.com/May-2005/The-Rise-of-the-Ephemeral-City/

Kotz, David M. 2003. "Neoliberalism and the SSA Theory of Long-Run Capital Accumulation." *Review of Radical Political Economics* 35, no. 3: 263–270.

Lefebvre, Henri. 1996. *Writings on Cities*. Cambridge, Mass.: Blackwell.

Meyerson, Harold. 2014. "The Revolt of the Cities." *The American Prospect*, May. Accessed February 27, 2016. http://prospect.org/article/revolt-cities.

Purcell, Mark. 2002. "Excavating Lefebvre: The Right to the City and Its Urban Politics of the Inhabitant." *GeoJournal* 58: 99–108.

Sassen, Saskia. 2001. *The Global City: New York, London, Tokyo*. 2nd ed. Princeton, N.J.: Princeton University Press.

Sennett, Richard. 2000. *The Corrosion of Character: The Personal Consequences of Work in the New Capitalism*. New York: W. W. Norton.

Skocpol, Theda. 2004. "The Narrowing of Civic Life." *The American Prospect*, May 17. Accessed February 27, 2016. http://prospect.org/article/narrowing-civic-life.

Skocpol, Theda, and Vanessa Williamson. 2013. *The Tea Party and the Remaking of Republican Conservatism*. New York: Oxford University Press.

Tarrow, Sidney. 1998. *Power in Movement: Social Movements and Contentious Politics*. New York: Cambridge University Press.

Taylor, Paul. 2014. *The Next America: Boomers, Millennials, and the Looming Generational Showdown*. New York: PublicAffairs.

Walliser, Andrés. 2013. "New Urban Activisms in Spain: Reclaiming Public Space in the Face of Crises." *Policy and Politics* 43, no. 3: 329–350.

Wilkinson, Richard, and Kate Pickett. 2010. *The Spirit Level: Why Greater Equality Makes Societies Stronger*. New York: Bloomsbury.

THE CONTRIBUTORS

STEPHEN ALEXANDER is an independent scholar who earned his Ph.D. from the University of Illinois at Chicago. He formerly was a research associate at DePaul University's Egan Urban Center and currently serves as a consultant to the Communitas Charitable Trust.

LARRY BENNETT teaches in the Political Science Department of DePaul University. His most recent book is *The Third City: Chicago and American Urbanism* (University of Chicago Press, 2010). Professor Bennett is co-editor of Temple University Press's Urban Life, Landscape, and Policy series.

MICHAEL BENNETT is associate professor of sociology at DePaul University in Chicago. He served as executive director of the Egan Urban Center, a major policy research center at DePaul, from 1997 to 2008.

CARRIE BREITBACH, adjunct professor of geography at DePaul University, received her PhD from Syracuse University. Her research has appeared in *Landscape Research* and *Gender, Place and Culture*.

SEAN DINCES, assistant professor of history and political science at Long Beach City College, earned his PhD in American studies at Brown University. Professor Dinces's research focus is the impact of sports on American society.

KENNETH FIDEL, a demographer and urban sociologist who earned his PhD from Washington University, St. Louis, recently retired from the Sociology Department at DePaul University.

ROBERTA GARNER is professor of sociology at DePaul University. She co-edited *The New Chicago* (Temple University Press, 2006) and is co-author (with Greg Scott) of *Doing Qualitative Research* (Pearson 2013) and co-editor with

Black Hawk Hancock of *Social Theory: Continuity and Confrontation*, 3rd edition (University of Toronto Press, 2014)

EUAN HAGUE is professor and chair of the Department of Geography and co-director of the Masters in Sustainable Urban Development at DePaul University. He is an urban and cultural geographer who has examined issues of gentrification, racism, whiteness, and national identity. His most recent book is *Regional and Local Economic Development* (Palgrave, 2011), co-authored with Cliff Hague and Carrie Breitbach.

BLACK HAWK HANCOCK is a cultural sociologist and associate professor of sociology at DePaul University. He is author of *American Allegory: Lindy Hop and the Racial Imagination* (University of Chicago Press, 2013).

CHRISTOPHER LAMBERTI earned his PhD in history at Brown University. He is an independent scholar and researcher for the Chicago and Midwest Joint Board of Workers United.

MICHAEL J. LORR is director of the Community Leadership Program and associate professor of sociology at Aquinas College. His work on urban, environmental, and cultural sociology has appeared in the *Journal of Contemporary Ethnography*, *Nature & Culture*, *Humanity and Society*, and the *Journal of Youth and Adolescence*.

MARTHA MARTINEZ is associate professor of sociology at DePaul University. A quantative sociologist, she focuses on economic topics. Professor Martinez's work has appeared in the *International Journal of Entrepreneurial Behavior and Research*, *Entrepreneurship Research Journal*, and *Case Research Journal*.

BRENDAN McQUADE, who earned his PhD in sociology from Binghamton University, is assistant professor of sociology at SUNY-Courtland. His work has appeared in *Science and Society*, *The American Journal of Cultural Sociology*, and the *Review of African Political Economy*.

ALEX G. PAPADOPOULOS is an urban and political geographer and a Europeanist, with specializations in urban morphology, queer space, and the history of cartography. His work has appeared in both European and North American academic publications and includes *Urban Regimes and Strategies: Building Europe's Central Executive District in Brussels* (University of Chicago Press, 1996).

RAJIV SHAH is an adjunct assistant professor in the Department of Communication at the University of Illinois at Chicago. His research seeks to understand the relationship between the design of technologies and society. He has published widely in computer science, communications, and the law and is frequently quoted as an expert on video surveillance in Chicago.

COSTAS SPIROU is professor and chair of the Department of Government and Sociology at Georgia College. His research interests center on the sociology and political economy of sports, downtown revival, and urban tourism. Professor Spirou is the author of *Urban Tourism and Urban Change* (Routledge, 2011). He is co-author (with Dennis Judd) of *Building the City of Spectacle: Mayor Richard M. Daley and the Remaking of Chicago* (Cornell University Press, 2016).

CAROLINA STERNBERG is assistant professor of Latin American and Latino Studies at DePaul University. She obtained her PhD in geography from the University of Illinois at Urbana-Champaign and received her MA in Geography from the Universidad de Buenos Aires, Argentina. Her main areas of research and teaching combine urban studies, Latin American studies, and local urban politics in both U.S. and Latin American settings. Her current research examines the extent of neoliberal contingency across global cities and critical debates about the future of neoliberal redevelopment governances in cities.

YUE ZHANG is associate professor of political science at the University of Illinois at Chicago. She is the author of *The Fragmented Politics of Urban Preservation: Beijing, Chicago, and Paris* (University of Minnesota Press, 2013). During the 2015–2016 academic year, Professor Zhang was a resident fellow at the Woodrow Wilson International Center for Scholars in Washington, D.C.

INDEX

tion growth, 58; race/ethnicity population trends, 59t

Calumet City, Ill., African American population, 55
Calumet Heights, Ill., poverty rates, 66
cameras, surveillance, 4; civil liberties concerns, 253–254; evolution of, 249–250; expansion of, 255; high visibility, 243–244, 245, 249; impact on crime, 252–253; redlight, 251, 255; speed, 251, 255
Campton Hills, Ill., 58
Carl Sandburg Village, 185
Carothers, Isaac, 244
car-sharing program, 102, 110–111
Castro District, San Francisco, 162, 168, 186n5
Center for Neighborhood Technology, 111
Central Loop TIF district, 87
Central Station development, 64
charter schools: expansion of, 10, 39–40, 85, 87, 91, 270; opening of, 2
Chaskin, Robert, 63
Chelsea neighborhood, New York City, 168
Chertoff, Michael, 244
Chicago: antisyzygy concept, 267–269, 271; Burnham's "Plan," 47–48; class and race-ethnicity in, 17–41; daily newspapers, 83–84; exurban development, 48, 52, 58–60; geography of inequality, viii, 47–67, 268; globalization and, 261–262; "greening" initiatives, 99–114, 155, 158; inner-ring communities, 52, 53, 55; landmark designation procedure, 204–205; as neoliberal city, 1–12, 261–273; as one-party city, 73–74; political evolution, 72–93, 271–273; population changes, 15, 49–50; post–World War II governance phases, 10; post–World War II urban development, 55–56; poverty rates, 65–66; rebranding of, 82; as "two cities," viii, 8–9, 10; vacant residential units, 60, 62. See also specific topics and locations
Chicago Alliance Against Racist and Political Oppression, 254
Chicago Anti-Eviction Campaign (CAEC), 225
Chicago Association of Neighborhood Development Organizations (CANDO), 157
Chicago Center for Green Technology, 111
Chicago City Council, 199, 238
Chicago Coalition to Protect Public Housing, 9
Chicago Emergency Communications Center (CECC), 248–249, 250, 253
Chicago Federation of Labor, 238
Chicago Gay Crusader, 168
Chicago Housing Authority (CHA): building
demolitions, 55, 63, 154; geographic consequences of public housing policy, 62–63; homeownership programs, 226–227; Plan for Transformation, 2, 4, 9, 60, 63, 66–67, 82, 84, 91
Chicago Infrastructure Trust, 89–90
Chicago Jobs Council, 238
Chicago Landmarks Commission, 199, 204
Chicago Metropolis 2020 vision, 8, 67, 85
Chicago Park District, 75, 145, 234, 236–238
Chicago Parking Meters, LLC, 90
Chicago Police Department (CPD): civilian deaths, vii–viii; civil liberties concerns, 253–254; evolving techniques, 252; Operation Disruption, 243, 253; professionalizing reforms, 247–248; Subversive Activities Unit (Red Squad), 247; surveillance, security, and intelligence-led policing, 4, 243–255; surveillance system impact on crime, 252–253
Chicago Public Schools (CPS): graduation rates, 20–21; overhaul of, 2, 39–40, 78, 82, 84–85, 270; racial demographics, 20–21; school closures, 8, 10, 21, 84–85, 91; standardized testing, 84–85; teacher reassignments, 84–85; TIF property taxes levied for, 3
Chicago Reader, The, 41, 86
Chicago Recycling Coalition, 109–110
Chicago State University, 269
Chicago Sun-Times, 83
Chicago Symphony Orchestra, 198
Chicago Teachers Union (CTU), 272; Emanuel's antagonism of, 87, 262; teachers' strike, 9, 254, 270–271
Chicago Transit Authority (CTA), 2, 102, 250
Chicago Tribune: changes, 83–84; "Chicago on Hold" series, 63–64; on Lakeside development plan, 152; on Lakeview commercial blight, 177; on LGBT community, 165; on Medinah Temple project, 201, 203; "New Plan of Chicago" suggestions, 269; on 1998 gay pride parade, 179–180; on Olympics bid, 234; red-light camera investigation, 251; on South Works site, 149–150
Chicago Velo Campus, 145
Chico, Gerry, 74
Chile, neoliberalism in, 6, 11n1
Chile Project, 11n1
Chinatown, gentrification in, 212
Cicero, Ill.: African American population, 55; poverty rates, 66

Cincotta, Gale, 225
Citizen and Law Enforcement Analysis and
    Reporting (CLEAR), 248
Civic Federation, 234
Civic Lab, 268
civil rights movement, curtailing of, 22–23
class division, growth of, 5–6, 37, 38, 40
class dynamics in Chicago, 17–41; "blue-
    collar" status and, 127–130; disengagement
    from voting and politics, 38–39, 272; dis-
    placement of marginalized, 38; economic
    restructuring and, 26–29; emerging class-
    ethnic structure, 29–37; environmental
    initiatives and, 99, 104, 106, 109–111, 156;
    hospital workers, 35; immigrants, 29–31;
    neoliberal definition of, 130–133; public
    sphere shrinkage, 38, 40–41; realigning
    significance, 34, 36–37; "smart choices" and
    "cultural values" narratives, 38, 39–40, 91
climate change, 102, 108, 111
Clinton, Bill, and administration, 81, 82, 86, 91
coal-burning power plants, 111–113
Coalition for an Alternatively Funded Arena
    (CAFA), 196
Coffee, Dan, 200
collective action, need for, 266–267
Commercial Club of Chicago (CCC), *Chicago
    Metropolis 2020* vision, 8, 12n2, 85
Commission on Chicago Landmarks, 198–
    199, 204, 205
Committee for Better Government, 77
Communities for an Equitable Olympics
    (CEO), 238
community organizing efforts, 268–269
Community Reinvestment Act (1977), 214,
    222–223
"complete streets" concept, 102
consumption-based city vision, neoliberalism
    and, 5–6, 7, 10, 150–151, 240–241, 262–263
Cook County, Ill.: African American popula-
    tion, 55; income demographics, 56; popula-
    tion changes, 52, 53t, 55t
Cooper, Marc, 6
Counter-Clout, 164
counter-neoliberalism, 230, 239, 264
Cowens, Tyler, 36
Cowie, Jefferson, 131
Cranford, Cynthia, 31
"creative class" as ideal urban residents, 7–8,
    18, 34, 36, 212
"creative destruction," 193
credit, homeownership and, 214; collapse of,
    218–219; subprime mortgages and, 215–217,

224, 226; tightening of, 221–223, *222*. *See
    also* foreclosure crisis
credit default swaps, 216
Crime Prevention and Information Center
    (CPIC), 4, 244, 248–249, 250, 252
Criminal History Records Information Sys-
    tem (CHRIS), 247–248
Cromidas, Rachel, 109
Cubs baseball team: admission and entertain-
    ment costs, *125*, 134n6; not seen as "blue-col-
    lar" team, 134n2; television broadcasts, 125
"cultural values" and "smart choices" narra-
    tives, 38, 39–40, 91
Cunningham, Lynne, 148, 151–152
Curran, Winifred, 106–7

Dahl, Robert, 272
Daley, Bill, 76
Daley, John, 76
Daley, Richard J., and administration: ma-
    chine politics of, 10, 72–75, 92; racial com-
    ponents of support, 74–75
Daley, Richard M., and administration: con-
    stituency-focused groups under, 77; dein-
    dustrialization under, 157; "greening" initia-
    tives, 99, 100–101, 102; LGBT community's
    relations with, 180–181, 184; machine poli-
    tics and, 73, 76; Medinah Temple preserva-
    tion, 199–200; Millennium Park project,
    80–81; neoliberal governance, 10, 74, 79,
    81–82, 84–86, 87, 91, 157; Olympics bid of,
    230–241; policing methods under, 243–244,
    249–250; political longevity, 85, 272; popu-
    larity of, 1; privatization under, 85–86, 90;
    pro-growth and pro-gentrification policies,
    64; public housing redevelopment under,
    82, 84; school reform under, 84–85; South
    Works redevelopment and, 149–152; special
    election (1989), 79; TIF program under,
    151–152; vision of Chicago's future, 2
Daly, Herman E., 108
databases, criminal, 247–248
Dave Matthews Band Caravan concert,
    154–155, 156
Davies, Richard, 134n2
Davis, Mike, 128
Davis, Morris Shadrach, 38
Dearborn Homes (public housing), 9
de Blasio, Bill, 272
deindustrialization: city's role in, 156–157; ef-
    fects of, 121, *122*, 123–124, 262; racial impact,
    23, 24, 26, 27; remaking spaces, 141–158
"delegate agencies," 78

Harold Ickes Homes (public housing), 9
Harris Bankcorp, Inc., 238
Harvey, David, 5, 156
Harvey, Ill., 24; African American population, 55; poverty rates, 66
Hasnain-Wynia, Romana, 21–22
Hayek, Friedrich, 6, 193
health indicators, race and, 21–22
Healy, Lori, 231, 238
Heartland Alliance Social IMPACT Research Center, 66
heat wave deaths (1995), 101
Henry Horner Homes (public housing), 62–63
Hertz, Daniel, 20
Highland Park, Ill., urban development, 56
high-tech jobs in Chicago, 9
highways, privatization of, 2, 85, 86
Hill, Christopher, 152
Hill and Woltersdorf architectural firm, 197
Hinrich, Kirk, 133
Hispanic communities. *See* Latino communities in Chicago area
Hispanic Democratic Organization (HDO), 77
historic preservation, 194; adaptive reuse and, 194–195; aldermen's power, 205–206; Illinois procedures, 203–206; in neoliberal context, 191–207, 262; as public good, 194, 205, 206–207
HIV-AIDS epidemic, 170, 187n13; race and infection rate, 21
hockey. *See* Blackhawks hockey team
Hodgkins, Ill., African American population, 55
Hoffman, David, 89
Home Investment Partnerships Program (HOME), 226–227
Homeland Security, Department of (DHS), 248
homeownership: broadening, through markets and policy, 224, 226–227; credit expansion and, 215–217; erosion of, in foreclosure crisis, 217–218; gentrification and, 212–213; as long-term savings, 226; mortgaged properties in Chicago, 218–220, 219t; viewed as social virtue, 211–212. *See also* foreclosure crisis
homicide "hot spots" in Chicago, 20, 22, 50–51
HOPE VI initiative, 82, 84
housing. *See* affordable housing; homeownership; public housing
Housing and Urban Development, U.S. Department of, 214
housing bubble. *See* foreclosure crisis
housing vouchers, 2, 4, 63

Huberman, Ron, 253
Huehl, Harris, 198
Huffington Post, 161
Human Rights Campaign's Municipal Equality Index, 184, 188n22
Humboldt Park neighborhood, gentrification in, 213
Hunt, D. Bradford, 88
Hureau, David, 252
Hyde Park neighborhood: gentrification, 75; LGBT community, 187n12; Olympics bid and, 4, 237
hypercommodification, 6
"hyper-incarceration," 20, 22, 24–25

Illinois FIRST funding, 200
Illinois Housing Development Authority, 226–227
Illinois Link card (SNAP), 104
Illinois Register of Historic Places, 198
Illinois Steel Company, 146
Immergluck, Dan, 157
immigrants: in emerging class structure, 18, 29–31, 32t, 33–34, 212; industrial employment, 146; job skills and, 27–28, 35; service sector employment, 5; subprime mortgages and, 216; suburbanization of, 52. *See also* Asian communities in Chicago area; Latino communities in Chicago area
incarceration rates, race and, 20, 22. *See also* "hyper-incarceration"
income inequality: Chicago's urban polarity, 268, 273; foreclosures and, 221, 263; home-ownership and, 212–213; race and, 19, 266; segregation and, 51
index of dissimilarity, 18, 41n1
Indianapolis, Ind., "blue-collar" rhetoric in, 133n1
industrial architecture, conversion of, 5
industrial spaces, redevelopment of, 141–158
Institute of Cultural Affairs, 111
"institutional ghettos," 24
intelligence-led policing (ILP), 244, 246–247; in Chicago, 247–253
International Monetary Fund, neoliberal policies, 7
International Olympic Committee (IOC), 229, 231–232, 236–237
Isackson, Noah, 250

Jackson, Jesse, Jr., 39
Jackson, Jesse, Sr., 39
Jackson, Sandra ("Sandi"), 39, 154

occupied and owner-occupied properties, 224t; racial composition and median income, 219t
London, England, neoliberal trends in, 4
Loop area, Chicago: bike sharing, 105; growth of, 47, 64–65; policing and surveillance, 38; tri-level street plan, 37
Lorr, Michael, 97, 262
Los Angeles, Calif., class inequality in, 37
Lovell, Sarah, 104
Ludwig, Jim, 173–174

Mabwa, Nasutsa, 143
MacArthur Foundation, 85
machine politics: of Richard J. Daley administration, 10, 72–74, 92; myth of, 74–77, 272; political machines distinguished from, 77–78; public employee participation in, 75
Maclean, John, 147
Madden Park–Wells–Darrow Homes (public housing), 9
Madigan, Lisa, 76
Madigan, Mike, 76
Mahany, Barbara, 165
Main, Frank, 252
Major League Baseball (MLB), salaries in, 129. See also Cubs baseball team; White Sox baseball team
Major Taylor Cycling Club, 106
Manhattan, Ill., population growth, 58
March on Washington (1963), 19
Marigny district, New Orleans, 178, 181, 185
Markham, Ill., 24; poverty rates, 66
Marriott Hotels, 196
Martinez, Anthony, 103
Martinez, Martha, 263
Marx, Karl, 38
mass transit. See public/mass transit
Mattachine Midwest, 163, 164
Mattachine Midwest (publication), 164
Mattachine Society, 187n6
Matteson, Ill., African American population, 55
Mayer Brown LLC, 86
McCaffery, Clayton, 143–144
McCaffery, Dan, 145, 155
McCaffery Interests, 142–143, 154–155, 156, 157
McCarron, John, 63–64
McCarthy, Deborah, 108
McCormick Place, 196, 233, 262
McDonald, Laquan, vii–viii
McHenry County, Ill., population changes, 52, 53t, 55t

McQuade, Brendan, 263
median income figures, race and, 19
Medinah Temple, 192; adaptive reuse, 195, 200–203; Richard M. Daley's preservation plan for, 199–200; landmark status for, 200, 204; original purposes, 191, 193, 198; renovation evaluation, 203–206
Medinah Temple Association, 199
Mell, Dick, 76
mental health facilities, closure of, 10
Meredith, Burgess, 197
Metcalfe, Ralph, 39
Metropolitan Pier and Exposition Authority, 196
Mexican community in Chicago, 17, 29, 30, 31, 33, 34, 53, 75, 112. See also Latino communities in Chicago area
Meyerson, Harold, 271–272
Michaels, Walter Benn, 132
Mickelson, Jerry, 155
middle-class professionals in Chicago, 17–18
Midway Airport, attempt to lease, 2, 85, 86
Midwest Generation, 112
Mier, Rob, 79
Milanovic, Branko, 33–34
Millennium Park: as Richard M. Daley's pet project, 80–81; security patrols of, 4
Million Dollar Blocks project, 268
Mitchell, Don, 6
Mitchell, Ross, 108
Molotch, Harvey, 7
Montes, Maria Elena, 148
mortgages. See credit, homeownership and
motor vehicle accident death rate, race and, 21
Mud to Parks project, 145
Municipal Equality Index, 184, 188n22
"municipal socialism" concept, 265

Naperville, Ill., African American population, 55
Naperville Community Unit School District 203, 56–57
Nash, Catherine, 162
Natarus, Burton, 200, 205
National Advisory Commission on Civil Disorders, report, 19
National Association for the Advancement of Colored People, 247
National Basketball Association (NBA), salaries in, 129. See also Bulls basketball team
National Council of Churches, 247
National Football League (NFL): player draft,

220; occupied and owner-occupied properties, 224*t*; Olympics bid and, 4, 237; racial composition and median income, 219*t*

Oakley, Charles, 128

Obama, Barack, 82, 232

Obama, Michelle, 232

Occupy Wall Street movement, 254, 266–267

Old Town neighborhood: gentrification in, 64, 185; LGBT community in, 165, 168, 170, 185

Olympics 2016 bid, 229–241; backers of, 232; benefits discussion absent from, 240–241; Chicagoans' lack of information about, 229–230; committee, 232–233, 236–241; community outreach, 236–238; decision to make, 230–232; failure of, 238–241; fiscal plan and economic impact, 234–236; memorandum of understanding and, 231–232, 236, 237–238; proposed physical plan, 233–234; protests against, 10, 230, 231, 237; South Side gentrification and, 4

One publication, 164

Operation Disruption, 243, 253

Operation PUSH, 247

"organic counter-neoliberalism," 230, 239, 264

Osborne, David, 81–82

Our Common Future (Brundtland report), 107

Pacyga, Dominic, 146

Palm Springs, Calif., 163

Papachristos, Andrew, 252

Papadopoulos, Alex, 263

Parfitt Brothers, 197

Paris, France, neoliberal trends in, 4

parking garages, privatization of, 85

parking meters, privatization of, 2, 10, 85, 86, 89, 90

Parks, Virginia, 26

Pasquinelli Development Group, Inc., 59

Pattillo (Pattillo-McCoy), Mary: *Black on the Block*, 19; *Black Picket Fences*, 25, 27

Peavy, Jake, 120, 133

Peck, Jamie, 185, 186n3

Pellow, David, 100, 110

People for Community Recovery, 111

Peotone, Ill., population growth, 58

"personal responsibility" ethos, 130–131

petcoke (petroleum coke) removal, 112–113

Peterson, Terry, 238

Phoenix, Ariz., 271–272

Pickett, Kate, 265

Pilsen Alliance, 112

Pilsen Environmental Rights and Reform Organization (PERRO), 111, 112

Pilsen neighborhood, gentrification in, 64, 212

Pinochet, Augusto, 6, 11n1

Pittsburgh, Pa., "blue-collar" rhetoric in, 133n1

Plainfield, Ill.: African American population, 55; population growth, 58

Plan for Economic Growth and Jobs, A, 88–89

Planning and Development, Chicago Department of, 99, 101–102, 150

Plano, Ill., population growth, 58

"Plan of Chicago" (Burnham), 47–48

plutocratization, 37, 264

Police Observation Devices (PODs), 243–244, 245, 249, 253–254

police shootings, vii–viii

policing. *See* Chicago Police Department (CPD); surveillance and policing in Chicago

Polish community in Chicago, 29, 34

political consciousness, expansion of, 266, 267, 272–273

political machines, concept of, 77–78

politics in Chicago, 72–93; contested politics in, 77–79, 81; demographic shifts and, 75; disengagement of marginalized and working class, 38–39; family dynasties, 76–77; incumbency advantage, 77; machine, 10, 72–77, 92, 272; neoliberalism and, 81–92. *See also specific mayors*

Pope, John, 155

Poppe, Molly, 109

Portage Park neighborhood: foreclosures in, 221*t*, 224; mortgaged properties, 219*t*; occupied and owner-occupied properties, 224*t*; racial composition and median income, 219*t*

poverty rates: racial disparity, 19, 22, 65–66; South Side of Chicago, 51; suburban, 65–66; West Side of Chicago, 51

power, electric: coal-burning plants, 111–113; failures, 101; and South Works, 151

"precariat," 26, 28

Preckwinkle, Toni, 39, 237–238

predictive analytics, 252, 255

print journalism in Chicago, decline of, 40–41

privatization: as neoliberal policy, 2, 5, 6–7, 39–40, 82, 85–86, 89–90, 91; protests against, 9–10; racial impact, 23; of urban spaces, 193–194

Provincetown, Mass., 162

public good: declining support of, 38; historic preservation as, 194, 205, 206–207

Public Health, Chicago Department of, 21–22, 99
public housing: crisis of, 82, 84; displacements, 154; scale-down of, 9. *See also* Chicago Housing Authority (CHA)
public/mass transit: in "better city," 265; employment and, 24, 213; environment and, 111; improvements to, 89; safety of, 113. *See also* Chicago Transit Authority (CTA)
public-private partnerships: environmental initiatives, 99, 107; as neoliberal policy, 2, 4, 5, 7, 10, 89–90, 229, 239–241
public-sector downsizing, 28, 30
public sphere, shrinkage of, 38, 40–41

Queer Bohemia district (North Loop and River North areas), 170, 173, 185, 187n14
Quigley, Michael, 73

Raby, Al, 39
race-ethnicity dynamics in Chicago, 17–41; crime and "hyper-incarceration," viii–ix, 20, 24–25; disparities in, 18–22; economic disadvantage, 19, 266; education, 20–21; environmental initiatives and, 99, 109–111; foreclosures, 22, 60–62, 217; health indicators, 21–22; historical perspective, 22–29; homeownership and, 212–213; hospital workers, 35; institutional racism, 24–25; neoliberalism and, 25–29; poverty rate and, 65–66; segregation and racial isolation, 18–19; settlement patterns, 47–67; sexuality equated to ethnicity, 180; stratification, 31, 32t, 33–34; subprime mortgages and, 216, 217; surveillance and policing, 252–254, 263
"racial steering" real estate practices, 24
Rakove, Milton, *Don't Make No Waves, Don't Back No Losers*, 72, 73
Rast, Joel, *Remaking Chicago*, 79
Reagan, Ronald, and administration, 7, 130
real estate development: under Emanuel's administration, 1, 2, 4, 87–89, 185–186; exurban, 48; globalization and, 37, 213; megaprojects, 2, 145, 193, 263; neoliberalism and, 4–5, 8–10, 157–158, 193–194, 263; Olympics bid and, 233–234, 235; redevelopment of industrial spaces, 141–158, 263; urban morphology of North Halsted–Broadway Corridor, 161–188; under Washington's administration, 78. *See also* gentrification; *specific projects*
recession. *See* Great Recession of 2008
recycling initiative, 100, 108, 109–111

Redflex Traffic Systems, 251
redlining practices, 23–24
Rendell, Ed, 82
Rice, Tamir, viii
Richton Park, Ill., African American population, 55
Riordan, Richard, 82
Riverdale, Ill., African American population, 55
River East Center development, 64
River East neighborhood, gentrification in, 64
River West neighborhood, gentrification in, 64
Robbins, Ill., African American population, 55
Robert Taylor Homes (public housing), 9, 62, 82, 84
Robinson, Renault, 39
Roenick, Jeremy, 130
Rogers, John W., Jr., 232
Romeoville, Ill., African American population, 55
Roosevelt, Franklin D., 92
Root, John Wellborn, 47
Rosati, Clayton, 6
Ross, Willie, 148
Rust Belt (term), 23, 27, 28, 121
Ryan, Patrick, 230

Sadowsky, Rob, 113–114
Safety Dynamics, 249
Sakamoto, Bob, 128
Salazar, Peggy, 157
Sampson, Robert, 20, 22; *Great American City*, 24–25
Sanborn Fire Insurance Atlas maps for Lake View, 174, 188n19
Sandel, Michael, 40
Sanders, Bernie, 267
San Francisco, Calif., class inequality in, 37
Sargent, John Singer, 197
Sassen, Saskia, 28, 261
Sauk Valley, Ill., African American population, 55
Scarborough Research, 125–126
Schaumburg Freedom Coalition, 251
Schmid, Richard Gustave, 198
Schmidt, John, 86
schools and education, Chicago-area: decentralization of, 84–85; suburban school spending, 56–57, 57t. *See also* charter schools; Chicago Public Schools (CPS)
Schrank, Andrew, 265
Schuler, Timothy, *Green Building & Design*, 158
Schumpeter, Joseph, 193

Schwartz, Adam, 254
Schwartzman, Kathleen, 27
Scott, Michael, 238
securities, mortgage-backed, 214–215
security: as neoliberal project, 4, 246–247; spatial reorganization and displacement and, 38. *See also* surveillance and policing in Chicago
segregation in Chicago, racial, 18–19; crime and, viii–ix, 50–51; degree of, 48, 49–51; economic disparity and, 24; environmental disparity and, 100; vs. other American cities, 50; post–World War II urban development and, 55–56; zoning and land use strategies, 56
Sellers, Rod, 146
Sennett, Richard, 267
Service Employees International Union, 271
service workers in Chicago, 9, 35
Shah, Rajiv, 263
Shakman, Michael, 75, 76
Sharkey, Patrick, *Stuck in Place*, 25
Shiller, Helen, 73
"shock doctrine," 11n1, 91
ShotSpotter, 249
Shriners, 198, 203
Silva, Jennifer, *Coming Up Short*, 36–37
Sirota, David, 130
Sites, William, 26
Skocpol, Theda, 40
Skogan, Wesley, 253
"smart choices" and "cultural values" narratives, 38, 39–40, 91
Smith, C. Gregory, 267
Smith, Sam, 129
social exclusion, neoliberalism and, 4, 5
social justice, "greening" initiatives and, 10, 101, 102, 107, 108, 111–114
social network analysis, 252, 255
social services, neoliberalism's cuts to, 7
Society for Human Rights, 163
Solo Cup Company, 152, 154
South Chicago neighborhood, 144, 146; foreclosures in, 220, 221t, 223; Lakeside development and, 149, 151, 152, 155; mortgaged properties, 218, 219t; occupied and owner-occupied properties, 224t; racial composition and median income, 219t; TIF district, 145, 151, 152, 154, 155
Southeast Chicago Development Commission, 148, 151–152
Southeast Environmental Task Force, 111, 112–113, 157

Southeast Side of Chicago, 146–147
South Lawndale neighborhood: foreclosures in, 221t, 224; mortgaged properties, 218, 219t; occupied and owner-occupied properties, 224t; racial composition and median income, 219t
South Loop neighborhood: gentrification in, 4, 60, 64, 212, 213, 272; TIF entertainment district, 196–197
South Side of Chicago: as Black Belt, 15, 48; crime in, 20, 22; environmental initiatives, 99; geographic consequences of public housing policy, 62–63; LGBT community in, 164, 170, 187n12; mass transit and, 24; Olympics bid and, 230–232, 233–241; poverty rates, 51; trauma center shortage, 22. *See also specific neighborhoods*
South Works U.S. Steel complex, 89, 141–146; community plan, 150; as cultural venue, 154–155; environmental legacy, 148; plant closure, 147–149, 156–157; redevelopment delayed, 149–152, 154; reinvisioning, 149; site history, 146–147
spectacular events hosting, neoliberalism and, 238–241, 262
SportsNet Chicago, 125
sports scene in Chicago: "blue-collar" values and, 119–134, 262–263; entertainment costs for, 123–125, 125, 134n6; neoliberal definition of social class and, 130–133, 262–263; Olympics bid, 229–241; premium seating, 124; television broadcast, 125–126, 126. *See also specific teams*
Stanton, Greg, 271–272
Star Tribune (Minneapolis), 180
Stateway Gardens (public housing), 9, 82, 84
Steel Workers Organizing Committee, 146
Stewart-Winter, Timothy, 180, 186n2
St. John, James Allen, 197
Stola, James, 203–204
Stroger, Todd, 39
subprime mortgages, 215–217, 220, 263
suburbanization of Chicago metro area, 48, 50, 51–58
Sugar Grove, Ill., population growth, 58
Sunstein, Cass, 41
Supplemental Nutrition Assistance Program, Illinois Link card, 104
"supply-side" economic policies, 6
Surkin, Marvin, 27
surveillance and policing in Chicago, 243–255; civil liberties concerns, 253–254; expansion of, 4, 5, 38, 249–251; facial recogni-

tion software, 250, 255; future of, 255; high visibility cameras, 243–244, 249–250; impact on crime, 252–253; intelligence-led policing (ILP), 244, 246–253; license plate recognition (LPR), 250–251, 255; predictive analytics, 252, 255; of private entities, 250; race-ethnicity dynamics, 252–254, 263; social networking analysis, 252, 255; video analytic software, 250, 255

sustainability. *See* urban sustainability

Sustainable Chicago 2015 Action Agenda, 102, 104

Sweet Beginnings, 268

Sydney, Australia, neoliberal trends in, 4

tax incentives for corporate headquarters, 2

Tax Increment Financing districts (TIFs), 2–3; adaptive reuse and, 194; Central Loop, 87; Emanuel's use of, 10, 87–88; funding for Millennium Park, 4; in Joliet, 59–60; Medinah block, 200, 202; for Olympic village, 234; South Chicago, 145, 151, 152, 154, 155; South Loop, 196–197

Tax Reform Act (1976), 194

Taylor, Dorceta, 100

Taylor, John, 104

Taylor, Paul, 267

Tea Party, 267

technology. *See* high-tech jobs in Chicago; surveillance and policing in Chicago

Thatcher, Margaret, 7

themed neighborhoods in Chicago, 10

Theodore, Nik, 185, 186n3, 193

Tootelian & Associates, 235–236

Torino, Italy, 28

Toronto, Canada: LGBT community in, 162; neoliberal trends in, 4, 18; race-ethnicity stratification, 33

toxic waste and polluted sites, 10, 100, 112, 114, 144–145, 147

"transfers out of the district," 21

Transportation, Chicago Department of, 105–106

trash collection, 87, 100, 109–110

Tree, Anna Magic, 197

Tree, Lambert, 197–198

Tree Studios, 191, *192*; adaptive reuse, 193, 195, 201–203; landmark designation, 204; original purpose, 193, 197–198; renovation evaluation, 203–206; sale and controversy over, 198–199

Trump Tower (Chicago), 37

Two Degrees of Association, 252

UIC Pavilion, 233

UN Committee against Torture, 254

unemployment rate, race and, 19, 22, 23–25, 26–27

unions. *See* labor unions

United Center sports arena, 233

United Kingdom: economic restructuring in, 28; neoliberalism in, 7

United Neighborhood Organization (UNO), 148

United States Olympic Committee (USOC), 231

United Steelworkers Union, 146, 147

University of Chicago, economists from, 6

University Village development, 64

Uptown-Edgewater neighborhood, 170

urban agriculture, 100, 104, 268

urban morphology, 161–163, 173–185, 186n1

urban populism, 10, 79, 93n4, 269

urban sustainability, 107–108; alternative forms, 110–114; bike lanes, 22, 100, 102; Chicago's accomplishments, 100–107; climate change and, 108; demographics of, 99, 104, 106–107, 108; grass-roots groups, 268; "greening" and, 99–114, 158, 262; UN goals, 107–108, 144

Urlacher, Brian, 127

"use value," 7

U.S. Green Building Council, 100

U.S. Steel (USX), 5; diversification of, 147, 156–157; South Works complex, 89, 146–147

Vallas, Paul, 84–85

Van Dyke, Jason, vii–viii

Verdi, Bob, 128–129

video analytic software, 250, 255

voting, disengagement of marginalized and working class, 38–39, 272

Vrdolyak, Ed, 78

Wacquant, Loïc, 26, 28, 38, 246

Waldinger, Roger, 31

Walley, Christine, 146

Walliser, Andrés, 266–267

Walsh, Higgins & Company, 150

Washington, D.C., African American suburbanization, 54

Washington, Harold, and administration: African American support for, 38–39, 78; initiatives of, 78–79; LGBT community's relations with, 180; machine politics' demise under, 76; TIF program under, 3; urban populism and, 10, 79, 269

The University of Illinois Press
is a founding member of the
Association of American University Presses.

Text designed by Jim Proefrock
Composed in 10.5/13 Minion Pro
with Venis and Avenir display
at the University of Illinois Press
Cover designed by Dustin J. Hubbart
Cover photo by David Schalliol
Manufactured by Cushing Malloy, Inc.

University of Illinois Press
1325 South Oak Street
Champaign, IL 61820-6903
www.press.uillinois.edu